D1074059

PHILIPPIANS AND PHILEMON

Sacra Pagina Series

Volume 10

Philippians and Philemon

Bonnie B. Thurston
Judith M. Ryan

Daniel J. Harrington, S.J.
Editor

A Michael Glazier Book

LITURGICAL PRESS
Collegeville, Minnesota

www.litpress.org

A Michael Glazier Book published by the Liturgical Press.

1 2 3 4 5 6 7 8 9

Library of Congress Cataloging-in-Publication Data

Thurston, Bonnie Bowman.
Philippians and Philemon / Bonnie B. Thurston, Judith Ryan ; Daniel J. Harrington, editor.
p. cm. — (Sacra pagina series ; v. 10)
"A Michael Glazier book."
Summary: "Translations with commentary of Paul's Letter to the Philippians and his Letter to Philemon. The letters are approached methodologically, with attention to historical and cultural contexts"—Provided by publisher.
Includes bibliographical references and indexes.
ISBN 0-8146-5820-2 (alk. paper)
1. Bible. N.T. Philippians—Commentaries. 2. Bible. N.T. Philemon—Commentaries. I. Ryan, Judith, 1952– II. Harrington, Daniel J. III. Title. IV. Series: Sacra pagina series ; 10.

BS2705.53.T58 2004
227'.6077—dc22

2004020780

CONTENTS

PHILEMON

Introduction

Translation, Notes, Interpretation

Indexes

EDITOR'S PREFACE

Sacra Pagina is a multi-volume commentary on the books of the New Testament. The expression *Sacra Pagina* ("Sacred Page") originally referred to the text of Scripture. In the Middle Ages it also described the study of Scripture to which the interpreter brought the tools of grammar, rhetoric, dialectic, and philosophy. Thus *Sacra Pagina* encompasses both the text to be studied and the activity of interpretation.

This series presents fresh translations and modern expositions of all the books of the New Testament. Written by an international team of biblical scholars, it is intended for biblical professionals, graduate students, theologians, clergy, and religious educators. The volumes present basic introductory information and close exposition. They self-consciously adopt specific methodological perspectives, but maintain a focus on the issues raised by the New Testament compositions themselves. The goal of *Sacra Pagina* is to provide sound critical analysis without any loss of sensitivity to religious meaning. This series is therefore catholic in two senses of the word: inclusive in its methods and perspectives, and shaped by the context of the Catholic tradition.

The Second Vatican Council described the study of the "sacred page" as the "very soul of sacred theology" (*Dei Verbum* 24). The volumes in this series illustrate how biblical scholars contribute to the council's call to provide access to Sacred Scripture for all the Christian faithful. Rather than pretending to say the final word on any text, these volumes seek to open up the riches of the New Testament and to invite as many people as possible to study seriously the "sacred page."

Daniel J. Harrington, S.J.

ABBREVIATIONS

Biblical Books and Apocrypha

Gen
Exod
Lev
Num
Deut
Josh
Judg
1–2 Sam
1–2 Kgs
Isa
Jer
Ezek
Hos
Joel
Amos
Obad
Jonah
Mic
Nah
Hab
Zeph
Hag
Zech
Mal
Ps (*pl.*: Pss)
Job
Prov
Ruth
Cant
Eccl (*or* Qoh)
Lam
Esth
Dan
Ezra
Neh
1–2 Chr
1–2–3–4 Kgdms
Add Esth
Bar
2 Bar
Bel
1–2 Esdr
4 Ezra
Jdt
Jub
Ep Jer
1–2–3–4 Macc
Pr Azar
Pr Man
Ps Sol
Sir
Sus
Tob
Wis
Matt
Mark
Luke
John
Acts
Rom
1–2 Cor
Gal
Eph
Phil
Col
1–2 Thess
1–2 Tim
Titus
Phlm
Heb
Jas
1–2 Pet
1–2–3 John
Jude
Rev

Other Ancient Texts

Apol.	Justin Martyr, *Apology*
Ann.	Tacitus, *Annales*
Ant.	Josephus, *Antiquities of the Jews*
Bell.	Josephus, *The Jewish Wars*
CD	Cairo Geniza copy of the *Damascus Document*
1-2 Clem.	1-2 Clement
Diss.	Epictetus, *Discourses*
Ep.	Pliny the Younger, *Epistle*
Ep.Mor.	Seneca, *Moral Epistle*
Herm. *Mand.*	Hermas, *Mandate*

Herm. *Sim.*	Hermas, *Similitude*
Hist. eccl.	Eusebius, *Historia Ecclesiastica*
Ign. *Eph*	Ignatius, *Letter to the Ephesians*
Ign. *Phld*	Ignatius, *Letter to the Philadelphians*
Ign. *Pol*	Ignatius, *Letter to the Polycarp*
Ign. *Smyrn*	Ignatius, *Letter to the Smyrnaeans*
m.	Mishnah
1QH	*Hodayot*
1QM	War Scroll
1QS	*Rule of the Community*
Sanh.	*Sanhedrin*
T. Benj.	*Testament of Benjamin*

Periodicals, Reference Works, and Serials

AB	Anchor Bible
ABD	*Anchor Bible Dictionary,* ed. David Noel Freedman et al.
ANRW	*Aufstieg und Niedergang der römischen Welt*
AsSeign	*Assemblées du Seigneur*
ATR	*Anglican Theological Review*
AUSS	Andrews University Seminary Studies
BBET	Beiträge zur biblischen Exegese und Theologie
BDAG	F. W. Danker, reviser and editor, *A Greek-English Lexicon of the New Testament and Other Early Christian Literature* (3rd ed.)
BDF	F. Blass, A. Debrunner and R. W. Funk. *A Greek Grammar in the NT* (Chicago: University of Chicago Press, 1961; revised 1990).
Bib	*Biblica*
BJRL	*Bulletin of the John Rylands Library*
BL	*Bibel und Liturgie*
BS	*Bibliotheca Sacra*
BTB	*Biblical Theology Bulletin*
BullBibRes	*Bulletin of Biblical Research*
BZ	*Biblische Zeitschrift*
BZAW	Beihefte zur Zeitschrift für die alttestamentliche Wissenschaft
ConBNT	Coniectanea Biblica, New Testament
CBNTS	Catholic Biblical New Testament Supplement
CBQ	*Catholic Biblical Quarterly*
CNT	Commentaire du Nouveau Testament
CSB/NAB	*Catholic Study Bible/New American Bible*
DPL	*Dictionary of Paul and His Letters*
EDNT	H. Balz and G. Schneider, editors, *Exegetical Dictionary of the New Testament* (3 vols.) Grand Rapids: Eerdmans, 1990–1993.
EKKNT	Evangelisch-katholischer Kommentar zum Neuen Testament
EstBib	*Estudios Bíblicos*
EvQ	*Evangelical Quarterly*
ExpTim	*Expository Times*

FB	Forschung zur Bibel
FTS	Freiburger Theologische Studien
HTKNT	Herders theologischer Kommentar zum Neuen Testament
HTR	*Harvard Theological Review*
HUCA	*Hebrew Union College Annual*
ICC	International Critical Commentary
Int	*Interpretation*
JBL	*Journal of Biblical Literature*
JETS	*Journal of the Evangelical Theological Society*
JSJ	*Journal for the Study of Judaism*
JSNT	*Journal for the Study of the New Testament*
JSNTSup	JSNT, Supplement Series
JSOTSup	JSOT, Supplement Series
JSPSup	Journal for the Study of the Pseudepigrapha Supplement Series
JTS	*Journal of Theological Studies*
KEK	Kritisch-exegetischer Kommentar über das Neue Testament
MM	J. H. Moulton and G. Milligan. *The Vocabulary of the Greek Testament. Illustrations from Papyrii and other Non-Literary Sources* (London: Hodder & Stoughton, 1930, repr. 1957).
NABPR	National Association of Baptist Professors of Religion
NAB Rev.	*New American Bible* Revised
Neot	*Neotestamentica*
NJB	*New Jerusalem Bible*
NovT	*Novum Testamentum*
NovTSup	Novum Testamentum Supplements
NRSV	*New Revised Standard Version*
NTD	Das Neue Testament Deutsch
NTM	New Testament Message
NTS	*New Testament Studies*
OTP	*The Old Testament Pseudepigrapha*, ed. James H. Charlesworth
PG	J.-P. Migne, ed., Patrologia graeca
PL	J.-P. Migne, ed., Patrologia latina
PRS	*Perspectives in Religious Studies*
ResQ	*Restoration Quarterly*
RevExp	*Review & Expositor*
RHR	*Revue de l'histoire des religions*
RB	*Revue Biblique*
RivB	*Rivista Biblica*
RSV	*Revised Standard Version*
RVV	Religionsgeschichtliche Versuche und Vorarbeiten
SBL	Society of Biblical Literature
SBLDS	SBL Dissertation Series
SBLMS	SBL Monograph Series
SNTSMS	Society of New Testament Studies Monograph Series
SNTSU	Studien zum Neuen Testament und seiner Umwelt
SUNT	Studien zur Umwelt des Neuen Testaments
TBT	*The Bible Today*

TDNT	Gerhard Kittel and Gerhard Friedrich. *Theological Dictionary of the New Testament* (10 vols.) Translated by Geoffrey W. Bromiley, Grand Rapids: Eerdmans, 1964–1976.
THKNT	Theologischer Handkommentar zum Neuen Testament
TLZ	*Theologische Literaturzeitung*
TynBull	*Tyndale Bulletin*
TZ	*Theologische Zeitschrift*
USQR	*Union Seminary Quarterly Review*
VT	*Vetus Testamentum*
WTJ	*Westminster Theological Journal*
WUNT	Wissenschaftliche Untersuchungen zum Neuen Testament
ZNW	*Zeitschrift für die neutestamentliche Wissenschaft*

Philippians

Bonnie B. Thurston

In thanksgiving for the ministries of

The Sisters of St. Joseph of Wheeling 1853–2003

"Connecting with the Dear Neighbor for 150 Years"

AUTHOR'S PREFACE

Although relatively brief, Philippians is one of the most interesting and beloved of Paul's undisputed epistles. The scholarly community has focused enormous attention on the "Christ hymn" of 2:6-11 and has struggled with the literary question of the letter's unity and the historical issue of the "enemies" addressed in chapter 3. Although except for 2:6-11 it is infrequently mined for theological content, Philippians reflects Paul's thinking on important theological issues, in particular justification by faith and theodicy. And Philippians provides a rare glimpse of Paul the man and shows him in a softer light than the one in which he usually appears.

A significant portion of this commentary deals with the Christ hymn (2:6-11), which is probably the oldest piece of Christian literature we have. My great difficulty has been to distill the enormous scholarly literature on that passage into a concise, but I hope not facile, reading of the text. I do not put forth any new theories. What may distinguish this commentary from others is its dogged insistence that the hymn be read as a hymn and not as a statement of systematic christology. Several important issues connected with the hymn (for example, the pre-existence of Christ or the Christ-Adam typology or the precise form of the hymn) are given short shrift in favor of viewing the passage as a hymn well known from a worship context and used as an example because it *is* well known by the Philippians. The pattern set forth in the hymn is central to every important issue Paul addresses in the letter, which is to say that Jesus Christ is at the heart of Philippians.

The scholarly debate about the unity of Philippians is lively, but I have tried to make a convincing case that canonical Philippians is as Paul wrote it, one letter. I do so much influenced by the lexical and structural studies of David Garland and the rhetorical analysis of D. F. Watson, but knowing that many scholars (among them, my teacher Jerome Murphy-O'Connor) disagree with my conclusion. With regard to the other great scholarly conundrum in Philippians, the identity of the "enemies" or "opponents," the "dogs" of 3:2, some readers will think I have "copped out" with the simple conclusion that the text does not give enough specific evidence to "name names," to know for certain who it is Paul confronts. Instead of making a case for one group, I suggest a range of possibilities and think, in fact, that at least two groups are probably in view, one addressed in chapter 1 and another in chapter 3.

What has struck me as I have worked with Philippians is the degree to which it reflects Paul's most mature theology. One seldom sees Philippians quoted in discussions of justification by faith, and yet it is at the heart of Paul's appeal in 3:8-11. Similarly, Paul's reflections on his own imprisonment and sufferings for the Gospel (1:12-14; 2:17; 4:10-20), the suffering and opposition the Philippian congregation is undergoing (1:27-30; 3:17–4:1) and the relation of both to the pattern of Christ's life set forth in 2:6-11 shed important light on Paul's understanding of the meaning of suffering and on the problem of theodicy. In Philippians, suffering is illuminated by the cross. Additionally, forms of the word for grace *(charis)* characterize the lexical field of Philippians and provide another instance of the letter's theological weightiness.

Most readers of the letter, however, are probably not drawn to it by these (sometimes arcane) matters. Many of us like the letter because we find the apostle Paul so approachable in Philippians and can observe how he interacts with a church in which his authority has not been called into question, in which "his gospel" has not been attacked. It is the evil-working "dogs" and mutilators (3:2) and not the Philippian Christians who draw Paul's ire. Although by genre Philippians is a hortatory letter, it is also a letter to dear friends by one who loves them deeply and cares very much for their welfare. In Philippians we see not only Paul's genius for friendship, an aspect of his considerable gifts that is frequently overlooked, but the delicacy with which he deals with his coworkers, both those who have overextended themselves on behalf of the Gospel (2:25-30) and those who threaten the unity of the church (4:2-3). The dominant mode of the letter is determined by the root word that occurs most frequently: joy (*charis,* which can also be translated "grace" or "divine favor"). But it is not a facile joy in the absence of suffering or difficulty; rather, it is a deep joy that issues forth from the prison cell (1:7, 13) and the suffering church (1:29-30), indeed, in the face of the very real possibility of martyrdom.

My methodological approach is traditional. I provide a literal translation of the text (more on this shortly), and the notes focus on the lexical meaning of important terms and their significance as well as on the implications for interpretation of interesting Greek constructions. I have tried to keep an eye to the larger units of what I take to be a unified letter and to the probable circumstances of the Christians in Philippi in the first century C.E. Because I am particularly interested in Christian spirituality and the life of prayer, I have highlighted passages in Philippians that illuminate those issues. I am happy to acknowledge my debt to other commentators on the text, and especially to Karl Barth, Gordon D. Fee, Morna Hooker, and Ralph P. Martin.

We are indebted to the many scholars who have made fine modern translations of the NT into the vernacular languages. We have come to take these excellent English translations for granted. Readers may, therefore, find my translation of Philippians rough. I have tried to remain as close to the Greek as possible both structurally and lexically and this has, perforce, led to a certain awkwardness in English. Occasionally I have had to add an English word. These words are indicated in brackets [ ]. I hope the resulting awkwardness is balanced by accuracy. Second, I have tried consistently to translate a single Greek word (or words from the same root) with the same word in English so that the reader of the English text can sense the lexical patterns in the original Greek. This may lead to some surprising renderings of familiar passages.

I have tried very hard to cite ideas that are not my own or to refer the reader to sources from which particular readings are taken. This is not altogether easy in a commentary without footnotes. And when one has worked on a project as long as I have worked on this one, ideas tend to rattle around in one's head. If I have neglected a citation or recorded one incorrectly, I would be grateful to have this pointed out so that corrections and proper credit can be given in future editions. I apologize in advance for any errors in the important matter of crediting others for their ideas. I am very grateful to the many scholars whose works appear here.

Indeed, I have many people to thank for their help, first and foremost the series general editor, Daniel Harrington, S.J., and my co-author Dr. Judith Ryan. I cannot imagine how anyone could have been more patient, gracious, helpful, encouraging, and kind than they have been to me. Second, I express my gratitude to the advanced Greek students at Pittsburgh Theological Seminary with whom I met once a week for the academic year 2001–2002 and worked through Philippians word by word. I learned an enormous amount from them, and this is as much their book as it is mine. All the librarians at Barbour Library at Pittsburgh Theological Seminary, and especially Anita Johnson and Ellen Little, were unfailingly cheerful, helpful, and encouraging. If they can't find it, it doesn't exist! James Lynn, Director of Computer Services, kept me "up and running"; Anne Rutledge, O.P., faculty secretary, provided great help and support; and Rodney Bryant and Daniel Holmes of the mail room got things where they needed to be. I am grateful to Sr. Loretta Fahey, V.H.M. for sharing her M.A. work on Philippians 2:5-11. The Cistercians at Our Lady of the Angels Monastery, Crozet, VA are a source of constant encouragement and support, but I am particularly grateful for the week we spent studying

Philippians together. The sisters' questions and prayerful responses opened new insights for me, especially into the Old Testament backgrounds of Paul's thought.

This has not been an easy book to write, in part because I have labored in the shadow of already existing and excellent scholarship on the letter. I only hope the reader will appreciate my enthusiasm for the apostle Paul and his profound experience and articulation of what it can mean to live life "in Christ" in crisis.

BONNIE B. THURSTON
Our Lady of Lourdes, 2004

PHILIPPIANS

INTRODUCTION

I. HISTORICAL BACKGROUNDS FOR THE STUDY OF PHILIPPIANS

1. *The City of Philippi*

Philippi was first mentioned about 490 B.C.E. in connection with the Persian invasion of Greece, although the city's Greek founding dates from about 360 B.C.E. when it was colonized by persons banished from Athens by order of Callistratus. About ten miles inland from the modern Greek city of Kavalla (ancient Neapolis), Philippi was bordered on the north and south by mountains and dominated by a high acropolis. The soil was fertile, and the area was noted for its many springs of water (thus the town was called Krenides), so there was good vegetation. There is some evidence for early mining in the area at Mt. Panagaion, and Thrace had gold deposits, which brought it to the attention of Philip II of Macedon. All this accords with the ancient description of Philippi by Appian in his *Civil Wars* 4.105-106.[1]

In 356 B.C.E. the residents of Krenides invited Philip to help them fight the local Thracian tribes. He subsequently annexed the region, renamed Krenides (which, itself, may have been built on the site of an older town called Datos) "Philippi" after himself, and began to mine the area. He also fortified the town because of its strategic location. The Romans occupied Philippi, which was subsequently transferred to the Empire in 167 B.C.E. under Aemilius Paulus. The construction of the Via Egnatia as a military road about 130 B.C.E. increased the trade and prosperity of the region. In October of 42 B.C.E. Mark Antony and Octavian defeated Brutus and Cassius in the Battle of Philippi and subsequently settled veterans there, thus in

[1]For the full text see Appian, *History*, trans. H. White. LCL (Cambridge, MA: Harvard University Press, 1913).

effect making the Greek city a Roman colony that included Neapolis, Oisyme, and Apollonia. (See Strabo, *Geography* vii, frag 41.) After the battle of Actium in 31 B.C.E. as many as five hundred more veterans were settled in Philippi by order of Octavian. (For a contemporary discussion see Dio Cassius, *Roman History* 51.4.6.)[2] In 44 C.E. Claudius conquered Thrace and officially made it a senatorial province of the Roman empire, although Thessalonica was the capital of the Roman province of Macedonia. While Latin was the official language of the Julio-Claudian period, the use of Greek continued into the third or fourth century of our era, especially by the indigenous inhabitants.

The Via Egnatia, which ran from Rome to the east, passed through Philippi, and it was on this route that Paul would have entered the city when he came from Neapolis. It has been estimated that the journey from Ephesus to Philippi would have taken about a week. From the Neapolis gate, the road went to the center of town. To the north were the forum, the theater, and the sanctuary of the Egyptian gods. Paul would have conversed with the magistrates (the *stratēgoi* of Acts 16:19-21) in the forum. In the lower city were the library and agora, in the upper, the temples. In Paul's day Philippi was a city of about 10,000. As it was primarily an agricultural colony, the mixed population of Thracians, Greeks, and Romans would have lived not only in the town proper, but in surrounding villages. Agricultural estates producing grain and wine were the economic units of the area. Philippi served as the market for the agricultural produce as well as a stopping place for travelers.

Philippi was governed by the *Ius Italicum*, Italian law, the highest honor a Roman province could attain. (Proud of this citizenship, Philippian Christians had to be reminded by Paul that their true citizenship is heavenly: Phil 1:27; 3:20.) This meant that Roman officials lived in Philippi (cf. Acts 16:22) and that its citizens had the right of ownership, transfer, and purchase of property, and the right to civil lawsuits. Additionally, they were at least theoretically free from provincial land and personal taxes as well as tribute.

Religiously, Philippi was as diverse as almost any city in the Empire, and its ethos was syncretistic. That is, people regularly participated in several of the city's many cults. The old Thracian gods, Apollos, Comaeus, and Artemis, continued to play an important part in the city's religious life. Mars was worshiped in his Thracian guise as Myndrytus. A votive monument to Apollo has been unearthed in the agora. There is also evidence of the worship of Dionysus. The Romans brought their own gods as well as those they had encountered in Asia Minor and the East. For

[2] Dio Cassius, *The Roman History*, trans. I. Scott-Kilvert. Penguin Classics (London: Penguin, 1987).

example, after 42 B.C.E. Philippi was placed under the protection of Isis. Also notable are the cults of Kabiroi and of Claudius. Lilian Portefaix has suggested that the city was divided into areas by religion. Inscriptions there also reflect the imperial cult. The south, along the Via Egnatia and town center, was devoted to Roman state religion. North of the Via Egnatia was the seat of folk religion, principally Cybele and other Magna Mater religions and devotion to various healing deities, where remains of the oriental cults have also been found.[3] Entering Philippi through the east gate from Neapolis via the Via Egnatia, Paul would have passed a spring and what is possibly a sanctuary to Cybele, the mother goddess.

Whether or not there were Jews in Philippi at the time of Paul is a matter for debate. Some archaeologists believe that finds from the western cemetery confirm the presence of Jews in Philippi, and a grave stele speaks of a fine to be paid to the synagogue if one puts another body in that place, but whether this evidence is from Paul's time is debated. As Murphy-O'Connor notes, "abundance of evidence for the religious preferences of the pagan population of Philippi makes the absence of any archaeological or epigraphic hint of a Jewish presence significant."[4] No Jews are listed among Paul's converts in Philippi, and in Acts 16 Lydia is specifically called a Gentile, as the jailer must have been. Murphy-O'Connor solves the problem of the place of prayer in Acts 16 by explaining that it was used by "Jewish travelers on the via Egnatia, who happened to be in the city on the sabbath."[5] There is certainly evidence of Jews in Philippi by the third century of our era, but this is much after the time of Paul.

For Reference and Further Study

Bakirtzis, Charalambos, and Helmut Koester, eds. *Philippi at the Time of Paul and After His Death.* Harrisburg, PA: Trinity Press International, 1998.

Blevins, James L. "Introduction to Philippians," *RevExp* 77 (1980) 311–23.

Bormann, Lukas. *Philippi: Stadt und Christengemeinde zur Zeit des Paulus.* Leiden: Brill, 1995.

Hendrix, Holland L. "Philippi," *ABD* 5:313–17.

Murphy-O'Connor, Jerome. *Paul: A Critical Life.* Oxford: Clarendon Press, 1996. Chapter 9, "Partnership at Philippi."

[3] Lilian Portefaix, *Sisters Rejoice. Paul's Letter to the Philippians and Luke-Acts as Received by First Century Philippian Women.* CBNTS 20 (Uppsala and Stockholm: Almqvist, 1988) 71. Chapter 4 of this study, "Deities of Importance to Women," contains an important discussion of the religious environment of Philippi.

[4] Jerome Murphy-O'Connor, *Paul: A Critical Life* (Oxford: Clarendon Press, 1996) 213.

[5] Ibid. 214.

Pilhofer, Peter. *Philippi. Die erste christliche Gemeinde Europas*. Vol. 1. Tübingen: J.C.B. Mohr, 1995.

Portefaix, Lilian. *Sisters Rejoice. Paul's Letter to the Philippians and Luke-Acts as Received by First-Century Philippian Women*. CBNTS 20. Uppsala and Stockholm: Almqvist, 1988.

2. *The Founding of the Church in the Acts of the Apostles*

Paul arrived in Philippi from Neapolis around 49 C.E. in the course of the second missionary journey recorded in Luke's Acts of the Apostles. It is appropriate to begin a study of Paul's letter to the Philippians with Luke's account of the founding of the church.

There are at least four sources available to those who wish to reconstruct Paul's ministry: information about Hellenistic Judaism and the Greco-Roman world; extra-canonical literature, which is late and legendary; Paul's own letters, which provide primary source material; and the Acts of the Apostles. An easily accessible discussion of the problems associated with using Acts uncritically as a source for the life of Paul is found in Günther Bornkamm's *Paul*.[6] Bornkamm notes that Acts was written at least forty years after Paul's life and letters and to address other matters. As a writer of Hellenistic history, Luke had a fair degree of freedom in composing the narrative and the speeches. Luke's picture of Paul is, at various points, at odds with what Paul reveals of himself in his letters, none of which are mentioned in Acts. In short, Luke wrote with a particular agenda, to show how the Gospel moved from Jerusalem to Rome and "the ends of the earth" (Acts 1:8). He puts the conventions of historical writing of his own day at the service of his various theological concerns.

Nevertheless, Paul dominates the second half of Acts. Thus it provides a background against which to understand Paul and offers historical touchstones that make dating the life of Paul possible. These include the famine in Palestine in the reign of Claudius ca. 46 C.E. (Acts 11:28); the death of Herod Agrippa I in 44 C.E. (Acts 12:23); Claudius' expulsion of the Jews from Rome in 49 or 50 (Acts 18:2); the arrival of the Roman governor Gallio in Corinth in 51 C.E. (Acts 18:12) and the accession of Festus in Caesarea in 56 or 59 C.E. (Acts 24:27).

In general, then, there are three scholarly positions about using Acts as a historical source for the life of Paul. Some hold that Acts is historically unreliable, and so one must depend exclusively on the epistles for information about Paul. Others maintain that while the epistles are primary,

[6] Günther Bornkamm, *Paul*, trans. D. M. G. Stalker (New York: Harper & Row, 1971). See especially pp. xiii–xxi of the Introduction.

and one must not skew their evidence to conform with that of Acts, Acts does provide some historically accurate information. Finally, still others hold that Acts and the letters give two different kinds of data (primary and secondary), and it may be best not to mix them.

But the material on the founding of the church in Philippi is a special case because at many points it is confirmed in the text of the letters. The description of the maltreatment at the hand of the magistrates is confirmed in 1 Thess 2:2 where Paul writes "we had already suffered and been shamefully mistreated at Philippi." Philippi is certainly one of the places Paul was beaten and imprisoned (2 Cor 11:23-25). Women were prominent in Macedonia, so the founding of the church among a group of women, and the prominence of women in the church (Lydia in Acts 16 and Euodia and Syntyche in Phil 4:2) is consistent. (For more on this matter see "Women in Philippi" below.) This, and other information, have led Gordon Fee to conclude: "there are no good historical reasons for doubting the picture that Luke presents."[7] At least with regard to the encounter with the magistrates, Murphy-O'Connor (quoting Justin Taylor) calls Acts 16 "a first-class source, indeed an eye-witness account [whose] details are historically exact."[8] What, then, does Luke report about the founding of the Philippian church?

Prior to the entrance into Macedonia there had been a general shakeup of missionary personnel (Acts 15:36-41). Barnabas, with whom Paul had been commissioned for service (Acts 13:1-3), proposed taking John Mark with them on a tour of previously established churches. Paul objected because John Mark had earlier turned back at Pamphylia. This disagreement about staffing the mission led to a parting of the ways between Barnabas and Paul. Acts 16:6-7 hints that the split resulted in a certain stagnation in the missionary work. Acts 16, then, begins with the addition of Timothy to Paul's missionary company and signals the beginning of a new mission.

Luke wants us to understand that this new mission is initiated under the guidance of the Holy Spirit. Acts 16:9-10 describes Paul's vision of a Macedonian (known to be Greek by his appearance? the style of his clothing? his unshaven face?) who pleads for their help. Verse 10 opens the enigmatic "we" source in Acts, which some take as evidence that Luke joined the party at this point and provides eyewitness accounts. The narrative-theological point for Luke, however, is God's direction of the work by means of the vision; visions are the way God gives direction.

[7] Gordon D. Fee, *Paul's Letter to the Philippians.* NICNT (Grand Rapids: Eerdmans, 1995) 27.

[8] Murphy-O'Connor, *Paul,* 214. O'Connor is here quoting Marie-Émile Boismard and Arnaud Lamouille, *Les Actes des deux Apôtres.* 6 vols. (vols. 4–6 by Justin Taylor). *V. Commentaire historique* (Paris: Gabalda, 1994).

The reader is to understand that the movement into Macedonia/Europe and Philippi is of divine origin and sanction.

Acts 16:11-15, 40 describes the founding of the church and introduces one of its prominent members, Lydia (whom Ernst Haenchen does not think Luke "invented"),[9] "a worshiper of God," " a dealer in purple cloth" (16:14). Paul and company (the "we" of 16:10-17; 20:5-15; 21:1-18; 27:1–28:16?) sail from Troas in Asia Minor to Neapolis and proceed straightaway to Philippi, "leading city of the district of Macedonia and a Roman colony" (16:12). (See above, "The City of Philippi.") Paul characteristically begins new missionary work in "hub" cities from which the Gospel might be carried to the surrounding countryside. In Philippi the nucleus of the new church is female. (See the following section, "The Place of Women in the Philippian Church.") On the Sabbath day Paul and company go "outside the city gate" (suggesting there is no synagogue *in* Philippi because there were not the requisite ten Jewish males to constitute it?) "by the river" (the Gangites), where they "supposed there was a place of prayer" (16:13).[10] The verse suggests not only that Judaism was not strongly established in Philippi at Paul's visit, but that he knew Greco-Roman religious custom; "pagan" religions often built temples by or worshiped near "living water" (springs or rivers). So Paul goes to meet religious seekers "on their own territory."

Paul meets Lydia, "a worshiper of God," probably a "godfearer," one like Cornelius in Acts 10 who worshiped the one God of Israel without having formally "converted" to Judaism. Lydia is not a native Philippian, but is from Thyatira, a Lydian city in the Roman province of Asia some twenty miles southeast of Pergamum that is famous for purple dyes. Some maintain that the purple dye was extracted from murex shells, the juice in the veins of shellfish that turned purple.[11] If this is accurate, then Lydia was perpetually ritually unclean by virtue of her work. Perhaps one is simply to understand that she sold luxury goods, purple being the color of royalty (see Dan 5:7; 1 Macc 10:20; Mark 15:17, 20; Luke 16:19-31). In any case, Lydia was a "professional woman," owner of a business and head of a household (16:14-15).

[9] Ernst Haenchen, *The Acts of the Apostles: A Commentary* (Oxford: Blackwell, 1971) 502.

[10] Murphy-O'Connor's discussion of this location is interesting and concludes that the place of prayer served not Jewish residents of Philippi, but Jewish travelers on the Via Egnatia. See *Paul,* 213–14.

[11] F. F. Bruce suggests that the dye was "derived from the juice of the madder root, for which her native region was famed as early as Homer's day." See his *Paul: Apostle of the Heart Set Free* (Grand Rapids: Eerdmans, 1986) 220, which cites Homer's *Iliad* (iv.141) in n. 31 for confirmation. See also Rosalie Ryan, "Lydia, A Dealer in Purple Goods," *TBT* 22 (1984) 285–89.

The text shows the inaccuracy of the popular view of Paul the misogynist, as he and his associates "sat down and spoke to the women who had gathered there" (16:13), sitting being the position of authority for a Jewish rabbi (see Matt 5:1). God's specific direction of the Philippian mission is reinforced as Luke records that "the Lord opened [Lydia's] heart to listen eagerly to what was said by Paul" (16:14). This is high praise of Lydia by Luke, in whose gospel only silent, listening women are commended by Jesus, and it provides divine sanction for Paul's inclusiveness. Lydia responded not just because of Paul's power as a teacher or speaker (a power Paul denies having in 1 Cor 2:1, 4-5), or because of her own needs, but because God had prepared the way for it. Lydia indicates her acceptance of Paul's message by submitting, with her household, to baptism (cf. Acts 2:37-42) and shows her understanding of what it meant by offering the service of hospitality (16:15). In this she parallels Peter's mother-in-law, who responds to her deliverance by her willingness to offer the service of hospitality (Mark 1:31). Conversion is confirmed by service.

The offer of hospitality was no small thing. As no male is mentioned in connection with her, Lydia was probably a single, female "head of household." How seemly would it have been to invite traveling male strangers, and Jews at that, to stay with her? What repercussions might it have had for her business, not to mention her personal reputation? In any case, Lydia was obviously persuasive, and again Paul was willing to overlook religious and cultural boundaries. The missionary team stayed with Lydia, and her home became the center of mission and the gathering point for believers to which Paul and Silas returned when released from prison (16:40). Perhaps it was to her home that Paul sent Timothy (Phil 2:19-24), Epaphroditus (2:25-30), and the Philippian letter itself.

The theme of the prominence of women in the founding of the Philippian church continues, albeit in a less direct way, in the exorcism by Paul of a slave girl, which leads to his imprisonment and the growth of the nascent church (Acts 16:16-39). The story is told in four dramatic scenes: the exorcism itself (vv. 16-18); the response of the populace (vv. 19-24); the experience in prison (vv. 25-34); the official response (vv. 35-39). It is especially interesting as one of the first confrontations between missionary Christianity and non-Jewish authorities. Paul had encountered religious disturbances at Pisidian Antioch and Iconium, but this is the first formal charge against him as a Christian.

As Paul and his associates are going to the "place of prayer" they encounter "a slave girl who had a spirit of divination," literally "a pythian spirit" (16:16). The python was the mythical snake of worship at Delphi and the adjectival form of the noun became the term used of one through whom the oracle spoke. This slave with an oracular spirit is of financial value to her owners, but a nuisance to Paul and company as she follows them crying out "These men are slaves of the Most High God, who proclaim to you [or "to us"] a way of salvation" (16:17). As was the case in the ministry of Jesus, here spirit recognizes spirit. "Most High God" is the same term used by spirits Jesus exorcises in Mark 5:7. While her cry is largely accurate, it apparently becomes annoying and, in the power of the name of Jesus, Paul orders the spirit to leave her (16:18). Technically this was probably some sort of violation of property rights.

The response of the slave girl's owners is predictable; they drag Paul and Silas to the magistrates. The term *stratēgos* is unusual, but it is a term of respect, perhaps reflecting Luke's apologetic attitude toward Rome. The charge is that Paul is preaching an illegal religion (*religio illicita,* cf. vv. 20-21); Christianity was an unrecognized religion in the empire. Ralph Martin points out that Roman patriotism was strong in Philippi, so that an unrecognized cult would have been a special affront.[12] Anti-Judaism may also have been involved. Judaism was legal and tolerated, but forbidden to proselytize. So many Romans had become Jews that Tiberius expelled the majority of Jews from Rome in 19 C.E., and Jews were again expelled from Rome by Claudius in 49 C.E. because of a disturbance in their community over one *Chrestus* (Christ?). Under Roman law, Roman precedent would have influenced governance in Philippi, so perhaps all Jews were suspect (another reason why none are clearly evident in Philippi?). In any event, the real issue is venality. The slave owners, deprived of their income, first accuse Paul and Silas and then turn the crowds against them, with the result that, contrary to Roman law, they are severely flogged and imprisoned. Verse 24 suggests they must have been perceived as a serious threat, for they are placed in "maximum security" conditions.

Their response to maltreatment is prayer and praise, which serve their evangelistic efforts since the other prisoners overhear (16:25). In darkest night ("about midnight") there is an earthquake (a characteristic feature of the geographic region and of biblical theophanies), and all the prisoners are released. The jailer, a Roman official or some sort of Roman retainer, must have known that Roman soldiers were put to death for being asleep on their watch (cf. Matt 28:11-15) and is prepared to commit suicide (16:27). But the mistreated Paul intervenes for his life, affirming that all the prisoners are accounted for. Having just survived earthquake and near loss of his own life, the jailer wishes to know what has transpired, and how he is to be saved. His question at 16:30 is exactly the one asked by those who heard Peter's Pentecost sermon (Acts 2:37). Paul responds with a shortened version of the early Christian *kerygma* and further

[12] Ralph P. Martin, *Philippians.* NCBC (Grand Rapids: Eerdmans, 1985) 5.

preaching (16:31-32), to which the jailer and his household respond positively. His conversion is attested by changed action (he serves his former prisoners and provides a fellowship meal; again, cf. Peter's mother-in-law in Mark 1:29-31a) and changed attitude. (Joy is the usual response to conversion; cf. 8:39.) The jailer's response to conversion is akin to that of Lydia; he offers hospitality. Although he, too, leads his household to be baptized, the jailer's name is never given, perhaps to protect his anonymity or perhaps because Luke knew that Lydia was the more prominent Christian in Philippi.

The response of the magistrates to their own bumbling is an all-too-familiar picture of authority gone awry (16:35-39). When they recognize their mistakes (indeed, their breach of law) and send word to release Paul, he insists on his rights as a citizen (16:36-37). The public flogging of a citizen without trial was illegal, and, at the very least, demanded public apology. The magistrates simply want to release Paul and Silas, but not to own their error publicly. In v. 37 Paul insists on his rights for the sake of the church in Philippi and its future. Here, again, is the Lukan theme that Christianity is not a threat to Roman order. Having "*ordered* them to be beaten with rods" (16:22), the magistrates now "*ask* them to leave the city" (16:39, italics mine). And, after visiting the Christian headquarters in Philippi, Lydia's home, "they departed" (16:40).

According to Luke, Paul made a second visit to Philippi on the "third missionary journey" (Acts 20:6; cf. 1 Cor 16:5-6; 2 Cor 2:13; 7:5). Paul founded the Philippian church, his first in Europe, with a foreign woman and her household and with a jailer working for Rome and *his* household. It is a startling picture of Paul the Pharisee breaking all sorts of barriers in carrying the Gospel to the Gentile world, and while this image serves Luke's purposes, it does not conflict with what Paul's letters reflect about the Philippian church.

For Reference and Further Study

Achtemeier, Paul J. "An Elusive Unity: Paul, Acts, and the Early Church," *CBQ* 48 (1986) 1–26.

Barrett, C. K. *Luke the Historian in Recent Study.* London: Epworth Press, 1961.

Bornkamm, Günther. *Paul.* New York: Harper & Row, 1971.

Bruce, F. F. *Paul: Apostle of the Heart Set Free.* Grand Rapids: Eerdmans, 1977, Chapter 20, "Antioch to Philippi."

Keck, Leander E. "Images of Paul in the New Testament," *Int* 43 (1989) 341–51.

Mattill, A. J., Sr. "The Value of Acts as a Source for the Study of Paul," in Charles Talbert, ed., *Perspectives on Luke Acts* (Danville, VA: Association of Baptist Professors of Religion, 1978) 76–98.

O'Toole, Robert F. "The Philippian Jailer," *ABD* 5:317–18.

3. *The Circumstances of the Church as Seen in the Letter*

Marvin R. Vincent's classic commentary on Philippians accurately sets forth the general character of the church in Philippi as it is reflected in the emotional tone of the letter. It is a church to which Paul had strong personal attachment and to which he wrote in almost wholly commendatory terms. Here there was no necessity for an official opening setting forth Paul's authority because it had not been challenged in Philippi. (For another view see the commentary on 1:1-2.) It is a church in which he has great confidence.[13] Indeed, it is a church in which he rejoices, one of the defining terms of the epistle (1:4, 18, 25; 2:2, 17, 28; 3:1; 4:1, 4, 10). And it is a church praised in glowing terms in 2 Cor 8:1-5. The letter reflects an organized, generous community that had supported Paul both financially and spiritually. But it was also a church facing internal struggles and external threats. While these matters will be taken up as they appear in the commentary that follows, a few reflections here by way of introduction are in order.

The organization of the Philippian church is indicated at the outset of the letter as Paul greets the saints "with the bishops and deacons" (1:1). They have been able to dispatch their own missionary, Epaphroditus, who has risked his life "for the work of Christ" (2:25-30). Further, the home church has "coworkers" with Paul (Euodia, Syntyche, Clement) who are well enough organized that Paul can ask one group of them to help the others (4:2-3).

This community has been an enormous support to Paul; they shared "in the gospel from the first day until now" (1:5). They sent him Epaphroditus, "your messenger and minister to my need" (2:25). The community's "revived concern" for Paul (4:10) carries on the tradition of their support sent to him in "the early days of the gospel, when I left Macedonia" (4:15), and in Thessalonica (4:16) with the current gifts sent via Epaphroditus (4:18). The long reflection on his present circumstances (1:12-26) indicates that Paul understands how deeply the Philippians care for him and are concerned for his welfare. Indeed, this is the only church he commends for "sharing [*koinōnia,* literally "fellowship" or "partnership"] in the gospel" (1:5) and the only one from which he accepts monetary aid. A great deal of recent analysis of the Philippian letter is carried out in the context of the rhetoric of friendship in the Greco-Roman world.[14] Paul viewed the Philippians not only as his converts and cowork-

[13] Marvin R. Vincent, *A Critical and Exegetical Commentary on the Epistles to the Philippians and to Philemon* (New York: Charles Scribner's Sons, 1906) xxxiv, xxxvi.

[14] See, for example, Gordon Fee's NICNT commentary; G. W. Peterman, *Paul's Gift from Philippi* (Cambridge: Cambridge University Press, 1997); Stanley K. Stowers,

ers but also as his friends, and this colors the rhetoric and contents of the letter.

But the Philippian church is not perfect, nor is it a community without difficulty or trials. Proud of their status as a Roman colony, the Philippians must be reminded that their citizenship is in heaven (3:20). Repeated reminders to be "one minded" (2:2, 5; 3:15; 4:2) and the difficulty between Euodia and Syntyche suggest there are internal (power?) struggles in the community, as do warnings against selfish ambition and conceit (1:17; 2:3). Paul would not have had to warn against behaviors that were not in evidence. That the church shares with Paul "both in my imprisonment and in the defense and confirmation of the gospel" (1:7), that they stand firm and "are in no way intimidated by . . . opponents" (1:28), and indeed that they have "the privilege not only of believing in Christ, but of suffering for him as well" and "are having the same struggle that you say I had" (1:29-30) suggest that they have faced, are facing, or soon will face persecution from outside the believing community (see 1:27-30 and 2:17). Persecution from without makes the matter of divisiveness within even more serious and brings into sharp focus the problem of Paul's opponents in chapter 3. Apparently the Philippians must contend with those who view the gospel very differently from Paul himself, persons who insist on male circumcision (3:2-3) and who live in ways inappropriate to "the cross of Christ" (3:17–4:1).

Finally, the text of the letter reflects several aspects of what is known of Greco-Roman Philippi and of the Lukan portrait of the founding of the church there. The focus on Christ as Lord *(kyrios)* is especially notable in a city in which public gatherings would include honoring the emperor by use of that title. Paul uses the language of sacrifice in 2:17, suggesting he is aware of the religious diversity of the city, and the virtue list of 4:8 is a catalogue of behaviors that would be praised in any Greco-Roman environment. The language of citizenship (1:27; 3:20) echoes the political realities in Philippi. Finally, Paul singles out women who "struggled beside me in the work of the gospel" (4:3). The prominence of women in both the Acts account of the founding of the church and in the Philippian letter calls for special comment in the subsequent section.

This picture of the Philippian church gleaned from the letter agrees with the view recorded in 2 Cor 8:1-7, a text that provides one other enigmatic bit of information. The passage appears in the section of the letter in which Paul is making an appeal for his collection to assist the Jerusalem

---

"Friends and Enemies in the Politics of Heaven: Reading Theology in Philippians," in Jouette M. Bassler, ed., *Pauline Theology* Vol. I (Minneapolis: Fortress, 1991) 105–21; Ben Witherington III, *Friendship and Finances in Philippi* (Valley Forge, PA: Trinity Press International, 1994).

church. Writing of "the churches of Macedonia" (8:1), the province that included Philippi and Thessalonica, Paul says that "during a severe ordeal of affliction, their abundant joy and their extreme poverty have overflowed in a wealth of generosity on their part. For, as I can testify, they voluntarily gave according to their means, and even beyond their means . . ." (8:2-3). Reinforced here is the picture of the Philippian church both as undergoing trials and as generous.

But what of the phrase "their extreme poverty"? The word for "extreme" *(bathos)* is a strong word meaning "depth" or "greatness." Suggested translations include "dirt poor" or "rock-bottom poor."[15] Because of the circumstances of the city and what is usually written about Christians there, one does not normally think of Philippian Christians as "dirt poor." Perhaps the reference is to Thessalonica to which Paul did, indeed, have to write about "work ethic" (1 Thess 2:5, 9; 4:10-12; 5:12; 2 Thess 3:6-13) and persecution (1 Thess 1:6-8; 2:14; 3:3-10; 2 Thess 1:4-8). Why might Christians in an otherwise affluent area have been impoverished? Was it due to the persecution alluded to in 2 Cor 8:2? Was it because the husbands of the women who were so prominent in the Philippian church, husbands who controlled the family resources, did not become Christians? Luise Schottroff's reconstruction of Lydia's position suggests that she was not a wealthy householder, but among the "working poor."[16]

What is clear is that Paul is using the example of the generous offering of those least in a position to donate to persuade the Corinthians to open their purses. He is depending on the emotional appeal of those who, though themselves persecuted, give generously. And as he has praised the Corinthians to the Macedonians, he does not want to be proved a liar if some of them accompany him to Corinth (2 Cor 9:1-5.). Second Corinthians 8:1-7, then, reinforces the portrait of the Philippian church as one that is suffering "a severe ordeal of affliction" but is nevertheless generous, and it introduces the possibility that this generosity comes not from wealth but from want.

For Reference and Further Study

Bloomquist, L. Gregory. *The Function of Suffering in Philippians.* JSNTSup 78. Sheffield: JSOT Press, 1993.

[15] Quoted in Veronica Koperski, "Philippians," in Catherine Clark Kroeger and Mary J. Evans, eds., *The IVP Women's Bible Commentary* (Downer's Grove, IL: InterVarsity Press, 2002) 709. My discussion here is heavily dependent on Koperski.

[16] See Luise Schottroff, *Lydia's Impatient Sisters: A Feminist Social History of Early Christianity* (Louisville: Westminster John Knox, 1995).

Peterman, Gerald W. *Paul's Gift from Philippi.* Cambridge: Cambridge University Press, 1997.

Reumann, John H. P. "Philippians and the Culture of Friendship," *Trinity Seminary Review* 19 (1997) 69–83.

Witherington, Ben III. *Friendship and Finances in Philippi.* Valley Forge, PA: Trinity Press International, 1994.

4. *The Place of Women in the Philippian Church*

A classic text on the Hellenistic world, William Tarn and G. T. Griffith's *Hellenistic Civilisation,* devotes a section to the position of women in the Greek cities, noting: "If Macedonia produced perhaps the most competent group of men the world had yet seen, the women were in all respects the men's counterparts. . . ."[17] He attributes the prominence of women in part to the Macedonian princesses and queens after Alexander, to the "trickle down" effect of their influence, and to Stoicism, which exhibited attitudes toward marriage that served to raise women's status. Tarn points to evidence in the ancient sources of women poets, scholars, and magistrates *(gynaeconomoi).* He also notes the special tragedy that infanticide (which was widely practiced in Greece) was for women.

It is a commonplace of scholarship that Greek women enjoyed increasing freedoms during the Hellenistic and Roman periods. As Carolyn Osiek notes, "literary and inscriptional evidence indicates that from Hellenistic times women in Macedonia . . . enjoyed more personal freedom and participation in social and economic life than women in most of the eastern Mediterranean lands."[18] During the Roman period some women owned provincial estates and were financially secure enough to be patrons in religious cults. Many Roman women in the provinces were freedwomen, with the attendant privileges. There is evidence that Greek women with Roman citizenship "held high civic office and were priestesses in the imperial cult in Asia."[19] This is not to argue against the fact of Roman patriarchy, but simply to say that the circumstances for women in Macedonia provided real opportunities for women of means. In any case, it is a universal truth that wealth makes for privilege, whatever one's gender.

This was especially true in the religious arena. Valerie Abrahamsen and Lilian Portefaix have done significant work on this topic, and my discussion here draws heavily on their conclusions. The cults of Diana and

[17] William Tarn and G. T. Griffith, *Hellenistic Civilisation.* 3rd ed. (London: Edward Arnold, 1959) 98.

[18] Carolyn Osiek, "Philippians," in Elisabeth Schüssler Fiorenza, ed., *Searching the Scriptures: A Feminist Commentary* (New York: Crossroad, 1994) 238.

[19] Witherington, *Friendship and Finances,* 108.

Isis were popular among Philippian women and both had "places of worship" in Philippi. The sanctuary of Diana (Roman Hecate) was cut into the rock of the Philippian acropolis and decorated with carvings in which female subjects greatly outnumber male. Diana's cult was immensely popular in Philippi, where she was worshiped in the aspect of Hecate, a deity of the lower world who transported persons to new life. The cult of Isis spread via the Romans from Egypt and was served by functionaries of both sexes. Her cult spoke directly to human need in the areas of fertility, healing, and the afterlife. The ecstatic cult of Dionysus also attracted women who could receive the emotional fulfillment of identification with the god. The fact that Philippi is normally considered to be a prosperous city may have contributed to its lively religious life. People had leisure for worship, and money to support the cults.

In his commentary Gordon Fee remarks: "Given the prominent place of women in Macedonian life in general, it is not surprising that the core group of first converts [to Christianity] were women, nor that the location of its first house church was in the home of a woman merchant."[20] Lydia in Acts 16 is a paradigm of a Macedonian woman. She is independent, head of her own household, active in public and religious life, indeed, the leading figure in a religious cult, and open to new spiritual ideas and experiences. Euodia and Syntyche became leaders in the Christian community, much as other women must have had leadership roles in pagan cults. Some of these cults also included the notion of a cosmic ruler with authority over heaven, earth, and the underworld. Indeed, since exclusivity (the idea that a person might worship only *one* god) was not a common concept in Greco-Roman religions, it might have been difficult to persuade women accustomed to participating in the cult of several deities that Jesus Christ was a "jealous God" and called for exclusive loyalty. (Certainly this was an issue in the church at Colossae.) Apparently the church after Paul did have to struggle with religious traditions that had powerful female deities. In any case, the leadership roles assumed by Christian women in Philippi would probably not have seemed unusual in that city's context.

Not only are women prominent in the NT records about Philippi, but their prominence also continues after the time of Paul.[21] Polycarp of Smyrna wrote to Philippi about the middle of the second century to commend the church, urge it toward further growth, and defend Paul's gospel.[22]

[20] Fee, *Paul's Letter,* 27.

[21] The following discussion is adapted from my book *Women in the New Testament* (New York: Crossroad, 1998) 47–51.

[22] Kirsopp Lake, *Apostolic Fathers I.* LCL (Cambridge, MA: Harvard University Press, 1912/1977).

Chapter 4 of Polycarp's epistle is devoted to instructions to wives and women, who are exhorted to behave in ways that will protect the church from disrepute. (In this respect it is very much like the canonical Pastoral Epistles.) Polycarp writes of the training of wives but does not limit their interest in the faith or their social access to men and women in the community. He alludes to an order of widows, who were expected to live exemplary lives and to offer public and private prayer for all. Virgins *(parthenous)* are exhorted "to walk with a blameless and pure conscience" (5:3), indicating that there existed a group of celibate women in the Philippian church. (Recall that the question of asceticism loomed large in the second-century church.) At the end of the letter Polycarp mentions Crescens' sister, who apparently is traveling to Philippi to be of service to the church (14:1).

The prominence of women in Philippi continues in later centuries. At least one apocryphal work mentions Philippi. *The Acts of Paul* (ca. 160–190 C.E.) has a fragment that mentions Philippi. In it Longinus orders the death of Paul and his own daughter, Frontina, whom the apostle has converted. She dies; Paul escapes, and later the girl is restored to life, leading to the conversion of many. Much later, in the fourth century, a basilica in the forum of Philippi and another outside the city walls were dedicated to Paul. By the sixth century there were four basilicas in Philippi. Inscriptions from these churches mention women as deacons and canonesses. One deacon, Agatha, was buried with her husband, John, and another, Posidonia, was buried with a woman named Pancharia, a canoness.

The picture of the church in Philippi in the first centuries of our era is one filled with prominent women. Luke reports they were the area's first converts, and Paul's letter to the community mentions two women by name. Women were addressed by the bishops of the apostolic period and appear in apocryphal materials, suggesting their importance in the popular traditions. As Valerie Abrahamsen notes, women continued to serve the Philippian church as deacons, canonesses, and "servants." The cultural context of Philippi itself, and the fact that Paul does not prohibit Euodia and Syntyche from Christian service, and in spite of their difficulties calls them "coworkers," sets the trajectory for the continuing prominence of women in the Philippian church.

For Reference and Further Study

Abrahamsen, Valerie. *The Rock Reliefs and the Cult of Diana at Philippi.* Th.D. diss., Harvard University, 1986. Ann Arbor: University Microfilms, 1986.

________. "Women at Philippi: The Pagan and Christian Evidence," *JFSR* 3 (1987) 17–30.

Gillman, Florence M. "Early Christian Women at Philippi," *Journal of Gender in World Religions* 1 (1990) 59–79.

Koperski, Veronica. "Philippians," in Catherine Clark Kroeger and Mary J. Evans, eds., *The IVP Women's Bible Commentary.* Downer's Grove, IL: InterVarsity Press, 2002, 706–13.

Luter, Boyd. "Partnership in the Gospel: The Role of Women in the Church at Philippi," *JETS* 39 (1996) 411–20.

Malinowski, Francis. "The Brave Women of Philippi," *BTB* 15 (1985) 60–64.

Osiek, Carolyn. "Philippians," in Elisabeth Schüssler Fiorenza, ed., *Searching the Scriptures: a Feminist Commentary.* New York: Crossroad, 1994, 237–49.

Perkins, Pheme. "Philippians," in Carol A. Newsom and Sharon H. Ringe, eds., *The Women's Bible Commentary.* Louisville: Westminster John Knox, 1992, 343–45.

Portefaix, Lilian. *Sisters Rejoice. Paul's Letter to the Philippians and Luke-Acts as Received by First-Century Philippian Women.* CBNTS 20. Uppsala and Stockholm: Almqvist, 1988.

Schottroff, Luise. *Lydia's Impatient Sisters: A Feminist Social History of Early Christianity.* Louisville: Westminster John Knox, 1995.

Thomas, W. D. "Lydia: A Truly Liberated Woman," *ExpTim* 95 (1984) 112–13.

________. "The Place of Women in the Church at Philippi," *ExpTim* 83 (1972) 117–20.

Torjesen, Karen Jo. *When Women Were Priests.* San Francisco: HarperSan Francisco, 1993.

Witherington, Ben III. "Lydia," *ABD* 4:422–23.

5. *The Philippian Church after the Time of Paul*

As the previous discussion suggests, the Philippian church not only received an epistle (or several epistles? see discussion in the essay on literary backgrounds of Philippians) from Paul and was mentioned in his other correspondence; it also retained prominence after the time of the apostle. This may be in part because Philippi itself grew after the apostolic period. The Via Egnatia was repaired during Trajan's reign (97–117 C.E.) and was expanded under Hadrian and Antoninus Pius.

Ignatius of Antioch visited Philippi in the early second century on his journey from Antioch to Rome, where he was to be martyred. His visit so impressed the church that they subsequently sought copies of his correspondence. Polycarp wrote to the Philippians about this matter. It is his only extant letter and not only gives advice to the church in Philippi but assists them with their project of collecting Ignatius' letters. The text of Polycarp's letter has many affinities with the Pastoral Epistles (which may have been written at about the same time) and supports "the wisdom of the blessed and glorious Paul" who "taught accurately and steadfastly the word of truth, and also when he was absent wrote *letters* to you, from the study of which you will be able to build yourself up into the faith given you" (3:2, italics mine). The verse not only suggests a problem with false teaching in Philippi but mentions multiple letters of Paul to that church, a matter that will be taken up below.

Philippi appears in at least two apocryphal texts, *The Acts of Paul* (discussed in the previous section), and the fragmentary *Acts of Andrew.* In the Philippian section of that work a wealthy Thessalonian, Exuos, renounces his inheritance and takes a vow of poverty when he is converted to Christianity. His furious parents ignite the house where he and Andrew are staying, but the fire is miraculously extinguished by the apostle with holy water. Additionally, Philippians appears in Pseudo-Clement (*Hom.* 9.16.3) in the context of an exorcism story and in the *T.Jos.* (8.5), which contains the story of an earthquake and hymn singing.

The earliest Christian building that has been identified in Philippi dates from the fourth century. It seems to have been an assembly hall built over a Macedonian tomb. There was a large fifth-century basilica built near the Via Egnatia and at least one other basilica of that period was not completed, its dome having collapsed during construction. Outside the walls of the city is another structure dating to the fifth century and known as the "Extra-muros Basilica." It is intriguing because it was built near an earlier church that had a mosaic giving the names of many bishops of the church in Philippi. The existence of many large basilicas and churches in Philippi suggests that it was a pilgrimage site in early Christianity and has led one scholar to posit that Paul was martyred and buried there.[23] There are extensive inscriptions from Philippi, many of which mention early Christians (both men and women) and the functions they carried out in the church.

All of this is to say that Philippi retained importance as an apostolic church after the time of Paul and well into the Byzantine period.

For Reference and Further Study

Abrahamsen, Valerie. "Women at Philippi: The Pagan and Christian Evidence," *JFSR* 3 (1987) 17–30.

Bakirtzis, Charalambos, and Helmut Koester, eds. *Philippi at the Time of Paul and After His Death.* Harrisburg, PA: Trinity Press International, 1998.

Hendrix, Holland. "Philippi," *ABD* 5:313–17.

[23] Allen Dwight Callahan, "Dead Paul: The Apostle as Martyr in Philippi," in Charalambos Bakirtzis and Helmut Koester, eds., *Philippi at the Time of Paul and After His Death* (Harrisburg, PA: Trinity Press International, 1998) 67–84.

II. LITERARY BACKGROUNDS FOR THE STUDY OF PHILIPPIANS

1. *Paul and the Greco-Roman Letter*[1]

Alexander the Great hoped that everyone in the "civilized" world would come to speak Greek, and, indeed, this largely occurred. By the first century the Greco-Roman world spoke the simplified form of Greek we now know as *koinē*, or "common" Greek. Because its forms vary from those of classical Greek, previous generations of scholars thought it might be a liturgical language. But the discovery in Egypt over the last one hundred years of hundreds of documents written on papyrus have dispelled that notion and have called into question the assumption of widespread illiteracy.

Many of these papyrus documents are written communications addressed to those from whom the sender was separated by distance; in short, letters. Such communications were originally transmitted orally, so the Greek word *epistolē*, from which we get the English "epistle," originally referred to oral communication. This may account in part for the importance of rhetoric in letter writing, as well as for the social stratification seen in such letters in the development of modes of address for one's equals, betters, and "lowers." Some of the early analysis of the ancient letter was carried out by Adolf Deissmann, who distinguished between true letters, which he defined as personal communications, and epistles, which he thought were literary or public communications.[2] This distinction has largely gone by the wayside.

Letters were so important in ancient literature that rhetorical handbooks existed to explain how to write various kinds of letters. Sometime between the second century B.C.E. and the second century C.E. Pseudo-Demetrius wrote *On Style* and listed twenty-one epistolary styles. Pseudo-Libanius (4th to 6th century C.E.) lists forty-one. In these handbooks letters were classified by content (for example, patronage letters or letters dealing with domestic matters), and these classifications generally followed Aristotle's divisions of rhetoric into the categories of judicial or forensic ("of the law courts," or "to persuade"), deliberative or hortatory (for public assembly, expediency) and demonstrative or epideictic (public celebration, to inspire or please). Much current New Testament scholarship has used the ancient rhetorical handbooks, especially their descrip-

[1] I was privileged to attend Jerome Murphy-O'Connor's lectures on this subject at the École Biblique in Jerusalem in 1993 and hereby acknowledge my debt to him. Any errors of interpretation are mine, not his.

[2] Adolf Deissmann, *Paul: A Study in Social and Religious History,* trans. William E. Wilson (New York: Harper & Brothers, 1957) Chapter 1.

tion of forms and of literary *topoi* (themes or commonplaces), to analyze canonical letters. In fact, the formal patterns in Pauline epistles have been a major focus of scholarly study over the past fifty years.[3]

There are some examples of Aramaic and Jewish epistolography, as well as the Mari and Ras Shamra letters, but in contrast to the number and variety of Greek letters there are relatively few distinctively Jewish epistles. However, Jewish authorities in Palestine did communicate with Diaspora communities by means of letters. Paul belies his Greco-Roman education, then, in using letters to communicate with his churches. Certainly the letter was the most popular literary form in early Christianity. There are twenty-two letters in the New Testament, twenty independent compositions and two embedded in the Acts of the Apostles (15:23-29; 23:26-30). They include letters from individuals to individuals or to groups and circular letters to specific communities. The letter form is also adapted as a framing device for the Revelation to John and the anonymous homily we know as the book of Hebrews.

Most letters in antiquity were written by a scribe or amanuensis. The scribe used a pen made from a reed with ink compounded of soot suspended in a gum base. Letters were written on papyrus, a highly refined plant product, or sometimes on *ostraca,* bits of pottery, or on wooden tablets covered with wax. Papyrus was graded for quality by its fineness, whiteness, stoutness, and smoothness. In the New Testament period the best paper was Roman. Ruled lines and margins were sometimes made with a disk of lead. Greek letters were placed on the lines; Hebrew letters hung from them. The unit of measurement by which a scribe charged for his work was the *stichos,* the average length of a Homeric hexameter line of poetry, or about sixteen syllables. In 310 C.E. the cost for a good scribe was twenty to twenty-five denarii per hundred *stichoi.* A day laborer might earn twenty-five denarii a day, a skilled craftsman fifty. So the writing and sending of letters could be an expensive undertaking.

Paul certainly used scribes to write his letters. In Rom 16:22 the writer names himself: "I Tertius, the writer of this letter." Sometimes Paul himself wrote letters (Phlm 19). When Paul adds his name at the end of a letter it may well be to authenticate contents written down by others (see, for example, 1 Cor 16:21; Gal 6:11; Col 4:18). This was characteristic of the time, as the sender's autograph, seal, or mark authenticated what the scribe had written. That Paul used amanuenses is clear; how extensively they influenced the content of the letters is unknown. To what extent did they influence the rhetoric of the letters? To what extent did co-authors of letters, Timothy or Sosthenes or Silvanus, for example, influence their

[3] For a cautionary discussion of this matter see Raymond E. Brown, *An Introduction to the New Testament* (New York: Doubleday, 1997) Chapter 15.

contents and rhetoric? Sometimes this is clear in the body of the letter as the pronouns shift from first person singular to plural, but sometimes we simply do not know. All of this is to say that, while the thought of the epistles is Pauline, the vocabulary and style may be influenced by others.

It is clear that Paul's letters followed the standard form of the Greco-Roman letter: opening formula; thanksgiving; body; closing formula. Philippians follows this pattern: opening, 1:1-2; thanksgiving, 1:3-11; body, 1:12–4:20; closing, 4:21-23. Letters opened with a formula that included the name of the sender *(superscriptio)*, the addressee *(adscriptio)*, and a greeting *(salutatio)*. Perhaps following the example of Roman diplomatic correspondence, Paul usually introduces himself with epithets ("apostle," or "slave," for example). A thanksgiving follows, which in Pauline letters normally sets forth in some way the theme of the letter and the degree of intimacy with those to whom the apostle writes. The body of the letter contains the heart of the message and the reasons for which it was written. Within this central section of the letter a number of conventions are evident. These include transitional formulas ("I do not want you to be ignorant," "I beseech you"), epistolary *topoi* (self-contained teachings perhaps only loosely connected to their context and often dealing with the themes of health, friendship, business, and/or domestic events), autobiographical statements, travel plans, and concluding paraenesis (that is, advice or exhortation to pursue virtue and avoid vice). Paul's letters also contain bits of early liturgy, benedictions, blessings, doxologies, hymns. The closing formula of a Greco-Roman letter includes a benediction, usually in the form of a "peace" wish. Paul's letters often add to this a request for prayer, secondary greetings, and an autograph.

Once a letter was authenticated by an autograph or mark it was rolled or folded, and the delivery instructions were written on the *verso* (back or rough) side. How it got where it was going was more complex. The Persians had the earliest postal system, a sort of "pony express." The Greeks had none. The Romans had a *cursus publicus*, but only for official communications. While the wealthy used their slaves to carry their letters to recipients, other persons had to send them with travelers going in the direction of the recipients. One can only speculate about how many letters went astray. We know from NT texts that Paul sent his letters by couriers known to the recipients (often Timothy). In the case of the Roman letter it may well be the deacon Phoebe who is carrying the letter, and because she was unknown to the Roman Christians, Paul appends a note of introduction to that letter (Rom 16:1-2), thereby employing another epistolary convention.

The questions of how many letters Paul wrote and when exactly he wrote them are complex and beyond the scope of this introduction. A careful reading of the NT text shows that Paul wrote more letters than we have (see, for example, 1 Cor 5:9; 2 Cor 2:4; Col 4:16). Some letters are clearly lost, and scholarship has posited that some we do have may be collections of fragments of multiple letters. Second Corinthians, Philippians, and Second Thessalonians have been described as composites. Some letters originally attributed to Paul were almost certainly written by his disciples. (See, for example, the Pastoral Epistles, 1 and 2 Timothy and Titus.) Such pseudonymity was widely practiced in the ancient world, which was not at all concerned with "intellectual property rights." It was understood that to use someone's name was to honor that figure (as, for example, Plato put his dialogues in the mouth of Socrates) and added the authority of the master to the disciple's work. Pseudonymous letters are not "forgeries" or "fakes," but authentic records of Paul's teachings as they were applied to the later circumstances of a growing and developing church.

In my view the letters of Paul are almost always occasional, that is, they were written to specific communities to address specific issues and served as substitutes for the apostle's presence. What we know of the community, and of its circumstances and issues, sets the limits of our interpretation. It is not manifestly clear whether Paul understood himself to be writing "scripture," especially since there is little precedent in Judaism for the use of letters as scriptural texts. For him "scripture" was the Jewish Scriptures, usually in the LXX form. It is clear that he believed he had the right to speak authoritatively and that he understood himself to be handing on a received, authoritative tradition, one that sometimes came directly "from the Lord" ("I received from the Lord what I also handed on to you," 1 Cor 11:23; "what I am writing to you is a command of the Lord," 1 Cor 14:37; compare Gal 1:11-12). It is important, then, to be alert to passages in which Paul alludes to his own authority and to that of his writing and its sources.

For Reference and Further Study

Aune, David C. *The New Testament in its Literary Environment.* Philadelphia: Westminster, 1987. See especially Chapter 5.

Bahr, G. J. "Paul and Letter Writing in the First Century," *CBQ* 28 (1966) 465–77.

Bradley, David G. "The *Topos* as a Form in the Pauline Paraenesis," *JBL* 72 (1953) 238–46.

Doty, William. "The Classification of Epistolary Literature," *CBQ* 31 (1969) 183–99.

________. *Letters in Primitive Christianity.* Philadelphia: Fortress, 1973.

Exler, F. X. J. *The Form of the Ancient Greek Letter.* Washington, DC: Catholic University of America, 1923.

Mahlerbe, Abraham. "Ancient Epistolary Theorists," *Ohio Journal of Religious Studies* 5 (1977) 3–77.

Mullins, Terence Y. "Formulas in New Testament Epistles," *JBL* 19 (1972) 380–90.

Murphy-O'Connor, Jerome. *Paul the Letter Writer. His World, His Options, His Skills*. Collegeville: Liturgical Press, 1995.

Stowers, Stanley K. *Letter Writing in Greco-Roman Antiquity*. Philadelphia: Westminster, 1986.

White, John L. *Light from Ancient Letters*. Philadelphia: Fortress, 1986.

2. *The Authorship, Provenance, and Date of Philippians*

Pauline authorship of Philippians has seldom been called into question. Origen and Eusebius assumed the work was written by the apostle Paul, as did Irenaeus and Clement of Alexandria. The first serious challenge to its authenticity was mounted by Ferdinand Christian Baur in the middle of the nineteenth century, and several scholars in the Tübingen school followed suit. Marvin R. Vincent's classic Greek commentary discusses the matter in detail and concludes that their objections to genuineness "are mainly imaginary."[4] Current scholarship assumes the letter to be Pauline. Philippians makes extensive use of the first person singular, and its tone is entirely that of a personal letter. A related matter, which will be treated in the commentary, is whether the "Christ hymn" of 2:6-11 was written by Paul. (See the commentary on the passage and Excursus I.)

Determining the provenance and date of the letter is much more complex. Philippians may be grouped with Paul's other "imprisonment epistles," Philemon, Colossians, and Ephesians, letters that allude to imprisonment. James Blevins says Philippians is ". . . a call from the jail cell, written by an apostle facing death, and directed to a church facing persecution and suffering."[5] References to imprisonment in Philippians (1:7, 13, 14, 17) provide the best clues by which to place and date the letter. But *where* was Paul imprisoned? There are at least four serious possibilities: Rome, Ephesus, Caesarea, and Corinth.

In an excellent rehearsal of the evidence for each location (to which my discussion is indebted), Gerald F. Hawthorne enumerates important information in Philippians to which one must attend in dealing with the issue.[6] Not only was Paul in prison when he wrote (1:7, 13, 14, 17), but his life hung in the balance (1:19-20; 2:17). This fact has led Paul Holloway to suggest that Philippians is a letter of consolation written to answer the church's discouragement over Paul's situation and their own suffer-

[4] Marvin R. Vincent, *The Epistles to the Philippians and to Philemon*. ICC (New York: Charles Scribner's Sons, 1906) xxvi. For the full discussion see pp. xxvi–xxx.

[5] James Blevins, "Introduction to Philippians," *RevExp* 77 (1980) 322.

[6] Gerald F. Hawthorne, "Philippians, Letter to the," in Gerald F. Hawthorne, Ralph P. Martin, and Daniel G. Reid, eds., *Dictionary of Paul and His Letters* (Downers Grove, IL: InterVarsity Press, 1993) 709. For his full discussion of the matter see pp. 709–11.

ing.[7] However, Paul had hopes of being released (1:24-25; 2:25). There was a praetorium where Paul was held (1:13), and members of Caesar's household (4:22). Paul was able to receive visitors (2:25-30); Timothy was with him (1:1; 2:19-23); and several trips were made back and forth between the place of imprisonment and Philippi. Wherever he was, his evangelistic efforts were ongoing (1:15-18).

The theory that the letter was written from Rome dates to the Marcionite prologues in the second century C.E. and is the traditional view. Certainly it fits much of the evidence. Acts reports that Paul was held in Rome for two years (28:30) under something like "house arrest." Soldiers guarded him (28:16), but he had access to visitors and was able to send and receive letters and to preach (28:17, 30, 31). Obviously there was a praetorium in Rome, as well as Caesar's household. And the church in Rome was both large and factional. But Rome is a long way from Philippi, seven hundred to eight hundred miles. Many scholars think this fact would preclude the many visits alluded to in the letter. Furthermore, there is no clear evidence that Timothy was with Paul in Rome, and Phil 2:24 suggests Paul plans to visit Philippi upon his release, although Rom 15:24-28 says his plan is to travel west to Spain.

Ephesus, on the other hand, is much closer to Philippi, about four hundred miles distant. The fact that Paul makes no direct reference to Ephesian imprisonment does not necessarily mean he was not in prison there, since he makes general reference to imprisonments (2 Cor 1:8 and 11:23). Certainly in 1 Cor 15:32 Paul says he fought wild beasts at Ephesus, and this might have been related to an incarceration. Many provincial residences would have had a praetorium and the possibility of members of Caesar's household in residence. Timothy was with Paul in Ephesus (Acts 19:22), which was a center of intense evangelistic activity (Acts 19:2-9). If, however, Philippians were written from Ephesus, why is there no reference to the collection for the church in Jerusalem, which was so important to Paul at that time? There is no particular evidence that Ephesus was a factional church, and it seems odd that Paul would say of his associates "all of them are seeking their own interests" (2:21, and see 1:15-17), since his friends Priscilla and Aquila were in Ephesus with him (1 Cor 16:19).

The case for a Caesarean imprisonment rests heavily on Acts 23–26, since Paul's letters mention no such imprisonment, although, as noted above, that does not necessarily preclude one. Luke reports that Paul was imprisoned in the praetorium of Herod at Caesarea, which had a Roman garrison (Acts 23:35). His imprisonment there was lengthy, but he had access to his friends (Acts 24:27; 24:23). In Caesarea Paul had made a defense

[7] Paul Holloway, *Consolation in Philippians* (Cambridge: Cambridge University Press, 2001).

for himself (Phil 1:7, 16; cf. Acts 24–26) and was awaiting its outcome. While the distance from Caesarea to Philippi is great, nine hundred to a thousand miles, the length of the Caesarean imprisonment might have allowed for multiple contacts. And although he was protected from the death sentence as a Roman citizen, as a Jew in Roman Palestine Paul might still have been under the Jewish law that prescribed death for one who had brought a Gentile into the Temple.

Finally, Corinth was close to Philippi, had a proconsul and thus a praetorium and "household of Caesar." Paul faced severe opposition in Corinth, but he was with Priscilla and Aquila, so the harsh remarks in the Philippian letter about associates seem untoward. The arguments for Corinth as the place of origin seem to me most problematic.

Through the years outstanding scholars have disagreed about the provenance of Philippians. William Barclay, Gordon Fee, J. B. Lightfoot, T. W. Manson, Wayne Meeks, James Moffatt and Johannes Weiss have supported the traditional, Roman location. On the other hand, Raymond E. Brown, Adolf Deissmann, G. S. Duncan, Robert Jewett, Wilhelm Michaelis, and Jerome Murphy-O'Connor assume an Ephesian location. Ralph P. Martin leaves the question open in his commentary. While I tend toward the theory of Ephesian origin, and I think the modern consensus is moving in this direction, the text of Philippians by itself does not provide enough information to be more than tentative about this conclusion. If the letter is from Rome, it is to be dated in the early 60's; if from Ephesus, in the early to mid-50's; if from Caesarea, the late 50's, and if from Corinth very early, about 50 C.E.

For Reference and Further Study

Blevins, James. "Introduction to Philippians," *RevExp* 77 (1980) 311–23.

Duncan, G. S. "Were Paul's Imprisonment Epistles Written from Ephesus?" *ExpTimes* 67 (1955–56) 163–66.

Hawthorne, Gerald F. "Philippians, Letter to the," in Gerald F. Hawthorne, Ralph P. Martin, and Daniel G. Reid, eds., *Dictionary of Paul and His Letters.* Downers Grove, IL: InterVarsity Press, 1993, 709–17.

Manson, T. W. "St. Paul in Ephesus: The Date of the Epistle to the Philippians," *BJRL* 23 (1958–59) 182–200.

Wansink, Craig S. *Chained in Christ: The Experience and Rhetoric of Paul's Imprisonments.* Sheffield: Sheffield Academic Press, 1966.

3. *The Unity of Philippians*

The discussion about whether Philippians is one letter or a composite of several is as lively as that about the provenance of the epistle. Even a cursory reading of the text reveals many kinds of material as Paul alternates among autobiography, exhortation, and polemic. In his own epistle to the Philippians, Polycarp alludes to *letters (epistolas)* the apostle Paul wrote to them in his absence (3.2). But the principal stumbling block to viewing Philippians as one letter appears at the beginning of chapter 3. Paul seems to be concluding ("Finally, my brethren," *to loipon, adelphoi mou,* 3:1), but then opens a new and polemical section of the letter at 3:2. Some scholars have noted that one can go from 3:1 to 4:4 with no break in thought, suggesting the intervening material might be an insertion. (For more on this "break" see the commentary on the text and Excursus II.)

Arguments against the integrity of Philippians first surfaced in the nineteenth century and have centered around some of the following observations: Polycarp mentions *letters* of Paul to Philippi. There is an apparent shift in substance and tone in the letter between verses 3:1 and 3:2. Several scholars have noted that a reader can jump from 3:1a to 4:4 without "missing a beat." And if Philippians is written at least in part to thank that church for its support to Paul (brought by Epaphroditus), why does he wait until the very end of the letter, 4:10-20, to allude to it? It is, according to Murphy-O'Connor, normally his practice to begin a letter with what is uppermost in his mind.[8]

Scholars who think Philippians is a composite of fragments of several letters disagree as to whether there are two or three letters represented and where, exactly, these fragments begin and end. Edgar J. Goodspeed, for example, thinks there are two letters. Letter A, 1:1–3:1a and 4:10-23, was written as Epaphroditus was returning to Philippi after his illness. Letter B, 3:1b–4:9, was written after Epaphroditus arrived from Philippi with their gifts to Paul. But other scholars think the two letters are (A) 1:1–3:1 and 4:20-23 and (B) 3:2–4:20. (Among those who hold the "two letter theory" are Günther Bornkamm, Joachim Gnilka, Edgar J. Goodspeed, and Leander E. Keck.) Scholars who think Philippians is a series of fragments hold that there are three (Karl Barth, F. W. Beare, J. F. Collange, Joseph A. Fitzmyer, Reginald H. Fuller, Helmut Koester, Eduard Lohse, Willi Marxsen, and Jerome Murphy-O'Connor). There are several reconstructions. One holds, for example, that Letter A is 4:10-20, Paul's "thank you note"; Letter B is 1:1–3:1a, 4:4-7, 21-23, a letter carried by Epaphroditus that reports on Paul's condition; and Letter C is 3:1b–4:3, 8-9, a letter attacking Philippian opponents of Paul. Murphy-O'Connor divides Philippians as follows: Letter A, 4:10-20; Letter B, 1:1–3:1, 4:2-9; and Letter C, 3:2–4:1.

[8] Jerome Murphy-O'Connor, *Paul: A Critical Life* (Oxford: Clarendon Press, 1996) 216.

While those holding the "fragment" theory believe that the irregular sequence is further proof of the fragmentary character of Philippians, other scholars see the inability to reach consensus on the number and exact division of fragments as an argument *for* its unity. Scholars who hold that Philippians is a single composition by Paul (L. Gregory Bloomquist, J. W. Dalton, Gordon Fee, David Garland, Robert Jewett, Werner G. Kummel, T. E. Pollard, D. F. Watson) often begin by refuting the external evidence. They point out that Polycarp's "letters" to Philippi may be a red herring since the plural *epistolai* can refer to *a* letter of importance, and in any case at 11.3 Polycarp's letter speaks of a single epistle from Paul. Adolph von Harnack thought that the reference in *PolPhil* 3.2 included the Thessalonian letters.[9] Philippians appears in no Greek manuscript in other than its canonical form, and according to Fee there are no known analogies for a "cut and paste" letter in antiquity.[10] In any case, why would a collector of Pauline fragments arrange them in this "random" way, since more logical possibilities are apparent? If, for example, 3:1 and 4:4 cohere, why would an editor break that unity by inserting unrelated material?

In my view the most substantive arguments for the unity of Philippians come from analysis of the internal evidence. First, there is the matter of the translation of "finally" *(to loipon)* at 3:1. It has been established that the phrase can be equally accurately translated "as to what remains." Margaret Thrall notes that in post-classical Greek it may simply be a transitional word; its function depends on its context.[11] David Garland's article listed below has pointed out the lexical unity of Philippians. Garland notes that the distinctive vocabulary of 2:5-11 pervades all of chapter 3 and that rare words that first appear at 1:27 recur at 3:20 and 4:1, 3, thus apparently marking out 1:27–4:3 as lexical inclusion. L. Gregory Bloomquist provides an extensive table of terms that recur in the various sections of Philippians, and W. J. Dalton has noted lexical parallels between 2:6-11 and 3:20-21. Finally, vocabulary in 1:3-11 reappears in

[9] For a more detailed discussion see Ralph P. Martin, *Philippians.* NCBC (Grand Rapids: Eerdmans, 1985) 11–13.

[10] Fee thinks 2 Corinthians is a different case, since it is attaching two letters in the assumed chronological order, not a "weaving together" of disparate material. Gordon D. Fee, *Paul's Letter to the Philippians.* NICNT (Grand Rapids: Eerdmans, 1995) 22. And see the discussion in Jan Lambrecht, *Second Corinthians.* SP 8 (Collegeville: Liturgical Press, 1999) 7–11.

[11] For more information see Margaret Thrall, *Greek Particles in the New Testament* (Grand Rapids: Eerdmans, 1962); H. G. Meecham, "The Meaning of *(To) loipon* in the New Testament," *ExpTim* 48 (1936–37) 331–32.

4:10-20, and this may, once again, indicate deliberate inclusion. (For more see Excursus II.)

Additionally, there are thematic repetitions that argue for the unity of Philippians. The themes of unity (1:27-28; 2:2; 3:16), one-mindedness (1:27; 2:2, 5; 3:15; 4:2), and suffering (1:29-30; 3:10-11) recur in the letter, as do images of humility (2:1-11; 3:1-11), emptying (2:5-11; 3:10), and glorification (2:10-11; 3:11). I have observed in each section of the letter a pattern of returning to the Philippians' conduct (1:27-30; 2:12-18; 3:17–4:1; 4:4-9). There are clear lexical and thematic ties between 1:27–2:18 and 3:17–4:1. And the whole letter is pervaded both tonally and lexically by joy (1:4, 18, 19; 2:2, 17, 18, 28; 3:1; 4:1, 4, 10). Finally, D. F. Watson's analysis of Philippians presents a convincing argument that the document is a single rhetorical unit addressing by means of deliberative rhetoric the appearance of a rival gospel in Philippi.

Although arguments about the unity of Philippians, or lack thereof, that rest on speculation about Paul's circumstances when writing Philippians are interesting, the analysis of lexical and thematic material in the document has convinced me that Philippians is a single letter. After the opening formula (1:1-2), there follows the customary thanksgiving (1:3-11) and a report by Paul of his circumstances (1:12-27). Following Garland, I am disposed to see 1:27–4:3 as a literary unit followed by paraenesis (4:4-9), an expression of thanks (4:10-20), and the usual closing formulae (4:21-23). I shall expand on the form of the letter in the section that follows, but give the final word to the always balanced Raymond E. Brown, who noted that "the debate over whether the preserved letter represents a compilation from two or three original letters is not of great importance to most readers. That affirmation may be tested by studying one of the theories of compilation and seeing if there are ways in which it affects the basic meaning of Phil."[12]

For Reference and Further Study

Bloomquist, L. Gregory. *The Function of Suffering in Philippians.* JSNTSup 78. Sheffield: JSOT Press, 1993.

Dalton, J. W. "The Integrity of Philippians," *Bib* 60 (1979) 97–102.

Fitzgerald, John T. "Philippians, Epistle to the," *ABD* 5:320–22.

Garland, David E. "The Composition and Unity of Philippians," *NovT* 27 (1985) 141–73.

Jewett, Robert. "The Epistolary Thanksgiving and the Integrity of Philippians," *NovT* 12 (1970) 40–53.

[12] Brown, *Introduction,* 498.

Koester, Helmut. "The Purpose of the Polemic of a Pauline Fragment (Philippians III)," *NTS* 9 (1961/62) 317–32.
Luter, A. B., and M. V. Lee. "Philippians as Chiasmus: Key to the Structure, Unity, and Theme Questions," *NTS* 41 (1995) 89–101.
Pollard, T. E. "The Integrity of Philippians," *NTS* 13 (1966/67) 57–66.
Rahtjen, B. D. "The Three Letters of Paul to the Philippians," *NTS* 6 (1959/60) 167–73.
Reed, Jeffrey T. "Philippians 3:1 and the Epistolary Hesitation Formulas: The Literary Integrity of Philippians, Again," *JBL* 115 (1996) 63–90.
Watson, D. F. "A Rhetorical Analysis of Philippians and its Implications for the Unity Question," *NovT* 30 (1988) 57–88.

4. *The Form and Structure of Philippians in Light of Its Purpose*

Over the last thirty years scholars have studied in detail the rhetorical patterns and forms of Greco-Roman letters and have analyzed Paul's epistles by using these methods. While the distinctions among the types of letters are not hard and fast, each type seems to exhibit particular structural forms and patterns of rhetoric. Philippians has been analyzed as a letter of friendship, as a letter of consolation, and as a family letter. These analyses have proved very fruitful for our understanding of the letter and the circumstances that gave rise to it.

Gordon Fee, John Reumann, and Ben Witherington III have all suggested that Philippians follows the conventions of the letter of friendship. They point out that friendship was a matter for serious philosophical inquiry in the Greco-Roman world. Aristotle, Cicero, Plutarch, and Seneca all wrote extensively on the subject.[13] It was generally understood that friendships could be between equals or between persons of different social standings. The latter often included patronage. Friendship between equals could be based on virtue, pleasure, or need. The highest form was based on virtue and included mutual encouragement toward virtue (so moral exhortation was a standard feature of letters of friendship) and reciprocity in giving and receiving gifts both material and "spiritual."

Noting the obvious affection Paul has for the Philippian church, Fee, Reumann, and Witherington suggest that the Philippian letter is a letter of friendship between equals. Paul avoids the "patron-client" conventions in favor of those that suggest mutuality and reciprocity. For example, he does not refer to himself as an apostle in the opening of the letter; he

[13] See, for example, Aristotle, *Nicomachean Ethics,* Book 8; Cicero, *De Amicitia;* Plutarch, *De Amicitia Multi;* Seneca, *Moral Epistles,* 11.

speaks of the mutual suffering he and the Philippians have undergone for the Gospel, and he commends Philippian Christians as his "coworkers." Perhaps most significantly, Paul accepts monetary gifts from the Philippians. The fact that he places the "thank you note" part of the letter at the end (4:10-20), and that he never really says "thank you" for their gift can be explained by the mutuality of the relationship he enjoys with that church (see commentary on 4:10-20). The paraenetic material in Philippians, of course, follows the conventions of moral exhortation as friends encourage friends toward greater virtue. Fee concludes that in terms of form, Philippians is a "hortatory letter of friendship."[14]

Similarly, Paul Holloway has suggested that Philippians is a letter of consolation written to encourage the Philippians in their discouragement over Paul's imprisonment. It is meant to console them in their worry about Paul and their own suffering for the Gospel. His strategy is to help them discern what is important and what is not. In 1:12–2:30 Paul addresses his own imprisonment and its effects, and in 3:1–4:1 he stresses that the one necessary thing is knowing, and rejoicing in, the Lord. Consolation comes from knowing that suffering is not random and meaningless. Paul's suffering, and that of the Philippians, serves to advance the Gospel and to unite them to Jesus, who suffered for them all.

Finally, Loveday Alexander has studied the formal patterns in family letters and concluded that Philippians is of this type. She has isolated seven features of such letters, all of which are evident in Philippians: (1) an address and greeting, 1:1-2; (2) a prayer for those receiving the letter, 1:3-11; (3) the author's reassurance to the recipients about him/herself, 1:12-26; (4) the sender's request for reassurance about the recipients (as in mutual friendship, see above), 1:27–2:18; 3:1–4:3; (5) exchange of information about mutual acquaintances, 2:19-30; (6) exchange of greetings with third parties, 4:21-22; (7) closing wish for health, 4:23. She concludes that the real purpose of Philippians is the strengthening of family ties; it is a *Verbindungsbrief,* a letter to bind Paul and the Philippian Christians more closely together in their work for the Gospel.

It is noteworthy that scholars who analyze Philippians according to the formal structures of types of Greco-Roman letters all conclude that it is one letter. Scholars who approach Philippians from the point of view of Greco-Roman rhetoric draw the same conclusion. They generally assert that Philippians uses deliberative rhetoric for a hortatory purpose. Aristotle points out that deliberative/hortatory rhetoric is for expediency. That is, its purpose is to convince in a particular situation. Paul's task is to encourage his friends in Philippi to greater unity, to convince them that this

[14] Fee, *Paul's Letter,* 14.

unity is both necessary for them and crucial to the progress of the Gospel. David Black, D. F. Watson, and Ben Witherington III have proposed that the structure of Philippians arises from Paul's use of deliberative rhetoric. In such rhetoric the *exordium* introduces the subject and seeks to dispose the audience favorably toward the speaker's point of view. The *narratio* explains matters at hand, and the *propositio* is the speaker's essential proposition or proposal. *Probatio* provides arguments to support the case; in *refutatio* the opponents' arguments are refuted, and the *peroratio* recapitulates the speaker's proposition and seeks to arouse the hearer's emotions in favor of his/her point of view.

Black notes that Philippians follows the structure of all Greco-Roman letters: opening (1:1-2); body (1:3–4:20); closing (4:21-23). The body opens with the usual thanksgiving (1:3-8) and prayer wish (1:9-11). According to Black the "body proper," 1:12–4:9, contains two sections, 1:12–2:30 and 3:1–4:9. Black notes a chiastic structure in the first part of the body with 1:12-26 as imprisonment news, 1:27–2:18 instructions for the church, and 2:19-30 news about companions. The second section of the body warns against those who threaten unity and uses Paul's own life as an example of the "right way." Following deliberative rhetoric, then, the letter is organized as follows: *exordium* (1:3-11); *narratio* (1:12-26); *argumentatio* (1:27–3:21); *peroratio* (4:1-9); *narratio* (4:10-20).

D. F. Watson also argues that Philippians is carefully constructed and organized according to the rules of deliberative rhetoric. The "rhetorical situation" is the appearance of a rival gospel that Paul must refute. The *exordium* of the letter is found in 1:3-26, which consists of the thanksgiving and prayer (1:3-11) and a personal narrative (1:12-26). The *narratio* in 1:27-30 sets forth the concerns to which the *exordium* has drawn attention and for which it has secured the good will of the recipients. The *probatio* in 2:1–3:21 is to encourage the Philippians to live lives worthy of the Gospel Paul has taught them. Finally, then, the *peroratio* of 4:1-20 recapitulates Paul's points and presents a last, emotional appeal. Watson concludes that Philippians is not "artless," but follows a rhetorical model that incorporates a variety of repeated patterns of words and ideas.

Similarly, Ben Witherington III understands Paul's primary focus in Philippians as that of securing concord in the church. The apostle employs deliberative rhetoric to that end. After the conventional letter opening, Witherington suggests the epistolary thanksgiving serves as the *exordium*. After a brief *narratio* explaining what gave rise to the letter (1:12-26), the *propositio* is set forth in 1:27-30. The greatest portion of the body of the letter, then, 2:1–4:3, serves as the letter's *probatio,* which is followed by the *peroratio* in 4:4-20. Witherington concludes that Paul uses positive and negative examples to exhort the Philippians to unity. Witherington notes that the letter reflects "considerable skill in rhetorical composition. This letter is far from artless prose lacking careful arrangement of form and content."[15]

One final analysis of the structure of Philippians is noteworthy. A. B. Luter and M. V. Lee have suggested that Philippians as a whole is a chiasmus. While I personally tend to think Pauline studies has gone a little "chiasmus mad," the reconstruction by Luter and Lee does speak intelligently to the structure and unity of Philippians. They propose that the overarching theme of Philippians is partnership in the Gospel. In the letter, A and A' deal with the theme of partnership in the Gospel (1:3-11; 4:10-20), and B and B' enumerate the results of Paul's partnership with the Philippians (1:12-26; 4:6-9). C and C' challenge the Philippians to remain united (1:27–2:4; 4:1-5), and D and D' urge them to do so by following examples of humility (2:5-16; 3:1b-21). At the center of the letter, then, are two examples of partnership in the Gospel, Timothy and Epaphroditus (2:17–3:1a). These two men provide examples to the Philippians of how they should live. Again, structural analysis reveals that Philippians is one, unified letter.

While the various rhetorical analyses of Philippians conclude that it is one letter, scholars divide the letter into differing rhetorical units. I suspect this is because they envision the reasons for the letter differently. Still, rhetorical analysis suggests a carefully constructed epistle. I am persuaded that Philippians exhibits conventions of both the letter of friendship and of the family letter and that rhetorical analysis gives important clues about how Paul structured his appeal to believers in Philippi. That said, it has been a challenge to divide the letter into units for commentary because there are several quite reasonable and defensible possibilities. This commentary follows the divisions of the Greco-Roman letter and, within the body of the letter, not a rhetorical schema, but what can be observed simply as the alternation of personal examples with instructions to the Philippians. My decision to divide the letter in this way was confirmed when I read an article by Stanley Stowers entitled "Friends and Enemies in the Politics of Heaven."[16] Stowers points out that Philippians is a hortatory letter of friendship. One of the rhetorical devices of such letters is the use of contrasting models. Stowers suggests that Paul uses positive and negative examples, demonstrating how friends behave and how enemies behave. This contrast, he believes, is the key to the letter's structure, and I concur in the following outline:

[15] Ben Witherington III, *Friendship and Finances in Philippi* (Valley Forge, PA: Trinity Press International, 1994) 20. Witherington's rhetorical analysis, which I have summarized in the text, is found on pp. 17–20.

[16] Stanley Stowers, "Friends and Enemies in the Politics of Heaven," in Jouette M. Bassler, ed., *Pauline Theology,* Vol. I (Minneapolis: Fortress, 1991) 105–21.

1:1-2	Opening Formula/Greeting	
1:3-11	Thanksgiving and Prayer Wish	
1:3-8	Thanksgiving	
1:9-11	Prayer Wish	
1:12–4:20	Body	
1:12-26	The Example of Paul	
1:12-14		Results of Imprisonment
1:15-18a		Motives in Ministry
1:18b-26		Paul's Dilemma
1:27–2:18	Instructions to the Philippians	
1:27-30		Their Manner of Life
2:1-4		Central Injunction
2:5-11		Christ Hymn
2:12-18		Their Manner of Life
2:19-30	The Examples of Timothy and Epaphroditus	
2:19-24		Timothy
2:25-30		Epaphroditus
3:1–4:1	Instructions to the Philippians	
3:1-4a		Instruction/Warning about "Dogs"
3:4b-14		Example of Paul
3:15–4:1		Instructions/Warning about Enemies
4:2-3	The Example of Euodia and Syntyche	
4:4-9	Instructions to the Philippians	
4:4-7		On Prayer
4:8-9		Virtue List and Final Exhortation
4:10-20	Thank You	
4:21-23	Final Greetings	

Note that both sets of instructions to the Philippians (1:27–2:18 and 3:1–4:1) have the example of a personal life at their center (Christ Jesus in 2:5-11 and Paul himself in 3:4-16) and alternate with the positive examples of Timothy and Epaphroditus (2:19-30) and the negative examples of Euodia and Syntyche (4:2-3).

For Reference and Further Study

Alexander, Loveday. "Hellenistic Letter-Forms and the Structure of Philippians," *JSNT* 37 (1989) 87–101.

Black, David A. "The Discourse Structure of Philippians: A Study in Text-Linguistics," *NovT* 37 (1995) 16–49.

Fee, Gordon D. "Philippians and Ancient Letter Writing," in idem, *Paul's Letter to the Philippians*. Grand Rapids: Eerdmans, 1995, 2–14.

Fitzgerald, John T., ed. *Friendship, Flattery and Frankness of Speech: Studies on Friendship in the New Testament World.* NovTSup 82. Leiden: Brill, 1996.

Holloway, Paul. *Consolation in Philippians*. Cambridge: Cambridge University Press, 2001.

Luter, A. B., and M. V. Lee. "Philippians as Chiasmus: Key to the Structure, Unity and Theme Questions," *NTS* 41 (1995) 89–101.

Reumann, John. "Philippians and the Culture of Friendship," *Trinity Seminary Review* 19 (1997) 69–83.

Russell, Ronald. "Pauline Letter Structure in Philippians," *JETS* 25 (1982) 295–306.

Swift, R. C. "The Theme and Structure of Philippians," *BSac* 141 (1984) 257–75.

Watson, D. F. "A Rhetorical Analysis of Philippians, and Its Implications for the Unity Question," *NovT* 30 (1988) 57–88.

Witherington, Ben III. *Friendship and Finances in Philippi.* Valley Forge, PA: Trinity Press International, 1994.

GENERAL BIBLIOGRAPHY

1. *General Studies*

Aune, David C. *The New Testament in its Literary Environment.* Philadelphia: Westminster, 1987.

Balch, David, et al., eds. *Greeks, Romans and Christians.* Minneapolis: Fortress, 1990.

Barrett, C. K. *Luke the Historian in Recent Study.* London: Epworth Press, 1961.

Bassler, Jouette M., ed. *Pauline Theology.* Vol. 1. Minneapolis: Fortress, 1991.

Becker, Jürgen. *Paul: Apostle to the Gentiles*. Louisville: Westminster John Knox, 1993.

Black, Matthew, and Georg Fohrer, eds. *In Memoriam Paul Kahle.* BZAW 103. Berlin: Töpelmann, 1968.

Bornkamm, Günther. *Paul.* New York: Harper & Row, 1971.

Brown, Raymond E. *An Introduction to New Testament Christology*. New York: Paulist, 1994.

________, Joseph A. Fitzmyer, and Roland E. Murphy, eds. *The New Jerome Biblical Commentary.* Englewood Cliffs, NJ: Prentice Hall, 1990.

Bruce, F. F. *Paul: Apostle of the Heart Set Free.* Grand Rapids: Eerdmans, 1977; 2nd ed. 1986.

Cannon, George E. *The Use of Traditional Materials in Colossians.* Macon, GA: Mercer University Press, 1983.

Deissmann, Adolf. *Paul: A Study in Social and Religious History.* New York: Harper & Brothers, 1957.

Doty, William. *Letters in Primitive Christianity.* Philadelphia: Fortress, 1973.

Dunn, James D. G. *Christology in the Making.* Philadelphia: Westminster, 1980.

Ellis, E. Earle, and Erich Grässer, eds. *Jesus und Paulus.* Göttingen: Vandenhoeck & Ruprecht, 1975.

Exler, F. X. J. *The Form of the Ancient Greek Letter.* Washington, DC: Catholic University of America, 1923.

Farmer, William R., and C. F. D. Moule, eds. *Christian History and Interpretation.* Cambridge: Cambridge University Press, 1967.

Fitzgerald, John T., ed. *Friendship, Flattery and Frankness of Speech: Studies on Friendship in the New Testament World.* NovTSup 82. Leiden: Brill, 1996.

Fortna, Robert, and Beverly Roberts Gaventa, eds. *The Conversation Continues.* Nashville: Abingdon, 1990.

Gamble, Harry. *The Textual History of the Letter to the Romans.* Grand Rapids: Eerdmans, 1977.

Gasque, W. Ward, and Ralph P. Martin, eds. *Apostolic History and the Gospels.* Grand Rapids: Eerdmans, 1970.

Green, Joel B., et al., eds. *Dictionary of Jesus and the Gospels.* Downers Grove, IL: InterVarsity Press, 1992.

Guthrie, Donald. *New Testament Theology.* Downers Grove, IL: InterVarsity, 1981.

Hawthorne, Gerald F., Ralph P. Martin, and Daniel G. Reid, eds. *Dictionary of Paul and His Letters.* Downers Grove, IL: InterVarsity, 1993.

Hooker, Morna D. *Not Ashamed of the Gospel.* Grand Rapids: Eerdmans, 1994.

Hengel, Martin. *Studies in Christology.* Edinburgh: T & T Clark, 1995.

Hurd, J. C., and G. P. Richardson, eds. *From Jesus to Paul.* Waterloo: Wilfrid Laurier University Press, 1984.

Jaeger, Werner. *Early Christianity and Greek Paideia.* New York: Oxford University Press, 1961.

Karris, Robert. *A Symphony of New Testament Hymns.* Collegeville: Liturgical Press, 1996.

Kroeger, Catherine Clark, and Mary J. Evans, eds. *The IVP Women's Bible Commentary.* Downers Grove, IL: InterVarsity, 2002.

Ladd, George E. *A Theology of the New Testament.* Grand Rapids: Eerdmans, 1974; 2nd ed. 1993.

Lederbach, Dennis. *Christ in the Early Christian Hymns.* New York: Paulist, 1998.

Murphy-O'Connor, Jerome. *Paul: A Critical Life.* Oxford: Clarendon Press, 1996.

________. *Paul the Letter Writer.* Collegeville: Liturgical Press, 1995.

Newsom, Carol A., and Sharon H. Ringe, eds. *The Women's Bible Commentary.* Louisville: Westminster John Knox, 1992.

Pfitzner, Victor C. *Paul and the Agon Motif.* Leiden: Brill, 1967.

Porter, Stanley, and Paul Joyce, eds. *Crossing the Boundaries.* Leiden: Brill, 1994.

Richards, E. Randolph. *The Secretary in the Letters of Paul.* WUNT 2nd Ser. 42. Tübingen: J. C. B. Mohr [Paul Siebeck], 1991.

Rienecker, Fritz, and Cleon Rogers. *Linguistic Key to the Greek New Testament.* Grand Rapids: Zondervan, 1980.

Sampley, J. Paul. *Pauline Partnership in Christ: Christian Community and Commitment in Light of Roman Law.* Philadelphia: Fortress, 1980.
Schmithals, Walter. *Paul and the Gnostics.* Nashville: Abingdon, 1972.
Schottroff, Luise. *Lydia's Impatient Sisters: A Feminist Social History of Early Christianity.* Louisville: Westminster John Knox, 1995.
Schüssler Fiorenza, Elisabeth, ed. *Searching the Scriptures: A Feminist Commentary.* New York: Crossroad, 1984.
Senior, Donald, ed. *Catholic Study Bible/New American Bible.* Oxford: Oxford University Press, 1990.
Stowers, Stanley K. *Letter Writing in Greco-Roman Antiquity.* Philadelphia: Westminster, 1986.
Sumney, Jerry. *Identifying Paul's Opponents.* JSNTS 40. Sheffield: JSOT Press, 1990.
________. *'Servants of Satan,' 'False Brothers,' and Other Opponents of Paul.* JSNTS 188. Sheffield: Sheffield Academic Press, 1999.
Thrall, Margaret. *Greek Particles in the New Testament.* Grand Rapids: Eerdmans, 1962.
Thurston, Bonnie. *Spiritual Life in the Early Church.* Minneapolis: Fortress, 1993.
________. *Women in the New Testament.* New York: Crossroad, 1998.
Torjesen, Karen Jo. *When Women Were Priests.* San Francisco: HarperSan Francisco, 1993.
Wansink, Craig S. *Chained in Christ: The Experience and Rhetoric of Paul's Imprisonments.* Sheffield: Sheffield Academic Press, 1966.
White, John L. *Light from Ancient Letters.* Philadelphia: Fortress, 1986.
Wiles, G. P. *Paul's Intercessory Prayers.* Cambridge: Cambridge University Press, 1974.

2. *Commentaries*

Barth, Karl. *The Epistle to the Philippians.* Richmond: John Knox, 1962.
Barth, Markus. *Ephesians.* 2 vols. AB 34, 34A. Garden City, NY: Doubleday, 1974.
Beare, F. W. *A Commentary on the Epistle to the Philippians.* 2nd ed. London: Adam & Charles Black, 1969.
Bockmuehl, Markus. *The Epistle to the Philippians.* BNTC. Peabody, MA: Hendrickson, 1998.
Bonnard, Pierre. *L'Epitre de Saint Paul aux Philippiens.* Paris: Delachaux & Niestle, 1950.
Bruce, F. F. *Philippians.* New York: Harper & Row, 1983.
Caird, G. B. *Paul's Letters from Prison.* Oxford: Oxford University Press, 1976.
Collange, Jean-François. *L'Epitre de Saint Paul aux Philippiens.* Paris: Delachaux & Niestle, 1973.
Craddock, Fred. *Philippians.* Interpretation. Atlanta: John Knox, 1985.
Fee, Gordon D. *Paul's Letter to the Philippians.* NICNT. Grand Rapids: Eerdmans, 1995.
Getty, Mary Ann. *Philippians and Philemon.* Wilmington: Michael Glazier, 1980.
Haenchen, Ernst. *The Acts of the Apostles.* Oxford: Blackwell, 1971.
Hawthorne, Gerald F. *Philippians.* WBC. Waco, TX: Word Books, 1983.

Hooker, Morna D. "The Letter to the Philippians," in Leander E. Keck, et al., *The New Interpreter's Bible.* Nashville: Abingdon, 2000, 9:467–549.

Koperski, Veronica. "Philippians," in Catherine Clark Kroeger and Mary J. Evans, eds., *The IVP Women's Bible Commentary.* Downers Grove, IL: InterVarsity Press, 2002, 706–13.

Lambrecht, Jan. *Second Corinthians.* SP 8. Collegeville: Liturgical Press, 1999.

Lightfoot, J. B. *Saint Paul's Epistle to the Philippians.* London: Macmillan, 1879.

Marshall, I. Howard. *The Epistle to the Philippians.* London: Epworth Press, 1991.

Martin, Ralph P. *The Epistle of Paul to the Philippians.* London: Tyndale Press, 1959.

________. *Philippians.* NCBC. Grand Rapids: Eerdmans, 1985.

Melick, Richard R., Jr. *Philippians, Colossians, Philemon.* Nashville: Broadman, 1991.

O'Brien, Peter T. *The Epistle to the Philippians.* NIGTC. Grand Rapids: Eerdmans, 1991.

Osiek, Carolyn. *Philippians and Philemon.* Nashville: Abingdon, 2002.

________. "Philippians," in Elisabeth Schüssler Fiorenza, ed., *Searching the Scriptures: A Feminist Commentary.* New York: Crossroad, 1994, 237–49.

Perkins, Pheme. "Philippians," in Carol A. Newsom and Sharon H. Ringe, eds., *The Women's Bible Commentary.* Louisville: Westminster John Knox, 1992, 343–45.

Plummer, Alfred. *A Commentary on St. Paul's Epistle to the Philippians.* London: Robert Scott, 1919.

Silva, Moises. *Philippians.* Chicago: Moody Press, 1988.

Vincent, Marvin R. *Epistles to the Philippians and to Philemon.* ICC. 4th impression. Edinburgh: T & T Clark, 1950.

3. *Studies on Philippi and Philippians*

Abrahamsen, Valerie. *The Rock Reliefs and the Cult of Diana at Philippi.* Th.D. dissertation, Harvard University, 1986. Ann Arbor: University Microfilms, 1986.

Bakirtzis, Charalambos, and Helmut Koester, eds. *Philippi at the Time of Paul and After His Death.* Harrisburg, PA: Trinity Press International, 1998.

Bartsch, Hans-Werner. *Die Konkrete Wahrheit und die Lüge der Spekulation.* Frankfurt: Peter Lang, 1974.

Bloomquist, L. Gregory. *The Function of Suffering in Philippians.* JSNTS 78. Sheffield: Sheffield Academic Press, 1993.

Bormann, Lukas. *Philippi: Stadt und Christengemeinde zur Zeit des Paulus.* Leiden: Brill, 1995.

Davis, Casey W. *Oral Biblical Criticism: The Influence of the Principles of Orality on the Literary Structure of Paul's Epistle to the Philippians.* JSNTS 172. Sheffield: Sheffield Academic Press, 1999.

Hawthorne, Gerald F. *Word Biblical Themes: Philippians.* Waco, TX: Word Books, 1987.

Hofius, Otfried. *Der Christushymnus Philipper 2, 6-11.* Tübingen: J. C. B. Mohr [Paul Siebeck], 1976.

Holloway, Paul A. *Consolation in Philippians: Philosophical Sources and Rhetorical Strategy.* Cambridge: Cambridge University Press, 2001.

Keller, M. Noël. *Choosing What Is Best: Paul, Roman Society and Philippians.* Unpublished doctoral dissertation. Chicago, IL: Lutheran School of Theology, 1995.

Loh, I-Jin, and Eugene A. Nida. *A Translator's Handbook on Paul's Letter to the Philippians.* Stuttgart: United Bible Society, 1977.

Martin, Ralph P. *Carmen Christi.* Cambridge: Cambridge University Press, 1967.

________. *A Hymn of Christ.* Downers Grove, IL: InterVarsity, 1997.

Martin, Ralph P., and Brian J. Dodds, eds. *Where Christology Began: Essays on Philippians 2.* Louisville: Westminster John Knox, 1998.

Mengel, Berthold. *Studien zum Philipperbrief.* Tübingen: J. C. B. Mohr [Paul Siebeck], 1982.

Moule, H. G. C. *Philippian Studies.* London: Hodder & Stoughton, 1897.

Oakes, Peter. *Philippians: From People to Letter.* MSNTS 10. Cambridge: Cambridge University Press, 2001.

Peterlin, Davorin. *Paul's Letter to the Philippians in Light of Disunity in the Church.* Leiden: Brill, 1995.

Peterman, G. W. *Paul's Gift from Philippi: Conventions of Gift-Exchange and Christian Giving.* Cambridge: Cambridge University Press, 1997.

Philhofer, Peter. *Philippi: Die erste christliche Gemeinde Europas.* Vol. I. Tübingen: J. C. B. Mohr [Paul Siebeck], 1995.

________. *Philippi: Katalog der Inschriften von Philippi.* Tübingen: J. C. B. Mohr [Paul Siebeck], 2000.

Portefaix, Lilian. *Sisters Rejoice. Paul's Letter to the Philippians and Luke-Acts as Received by First-Century Philippian Women.* CBNTS 20. Uppsala and Stockholm: Almqvist, 1988.

Reed, Jeffrey T. *A Discourse Analysis of Philippians.* JSNTS 136. Sheffield: Sheffield Academic Press, 1997.

Verwilghen, Albert. *Christologie et Spiritualité selon Saint Augustin: L'Hymne aux Philippiens.* Paris: Beauchesne, 1985.

Wick, Peter. *Der Philipperbrief: Der formale Aufbau des Briefs als Schlüssel zum Verständnis seines Inhalts.* Stuttgart: Kohlhammer, 1994.

Witherington, Ben III. *Friendship and Finances in Philippi.* Valley Forge, PA: Trinity Press International, 1994.

TRANSLATION, NOTES, INTERPRETATION

OPENING FORMULA/GREETING: 1:1-2

1. Paul and Timothy, slaves of Christ Jesus, to all the holy ones in Christ Jesus who are in Philippi, with bishops and deacons, 2. grace to you and peace from God our Father and [the] Lord Jesus Christ.

Notes

1. *Paul and Timothy, slaves of Christ Jesus:* Timothy is a Pauline coworker who appears as co-author in several epistles (2 Cor 1:1; Col 1:1; 1 Thess 1:1; 2 Thess 1:1; Phlm 1) and figured prominently in the work in Philippi (2:19-24). He may have served as Paul's amanuensis, but more important is the point that Paul did not work alone; he acted in collaboration with others with whom he had long-term working relationships. Paul frequently introduces himself to congregations as "apostle of Jesus Christ" (1 Cor 1:1; 2 Cor 1:1; Gal 1:1; Eph 1:1; Col 1:1; 1 Tim 1:1; 2 Tim 1:1), but here (and in Rom 1:1 and Titus 1:1) he calls himself and Timothy slaves *(douloi).* At the heart of the letter is a call for greater unity to be achieved through humility like that demonstrated by Jesus Christ who "took the form of a slave" (*doulos,* 2:7). So Paul does not claim apostolic authority here, but subtly suggests that, in the words of Jesus, "whoever would be first among you must be your slave" (Matt 20:27). Slaves are those who have no autonomy, who are completely at the beck and call of their owner; here Jesus Christ is the one who, Paul says elsewhere, has "bought" Christians ("you were bought with a price," 1 Cor 6:20) and therefore "owns" them. Paul and Timothy belong to Christ and are in his service.

   to all the holy ones in Christ Jesus who are in Philippi: Paul and Timothy are not the only ones owned by Christ; they share this with the "holy ones" in Philippi. To be holy *(hagios)* is to be "set apart," in Hellenistic Greek "devoted to the gods." "Saints" appears in the plural in the NT as a common designation for those who believe in Jesus, and it is one of the terms Hebrew Scripture uses for Israel, the people of God (see Lev 19:2; Deut 7:6; 14:2; Ps 147:20). "In Christ Jesus" describes the means by which the community is constituted and sanctified, made holy. Christ is also, so to speak, the matrix within which the believers dwell. Again there is a subtle connection to the body of the letter. Verse 14 says "the majority" are persuaded. But not all of them? Similarly, 1:15-18a indicates not all preach from "holy" motives, and 3:1–4:1 suggests that not all the believers in Philippi were "holy." Some had strayed from the Pauline gospel. Are we to understand that the apostle is not greeting them? Are there "unholy" ones whose Paul's greeting subtly excludes?

with bishops and deacons: "With" *(syn)* can be used inclusively ("including") or exclusively ("together with"). I find the latter use here. In addition to the "holy ones," the general category of faithful Christians in Philippi, Paul greets a special group, bishops and deacons. This is the first designation of its kind in Paul's letters, and the only letter in which he makes reference to local officials. Unfortunately, it is not manifestly clear either who the bishops and deacons would have been at this point in the church's history or what they did, what their duties were. "Bishops" *(episkopoi)* is a secular title used for the commissioner of a new colony. Its root word *episkopē* means "visit," and in nonbiblical Greek the noun denoted an "overseer" or "watcher." The term is used several times in the NT (Acts 20:28; 1 Tim 3:1-7; Titus 1:5-9; 1 Pet 2:25, and perhaps 5:2-3) and suggests some leadership position, although exactly what it was is not self-evident. By the second century, the *Didache* (15) describes local bishops and presbyters over whom they have precedence by the time of Ignatius of Antioch (see Ign. *Magn* 6:1; 13:1; *1 Clem* 42). Deacon *(diakonos)* comes from the verb that means "to wait at table" which also, as H. W. Beyer points out in the *Theological Dictionary of the New Testament* (2:81), has the wider meaning of "a service of love." In the NT the term is used both generally for servants of Christ and for a specific office (see 1 Tim 3:8, 12). Diaconal duties were apparently those of both service and administration, and they were in some way related to bishops. Both men and women served as deacons (see Rom 16:1; 1 Tim 3:11). (For more on why Paul used these terms here, see the Interpretation below, and see the Note on 1:1 in *CSB/NAB*.)

2. *Grace to you and peace:* Grace *(charis)* and peace *(eirenē)* is the standard Pauline greeting; it yokes a Greek salutation (grace) with the Hebrew "peace." Some form of *chairein* plus a family modifier characterized the greeting in Greco-Roman "family" letters. *Chairē* was a Greek morning greeting, and the related *chara* implied "festal joy" (see also Deut 2:7 LXX). It is a Greek equivalent for the Hebrew *ḥesed*, God's merciful loving-kindness. For Paul it connotes the free giving of God to human beings and so is related to God's blessing. It is given, not earned or achieved. Similarly, peace is not absence of conflict, but a deep, inner confidence bestowed by God, the "peace of God which passes all understanding" (4:7). God's grace bestows such peace.

   from God our Father and [the] Lord Jesus Christ: The grace and peace Paul bestows on the Philippian holy ones is not of human origin, but comes only from God, who is understood as their common parent (as Jesus taught in calling God *Abba*), and the "Lord" *(kyrios)* Jesus Christ. For the Philippians "Lord" was a political term, a designation for the Caesar. As Philippi was governed by Roman law and closely connected to Rome, to call anyone other than the

Caesar "Lord" was bold and probably dangerous. (Recall that the Philippians were subjected to persecution, Phil 1:28-29, 2 Cor 8:1-7.) The phrase is standard in Pauline greetings (1 Cor 1:3; 2 Cor 1:2; Gal 1:3; Eph 1:2; 2 Thess 1:2; 1 Tim 1:2; 2 Tim 2:2; Phlm 3), suggesting how firmly convinced the apostle was of the source of grace and peace. "Lord Jesus Christ" also echoes the earliest Christian confession, "Jesus Christ is Lord," and, as do the terms "grace" and "peace," brings together a Greco-Roman title (lord) with a Jewish concept, Christ, the Greek word for the Hebrew "Messiah," or "anointed one."

INTERPRETATION

These two verses follow the standard form of greetings in Greco-Roman letters, which are intended to establish the bond of friendship between sender and recipient and to give emotional expression to it. The elements of such greetings included a greeting verb, an indication of who is doing the greeting, the name(s) of the one/ones greeted, and "elaborating phrases" intended to stress the warmth of the greeting. In Paul's letters the greetings often give subtle expression to what is to follow in the letter, and that is the case here. As is also characteristic of Paul's letters, the names of the senders appear in the nominative case and the recipients in the dative.

Jerome Murphy-O'Connor and others have suggested that we must take seriously "co-authorship" of the Pauline letters. Timothy is to be understood in this capacity in Philippians. But was he more than simply Paul's companion or even secretary? This is hard to assess, and one can only imagine how he might have felt in recording 2:19-24 as he is both highly praised by Paul ("I have no one like him" 2:20) and lifted up as an example of the behavior Paul hopes to encourage in the Philippians (2:4, 20-21).

It is noteworthy that Paul omits any reference to his own authority, his "apostleship," which is so often at the fore in his greetings. Such assertion of authority would be misguided here. In a letter in which Christian humility is a major theme (2:5-8, 19-20, 30, for example), Paul begins by stressing his own lowliness. He and Timothy are slaves, the lowest of the low in worldly terms, but the greatest in the Christian community (see Mark 10:44). Perhaps this gives some clue as to why "bishops and deacons" appear only in this letter. In fact, outside the Pastoral Epistles there is little reference to church office. Paul himself prefers to discuss "gifts for ministry" (see Rom 12:3-8 or 1 Cor 12:1-31). By referring to himself and Timothy as slaves, is Paul subtly chiding those who think "titled roles" in ministry are important? One wonders, for example, why they are not singled out in 4:10-20 when he thanks the community for their support. Is it because Paul disapproves of those who would insist on the dignity of their office? Certainly the use of *douloi* serves to introduce the themes of suffering and service that follow in the body of the letter.

For Reference and Further Study

Best, Ernst. "Bishops and Deacons: Philippians 1:1," in F. L. Cross, ed., *Studia Evangelica* IV/1. Berlin: Akademie, 1968, 371–76.

Garland, David E. "Phil 1:1-26: The Defense and Confirmation of the Gospel," *RevExp* 77 (1980) 328–31.

Mullins, Terence Y. "Greeting as a New Testament Form," *JBL* 87 (1968) 418–26.

Murphy-O'Connor, Jerome. *Paul the Letter-Writer.* Collegeville: Liturgical Press, 1995.

Richards, E. Randolph. *The Secretary in the Letters of Paul.* WUNT 2nd ser. 42. Tübingen: J. C. B. Mohr [Paul Siebeck], 1991.

Russell, Ronald. "Pauline Letter Structure in Philippians," *JETS* 25 (1982) 295–306.

THANKSGIVING/PRAYER WISH: 1:3-11

Thanksgiving (1:3-8)

> 3. I thank my God upon all the remembrances of you, 4. always, in all my petitions for all of you, praying with joy 5. because of your fellowship in the gospel from the first days [until] now, 6. having been persuaded about this, that One Who began a good work in you will complete [it] until [the] day of Christ Jesus, 7. just as it is right for me to think this of you all, to have you in my heart, all of you being fellow sharers with me of the grace, in my bonds and in the defense and guarantee of the gospel. 8. For God [is] my witness how I long for you all with [the] compassion of Christ Jesus.

Notes

3. *I thank my God:* Greco-Roman letters typically begin with an expression of thanks. "I thank" *(eucharistō)* is the first finite verb in the letter and sets the tone for all that follows. The "I thank my God" formula is normally, as here, followed by participial phrases and/or a *hoti* (because) subjunctive clause explaining the reason for the thanks.

upon all the remembrances of you: The phrase expresses more than simply Paul's pleasure in his memories of the Philippian church. The preposition "upon" in Greek is *epi* with the dative case, which can mean "at" or "upon," suggesting temporality ("I thank God when I remember you") but also "because of," suggesting causality. Part of the reason for the letter to the Philippians is to thank them for their support of his ministry (4:10-20), thus "I thank my God for every remembrance of you" may suggest, in part, "because of what you sent me," in effect, "thank you for remembering *me.*" (For a discussion of this matter see G. W. Peterman, *Paul's Gift from Philippi,* 93–99.)

4. *always, in all my petitions:* Verse 4 opens with a double stress on "all," all the time and in all his prayers. "Always" *(pantote)* is a strong, compound adverb in Greek. There are several words for prayer in Greek. The word used here, *deēsis,* means literally "request," and is used for petitionary prayer.

for all of you: Paul is praying inclusively, for all the Philippians, not only the "holy ones" (see commentary on v. 1 above), but also those whose motives may not be pure (1:15) and perhaps even for the "dogs" and "evil-workers" (3:2).

praying with joy: Repetition of a form of *deēsis* (prayer) stresses supplication. The prepositional phrase describes the quality of Paul's prayer and is the first use of the root word *chara,* which characterizes the Philippian letter, Paul's epistle of joy and rejoicing. It is the only use of the word in Pauline thanksgivings and sets the emotional tone of this whole epistle.

5. *because of your fellowship in the gospel:* Verse five explains the second reason for Paul's joy. Fellowship *(koinōnia)* is a particularly strong and evocative word in early Christianity. It implies more than simple association. Those in fellowship with one another were responsible for each other, and this included fiscal responsibility which, of course, the Philippians have showed toward Paul. *Koinōnia* is a term that is also used by Paul in reference to the collection for the church in Judea (2 Cor 8:3; 9:13). Such a deep bond of fellowship is not created by human preferences, but is "in the gospel." This phrase, "fellowship in the gospel," is, in fact, unique to Philippians. The good news of what Jesus Christ has done for all brings believers into mutual responsibility for each other. This is the first use of the term "gospel," which appears nine times in the letter and is an important source of the mutuality Paul feels with the Philippians.

from the first days [until] now: Since their first association Paul and the Philippians have been bound together by the Gospel, their mutual acceptance of what Jesus Christ has done for them all. From the outset they cared for Paul, and he responded with joy, thanksgiving, and prayer for them. This phrase indicates that Paul's friendship with the Philippians has a history. But Paul's pleasure in them is not just for past goodness, as the next verse makes clear.

6. *having been persuaded about this:* The Greek word is the perfect active participle for "persuade" *(pepoithōs).* It has a causal force, which leads many to translate the word "confident." "About this" is an emphatic combination intended to communicate "about this same thing," that is, either their past "fellowship in the gospel" or the fulfillment or perfection of it, which Paul next addresses.

that One Who began a good work in you: By use of a participial form for "begin" Paul accomplishes an oblique reference to God that is characteristically rabbinic. The idea is that, just as their fellowship is brought about by the Gospel, their good work comes from God. The point is God's grace, not human accomplishments. It is God who provides laborers for the Gospel, as 2:13 makes clear. The implication of the phrase is also that God's "work" in them is not complete, but ongoing; it is "begun" and will be, but is not yet, complete.

will complete [it] until [the] day of Jesus Christ: What God has begun to do, God will continue to do. The root of "complete" *(epitelesei)* means not only "finish," but "fulfill" and "perfect." The preposition "until" carries the idea that something that is presently going on will continue to a certain point. In Paul's mind that point in time is the Second Coming of Jesus. "The day of Jesus Christ" hearkens back to the idea of the "day of the Lord" (see, for example, Amos 5:18-24) in Hebrew Scripture. In the NT it is one way of speaking of the *parousia,* the return of Jesus Christ, an idea Paul had worked with extensively in earlier correspondence (see 1 Cor 1:8; 5:5; and especially 15:24-28; 2 Cor 1:14; 1 Thess 5:2). The "day of Jesus Christ" will be the day when the cosmic worship of Jesus described in 2:10-11 becomes a reality, when all good work is completed and perfected.

7. *just as it is right for me to think this of you all:* The verse opens with a comparative conjunction that can either link the new phrase to the previous material or begin a new sentence as a transitional expression. "It is right for me" is a figure of speech and does not imply moral rightness. "To think" *(phronein)* introduces another of the key terms in the Philippian letter. Forms of it appear some twelve times (see, for example, 2:1-5; 3:15, 19; 4:2, 10). The term means "to be of a mind," "to form an opinion," or "to judge." It implies having an attitude toward something, being disposed in a particular way, so it is an activity of head and heart, intellect and emotion, a disposition of the whole person.

to have you in my heart: The phrase expresses the deep emotional bond Paul has with the Philippians, but also the notion of *koinōnia* from v. 5, because the "heart" was not only the center of emotional life but was understood as the very core of the person, the center of being, the locus of will. Paul says he has the Philippians in the very center of who he is.

all of you being fellow sharers with me of the grace: "Fellow sharers" *(sygkoinōnous)* has as its root *koinōnia* and is the word Paul picks up and uses again at 4:14 when he speaks of their sharing in his suffering (and compare 3:10). The grace in question is that given by God, and the verse implies that it extends both to suffering and ministry. On "grace" see the Note on 1:2.

in my bonds and in the defense and guarantee of the gospel: One reason Paul feels so close to the Philippians is that they share with him both suffering ("my bonds") and ministry ("the defense and guarantee of the gospel"). A "defense" is what is classically known as an "apology," an explanation of ideas that anticipates the audience's objections and answers them as the idea is presented. It is the language of the courtroom in the sense of a defense against an accusation. "Guarantee" *(bebaiōsis)* is the language of banking, a technical legal term for guaranteeing a security. Many interpreters think the reference is to Paul's upcoming trial as an occasion for proclamation of the Gospel. But perhaps this word contains a veiled reference to the Philippians' financial support of Paul's ministry. The notion that Paul and the Philippians are brought together in the Gospel was introduced at 1:5.

8. *For God [is] my witness:* This is a mild oath form. Interestingly, unlike the rabbis, Paul here speaks the Divine Name and, following the practice of the LXX and of much Jewish writing, uses the definite article with the noun for God *(ho theos).* Such usage is common in this letter. This is no anonymous Greco-Roman deity, but the One God, the Father of Jesus Christ. "Witness" continues the courtroom language of the previous phrase.

   how I long for you all with [the] compassion of Christ Jesus: The verb "long" *(epipothō)* is a compound, and the prepositional prefix *(epi)* has a directional force and implies eagerness. It is a word Paul uses elsewhere to describe his desire to be with friends (Rom 1:11; 1 Thess 3:6). The first of several athletic metaphors in Philippians, the word is used of an athlete straining forward to reach the finish line when victory is within sight. Paul longs toward them or yearns after them. Even in view of his precarious circumstances (1:12-26), Paul communicates certainty of victory. The emotional strength of the statement is reinforced by the use of the word "compassion" which, at root, means "innards," "guts," or perhaps "womb," and thus "womb feeling," a maternal image (compare Gal 4:19). And this is like the compassion of Christ Jesus, who went to the cross for them. Forms of the word *splanchna* or its verbal form *splanchnidzomai* are frequently used in the gospels to describe Jesus' reactions (see, for example, Mark 1:41; 6:34; 8:2). I have translated the preposition *en* as "with," that is, Paul shares the compassion that is Christ's for them. But it might also be rendered "in," the locative sense suggesting that both Paul and the Philippians are encompassed by, dwelling within, Christ's compassion.

Interpretation

The thanksgivings of Greco-Roman letters grew out of their epistolary situations and thus give some sense of the life-setting of a letter. They typically began with a verb of thanksgiving ("I thank"), followed by a modifier ("my God"), the object of the thanksgiving ("in . . . remembrance of you"), and the substance of the thanksgiving ("for . . ."). Paul expanded on this simple pattern by following the finite verb of thanksgiving with several participial phrases including a causal "because" *(hoti)* clause. That practice allows for several possible ways to see the structure here. While vv. 3-8 are one long, rambling sentence in Greek, translators into English variously indicate vv. 3-7 as one long complex sentence, or make vv. 3-6 a sentence with vv. 7 and 8 separate sentences. (For more on structure see Fee's commentary, 74–77.) In terms of logical content, vv. 3-4 express thanksgiving, vv. 5-7 the reason for it, and v. 8 the writer's emotional longing for the recipients of the letter. It is clear from this thanksgiving that the relationship between Paul and the Philippians is very cordial indeed. Paul is not only genuinely thankful for them, he longs to be reunited with them. Thus instead of saving his expressions of confidence in them for the closing of a letter as was his more usual practice, he opens Philippians with such expressions.

As R. C. Swift has pointed out, vv. 3-6 are a cameo of the whole letter. The opening verses of the thanksgiving set forth Paul's deep affection for the church because of the fellowship they share in the Gospel. Paul's happy task here is not to correct grave error (as, for example, he must in writing to the Corinthians or the Galatians), but to encourage toward perfection what is already well under way. The language of the thanksgiving introduces the root lexical field that dominates the rest of the letter: joy, fellowship, gospel, think. The major themes of the letter, suffering, joy, and the Christian's proper attitude ("mindedness"), also appear.

Paul is grateful to the Philippians for a number of reasons, but primarily for their fellowship in the Gospel, which has included not only provision for his ministry but also their own proclamation of it. This binds Paul and the Philippians Christians to each other in a number of ways. First, they are bonded in *koinōnia,* which has included the Philippians' material provision for Paul and his ministry (see 4:10-20). Second, they share a certain "bondage" to Roman authority, the authority that has imprisoned Paul and may well be at the root of persecution in Philippi. They are suffering together for the Gospel, what in 3:10 Paul calls the "fellowship of suffering" (see also 1:29-30). Third, they are bound by ministry. Both Paul and the Philippian Christians are anxious to communicate the Gospel. The issue in the letter is not whether, but how.

We learn a great deal about prayer in this section of the letter. Paul is deeply connected to the Philippians, not just because of their material provision for him, but by a spiritual bond formed as they pray for each other. Note that Paul prays for the Philippians both constantly ("all my remembrances," "always") and individually as the repetition of forms of "all" and "all of you" makes clear (vv. 3, 4, 7, 8). The words Paul uses to describe how he prays are strongly affective words; he prays with joy (v. 4), confidence (v. 6) and longing (v. 8). Paul is praying for them from prison (as, indeed, Luke reports he prayed in prison in Philippi, Acts 16:25), and they are, themselves, suffering (1:29), but his purpose is to share with the Philippians his joy in Christ, a joy that includes suffering. (See 2 Cor 11:24-27.) Thus the theological issue of theodicy, which is treated at several points in the letter, first appears at the outset. The key words are "joy" and "mind," the gift and its means of communication.

FOR REFERENCE AND FURTHER STUDY

Jewett, Robert. "The Epistolary Thanksgiving and the Integrity of Philippians," *NovT* 12 (1970) 40–53.

Mullins, Terence Y. "Formulas in New Testament Epistles," *JBL* 91 (1972) 380–90.

Peterman, G. W. *Paul's Gift from Philippi.* Cambridge: Cambridge University Press, 1997.

Swift, R. C. "The Theme and Structure of Philippians," *BSac* 141 (1984) 257–75.

Prayer Wish (1:9-11)

9. And this I pray, that your love might overflow more and more in knowledge and all insight 10. to discern what is excellent that you might be genuine and without offense in [the] day of Christ, 11. having been filled [with the] fruit of righteousness [that comes] through Jesus Christ to [the] glory and praise of God.

NOTES

9. *And this I pray:* Paul moves from an expression of thanksgiving to the substance of his prayer for them, to intercession. The verb for "pray" changes from v. 4. Here it is *proseuchomai,* a more general word for prayer, and the one Paul uses for praying in a tongue, in the spirit (1 Cor 14:14-15). James uses this word for earnest prayer (5:17). In this period the term is used most frequently for requests made to a deity.

that your love might overflow more and more: The first purpose clause of the thanksgiving begins here. "Your love" is the Philippians' mutual love, which should reflect the very nature of God. Paul assumes a loving community and asks for increase of that fruit of the Spirit. The tense of "overflow" is progressive and expresses desire. The image created by the phrase is of growing abundance, and it employs a typically Pauline rhetorical device, the compounding of comparative adjectives (see 2:23; 2 Cor 4:17).

in knowledge and all insight: The "fruit" of the love is seen in knowledge and insight. "Knowledge" *(epignōsis)* and its cognates are frequently used by Paul and imply knowledge from personal experience, not just "intellectual" knowing, but "heart" knowing, whole person knowing (see the Note on "heart" at 1:7). The word for insight *(aisthēsis)* is what is called "discernment" in the spiritual life (see, for example, LXX Prov 1:7; 5:2). Originally the Greek word was used for sense perception, but it later denoted aspects of the inner world, moral and spiritual perception as it related to "practice." Paul prays that their love will lead to clear perception about what, practically, they should do.

10. *to discern what is excellent:* The word translated "discern" *(dokimazein)* means literally "prove," as in "test out." Experientially and practically, the Philippians are to "approve" what is worthwhile, and more than that, what is "excellent."

that you might be genuine and without offense in [the] day of Christ: The second purpose clause of the thanksgiving begins here. "Genuine" (also translated "pure" or "transparent" by Moffatt) literally means "tested by sunlight." In the Roman world one held wine up to the light to see if it was clear and thus "pure," much as our grandmothers did their jars of jelly. This is the only adjectival use of the word in Paul. "Without offense" comes from a word that means "without stumbling," thus "without giving offense" (compare 1 Cor 5:32). Paul's prayer is that they might be blameless in people's sight, that they might not cause "blame" or stumbling. On the *parousia,* "the day of Christ," see the Notes on v. 6 above. Paul often seeks to prepare his churches for the *parousia,* and such an eschatological remark is a characteristic indication that a thanksgiving is coming to an end.

11. *having been filled [with the] fruit of righteousness:* "Filled" has as its root the word that means not only "completed" but "brought to maturity" and even "perfected." The root word has already appeared in v. 6, and the idea is not only spatial, but moral and spiritual. "Fruit of righteousness" is a metaphor from Hebrew Scripture (see, for example, Prov 11:30; Amos 6:13).The metaphor of fruit will recur at 1:22 and 4:7. "Righteousness" is a heavily theological word for Paul encompassing all that one does to be in right relationship with God. In Rom 5:1 Paul says God grants it to believers. Here the genitive can mean either fruit that *is* righteousness or that *comes from* righteousness. In this context, I favor the latter. Elsewhere (Rom 13:8-10, Gal 5:14) Paul stresses love as fulfillment of the law, the same love for which he has just prayed. There may be an extended metaphor here, if the term for "genuine" in v. 10 is tied to the metaphor of "fruit" (what is produced in a moral sense; see Rom 6:21-22; Gal 5:22) in v. 11. (Compare Gal 5:22-25 and see "Pauline Theology" 82:68–70 in *NJBC.*)

[that comes] through Jesus Christ to [the] glory and praise of God: One does not achieve righteousness on one's own, as Paul so clearly understood and explained so eloquently in 3:4b-9, especially v. 9. Righteousness comes by means of all that Jesus Christ has done. Put another way, Jesus Christ is the efficient cause of the Philippians' righteousness. And what Jesus did, and the Philippians received by means of Jesus, is for God's praise and glory. Their knowledge and discernment, their righteous lives, are to reflect not on themselves, but on the God they serve. This is consistent with the conclusion of the Christ hymn in 2:11. The opening verses of Philippians stress the initiative of God and the agency of Jesus Christ in all Christian "fruitfulness," all good deeds, actions, attitudes (cf. v. 6 and 2:12-18; 3:9), and, indeed, in their perfection. As is characteristic of Pauline prayers, this one closes with doxology. The section begins with thanksgiving (v. 3) and ends with doxology (v. 11), as does the "thank you" section that closes the letter (4:10-20).

Interpretation

The "prayer wish" in vv. 9-11 completes the epistolary thanksgiving in which Paul announces prayers for the Philippians (vv. 3-5), encourages them (vv. 6-8), and shares personal feelings (vv. 7-8). G. P. Wiles points out that vv. 9-11 "forecast" the upward movement of the whole epistle; they press forward toward doxology (compare 3:13-16; 4:10-20).

The Greek structure of the verses makes the substance of Paul's prayer for the Philippians clear. He prays that their love may abound and be manifest in knowledge and insight and that they might discern what is pure and without offense. Paul prays that their love may be manifest in knowledge and judgment and that their lives may be blameless. This is a potent prayer under the circumstances. Greco-Roman religions promised knowledge of the mysteries. Paul prays for knowledge that will allow practical action. Indeed, the first purpose clause of the prayer alludes to two practical matters the body of the letter will address. First, there is clearly teaching contrary to Paul's in Philippi (see 3:2-3), so the Christians there need judgment and discernment to determine what is genuine. Second, in a community so interested in spreading the gospel, the lives of Christians are particularly important. They must live so that others may see the beauty of Christianity. As v. 11 makes clear, how they live reflects on their God. Again, we know from the text of the letter that not everyone in the community was blameless or "lived beautifully." Throughout there is an appeal to unity, and specifically two women are urged to be "of the same mind in the Lord" (4:2). The practical cast to Paul's prayer for the Philippians suggests that he has these matters in mind as he writes to them and prays for them.

Paul's concern in the prayer is that the "good work begun in them" (v. 6) be brought to perfection or maturity. And the good news is that, since the day of Christ has not yet come, there is opportunity for precisely this.

For Reference and Further Study

Fee, Gordon D. *Paul's Letter to the Philippians.* NICNT. Grand Rapids: Eerdmans, 1995, "Prayer as Petition," 95–105.

Garland, David E. "Phil 1:1-26: The Defense and Confirmation of the Gospel," *RevExp* 77 (1980) 328–31.

Perkins, Pheme. "Philippians," in Leander Keck, et al., eds., *The New Interpreter's Bible.* Nashville: Abingdon, 2000, 9:485–86.

Wiles, G. P. *Paul's Intercessory Prayers.* Cambridge: Cambridge University Press, 1974, 202–15.

THE EXAMPLE OF PAUL: 1:12-26

In the opening of the body of the letter, Paul provides the Philippians with news of his imprisonment. The passage has three sections: vv. 12-14, reassurance that his imprisonment has been for the good; vv. 15-18a, reflection on motives in ministry and rejoicing in the Gospel's proclamation; vv. 18b-26, reflection on the eventual outcome of his present circumstances of imprisonment. The section is closely linked to 4:10-20, with which it shares many words and phrases and which also reflects Paul's circumstances vis-à-vis the church in Philippi.

Results of Imprisonment (1:12-14)

> 12. Now I want you to know, brethren, that the things that have come to me, on the contrary, have served to advance the gospel, 13. so that my bonds in Christ have become known in all the praetorium and to all the rest, 14. and the majority of the brethren in the Lord, being persuaded by my bonds, abundantly, without fear, dare to speak the word.

Notes

12. *Now I want you to know, brethren:* The transitional particle *de* (now) marks a new section, and with the disclosure formula ("I want you to know") provides the transition to the body of the letter (compare 1 Thess 4:13; 1 Cor 10:1; Rom 1:13). In the disclosure formula a verb of desire in the first person indicative (I want) is followed by the vocative of address (brethren) and a subjective clause introduced by *hoti* (that). Paul is providing accurate information about something of which they have heard. The Greek *adelphoi* is best translated in an inclusive sense,"brethren," or "brothers and sisters," male and female believers, not just "brothers." Christians are God's children and siblings to one another.

    that the things that have come to me, on the contrary, have served to advance the gospel: The Greek *mallon,* which is sometimes translated "rather," suggests that something other than what was expected has happened. Paul is correcting a misperception, describing what "really happened." His current imprisonment is not, in fact, a setback for the Gospel. "Advance" *(prokopē)* carries the connotation of forward movement in spite of obstructions. In Greek philosophy the word is used for progress toward wisdom. The fact that the word is repeated in 1:25 suggests an *inclusio* in this section of the body of the letter, the subject of which is the attitude of those who proclaim the Gospel. What might appear to be a drawback or hindrance is, in fact, a means of progress, of accomplishing goals.

13. *so that my bonds in Christ:* "So that" has an explanatory force. The idea is that Paul's bonds, his imprisonment, is for or because of Christ (but also "in Christ," within Christ's sphere of influence). The phrase explains the reason for Paul's imprisonment. "Bonds" is repeated in vv. 14 and 17. Paul keeps his circumstances clearly in the Philippians' field of vision; his imprisonment gives emotional force to his words.

have become known in all the praetorium and to all the rest: The infinitive "become" used with the participle here expresses actual result. The result of Paul's bonds is knowledge on the part of others. The verse is one of the interpretive cruxes of Philippians because of the term "praetorium," a Latin loan word, which is used in several ways. The Praetorian Guard was the emperor's bodyguard in Rome. A "praetorium" was the headquarters of a Roman official who administered a region and normally included his home. Many commentators have taken the reference to the praetorium here as evidence that Philippians was written from Rome (compare 4:22). But the Praetorian Guard would be with the emperor or members of his family in any of his residences, and most cities that were headquarters for Roman administration had a praetorium. This served Paul's evangelistic purpose, as the guard changed every four hours, giving Paul access to many soldiers. At the very least the term suggests that Paul has been imprisoned by the Romans and is being held in an administrative center where legal judgment can be rendered. Paul's point is that instead of hindering the progress of the Gospel, his imprisonment has advanced it because all of those guarding him, all of those in the administrative center, have been introduced to the Gospel.

14. *and the majority of the brethren in the Lord:* It is not only nonbelievers upon whom Paul's imprisonment has had good effect. Most of his fellow believers (but not all?), the Christians where he is imprisoned, have also been encouraged. That they are all "brethren" should be recalled in what follows in 2:15-18.

being persuaded by my bonds: The word for "persuaded" *(pepoithotas)* means utterly convinced. Paul's imprisonment has convinced (or even "convicted") them of what they, too, must do. Again, the chains of imprisonment are persuasive and not a hindrance (compare v. 12).

abundantly, without fear, dare to speak the word: The phrase describes what Paul's bonds have convinced his fellow believers to do: boldly proclaim the Gospel. They do so generously or even lavishly and fearlessly. The Greek adverb *aphobōs* literally means "without fear," an astonishing claim if Paul is writing from Nero's Rome. That they "dare" to do so suggests there is some danger involved in the activity. So, in effect, the believers where Paul is imprisoned become to him what the Philippians are, "sharers . . . in the defense and guarantee of the gospel" (v. 7). Apparently seeing Paul spreading the Gospel to his captors while in prison has emboldened the Christians in the area to preach the Gospel fearlessly.

INTERPRETATION

Following the convention in letters of friendship, Paul begins by reassuring the Philippians about both himself and his work, the progress of the Gospel. Because he cares for them, he wants first of all to assuage their anxiety about his circumstances, to correct their misunderstanding about those circumstances and their effect. Some scholars understand Philippians to be a letter of consolation written to address that church's discouragement about Paul's imprisonment and their own suffering for the Gospel. They see 1:12–2:30 as focusing on Paul's imprisonment and its effects.

In any case, the Philippians' concern for Paul results in a biographical prologue to the letter, 1:12-26, in which Paul himself exhibits virtues mentioned in the prayer of 1:9-11. Paul is "discerning what is best" in his situation, acting in ways that do not give offense (indeed, which draw others *to* the Gospel), and thereby glorifying God. As R. C. Swift has remarked, 1:12-26 demonstrates that Paul "practiced what he preached" in 1:3-11. It is unusual in Pauline letters for the author to devote much space to his own circumstances. That he does so here is indicative of the depth of his friendship with the Philippian church.

These verses exhibit a pattern frequently seen in the transition from the thanksgiving to the body of a Pauline letter. A first person finite verb (here "I want") and the particle *de* precede references to the recipients (the accusative *hymas,* you) and the vocative "brethren." There follows an injunction introduced by *hoti* ("that" or "because"). The opening formula in the body informs the recipients about a subject, here Paul's imprisonment. The section is a single sentence in Greek.

Once again, the Philippian letter emphasizes that the faithfulness of Christ does not exclude believers from trials. The joy the letter reflects is not the absence of suffering; quite the contrary. The point here is what the results of Paul's own trials have been: the Gospel has been advanced (see Acts 9:15-16). It is to be recalled that Acts 16:16-34 records a similar outcome for Paul's Philippian imprisonment. Paul's response to adversity has encouraged others. As Karl Barth points out, Paul's real concern is not his own circumstances, but the Gospel. It is a timeless truth that how Christians handle their own trials and sufferings has a profound effect both on other believers and on non-Christians. Faith, even joy, in adversity is a powerful recommendation of Christian faith.

FOR REFERENCE AND FURTHER STUDY

Holloway, Paul A. *Consolation in Philippians.* Cambridge: Cambridge University Press, 2001.

Omanson, Roger L. "A Note on the Translation of Philippians 1:12," *BT* 29 (1978) 446–48.
Sanders, Jack T. "The Transition from Opening Epistolary Thanksgiving to Body in the Letters of the Pauline Corpus," *JBL* 81 (1962) 348–62.
Swift, R. C. "The Theme and Structure of Philippians," *BSac* 141 (1984) 257–75.
White, John L. "Introductory Formulae in the Body of a Pauline Letter," *JBL* 90 (1971) 91–97.

Motives in Ministry (1:15-18a)

15. Indeed, some even preach the Christ because of envy and strife, but others also because [of] goodwill, 16. the ones from love, knowing that I am destined for the defense of the gospel, 17. the others from selfishness preach the Christ, not purely, imagining to raise tribulation for my bonds. 18a What then? except that in every manner, whether in pretense, whether in truth, Christ is preached, and in this I rejoice.

Notes

15. *Indeed, some even preach the Christ because of envy and strife:* The verse addresses the motives for proclamation of *the* Christ, a subtle reminder in the Greek text of the uniqueness of God's messiah. *Dia,* "because of" or "on account of" indicates motive. The word translated "envy" also means "spite," which is more nearly opposite to "goodness" in the latter part of the verse. "Strife" implies selfish rivalry; the root reappears in v. 17 and in an absolute prohibition in 2:3. Envy and strife are anti-social vices that appear in a vice list in Gal 5:20-21 and in Rom 1:29. Both militate against the unity Paul commends to the Philippian church. The questionable motive of self-seeking also occurs in 2:21.

    but others also because [of] goodwill: The second half of the verse is parallel to the first, though it communicates the opposite motive and is an example of the antithetic parallelism that characterizes Hebrew poetry. "Goodwill" implies benevolence and is the positive motive for work in 2:13, a motive that is God-given.

16. *the ones from love:* The opening words of vv. 16 and 17 are a Greek construction of comparison, "the ones . . . the others," and carry the idea "on the one hand/on the other hand." The motive of Christian love *(agapē)* mirrors the nature of God and the motive of Jesus himself in his actions. In this context love means disinterestedly wishing and working for the deepest good of others.

knowing that I am destined for the defense of the gospel: The word for "destined" *(keimai)* literally means "to lie" or "to recline," but is a metaphor for "appointed" or "destined." At many points Paul says that he was chosen by God to preach the Gospel to the Gentiles, that he is an apostle by God's will (see, for example, Rom 1:1; 2 Cor 1:1, and Gal 1:15). The word "defense," literally "apology," has already appeared at 1:7 (see Note above) and alludes to Paul's understanding of the method involved in communicating the Gospel.

17. *the others from selfishness preach the Christ:* "Selfishness" here is the same root as "strife" in v. 15. It is used in parallel literature for the character of one who works for pay, a hired laborer or a mercenary—in other words, one who works for his or her own interests. Such a one is, of course, in contrast to the positive examples that follow: Jesus (2:6-11), Timothy and Epaphroditus (2:19-30), and Paul himself (3:4-14). The word "preach" is a compound beginning with *kata,* which intensifies the meaning to something like "make fully known." The motive may be incorrect, but the proclamation is complete, and the subject, Christ, is correct.

not purely: The adverb with the negative *(ouk hagnōs)* means "mixed" or "impure." Some preach Christ for "mixed motives," their own aggrandizement or even monetary gain. But the fact that they do preach is positive and, in fact, the most important thing according to Paul.

imagining to raise tribulation for my bonds: The word for "imagining" *(oiomenoi)* can also be translated "supposing" and implies beliefs based on one's own feelings, not the facts of the case. "To raise tribulation" might be rendered into English with the colloquialism "kick up dust," in other words, cause trouble. The "mixed motive" preachers cause Paul trouble in his imprisonment because he can do little about it, and one presumes the "trouble" they cause is to point to Paul's imprisonment with derision. It is always dangerous to psychologize across the centuries, but perhaps in their envy of Paul's success as a preacher (v. 15) they point to his imprisonment as a way to discredit him, to undercut his authority and success, rather in the way one losing an argument attacks *ad hominem.* "What sort of preacher is *this,* imprisoned like a common criminal?!?"

18a. *What then?:* A colloquialism that might be rendered "so what?"

except that in every manner, whether in pretense, whether in truth: The phrase begins with an adverbial particle *(plēn)* used as an adversative conjunction and might also be translated "nevertheless." As in vv. 15, 16, 17, Paul's construction is comparative, "on the one hand/on the other hand." "Pretense" and "truth" are used appositively. What is at issue is the motive of the preachers, not the substance of the preaching, which is Christ. Whether the preachers are "pretentious," or acting for a false reason, or are genuine is not so important as the communication of the message itself.

Christ is preached, and in this I rejoice: The important thing is the proclamation of the Messiah, not the motives of the proclaimers. Because Christ *is* being proclaimed, Paul rejoices. Forms of "rejoice" characterize the letter.

Interpretation

Verses 15-18a comprise a self-contained unit that is closely linked to its context. The repetition of motives for preaching in vv. 15 and 18 frames the unit. Verses 16 and 17 elaborate on the statement made in v. 15, and v. 18 is Paul's response. The whole section is carefully composed using antithetical parallelism to contrast the motives of two groups of preachers; one is envious and rivalrous, the other sincere and of good will. The chiastic structure seems clear:

A some even preach the Christ because of envy and strife

B but others also because [of] good will

B' the ones from love . . .

A' the others from selfishness preach the Christ . . .

Much speculation exists about who the falsely motivated preachers were, but "some" *(tines)* in Greek gives no clue to their identity. All we know is that they were part of the Christian community where Paul was imprisoned and apparently found his imprisonment distasteful. It would seem that these factional preachers are other than "the majority of the brethren" of v. 14, but I take them to be members of that same community. They are preaching where Paul is imprisoned (the logical inference from v. 17) and, oddly enough, they seemed to be simultaneously envious of Paul and disdainful of his imprisonment. It is clear that the esteem in which later Christianity held *the* apostle Paul was not universal in his lifetime.

Seemingly not terribly concerned about his lack of universal popularity, Paul says that his suffering allows him to rejoice because it has caused him to face what is and what is not important. Suffering has given perspective. As he will momentarily write, "to live is Christ" (1:21). That being the case, Paul also had the perspective to see that the proclamation of Christ is of paramount importance, much more important than rivalry between preachers. His theological lens is wide angle. Paul has the big picture in view, and it includes the fact that God's work in the world was accomplished through the suffering of Jesus Christ (see 3:10-11). More important than his own circumstances or the motives of preachers is the proclamation of the Gospel. Evangelism is more important than the evangelists, and judgment is best left to God (compare Rom 14:4a).

For Reference and Further Study

Hawthorn, T. "Philippians 1:12-19 with Special Reference to vv. 15, 16, 17," *ExpTim* 62 (1950–51) 316–17.

Paul's Dilemma (1:18b-26)

18b. Furthermore, I will rejoice 19. for I know that this will result in my salvation through your petition and supply the spirit [of] Jesus Christ, 20. according to my eager watching and hope that in nothing I shall be ashamed, but in all boldness, as always, also now, I shall magnify Christ in my body, whether through life, whether through death. 21. For me, to live [is] Christ and to die [is] gain. 22. But if [it is to be] life in the flesh, this [is] fruitful labor for me, and I do not know what I shall choose, 23. for I am pressured by the two, having the desire to depart and to be with Christ, for this [is] much better; 24. but to remain in the flesh [is] more necessary on account of you. 25. And knowing this, I shall remain and serve with you all for your advance and joy in the faith, 26. in order that, through my presence with you again, your boast in me should abound in Christ Jesus.

Notes

18b. *Furthermore, I will rejoice:* The Greek sentence begins by combining two particles which gives a progressive sense that is continued in the shift to a future tense verb that also has a volitional sense. The phrase suggests a strong decision to do something, in this case, rejoice. Forms of the word occur twice in v. 18. Paul cannot choose his circumstances, but he can choose how he will respond to them. The freedom to choose how one responds to one's circumstances is a freedom no imprisonment or misfortune can take away (as, indeed, the Stoics taught). Now Paul's rejoicing is because of the anticipated outcome of his own circumstances, whichever eventuates.

19. *for I know that this will result in my salvation:* "I know" expresses strong confidence. The word translated "result" literally means "come back," metaphorically "turn out to." The idea is that the prayers of the Philippians will result in Paul's liberation, which brings "returns" to them. It is a "cast your bread upon the waters" scenario. The phrase echoes Job 13:16 (LXX), a passage in which Job passionately avows his innocence and seeks divine vindication. The Psalms frequently speak of God's defense of people for God's glory (Pss 34:3-5; 35:26-27; 40:16-17, LXX). There are three possible "salvations" or "deliverances" available to Paul: release from prison, vindication at his Roman trial, or God's final approval of his life's work at his death. In the context, I tend to favor the first possibility.

through your petition and supply the spirit [of] Jesus Christ: Two things inspire Paul's confidence, the Philippians' prayers and the Holy Spirit. He has human and divine assistance. The form of prayer being offered is petitionary, and it reflects another aspect of spiritual *koinōnia* as Paul prays for them and they pray for him. Its result is Paul's liberation (compare 2 Cor 1:11). Its effectiveness is already evident in his attitude. "Supply" is used in marriage contracts in the context of providing for the spouse and in medical texts of the ligament that supports. I translate the genitive "Jesus Christ" here as subjective; that is, "the supply that the spirit of Jesus Christ gives" (see Gal 3:5). Paul is "liberated" by the Philippians' prayers and by Christ's Spirit.

20. *according to my eager watching and hope:* "Eager watching" is an attempt to render a verb composed of a preposition that means "away," a noun meaning "head," and the verb "to watch." Barth suggests "looking out for something with head held high." We might envision someone craning the neck to catch a glimpse of something ("rubbernecking"). The word means "intense watching" and is used in Rom 8:19 for creation's eager watching for its redemption. This sort of watching and hope are experientially synonymous.

that in nothing I shall be ashamed, but in all boldness, as always, also now: "In nothing . . . in all" sets up the contrast in the verse. It is unlikely that one who has faced the hardships Paul has (see, for example, 2 Cor 11:21b-29) would be worried about physical courage in the face of a "guilty" verdict. "Shame" for him would be the defeat of the Gospel, which he knows to be impossible. The word for boldness implies forthright speech, "plain speaking," but can also mean "openness" as opposed to fearfulness or reserve. Paul has not heretofore been ashamed of his work for the Gospel and aspires to continue his bold witness whatever his circumstances.

I shall magnify Christ in my body, whether through life, whether through death: "Magnify" *(megalynthēsetai)* is literally "made large." "Body" *(sōma)* here, as in Rom 12:1, means the "whole person, the enduring self" (not just the transitory flesh, *sarx;* see Note on v. 22). The idea is that it is Christ who is "increased" by what befalls Paul. Again, as characterizes this whole section, there is antithetic parallelism: life/death. Paul's hope and confidence is that, just as in the past, now and in the future his life and/or his death will glorify God.

21. *For me to live [is] Christ and to die [is] gain:* The last phrase of v. 20 apparently leads Paul to speak of his view of his life and death. The sentence begins with an emphatic pronoun in Greek, and the "for" indicates that what follows explains what preceded. The antithetical nouns in v. 20 (life/death) reappear as infinitives in v. 21 (to live/to die). "To live" in Greek is an articular infinitive that carries a present, continuous sense ("living"). The word for "gain" is usually found in reference to money and thus normally denotes profit. In the Greek, "Christ" and "gain" *(kerdos)* alliterate, which adds drama to a statement written to be heard when the letter was read aloud. What Paul is saying is that his will is so conformed to Christ's that, for him, living *is* Christ, and dying is "gain" (profitable) because it means going to or being with Christ. Galatians 2:20 sheds light on the idea (compare Rom 6:3-11 and 2 Cor 5:2-8). For Paul, eternal life has already begun because his life in Christ *is* Christ. Unlike 2 Cor 5:1-10, here Paul is not speaking of the future but of the present. Anglicans hear the idea at the communion rail. As they receive the elements, the priest or eucharistic minister says, "the Body of Christ *keep* you in eternal life." Eternal life has already begun for Christians; we are "in it." Paul is not the only Greek writer to express the idea that death is gain. There are many examples in Greek literature of the idea that death is preferable to suffering, and many of these use the term "gain" *(kerdos).* Euripides in *Medea* (145-47)

expresses the idea that death is gain because it is an end to a hateful life. A similar idea is expressed in Sophocles' *Electra* (814-22), Euripides' *Trojan Women* (630-42), Plato's *Apology,* and Josephus' *Antiquities* (15.158). Libanius (*Oratio* 26) says, "death is gain for those for whom living is a burden." What is different here is that Paul sees a positive, if for him personally difficult, result if he remains. And in any case Christ is his life *whether* he lives or dies; living or dying, he is Christ's (Rom 14:8). This is an expression of deep intimacy with Christ.

22. *But if [it is to be] life in the flesh:* "Flesh" here denotes "creaturehood." Flesh *(sarx)* contrasts with body *(sōma)* in v. 20. "Flesh" is literally "meat," that which decays, which is impermanent. At 3:21 Paul will suggest that God has an eternal purpose for the body *(sōma).* (Parenthetically, Paul records in 1 Cor 11:24 that at the Last Supper Jesus said, "this is my body *(sōma),*" my whole, enduring self.)

this [is] fruitful labor for me: An alternative translation closer to the Greek is "this is for me the fruit of labor," in other words, a harvest, that which follows hard work.

and I do not know what I shall choose: Here one sees Paul "thinking out loud" as it were, deciding between two alternatives. Paul seems genuinely indecisive. His desire, his own choice, is at odds with what he thinks is best for the Philippians. In a very helpful article, however, N. Clayton Croy has pointed out that there was a rhetorical trope known as *aporia* or *diaporesis,* "feigned perplexity." The writer or speaker pretends to be uncertain and poses a question as a way of strengthening the argument he is making. *Diaporesis* in particular is an expression of uncertainty about what course of action to take. Croy suggests that 1:19-26 is an example of this rhetorical device.

23. *for I am pressured by the two:* The Greek particle *de* introduces an explanation. The word "pressured" here literally means "held together," thus pushed from both sides or "pressured." The two alternatives are closing in on Paul.

having the desire to depart: "Desire" *(epithymia)* is a strong word for a preference and is often found in pejorative contexts in Paul. "To depart" is a euphemism for death (see v. 21 above). The word means "break up," "undo," or "loose" and is found in parallel literature for a ship breaking from its moorings and soldiers breaking camp. (For the latter see 2 Macc 9:1 and compare 2 Cor 5:1.) It is rendered by the Vulgate "desiring to be dissolved," and by Calvin "being unbounded." It denotes a serious break.

and to be with Christ: The phrase has occasioned much discussion, but in this context it seems to aver to dying and rising with Christ, a matter frequently addressed by Paul. Romans 6:1-11; 1 Cor 15:18; 1 Thess 4:14 speak of being in/with Christ in death. Death, then, is the vehicle that takes Paul to Christ's presence (see Excursus 2 in Collange for a discussion of the phrase). As such, it is nothing to be feared or avoided. The idea is like that encountered in Sufi poetry and Islamic mysticism, that death is the friend who takes one to God.

for this [is] much better: The last phrase compounds comparative terms, literally reading "much rather better." Paul clearly feels it would be better for him, personally, "to be with Christ," but his personal preferences are no longer his motivation for action. In this he is in direct contrast to the preachers who preach "from selfishness" (v. 17), but he mirrors the activity of Timothy, whom Paul will commend in 2:19-24 precisely for putting others' interests first.

24. *but to remain in the flesh [is] more necessary on account of you:* As in v. 22, flesh *(sarx)* is again contrasted with body *(sōma)*. Flesh is the impermanent, limited part of the person that is set aside in death. "Remain" *(epimenein)* has the connotation of a protracted stay. Another form of the same word is used by the evangelist John to describe the "dwelling with" believers of the Holy Spirit (14:17) and their "abiding" in Christ the vine (15:4-7, 10). The comparative adjective "more necessary" may carry the implication of divine necessity (see 1 Cor 9:16).

25. *And knowing this:* The coordinating conjunction signals a strong connection to v. 24. "Knowing" reflects Paul's conviction and reflects a confidence formula. Some commentators think it signals a shift in Paul's thought from contemplation of martyrdom to assurance that he has a future in his life with the Philippians.

I shall remain and serve with you all: Literally, "I remain and shall remain." While the root "remain" is the same as in v. 24, the form *(paramenō)* here is slightly different and means to remain with the idea of serving or "waiting on." Verses 24-25 have three different words, each with the same root, "remain," but with slightly different connotations. This contributes to the sense that Paul's decision is clear. Both Paul and the Philippians are servants of the Gospel. Significantly, he suggests that he serves *with* them, not he "serves them." And Paul serves with them *all,* excluding no one, not even the "mixed motive preachers" of 1:15-18 or the "dogs" of chapter 3.

for your advance and joy in the faith: The pronoun "your" modifies both nouns. Paul remains for their benefit, not his own. "Advance" here is used in the sense of "progress," moving forward. It is the same word that appeared in v. 12 and, with the repetition of "joy" in both verses, signals an inclusion. What has happened to Paul has advanced the Gospel (v. 12), and what he now is choosing will advance the Philippians. The emphasis is on "joy in the faith," a theme of the letter and another mark of Paul's closeness to the community at Philippi, as he knows his return would bring them joy.

26. *in order that, through my presence with you again:* "Presence" *(parousias)* carries the idea of return and is used in the NT for the second coming of Jesus Christ. Obviously, Paul has spent time with the Philippians before. It is the reunion with them that Paul hopes will encourage them. Acts 20:1-6 suggests Paul did have a second visit to Philippi after the founding one recorded in 16:11-40.

your boast in me might abound in Christ Jesus: Kauchēma is usually translated "boast," but can also mean "glorying." In this context the connotation is positive. This is "big time" boasting; the word "abound" means "overflow" (compare 1:9; 4:12, 18 and the adverbial use in 1:14). But the boasting is not ultimately because of Paul's return; it is "in" (or "because of") Christ Jesus. The ultimate aim of what happens to Paul is that Christ might be glorified (compare 1:10-11). The idea of the rather difficult Greek is that because of

Paul's returning to them, coming to them again, their boasting or "grounds for glorying" (Fee) might be in Christ Jesus.

Interpretation

Although not unique in the Pauline corpus, this text is unusual in that in it Paul reflects at length on his own situation. We overhear Paul thinking out loud, reasoning out a decision to be made. He had found a new center of life on the Damascus road, one that meant that his own best interests were no longer central, no longer the determining factor in his decisions. In this Paul is following the model of Jesus Christ (cf. 2:6-11) and is "looking not to his own interests, but the interests of others," precisely what he asks the Philippians to do at 2:4 and what he commends Timothy for at 2:20. Similarly he is exhibiting the virtues he taught in vv. 9-11, practicing what he preached, "walking the talk." Rhetorically, Paul echoes the OT motif of the distressed believer who looks to God for vindication. Fee suggests that the figure of Job is a good point of comparison. As in other instances where Paul alludes to his own biography, the intent is as much didactic as informational. Paul includes his biography to illustrate something he wishes to teach.

Verses 18b-20 are one complex Greek sentence. Verses 19-20 explain why Paul rejoices and are particularly closely tied to vv. 12-14 because the sense is that no matter what happens, God can bring good from it, good either for Paul personally or for the Philippian church. This is the Christian hope that "in everything God works for good with those who love him, who are called according to his purpose" (Rom 8:28). So what is at issue here is not deliverance *per se*, but the *kind* of deliverance, that is, from prison/death to the church or from biological life to Christ. The key note of the verses is expectant hope and joy *either way*.

Verses 21-24 present a hypothetical or rhetorical discussion between the two alternatives of life or death. Rhetorically what seems to be operative is epideictic or deliberative rhetoric designed to advise the Philippians on the course of action they should take in the future. This is subtle because Paul does not come out and say "do this" so much as offer himself as the example to follow. Paul is the example of how to accept suffering in the hope that God can bring good from it, how to deal with jealousy and rivalry without adopting those actions and attitudes himself. In these verses life (vv. 20, 21a, 22, 24) and death (vv. 20, 21b, 23) alternate dramatically. This section is at the heart of the passage. They depict Paul with a clear, personal preference that he sets aside in favor of the Christian community's greater good. This is precisely what he asks the Philippians to do (2:1-4; 3:17; 4:11, 13) and what Jesus did (2:5-11).

Verses 21-24 are illuminated by 2 Cor 5:1-10, which describes the dissolution of the "earthly tent," the flesh *(sarx)*. Paul explains to the Corinthians that when Christians are "at home in the body" they are "away from the Lord" (5:6). While being with the Lord is preferable, the real issue is that, no matter what the circumstances, "we make it our aim to please him" (5:9). That is the motivating factor here in Philippians. Paul would prefer to "depart" to be with the Lord, but will remain if that most assists the Philippians, advances the Gospel, and thus pleases the Lord. One is again struck by the profound connection between Paul and the Philippians, one that is forged "in the Lord" whom they both serve.

Verses 25-26, a single Greek sentence, mark the transition from Paul's circumstances (1:12-26) to those of the Philippians (1:27–2:18).

For Reference and Further Study

Bertram, Georg. "APOKARADOKIA (Phil. 1, 20)," *ZNW* 49 (1958) 264–70.

Croy, N. Clayton. "'To Die is Gain' (Philippians 1:19-26): Does Paul Contemplate Suicide?" *JBL* 122 (2003) 517–31.

Dailey, Thomas F. "To Live or Die: Paul's Eschatological Dilemma in Philippians 1:19-26," *Int* 44 (1990) 18–28.

Droge, Arthur J. "*Mori Lucrum:* Paul and Ancient Theories of Suicide," *NovT* 30 (1988) 262–86.

Garland, David E. "Phil 1:1-26: The Defense and Confirmation of the Gospel," *RevExp* 77 (1980) 328–31.

Lee, G. M. "Philippians 1:22-23," *NovT* 12 (1970) 361.

Palmer, D. W. "'To Die is Gain.' Phil 1:21," *NovT* 17 (1975) 203–18.

Vogel, C. J. De. "Reflexions on Phil 1:23-24," *NovT* 19 (1977) 262–74.

INSTRUCTIONS TO THE PHILIPPIANS: 1:27–2:18

This section of the letter is crucial to its purpose as Paul exhorts the Philippians to greater unity on the basis of the model of Christ. The startling imperative toward humility and servanthood are, in Paul's mind, the means to unity. He calls for the application of "Christ-mind" to personal and public issues in Christian life. The section moves from what Paul wants the Philippians to do (1:27-2:4), to the example of Christ which models the behavior Paul calls for (2:5-11, the "Christ Hymn"), to a description of the practical response Christ's model calls for in their lives

(2:12-18). And this leads Paul in 2:19-30 to describe two people known to him and to the Philippians who follow this model.

Many commentators have suggested that the section is chiastic in form.

A An appeal to fortitude and unity in difficulty (1:27–2:4)

B The Example of Christ (2:5-11)

A' An appeal for fortitude and unity in difficulty (2:12-18).

Their Manner of Life (1:27-30)

27. Only live your life worthily of the gospel of Christ, so that whether coming and seeing you or being absent, I hear about you, that you stand firm in one spirit, one soul, struggling together for the faith of the gospel 28. and not being frightened in anything by the opposing ones, which is evidence of their destruction, but of your salvation, and this [is] from God. 29. For you were graciously given, on behalf of Christ, not only to believe in him, but also to suffer on behalf of him, 30. having the same struggle which you saw in me and now you hear in me.

NOTES

27. *Only live your life worthily of the gospel of Christ:* "Only" signals a rhetorical shift to exhortation. "Live your life" reflects a fascinating Greek word, *politeuomai,* which is used only here and in Acts 23:1, and means "be a citizen," "behave as a citizen." The rarity of the word in the NT and parallel literature suggests it has a technical meaning. Hellenistic writers use it in relation to pledging one's self to some form of government. In Philo it is used to connote allegiance to heavenly order, and in Acts 23:1 it is used of Paul's allegiance to divine will. (For a full discussion of the parallels see Raymond R. Brewer's article listed below.) The noun form of the word occurs in 3:20, where Paul reminds the Philippians that their authentic citizenship is in heaven. The word is particularly interesting in the context of the Praetorian Guard, which would have sworn loyalty to Caesar, and of the pressure brought to bear on the Philippians to participate in the imperial cult. The term serves as a subtle reminder by Paul that Christ's name is above all others (2:9-11), that he and not Nero is Lord, and that citizenship is heavenly rather than Roman (3:20). As Brewer points out, it is used with reference to conduct relative to law of life. The Philippians are to live the lives of those who are loyal to the Gospel of Christ, to live as citizens of heaven. The practical point is simple: what we do shows

whose we are. The conduct of the Christian's life should have the merit of the Gospel itself. In any age, a worthy life is the Gospel's greatest recommendation. As St. Vincent de Paul is reputed to have said, "if God is the center of your life, no words are necessary. Your mere presence will touch hearts."

so that whether coming and seeing you or being absent: Here begins a purpose clause using the comparative form that was so effective in 1:12-26. "Absent" can also be translated "away from." The phrase serves as a link to the previous discussion of Paul's "life options" in 1:19-26. "Coming and seeing you" is a straightforward reference to a visit. "Being absent" implies, at best, remaining in prison and perhaps even Paul's death.

I hear about you, that you stand firm in one spirit, one soul: Presumably Paul hopes to hear about them from Timothy (2:19). The term for "stand firm" suggests a soldier who does not leave his post. Repetition of adjectival forms of "one" (*heni* and *mia*) emphasize the unity for which Paul calls. "One spirit, one soul" is a prelude to the "one-mindedness" Paul commends in 2:2, 5 and serves to link the two passages lexically. "Spirit" here is probably not the Holy Spirit, but a metaphorical way to speak of the Philippians' common attitude. Their attitude and their life principle (which *psychē* suggested at the time) are to be one, which recalls a basic reason for the letter: to encourage the unity of the Philippian church.

struggling together for the faith of the gospel: "Struggling together" represents a Greek compound verb used only here and at 4:3, where Paul urges Euodia and Syntyche to work together. Its root word is "athletics" and connotes team spirit. In Hellenistic Greek it was used of athletics, but in classical Greek in contexts of war or battle. The root verb is compounded with *syn* (with), a subtle reinforcement of Paul's purpose, urging them toward greater unity. The dative construction of the phrase is a dative of interest, so "for" means "on behalf of." Paul is a wise psychologist and understands that a powerful way to unify any group is to have the individuals in it working toward a common goal. Verses 27-30, indeed the whole epistle, suggests that the "common goal" for the Philippians is the Gospel. Karl Barth points out that the struggle is not *against* adversaries, but *for* the Gospel, which is consistent with Paul's views in 1:15-18.

28. *and not being frightened in anything by the opposing ones:* The word for "frightened" means "startled," as an animal by a sudden noise, as well as "intimidated." Both are germane to the context. Paul is giving them information that will prevent their being surprised or startled or intimidated (by Roman authority?). The Philippians now know that Paul's imprisonment has served to advance the Gospel (1:12-14) and that he is unperturbed by those who preach from bad motives or "afflict" him in prison (1:15-18). If his difficulties have advanced the Gospel, theirs might as well. In any case, standing firm in Christ, they cannot be intimidated, by enemies or by anything else. "The opposing ones" is literally those who "line up against," thus "adversaries," "enemies." The reference may be obliquely to the Philippian persecution (1:29). Whether these persons are outside the church (Roman officials, as their "destruction" suggests?) or Christians (the partisan preachers of 1:15-18 or the "dogs" of

ch. 3?) is not clear. We are given a hint of strife in Philippi, but its exact nature is not articulated. In either case the phrase both keeps opposition to the Gospel in Philippi clearly in view and encourages those believers.

which is evidence of their destruction, but of your salvation: In lining up against the Philippians, the enemies are lining up against God and the Gospel, and this is, of necessity, destruction. "Evidence" is a term found in Attic law meaning "proof" or "demonstration." Ralph P. Martin translates it "clear omen," a phrase that alludes to the eventual destruction of the "opposers." The word for destruction *(apōleia)* is particularly strong and might be translated "perdition," since its opposite in this context is "salvation" (compare 3:19). Those who oppose the Gospel ultimately, perish ultimately.

and this [is] from God: Although the antecedent of "this" is ambiguous ("their destruction?" "your salvation?" both?), the final clause is an explicit expression of causation. Clearly the salvation of the Philippians has its origin in what God has done and will do. Paul says God gave salvation, and God will eventually destroy those who oppose the Gospel (compare 1:6, 18b-19). To a persecuted community this would be a word of hope.

29. *for you were graciously given on behalf of Christ:* The conjunction "for" suggests a reason. Vincent thinks it has special reference to "salvation" in the previous verse. The verb for "given" *(echaristhē)* has as its root "grace." The form is a "divine passive," which serves as a reminder that belief itself is from God (compare, for example, Eph 2:8). What is given is more than a gift, as positive as gifts are generally taken to be; it is given freely and "on behalf of Christ." The gift is, in short, Christ's gift to them. "On behalf of" suggests "for the sake of." The gift is from Christ and to be used for his purposes. The following two phrases make the gift's startling content clear.

not only to believe in him: Here is a clear statement of a Pauline principle, that belief itself is neither achieved nor earned, but gift, grace (compare Rom 3:21-28; Gal 2:15-16; Eph 1:3-8; 2:4-9). Belief is "in Christ," which I take to be a pun, a *double entendre.* Christ is the object of their belief, but belief also is "in," that is, because of Christ. This is the "plus" side of the gift.

but also to suffer on behalf of him: At this point there is a "twist." One can see how belief is a good gift. Now Paul is suggesting that to suffer for Christ's sake is also a good gift. God gives some people the grace of suffering for Christ. The articular infinitive "to suffer" is used as the subject of the verb. The parallel construction makes "to believe" and "to suffer" two aspects of the same thing (i.e., life in Christ). Faith implies fellowship with Christ and thus with his sufferings, as Paul wrote in Rom 8:17 and especially here in 3:10. Paul's exhortation to unity has taken a decidedly theological turn toward theodicy, explaining suffering, or at least presenting it in its Christian context.

30. *having the same struggle which you saw in me and now you hear in me:* While the Greek is a bit obscure, the meaning is clear. The Philippians and Paul both have received the "gift" of belief and of suffering. The Philippians have the same "struggle" or conflict, and probably from the same source, Roman authority. One hears in the Greek *agōna* the English cognate "agony" and is re-

minded that the Greek word was used of contests in the arena. This is serious suffering, not some minor inconvenience. The Philippians had seen Paul's previous struggles during his imprisonment in Philippi (see Acts 16:19-40 and Paul's remark in 1 Thess 2:2) and now, by means of the epistle and of Epaphroditus' report, they hear of it again. And Paul knows that they, too, have suffered "on behalf of Christ." But, as the following verses make clear, suffering in Christ and for the Gospel is not pointless or "unredeemed." Indeed, it is part and parcel of the experience of their Lord.

INTERPRETATION

These verses open a new section of the letter closely linked by v. 27 to what precedes it. Having decided that he probably will return to Philippi, Paul is giving the church counsel in preparation for his arrival. The imperative mode is much in evidence. In essence his advice is encouragement toward greater unity based on the example of Christ's humility and self-giving. The previous section focused on Paul; this one focuses on the Philippians, an example of what I take to be the overall pattern of the letter: specific examples alternate with instructions to the Philippians. This new section of the letter is framed by references to their conduct (1:27-30 and 2:14-18) in the context of suffering for the Gospel, a suffering that is itself a gift from God. At its heart is the example of Christ himself, the famous "Christ hymn" of 2:5-11. Verses 27-30 are one long, complicated Greek sentence. As Morna Hooker points out in NIB, many of the ideas in 1:27-30 recur at 3:17–4:1, a section of the letter that is also devoted to instructions to the Philippians in the context of "opposers" of the Gospel. The two passages may mark off an inclusion.

The opening phrase in the imperative governs the whole: "Live your life worthily of the Gospel of Christ." Paul reminds the Philippians that conduct worthy of the Gospel refuses to be intimidated and accepts suffering for the Gospel as gift. In these verses Paul enumerates characteristics of a person "in Christ." The Gospel is evident (or not) in his or her manner of life (v. 27). It is manifested in union with other believers in "one spirit, one soul" (v. 27), and in a life of testimony and witness (v. 27) that is without fear (v. 28) and accepting of the grace of suffering (v. 29). All of these characteristics Paul himself has exhibited.

Another mark of the Philippians' closeness to and union with Paul is that they, too, suffer for Christ, have had "the same struggle" as Paul. Several commentators remark, and I agree, that this section of the letter is a theodicy, an explanation of Christian suffering in light of what God did in Jesus Christ. It should be noted, however, that what is in view is specifically suffering "for the Gospel," and not the more general "slings and arrows that flesh is heir to." (For Paul's thoughts on that see Rom 8:17-30.)

As such it cuts both ways, reminding Christians that they can expect suffering precisely because they *are* Christians. This is a divine promise: "in the world you face persecution" or "you have tribulation" (John 16:33, and compare 2 Tim 3:12-13). But at the same time there is consolation and meaning in that suffering. God's Christ suffered to effect human salvation. For the Christian, suffering for the sake of others, especially to bring them the salvation of the Gospel, is not an evil to be avoided, but a paradigm to be embraced, a grace, albeit a severe one. It is also, as 3:10 makes clear, a means of knowing resurrection power.

For Reference and Further Study

Brewer, Raymond R. "The Meaning of *Politeuesthe* in Phil 1:27," *JBL* 73 (1954) 76–83.

Pfitzner, Victor C. *Paul and the Agōn Motif.* Leiden: Brill, 1967.

Stagg, Frank. "The Mind in Christ Jesus: Phil 1:27–2:18," *RevExp* 77 (1980) 337–47.

Central Injunction (2:1-4)

> 1. Therefore if [there is] any comfort in Christ, if any consolation of love, if any fellowship of spirit, if any compassion and tenderness, 2. fulfill my joy, having the same opinions, the same love, one-souled, thinking the one [thing], 3. [doing] nothing from selfish ambition, nothing from empty glory, but in humility counting others superior to yourselves, 4. each one not considering the things of themselves, but [also] the things of others.

Notes

1. *Therefore if [there is] any comfort in Christ:* Verses 1-4 are one complex sentence that opens with four conditional clauses. The Greek construction implies an answer in the affirmative. The effect is that Paul is saying, "If there is any comfort in Christ (and there IS), if any consolation of love (and there IS), if any fellowship of spirit (and there IS), if any compassion and consolation (and there IS)." The issue is not in doubt. The conditional form is used to prepare for a request. Because the Philippians do, indeed, experience these things, Paul can go on to ask of them perfection (*plērōsate,* v. 2). His call is to "fill up" what is already in evidence. "Therefore" ties Paul's appeal here to the immediately preceding text, 1:27-30, which urged that the Philippians' manner of life, especially in suffering, must be worthy of the Gospel. This should be kept

in view. In suffering there is comfort in Christ and in the love and fellowship of the community (see 1:19). "Comfort" *(paraklēsis)* has as its Greek root the familiar Johannine term *paraklētos,* "advocate," one called alongside to help. The root idea is of one, here Christ, "called alongside."

if any consolation of love: Paul again chooses a Greek word with the prefix *para,* "beside" or "with." The word literally means "beside-care," thus "consolation" or "encouragement." The parallel word forms mirror the parallel conditional clauses. The word for love is, naturally, *agapē,* the disinterested well-wishing and doing good for others that characterizes the mature Christian. Recall that the context of love's consolation is suffering.

if any fellowship of spirit: Fellowship, *koinōnia,* is precisely what Paul hopes to encourage in Philippi (see 1:5). This much is clear. The remainder of the phrase is debated. Is this a subjective genitive (fellowship created *by* the Holy Spirit) or an objective genitive (fellowship *in* the Holy Spirit)? "Spirit" is read by some scholars as it was used in 1:27, not to refer to the Holy Spirit but to describe the attitude or disposition of the community. Others suggest the phrase means "fellowship *in* the Holy Spirit," the sharing the Philippians have with each other because of the sharing *each* has with the Holy Spirit. If the latter is correct, the verse's underlying structure is Trinitarian. My own sense is that "spirit" here refers to the shared life of the community. "Comfort," "consolation," and "fellowship" in the face of suffering are found in the life of the community redeemed by Christ and sustained by the Holy Spirit, which mediates his Risen Life to it.

if any compassion and tenderness: Paul's appeal is couched in deeply affective language. "Compassion" *(splanchna)* is a fascinating word. Literally it means "innards" or "guts" and was understood by the ancients as the center of emotional life. Paul used this strong word at 1:8 to describe his longing for the Philippians. Compassion is "gut feeling," the feeling a mother has for her child, since recent scholars have suggested the word referred to the womb and thus carries the connotation of maternal love and nurture. "Tenderness" *(oiktirmoi)* suggests pity or mercy expressed affectively, with "feeling." The two terms also occur together at Col 3:12.

2. *fulfill my joy:* Verse 1 is the "if" clause; v. 2 begins the "then" completion of the thought. "Fulfill" *(plērōsate)* means not only "complete" or "fill up" with a spatial connotation, but "perfect" or "mature." The construction of v. 1 suggests that the Philippian congregation already has those qualities in some measure. Paul now calls for their perfection. (Compare 1:6, which uses the same root word.) "Joy" is a keynote of the letter and certainly the primary term Paul uses to describe his own disposition throughout it (e.g., in 1:4, 18, 19; 2:17). The basis of the apostle's appeal is not only emotional, but very personal.

having the same opinions, the same love: "Having opinions" *(phronēte)* suggests a mental attitude. It is a crucial term in the letter (see 1:7; 2:5; 3:15, 19; 4:20). Paul is asking that they be "minded" or "disposed" in a certain way, literally "think the same." The term is characteristically Pauline; he uses it twenty-three times, with at least ten occurrences in this letter. It means "like-minded" (NIV) or "of the same mind" (RSV) and implies a habitual attitude that is a combination of intellectual and affective activity. The form of "love" is the same as that in 2:1 and points back toward it. The Philippians are to love as they have been loved. The repetition of forms of "same" underscores Paul's plea for unity, as does the repetition of nearly synonymous phrases.

one-souled, thinking the one [thing]: There is no good English equivalent for *sympsychoi,* which I have translated "one-souled." It means "of one accord." William Barclay points out that *psychē* is the term the Greeks use for physical life. Thus Paul is asking the Philippians to share the same life principle. Theirs is to be a somatic unity. "Thinking" here is another form of the word "opinion," with which the verse opens. The Philippians are encouraged to "think one thing" (compare Rom 12:16, 15:5; Phil 4:7). There is sublime ambiguity here, for the phrase can mean "be like-minded," but also, poetically, "have one focus," that is, Christ (compare 1:18, 21 and, parenthetically, Luke 10:41-42). Verse 2 picks up many of the terms and ideas from Paul's imperatives in 1:27.

3. *[doing] nothing from selfish ambition, nothing from empty glory:* Verse 3 has no verb. I have supplied "doing" to render the English more smoothly. The Greek construction has the force of an imperative. As was the case in vv. 1 and 2, here there is a series of parallel phrases in the Greek; two "nothing from" phrases are in apposition to the phrases in the second half of the verse so that selfish ambition and humility, empty glory and superiority are contrasted. "Selfish ambition" has as its root *eritheia,* the work done by a day laborer, i.e., done only for hire. In Aristotle it is used of political ambition, and Paul used the term in 1:17 for the partisan preachers he contrasts with those who act from love (1:16). Indeed, 1:15-17 describe the very behaviors Paul here prohibits. *Kenodoxia* is literally "empty glory" or "vainglory" and is a *hapax legomenon.* In Greco-Roman literature it is used of those who think highly of themselves—with no foundation in fact, appearance without reality. It indicates self deception. In the NT "glory" *(doxa)* usually appears in reference to God. "Vainglory" can be understood as an attempt to rival God, and thus is opposite to the humility Paul commends.

but in humility counting others superior to yourselves: "Humility" would have been a startling word in the ears of the original audience because it was a slave virtue, not a quality touted for proud citizens of a Roman city. As I-Jin Loh and Eugene Nida point out in their translators' notes, Greek moralists viewed humility as the subservient attitude of a lower-class person. It involved distasteful self-abasement. The root word *tapeinoō* literally meant "to level a mountain," and that gives important insight into its meaning as a Christian virtue. The "mountain" *chooses* to be "made low"; the "mighty" *gives up* the throne. The choice is not for enforced servility or obsequiousness, but for chosen service after the model of Christ. The term develops a positive meaning as exemplified by Christ's own humility, which is the subject of the next section of the letter, 2:6-11, especially v. 8. "Humility" becomes the virtue describing lowly service chosen and executed by a noble person (and best exemplified by the foot-washing in John 13), a "tall one" who "levels" him- or herself. In Matthew's gospel this same root word *(tapeinos)* is used by Jesus to describe himself (Matt 11:29). Qumran texts use the equivalent Hebrew term for those obliged to exhibit truth and humility in the common life (1QS 5:3) and for the correct attitude toward God and other members of the community (1QS 2:24; 4:3; 5:23, 25). The verb "count on" or "consider" recurs at 2:6 in the context of Christ's own self-consideration. "To count others superior" is not to practice "doormat-ism" or insincere self-denigration. It is to understand one's own proper place in relation to Christ and, therefore, in relation to others. Christ's love for believers makes them equals. To put it boldly, all Christians are slaves of the same Master. A believer learns to see in the other the Christ who loved him or her. Verse 3 then contrasts two negative attitudes that militate against unity (selfish ambition and empty glorying) and two positive attitudes that promote it (humility and counting others as better than oneself). Paul commends what makes for a unified community and prohibits what prevents it.

4. *each one not considering the things of themselves, but [also] the things of others:* Grammatically the verse consists of a final adjectival participle that has the sense of an imperative. As in the previous verses in this section, the phrases here are carefully constructed to be parallel. "Each one"/"themselves" contrasts with "others." "Considering" has as its root a word involving sight, that is, "consider" in the sense of "look at closely," or "concentrate on." It suggests that some effort is required to "see" the concerns of others. If there were ever a countercultural suggestion, this is it!

Interpretation

In 1:27-30 the context was suffering that the Philippian believers experienced, probably caused by those outside the community, those destined for "destruction" (1:28). At 2:1 Paul's focus changes to become intra-church, stressing the danger of division and divisiveness *in* the community. Apparently dissension within the church was occurring at the same time that it faced persecution from without. Paul recognized this as an especially perilous position. In the long run only internal unity would allow the Philippians to "stand firm in one spirit, one soul" (1:27) against external pressure.

Verses 1-4 are, again, one complex sentence in Greek. Paul repeats key concepts that have already appeared in the letter (joy, fellowship, love, unity, "mindedness"), then intensifies the appeal for unity by making the shocking statement that the slave virtue of humility is the means to that unity. (See the Note on "humility" in 2:3.) Such an appeal can only be made on the basis of the example of Christ, which follows in 2:5-11. The Greek construction with which this section opens implies an answer in the affirmative. The if/then format suggests that because one is united to the church, certain actions are expected. The language at the end of v. 1 is highly emotional and personal. The heart of the matter appears in v. 2

with the finite verb "fulfill" or "perfect" governing Paul's appeal. Paul's joy in them will be perfect when they exhibit "one-mindedness." The hindrances to it, and their correctives, are spelled out in vv. 3-4.

Karl Barth's commentary on these four verses is particularly helpful. He finds 2:1-11 "a little compendium of Pauline testimony" (p. 49). Here, for Barth, is the heart of the Pauline ethic: ". . . each is to climb down from the throne on which he sits, and to mind and seek after the *one* end, which is then also that of the *others* and in which all *must* find their way to unity" (p. 50). Barth reminds one that she or he "climbs down" from the throne of self in order to mind "that which is minded *in Christ Jesus*" (p. 50). Ironically, our unity as believers comes precisely from understanding our equality as sinners redeemed by Christ. Our response must be to "unthrone" ourselves for the good of others and the community, trusting that *they* are doing precisely the same thing for *our* benefit. What is required is a staggering mutuality, one seldom understood by those formed in the western ethos of "rugged individualism."

In the context of the Philippians' situation, Paul's point in this passage is to encourage unity. Normally one does not underscore the need for something that already exists. Several passages suggest internal divisiveness in the Philippian church (1:15-17; 3:2-4; 4:2-3). Whatever the exact circumstances that are causing division, selfishness, personal conceit, and self-interest will exacerbate the problem. Humility and concern for others always calm troubled relational waters. But when people are focused only on themselves and their own concerns, others are easily viewed as threats and unfortunate clashes result. Paul has already reminded the Philippians that they are "in Christ." That is the real origin and locus of their unity. But *their own* behavior will either fracture or strengthen that unity.

Paul's point is that true humility on the part of all community members is essential to church unity, and church unity is essential in the face of external persecution. The nature of such humility is exemplified in the life of Jesus Christ (2:5-11), which calls the Philippians to a particular "mindedness" or "mindset."

For Reference and Further Study

Barclay, William. "Great Themes of the New Testament: Phil 2:1-11," *ExpTim* 70 (1958) 4–7.

Barth, Karl. *The Epistle to the Philippians.* Richmond: John Knox, 1962, especially pp. 49–59.

Loh, I-Jin, and Eugene Nida. *A Translator's Handbook on Paul's Letter to the Philippians.* Stuttgart: United Bible Societies, 1977.

Stagg, Frank. "The Mind in Christ Jesus: Phil 1:27–2:18," *RevExp* 77 (1980) 337–47.

EXCURSUS I

HYMNS IN EARLY CHRISTIANITY

The first records of what early Christians thought about Jesus of Nazareth, the Christ, are found in hymns embedded in books in the New Testament. These hymns were originally composed under the guidance of the Holy Spirit and sung or chanted in public worship. Hymns in Christian worship were understood to be a gift of the Holy Spirit, spontaneous compositions "given" by the Spirit. Their content was the saving acts of Jesus Christ. The major hymnic passages in the NT are almost exclusively about Jesus for the simple and profound reason that Jesus was centrally important to early Christians.

Paul himself gives evidence of the practice just described in writing to the church at Corinth. First Corinthians 14 contains the earliest description of Christian worship: "When you come together, each one has a hymn, a lesson, a revelation, a tongue or an interpretation" (14:26; see 1 Cor 11:17-34 for the first description of the Eucharist). Note that the first item in the list of "worship contents" is a hymn. Verse 15 says that these hymns of praise are sung with the spirit and with the mind, suggesting they are both affective, what we might call "moving," and have serious intellectual content. The Roman official Pliny the Younger corroborates Paul's picture. He wrote to Trajan (*Ep.* 10.96) that Christians come together on a regular day "to sing a song alternately to Christ as god." The remark suggests antiphonal singing of Christ hymns.

The foundation for early Christ hymns was, first, knowledge of the events in the life of Jesus, especially his Passion, and, second, the Scriptures of Judaism, particularly the Psalms and Wisdom literature. Martin Hengel has long argued that the earliest Christian hymns were messianic readings of Psalms 2, 8, 22, 110, and 118, and that the earliest Christians interpreted their experience of the risen Lord and his Spirit on the basis of the Psalms. Wisdom literature also provided precedents. Hengel explains: "early Christian thought was faced with the task of expressing the unique and surpassing worth of the revelation of God in His Christ, Jesus of Nazareth, in such a way that all previous Jewish exaltation and mediator conceptions of men of God, teachers, prophets, and angels paled beside it. The linguistic means to express this worth was supplied out of hand by Jewish Wisdom teaching alone" (*Studies in Early Christology,* 116). Certainly Jesus used Wisdom language and images for himself (see, for example, Matt 11:28-30). It is hypothesized that this material made its way into the sayings source called "Q." By the late 40's, Christians were singing "Jesus Wisdom hymns" in their worship, and those hymns served the dual purpose of worship and catechesis. Hymns were teaching tools, the expression of earliest christology. Early Christians were not interested in the "gender" of God (focal in some recent studies of the Wisdom tradition), but in finding a language that would be exalted enough to describe their experience of what God had done in Jesus Christ. Wisdom texts that were frequently mined for what they could offer in this regard included Job 28, Proverbs 1 and 8, Sirach 1 and 24, and Wisdom of Solomon 6–9.

Some of these Christ hymns were incorporated by writers of the NT into their works and served various purposes. NT texts generally taken by modern scholarship to be hymns or hymn fragments include Phil 2:6-11; Col 1:15-20; John 1:1-14; Heb 1:3; 1 Tim 3:16; 1 Pet 2:21-25. Some scholars have suggested that Eph 2:14-16; 1 Tim 2:5-6; 2 Tim 2:11-13; Titus 3:4-7; 1 Pet 3:18-21 are also hymns or fragments thereof. Additionally, the book of Revelation is a particularly rich source for early Christian hymnody (1:4-8; 4:8; 5:9-10, 12; 11:15, 17-18; 15:3-4; 22:17). An accessible description of how these passages were determined to be hymns is found in Markus Barth's Anchor Bible Commentary, *Ephesians 1:7-8*. Generally speaking, they are marked off in some way from their context in the letters; they exhibit the compressed language of poetry and often scan or can be divided into lines and stanzas on the basis of beats or syllables; they exhibit other elements of careful structure (such as parallelism, ring composition, and inclusion) and reflect unusual lexical features (e.g., *hapax legomena*). In content the christological hymns speak of the equality of Jesus and God, Jesus' role in the creation, its sustenance and redemption, and, therefore, of his death, resurrection, and exaltation by which both humanity and the cosmic powers are subjected to him.

Christians first began to articulate what they thought about Jesus by means of spirit-inspired hymns in the context of worship. Those hymns reached back into Jewish tradition (and some would argue Greco-Roman tradition) for their language and metaphors. The songs were not only a means of praising and thanking God, but were a means of teaching *about* Jesus Christ and about morality, as hymnody was accessible to both Jewish and Gentile Christians. The hymn to Christ served as a living medium for the development of christology in the early church. It began with messianic psalms, moved into the Wisdom tradition, and culminated in the prologue to the Fourth Gospel. In a very real sense early Christian theology grew out of the worship of Christ in some liturgical form as it was experienced in the community of believers. Since singing hymns to the deities characterized the religious cults of the Greco-Roman world, the "Christ hymns" were "ready made" tools for use in worship and in evangelism to express the unity of Christian belief. Men and women commonly and universally took full part in liturgical singing since *koinōnia* (the common life) was expressed by means of it. Spontaneous singing of hymns in Christian worship was greatly cut back after the second century because such "charismatic" worship was thought to characterize "heretical" groups. We begin to see such limitation in 1 Corinthians.

The text that follows, Phil 2:6-11, is almost universally taken to be one of these early Christian hymns. It is a self-contained unit of material that was probably first sung in early Christian worship as an ode to Christ. It presents a "soteriological drama" concerned with what Jesus accomplished, how he accomplished it, and God's response, which effected Jesus' ultimate lordship. While almost all scholars admit that this is a hymn, subsequent commentary on the passage often loses sight of the reality of the genre. A hymn is a poem, a song, an element of worship. While it may reflect christology, its intention is not systematic theology, but praise and worship. Another way to say this is that Paul inserts a hymn at this point in Philippians for a pastoral reason, to address a problem in the Philippian church about which he is concerned. He does not quote a hymn to offer a definitive answer to questions about the relationship between Adam and Christ, the pre-existence of Christ, or the relationship between the first two persons of the Trinity. These are important issues for christology, but they are not the reason Paul inserts the hymn, nor is the hymn form the best means to address them. In the commentary that follows I skirt these (and other) much discussed and important issues in favor of trying to take extremely seriously the *genre* of the text. As Paul Minear wrote in "Singing and Suffering in Philippi," ". . . music is not the place to look for theological precision" (204). I try to treat the hymn as hymn, not as a statement of systematic christology. I do, however, allude to the scholarly christological discussions and provide references that will allow readers to follow those important lines of inquiry.

For Reference and Further Study

Barth, Markus. *Ephesians.* 2 vols. AB 34, 34A. Garden City, NY: Doubleday, 1974.

Bischel, M. Alfred. "Hymns, Early Christian." *ABD* 3:350–51.

Brown, Raymond E. *An Introduction to New Testament Christology.* New York: Paulist, 1994.

Dunn, James D. G. *Christology in the Making.* Philadelphia: Westminster, 1980.

Guthrie, Donald. *New Testament Theology.* Downers Grove, IL: InterVarsity Press, 1981.

Hengel, Martin. *Studies in Early Christology.* Edinburgh: T & T Clark, 1995.

Karris, Robert. *A Symphony of New Testament Hymns.* Collegeville: Liturgical Press, 1996.

Ladd, George E. *A Theology of the New Testament.* Grand Rapids: Eerdmans, 1974/1993.

Lederbach, Dennis. *Christ in the Early Christian Hymns.* New York: Paulist, 1998.

Minear, Paul S. "Singing and Suffering in Philippi," in Robert Fortna and Beverly Roberts Gaventa, eds., *The Conversation Continues.* Nashville: Abingdon, 1990, 202–19.

The Christ Hymn (2:5-11)

5. Have this mind among you which [is] also in Christ Jesus, 6. who, being in essence God, did not consider equality with God to be grasped, 7. but emptied himself, taking [the] essence of [a] slave, being in likeness human and being found in appearance as human, 8. he humbled himself, being obedient unto death, even death of [a] cross. 9. And therefore God exalted him and gave to him the name that [is] above all names, 10. that at the name of Jesus every knee should bow in heaven and upon earth and under earth, 11. and every tongue should confess that Jesus Christ [is] Lord to [the] glory of God [the] Father.

Notes

5. *Have this mind among you:* The Greek verb for "have . . . mind" *(phroneō)* has already figured prominently in the letter (1:7; 2:2) and will recur (3:15, 19; 4:2, 10). Here it means "disposition" or "habitual attitude." "You" is plural. Paul commands (the verb is imperative) the community as a whole to have a particular "cast of mind." *En* can be translated either "within" (as in an individual) or "among" (as in a community). I think the plural pronoun calls for the latter. Paul has the whole Philippian church in view. But, of course, for the whole church to be "Christ-minded," each individual member of it must also be so disposed.

   which [is] also in Christ Jesus: At the outset it is clear that the model Paul is commending is that of Christ Jesus. The Philippian community is commanded to have the attitude or "mindedness" that Jesus Christ had. The verse has no verb; it is implied. I have supplied "to be," although other scholars suggest some form of "to have." The Philippians are either to imitate Christ or to be what they already are in him (or both!). In my view the "to be" form of the verb places the focus on Christ, who is being commended as a model. (For an extended discussion of the verb issue see Ralph P. Martin's *Philippians,* 91–93, and Hooker in *NIB* 11:506–507.) Verse 5 suggests to many scholars that what follows is to be seen as "exemplification," and for reasons that will become apparent in the Interpretation, I agree.

6. *who, being in essence God:* Verses 6-8 describe the "mind" that v. 5 commended. The present active participle expresses the continuation of a former condition; Jesus continued to be in some mysterious way essentially God, whatever his

"form" was. He always had the "essence" of God; he was "in nature God." *Morphē* (essence) has been interpreted in three ways: (1) as a philosophical term (my own preference); (2) as akin to the words *eidos* or *homoiōma* in the LXX and meaning "outward form"; (3) in the context of Hellenistic Gnostic sects as a term for divine nature. Certainly *morphē* was a Greek philosophical term used by Aristotle to express true Being, a reality that never changes. "Visible form" would not have been the connotation of the term for those who knew that God does not have a "form" that can be seen (compare John 4:21-24, especially v. 24. However, Markus Bockmuehl has isolated Jewish literature containing the idea that God has a form, but one that cannot be seen by human beings). In my view the "essence" of God would include the idea of "condition" or "status" of divinity (as per Eduard Schweizer). *Morphē* is used three times in the NT, twice in the hymn (vv. 6, 7). Discussions of the relationship of Christ to the figure of Adam begin with the equation of the terms *morphē* and *eikōn*, the latter of which appears in Gen 1:26 LXX (compare Col 1:15 and John 1:18). Some scholars suggest that the two words are used in similar contexts with a common referent and from this articulate a Christ/Adam typology in the hymn. (See, for example, the article listed below by Charles H. Talbert, "The Problem of Pre-Existence in Phil 2:6-11.") A convincing case against the two terms as synonyms is made by Dave Steenburg, who concludes that *morphē* is used in the description of the creation of humanity in God's image precisely because it connotes what *eikōn* does not. The phrase "being in essence God" is a strong assertion of the divinity of Jesus. On the basis of it some scholars have argued that the phrase indicates the pre-existence of the Christ, especially since the classical use of *ousia* indicates essence.

did not consider equality with God to be grasped: The Greek word for "grasped" *(harpagmos)* is a notable *hapax legomenon.* The word does not appear in the LXX and is rare in extra-biblical materials. In essence it means "robbery," with the connotation of abrupt taking or usurpation. It seems to be an abstract word meaning "the act of snatching." In other contexts it is used of rape! (See the article by C. F. D. Moule listed below, 268.) The modern idiom "ripped off" catches the connotation. In parallel literature it is used of a prize to be seized or held onto and of a piece of good fortune. The most extended and technical discussion of the term appears in the article by N. T. Wright listed below. He concludes that the word is crucial to understanding the whole hymn. It emphasizes that Jesus refused to take advantage of the position that was his (as opposed to oriental despots who used their positions for their own advantage) and, in fact, understood his position to mean the self-negation described in vv. 7-8. As Wright says, his position did not excuse him from the task of redemptive suffering, but uniquely qualified him for it (Wright, *"Harpagmos,"* 345). Wright's reading is bolstered by Roy W. Hoover's philological study, which concludes that the term means "something to take advantage of" or "something to use for one's own advantage." "Grasped," then, has a passive sense. Jesus refused to exploit his position for his own advantage. *If* "in essence God" echoes Gen 1:26 (and I am far from convinced of this), the contrast is between Adam who *did* grasp at equality with God and Jesus who did not.

In any case, equality with God is what Jesus did *not* steal, as it was *already* his. As Karl Barth puts it, Jesus "is so much God's Equal [sic] that he does not . . . have to make of his equality with God a thing to be asserted tooth and nail . . . it is beyond dispute" (*Epistle to the Philippians*, 62). Hooker notes this verse is unique in Paul in its depiction of what Jesus Christ did *not* do.

7. *but emptied himself*: Verse 6 tells us what Christ did not do; vv. 7-8 reveal what he did. In Greek the pronoun precedes the verb and is therefore emphatic. "Emptied," *ekenōsen,* is a key verb describing Jesus' choice of renunciation of privilege (see Wright's article, and compare Rom 4:14; 1 Cor 1:17; 9:15; 2 Cor 9:3). "Emptied himself" is not only graphic, but emphatic. Jesus chose to do this *to* himself; he is both subject and object of the verb. This matter of "emptying" has great implications for christology. Does the fact that Jesus "emptied himself" mean that his status of equality with God was temporarily suspended during his earthly life (as in the nineteenth-century kenotic theory of incarnation)? Or is it to be understood as Jesus' self-abrogation, his humility and refusal of self-aggrandizement? If, indeed, Jesus was in form/essence God, then certainly there was some continuity between his pre-existent and his incarnate state. But these are matters for systematic theology and not hymnody. (See Excursus I above.)

taking [the] essence of [a] slave: The hymn repeats the term "essence" *(morphē)* used in v. 6 (and discussed there) to stress that, just as Jesus was really divine, he was also really a slave. John 13:5-17 presents a dramatic example of slave imagery in the life of Jesus. "Slave" is both a term Paul used for himself (Rom 1:1; Phil 1:1) and his common description of the Christian life (Rom 7:6, 25; 12:11; Gal 5:13; Phil 2:22). It would have had potent associations for the recipients of the letter. The slave is one absolutely without rights; slaves were entirely dependent upon the will of their masters (compare Wis 9:4-7, and see Col 3:22–4:1 and Eph 6:5-9). The comparison being made is that of the highest form of being (God) to the lowest form of being (slave). A shocking contrast exists between v. 6 and v. 7 in the antithesis "essence of God/essence of slave." Jesus emptied himself of the first to assume the second. He chose to do so.

being in likeness human and being found in appearance as human: These are the first two of a set of participles of manner, participles used as adjectives to describe what Jesus was like or appeared to be (versus what he *really* was, v. 6). Here the term shifts from "essence" to "likeness." "Likeness" *(homoiōma)* means "appearance," what something is made to look like, and it implies that something might not be what it appears to be. The Greek word for "human" is *anthrōpos.* It is significant that the writer of the hymn did not use the Greek word for "man," *anēr.* What is being stressed here is not Jesus' maleness (which is not in question) but his *human*-ness. The hymn neatly answers the feminist question "can a male savior save women?" by stressing that Jesus became completely *human.* "Appearance" *(schēma)* is the opposite of "essence" *(morphē).* It means something like "demeanor," or what can be outwardly known, and implies what is changeable and external. Its only use in the LXX is Isa 3:17. Jesus "looked like" a human being; that was not his only reality (compare 1 Cor 7:31). The contrast is between "outward appearance," which can change *(schēmati),* and the reality or unchanging essence *(morphē).* What seems to be the case, rather than the reality, is stressed in this verse. God cannot stop being God. What Jesus relinquished was "privilege, not essence" (see Frank Stagg, "The Mind in Christ Jesus," 344).

8. *he humbled himself:* The phrase echoes "emptied himself" at the beginning of v. 7. Again, the term "humility" has already been used by Paul to dramatic effect (see the Notes on 2:3). Humility was a slave virtue, and so the verb aptly describes the "emptied condition" of Jesus in the previous verse. The aorist verb implies one definite action in the past, which was the "emptying" and choice of the cross, but its effect continues.

   being obedient unto death: That Jesus was obedient or "subject" suggests that the death was not random, but part of a plan (compare Isa 53:8, 12). Jesus was obedient *to* someone and something: God and God's plan of salvation (compare Eph 1:3-14). The suggestion has been made that the root idea is that Jesus chose the role of the *ʿebed* YHWH of Isaiah's "Servant Songs." His choice, of course, is one that leads to death, a terrible sort of death.

   even death of [a] cross: This second phrase is explanatory, and chilling. Not only did Jesus submit to death ("*even* death"; compare Rom 5:6-8), but death of the most horrible kind. The cross was reserved as the punishment for the most heinous criminals. Only non-Roman citizens could be tortured to death in this way. Crucifixion was for the lowest order of society; slaves died by crucifixion (see v. 7). Morna Hooker calls it the "nadir of humiliation." Many scholars think the phrase is a Pauline addition to a pre-existing Christ hymn, but it strikes me as a most dramatic and forceful conclusion for the kenotic phase of the hymn. (For a contemporary view of crucifixion see Cicero, *Pro Rabirio* 5.10. One of the best recent explanations of the meaning of "cross" to Paul's original audience is found in Morna Hooker's book, *Not Ashamed of the Gospel: New Testament Interpretations of the Death of Christ* [Grand Rapids: Eerdmans, 1994].)

9. *And therefore God exalted him:* In the terms of Greek drama this is the *peripeteia,* the reversal or change of fortune of the hero. Verses 6-8 describe a "great plunge," the descent from godliness to human-ness to slavery to death. All of this happens by the choice of Jesus, who *made himself* nothing, *took form* as a slave, *humbled himself,* and *was obedient.* The focus has been on what Jesus chose to do. Now in vv. 9-11 the focus shifts entirely: the "direction" of the hymn is no longer "down," but decidedly "up," and the actor is not Jesus, but God. "Therefore" is particularly strong. God's action is the result of Jesus' obedience. Verses 6-8 describe Jesus' actions; he is the subject of the verbs. But vv. 9-11 describe God's action; God is the subject, Jesus the object. Acts 2:36 provides an important gloss on the verse and this section of the hymn: ". . . God has made him both Lord and Christ, this Jesus whom you crucified" *(RSV).* "Therefore" *(dio)* suggests reward or recompense, although the Reformers resisted this idea. The inclusion of the definite article *(ho theos),* as per Semitic usage, suggests that the phrase is very early in Christian articulation and also makes a subtle point. Verse 6 speaks of divinity in general, godly essence. But at v. 9 the hymn makes explicit for Greco-Romans *which* god: the

God of the Hebrews, the God whom Jesus invites his followers to call "Father" *(Abba)* (as per v. 11). "Exalted" is a compound verb meaning, as Loh and Nida point out, "God hyperexalted him" (*Translator's Handbook,* 61). It is superlative, and contrasts with the absolute degradation described in v. 8.

and gave to him the name that [is] above all names: The verb for "gave" *(echarisatō)* has as its root the word "grace." God gave the name "Jesus," which is derived from a Hebrew word that means "savior," as an act of grace. To give a name is to bestow status, authority, even power. To receive a new name (here "Lord," as per v. 11) also signals a new stage in life (see Gen 17:5; 32:28). The hymn suggests that Jesus chose to act in absolute conformity to the meaning of his name. (For an extended discussion of the importance of "the Name" in early Christianity see Bonnie Thurston, *Spiritual Life in the Early Church* [Minneapolis: Fortress, 1993], Chapter 4, "The Name in Acts 1–10.") Charles Talbert points out the parallelism between "exalted" and "gave" in this verse. What Jesus "gave up" in vv. 6-8, God "gives back" in vv. 9-11.

10. *that at the name of Jesus every knee should bow:* "That" *(hina)* suggests the purpose of Jesus' exaltation. Several scholars have pointed out that the "name" that is important here is "Jesus," with its connotation of salvation, rather than the title "Lord," which will be focal in the next verse. The subjunctive form of the verb is a subjunctive of purpose (compare Rom 11:4; Eph 3:4). In the Philippians' world one bowed the knee to the emperor. The image is not that of prayer (which the modern reader might assume), but of fealty or subjugation to one's liege. Only the name "Jesus" commands the Christian's obeisance (compare Isa 45:18-24, especially v. 23). The overall image is that of an enthronement; Jesus is exalted, and his "subjects" kneel before him.

    in heaven and upon earth and under the earth: In the Greek text there are three parallel compound adjectives formed of a preposition of place and a noun. These adjectives function as nouns and are intended to describe the cosmic extent of Jesus' reign as they describe the three-tiered universe of Greek cosmology: heaven, earth, the netherworld (under the earth). The point is that nothing in creation is outside the realm of Jesus' lordship. The same point is focal in the Colossian Christ hymn, 1:15-20.

11. *and every tongue should confess:* "Tongue" functions as a personification of an individual and of groups of people, since "tongues" are languages. Every individual person and every person who speaks a language (every "people's group") is destined to confess the lordship of Jesus. "Confess" is another subjunctive of purpose (see previous verse). The verb means "admit openly," and implies an unguarded, public profession of faith in Jesus' lordship. In Roman Philippi this represents a very bold action, implying, as it does, that one other than the Caesar is Lord. This is one of the reasons why the hymn is so relevant to the pastoral situation Paul addresses.

    that Jesus Christ [is] Lord: So far as we know, this is the substance of the earliest Christian confession. First, Jesus is the looked-for Messiah, with all that implies. Second, *kyrios* is used to translate the Hebrew *adonai* and the Aramaic *mar* (see 1 Cor 16:22). It is found in the LXX as translation for both *adonai* and

YHWH. In general it is used in the NT for an owner (Matt 20:8), a master (Matt 25:18), and as a title of respect (Matt 21:30). Its general sense, then, is "master" or "owner," one with legitimate authority. The term is used 717 times in the NT, predominantly in the writings of Luke and Paul, suggesting that as a title for Jesus it developed in the Hellenistic environment. The title seems not to have originated with Jesus (but see John 13:13), but to be post-resurrection. It is clearly a confessional formula in Paul (Rom 10:9; 1 Cor 12:3), 1 Peter (3:22), and John (20:13, 28). In the Philippian context *kyrios* would have been the title given to the Roman emperor and the prefix used before the names of Greco-Roman gods, especially deities who could answer prayer.

to [the] glory of God [the] Father: To confess that the Son is Lord gives glory to the Father to whom he has been obedient and who responds to that obedience by exalting the Son. Christ's lordship does not compete with God's sovereignty (compare 1:1).

INTERPRETATION

Philippians 2:5-11 is one of the most frequently commented upon passages in the NT. William Barclay quotes A. B. Bruce that "the diversity of opinion prevailing among interpreters is enough to fill the student with despair, and to afflict him with intellectual paralysis" (see Barclay, "Great Themes," 4). This student can only add her hearty "AMEN!" Any serious study of the passage must begin with Ralph P. Martin's magisterial *A Hymn of Christ: Philippians 2:5-11 in Recent Interpretation & in the Setting of Early Christian Worship* (1997). Interpretations of the text generally focus on either the hymnic form or the christological content. My modest intention here is to introduce some of the discussion of the hymn's (1) origin and authorship, (2) conceptual backgrounds, (3) form and structure, and (4) purpose in Philippians. The attempt will keep clearly in mind that this is a hymn devised for and taken from the context of public worship, not a work of systematic theology or christology.

(1) *Origin and authorship:* As noted in the introductory essay, the letter is almost universally taken to be authentically Pauline. While there has been debate about whether Philippians is a unified letter or a series of letter fragments, almost no one has suggested it (or they) was/were not written by Paul. The question here is whether or not the hymn was written by Paul or existed in the church and was inserted by the apostle into the letter to serve his purposes.

Philippians 1:27–2:18 is a tightly structured unit within the letter, the dominant note of which is exhortation, what I call "Instructions to the Philippians." While clearly related to the theme of the section, Phil 2:5-11 reads in the Greek like a "literary interruption." In content the hymn both gives the reasons for and serves as an example of the behavior Paul wants the Philippians to exhibit, but in literary style it is different from what precedes and follows it. The *hos* ("who") in v. 6 intimates that what follows will be some sort of creed. While Ernst Lohmeyer's case for a Semitic original (that the hymn was written in Greek by someone whose native language was Hebrew or Aramaic) is now called into question, it does seem that the unusual vocabulary of the hymn, with its many *hapax legomena* (see commentary on individual verses above), the careful parallel construction (see "form and structure" below), and the rhythm of the Greek original all suggest a pre-existing hymn. The passage is different in tone from what surrounds it, uses many non-Pauline terms and the sort of servant language that is largely absent from Paul's other letters. On stylistic grounds it seems that Paul, like a good preacher, is using a pre-existing hymn illustratively in his exhortation to the Philippian congregation. Just as modern preachers may use a stanza or two of a well-known hymn to illustrate a point in a sermon precisely because the hymn *is* well known to the hearers, Paul is using a similar approach here.

On the other hand, the hymn bears striking similarity to other Pauline texts (1 Cor 13 or Rom 8:35-39, for example) and has lexical and conceptual parallels with 3:20-21. Paul S. Minear has pointed out that it is precisely Paul's own circumstances that give emotional force to the use of the hymn. In Acts 16:25 Luke reports that during his Philippian imprisonment Paul sang hymns. Minear suggests that this hymn in a later imprisonment (1:7, 13) is a "Passion chorale," a sort of prophetic disclosure. What happened to Jesus is a model for all Christians, and certainly for the imprisoned Paul, who does not know the outcome of his imprisonment (1:12-26), only that God's exaltation of Jesus after his suffering is part of God's design for all things. Jesus' own choice was for slavery and death. For this "God highly exalted him" (2:9). Paul's circumstances are (albeit imperfectly) parallel. Paul, the slave of Jesus Christ (1:1), has set aside his accomplishments for the sake of the Gospel (3:4-6) and "suffered the loss of all things" (3:8). Thus Paul can expect God's exaltation in his own resurrection (which he does at 3:11, 21). If Paul did not write the hymn, nevertheless it not only serves his purposes but also reflects his circumstances and implicitly those of the Philippian Christians.

While it is my sense that Paul employs an existing hymn in the Philippian letter, scholarship evinces no clear consensus. British and American evangelical scholarship tends to assume that Paul wrote the hymn. Continental scholarship (particularly German and French) leans to the position that Paul is working with a pre-existing hymn of Semitic origin. This leads, then, to the issue of the hymn's background.

(2) *Conceptual backgrounds:* Again, scholarship is divided about whether the conceptual backgrounds of the hymn are, following Lohmeyer, Semitic (a pre-Pauline two-stanza hymn) or, following Ernst Käsemann, Hellenistic (a mythic soteriological drama), or a synthesis of the two.

Those looking at the hymn from the point of view of Hebrew Scripture can hardly fail to see its many similarities to some psalms and prophetic literature. Of particular interest are Old Testament passages that discuss the Servant of Yahweh, his obedience, submission to God, and eventual glorification (compare, for example, what is said of YHWH in Isa 45:23 with what is said of Jesus in the hymn). In particular, attention has been drawn to parallels between Isa 52:13–53:12 and the hymn, even though the word for "servant" there is *pais* (child) and not *doulos* (slave). Scholars also point out the Adam/Christ contrast in the hymn: Adam snatched at equality with God; the Christ did not. (Other Pauline passages comparing the two include Rom 5:12-21 and 1 Cor 15:21-24.) Christ is the pattern *(morphē?)* of what human beings (Adam) were *intended* to be: obedient to God, in whose image they are made.

One sees in vv. 9-11 a reflection of the Vindicated One of Ps 110:1. Psalm 110:1-2 and Phil 2:9-11 share an enthronement theme. In both, God vindicates the sufferer. Other aspects of the hymn also appear in the psalm. The "pre-existence" of 2:6 can be seen in 110:3 ("yours is princely power from the day of your birth. In holy splendor, *before the daystar,* like the dew I begot you" [*NAB,* italics mine]). "Like dew I begot you" is an adoption formula. "Like Melchizedek you are a priest forever" (110:4 *NAB*) was picked up by the writer of Hebrews. There, in chapter 7, Melchizedek is a type of Christ. Certainly the mysterious origins and end of Melchizedek parallel those of Jesus in the hymn, who is also a "priest forever" (compare Heb 7:15-16, 25-26). Finally, in Phil 2:9-11 one sees enacted the promise that God will "lift up his head" (110:7b), that is, restore the status of or vindicate Jesus. In pondering Phil 2:6-11 and Psalm 110 together, I have come to wonder whether the hymn's author might have had the ideational content of the psalm in mind as he wrote.

There are also clear parallels in the hymn to Wisdom literature, in particular Prov 8:22-31 and Wis 9:9-10. J. A. Sanders has discussed the thought source of the hymn in connection with the *Corpus Hermeticum* and has noted that *Enoch* is an important source for the idea of the humble *deus descensus.* Also noted as possible parallels is material in the Qumran documents from Caves 4 and 11. (For a Semitic reconstruction of the hymn see Lohmeyer, Martin, and the article by Joseph A. Fitzmyer, "The Aramaic Background of Philippians 2:6-11.")

While there is strong evidence in favor of the Jewish origins of the hymn's thought, it is important to note that the origin of the Philippian church was notably Gentile. According to Acts 16 Paul found no synagogue in Philippi. Would he have used (or written?) a document so dependent on Hebrew Scripture in such a pivotal way with people who themselves were not deeply versed in that Scripture? Perhaps for this reason other scholars have seen behind the hymn a Gnostic redeemer myth that celebrates the descent and exaltation of a savior figure. In this mythic pattern a hero becomes subject to hostile powers and, in a cosmic drama of salvation, is delivered. It is argued that in Phil 2:6-8 Jesus is subjected to hostile forces that are defeated in 2:9-11. In spite of the context in Gentile Philippi, in my view this position can be held only by playing down, first, the *kenosis* of Jesus, his *choosing* to "come down," and, second, his refusal of status (see discussion on *harpagmos* at 2:6 above). And there is no clear evidence that Paul encountered Gnosticism in Philippi.

Finally, then, the Philippian hymn exemplifies what I have called elsewhere Paul's "dual purpose vocabulary." Paul had a genius for choosing language that had connotations in *both* Jewish and Hellenistic ideational worlds. While this is particularly evident in the lexical fields of Colossians and Ephesians, the same technique is at work in this letter to another Greek city. Paul either composes or chooses a hymn that has material that can be recognized both by those who know Jewish thought and by those familiar with Hellenistic thought. From whichever direction the hymn is approached, the picture of Jesus as presented serves Paul's purposes exactly in the context.

(3) *Form and structure:* While there is a great deal of discussion about whether the hymn scans in Greek, that is, whether it exhibits a discernible rhythmic pattern, most scholars remark on the poetic quality of the hymn (which is printed in stanza form in the *NIV, NRSV,* and *NAB*). While it does not seem to follow the rules of Greek poetry, the patterns of regular stresses, and especially the parallelism, are reminiscent of Hebrew poetry.

Basically there are two views of the structure: the hymn has either two or three stanzas. The two-stanza theorists basically follow Ernst Lohmeyer, who suggested that the hymn depicts a pattern of descent (vv. 6-8) and ascent (vv. 9-11). Verses 6-8 focus on the decision and activity of Jesus and vv. 9-11 focus on God's responses. The two-stanza structure places the focus on Jesus' actions: what he did, a functional view of Jesus. On the other hand, Joachim Jeremias suggests that the hymn is a christological statement about the pre-existent Christ (vv. 6-7a), the earthly Jesus (vv. 7b-8), and the exalted Christ (vv. 9-11). The three-stanza structure places the focus on who Jesus was, an essentialist view of Jesus. In both cases it is God who acts in the exaltation of Jesus, and more than one scholar has noted the parallels between vv. 9-11 and ancient enthronement ceremonies and enthronement liturgies.

Diverging from the traditional "two or three" stanza suggestions are Charles Talbert and Robert Gundry. Talbert has divided the hymn into four strophes of three lines each, vv. 6-7b; 7c-8; 9; 10-11 (see Talbert, "The Problem of Pre-existence"). Gundry has pointed out both the concentric and chiastic patterns in the hymn. In "Style and Substance in 'The Myth of God Incarnate'" he suggests the following structure:

A. Preexistent divine being

B. Slave-like death

C. Incarnation as human being

B' Death on a cross

A' Postexistent acknowledgment as divine

More recent scholarship on the issue has taken as its point of departure not simply the form of the hymn itself, but rhetorical and structural analysis of the whole letter, examining the hymn within the overall rhetorical structure of the Philippian letter. D. F. Watson and David A. Black provide two examples of such analysis. Watson ("A Rhetorical Analysis of Philippians") argues that Philippians is a single rhetorical unit that can be analyzed as a whole. He believes that the rhetorical situation of the letter is the appearance in Philippi of a rival gospel that Paul seeks to counter. Thus the letter is an example of deliberative rhetoric in which Paul seeks to advise and dissuade about a course of action. Within that overall structure the hymn appears in the *probatio* of the letter (2:1–3:21), which is intended to encourage the Philippians to "live life worthy of the gospel." Chapter 2, vv. 1-11 contains a restatement of the proposition (vv. 1-4) and an "exemplification" (vv. 5-11, the hymn). Verse 5, he thinks, makes clear that vv. 6-11 are an example of what Paul wants done.

Similarly, Black ("The Discourse Structure of Philippians") thinks that Philippians is an integral epistle whose primary rhetorical function is deliberative. He, however, thinks the letter is written to solve the problem of disunity. In the *exordium* (1:1-11) Paul seeks the Philippians' attention and good will. In the narration (1:12-26) he presents the facts, and in 1:27-30 the proposition. This is followed by three examples in 2:1-30 (Christ, 2:6-11; Timothy, 2:19-24; Epaphroditus, 2:25-30). Chapter 2, vv. 1-11, then, is part of an exhortation to unity and humility. Verses 1-4 appeal for unity in the face of divisions and vv. 5-11 consist of three strophes that exhort the Philippians to Christlike humility. Christ is the first and foremost example of behavior that makes for unity. The emphasis, Black thinks, is ethical; the hymn provides support for the exhortation in vv. 1-4. Such rhetorical analysis leads directly to a consideration of the purpose of the hymn.

(4) *Purpose in Philippians:* That Phil 2:6-11 is a hymn determines its purpose in the letter. As Paul S. Minear has pointed out so persuasively, Paul is not writing a literary essay (or, I would add, a work of systematic christology), but is addressing a pastoral crisis. The nature of that crisis, and what William Barclay rightly notes moved Paul to his most eloquent appeal (1:27; 2:14, 21; 3:2; 4:2), was the danger of division in the church

due to dissension. Paul's purpose in the passage is practical: to maintain the unity of the church in Philippi.

In chapter 1 Paul discusses his own persecution/suffering and the Philippians' conduct in relation to threats (like the one he was facing) from outside the community. In chapter 2 he turns to an internal problem, that of a divided church. In 2:1-4 he speaks of harmony in the church, and in 2:5-11 he uses the life of Jesus Christ as the model for the lives both of individual Christians and of the Christian community. He will follow this with two further positive examples, both known to the Philippians, that of Timothy (2:19-24) and of Epaphroditus (2:25-30). But to paraphrase what Paul "says" in 2:5-11: What Jesus did is the model for us. Our wholeness and unity as a community come through renunciation of the natural, selfish state and the appropriation of Jesus' self-giving, to which God responded positively. At first glance vv. 5-8 seem more clearly related to Paul's purpose than vv. 9-11. The example of Jesus' humility seems more to the point than God's vindication and elevation of him. But the lordship of Jesus is the point of the passage. Paul calls the Philippians to follow his example and to live under his lordship. Ralph P. Martin quotes Pierre Bonnard, "The obedient one is to be obeyed" (lii).

Philippians 2:6-11 is a self-contained unit of material, a hymn sung as an ode to Christ as part of a service of worship and recognized as such by the Philippians. It is a "soteriological drama," concerned with what Christ accomplished, and it stresses his ultimate lordship, his exaltation by God. This beautiful "upswing" at the end of the hymn (what in Aristotelian terms would be the "poetic justice") must not obscure why Paul used it in the letter. He wants to influence the conduct of the people in the Philippian church. As Martin notes, "the entire quotation of the hymn is meant to enforce an ethical appeal" (xlix). Paul apparently felt the Philippians were leaning toward selfishness, ambition, vainglory, and self-centeredness that should have no place in God's realm and reign. One does not warn against faults not in evidence! The remedy Paul proposes is the humility of Jesus Christ himself, something he has already called for ("count others better than yourselves," 2:3; look to others' interests as well as your own, 2:4), and the Philippians' humble submission to Christ.

As Fred Craddock has pointed out in his Interpretation commentary on Philippians, "The central event in the drama of salvation is an act of humble service" (p. 42). The Christ hymn in Philippians is one of the most moving and comprehensive statements about the Christian life in the NT. It says that the one who could claim equality with God, and all the power and position and glory and prestige that came with it, "emptied himself" of that equality, a mystical term of complete self-renunciation. Jesus chose "downward mobility." Much current feminist and liberation thought suggests that some populations in the Christian community have heard too much about "self-emptying" and "self-giving" and "setting self aside." Certainly perversions of the pattern have been taught and even enforced by those in authority. But the point is that Christ did not "give himself away" without first possessing himself. As the hymn points out, he *knew* his identity, *knew* who he was. (This is why the discussion of pre-existence in the hymn is so practically and pastorally important.) *Then* (and not before) he *chose* to renounce it all. Nobody forced him to do so. He could not have emptied himself of what he did not have. I find no conflict between the *kenōsis* of Christ and feminist/liberation thought, which seeks to empower persons to claim the fullness of their identity.

When Jesus is seen as the NT sees him it is in the light cast by Phil 2:6-11: from his incarnation, to his stooping to wash feet at the Last Supper, to his giving of his very self (his body, *sōma*) and his life (his blood) on Calvary's cross. It was no easier for the Philippians than it is for us, but it is only through chosen acts of self-emptying, only through looking to others' welfare as well as our own (2:4) that we are brought into the sphere of Jesus, his life and his power. It is in imitating his *kenōsis* that we are "raised up." Paul knew this in his own life and situation (3:7-11) and knew it would be true for the Philippians. The great consolation set forth in the final two verses of the hymn is that there is nothing in creation outside Christ's power. Jesus Christ has ultimate authority over all that endangers. When, through self-giving, Christians place themselves in his hands, they are delivered from all that can ultimately destroy. This is certainly the lesson of the Ignatius of Loyolas and the Charles de Foucaulds!

Christ's humility sets the example and provides the corrective to the Philippian church's internal problem of divisiveness caused at least in part by self-assertion. And God's response to Jesus' obedience speaks to threats from secular authorities outside the community. Jesus Christ is made lord of all creation, even that powerful human creation the Roman empire, and, to paraphrase Romans 8, nothing can separate the believer from his love.

For Reference and Further Study

Note: for a comprehensive bibliography see Ralph P. Martin, *A Hymn of Christ* (1997).

Bakken, Norman K. "The New Humanity, Christ and the Modern Age: A Study Centering in The Christ Hymn Phil 2:6-11," *Int* 22 (1968) 71–86.

Barclay, William. "Great Themes of the NT: Phil. 2:1-11," *ExpTim* 70 (1958) 4–7.

________. "Great Themes of the NT: Phil. 2 cont.," *ExpTim* 70 (1958) 40–44.

Black, David A. "The Discourse Structure of Philippians: A Study in Textlinguistics," *NovT* 37 (1996) 16–49.

Bockmuehl, Markus. "The Form of God (Phil 2:6). Variations on a Theme of Jewish Mysticism," *JTS* 48 (1997) 1–23.

Craddock, Fred. *Philippians.* Interpretation. Atlanta: John Knox, 1985.

Fitzmyer, Joseph A. "The Aramaic Background of Philippians 2:6-11," *CBQ* 50 (1988) 470–83.

Gould, Nicholas D. "'Servants of the Cross' Theology in Philippians," *ResQ* 81 (1975) 93–101.

Gundry, Robert H. "Style and Substance in 'The Myth of God Incarnate,'" in Stanley Porter and Paul Joyce, eds., *Crossing the Boundaries.* Leiden: Brill, 1994, 271–93.

Hooker, Morna D. "Philippians 2:6-11," in E. Earle Ellis and Erich Grässer, eds., *Jesus und Paulus.* Göttingen: Vandenhoeck & Ruprecht, 1975, 151–64.

________. "The Letter to the Philippians," *NIB.* Nashville: Abingdon, 2000, 11:467–549.

Hoover, Roy W. "The *HARPAGMOS* Enigma: A Philological Solution," *HTR* 64 (1971) 94–119.

Howard, George. "Phil 2:6-11 and the Human Christ," *CBQ* 40 (1978) 368–87.

Hurtado, Larry W. "Jesus as Lordly Example," in J. C. Hurd and G. P. Richardson, eds., *From Jesus to Paul.* Waterloo: Wilfrid Laurier University Press, 1984, 114–26.

Käsemann, Ernst. "Pauline Theology of the Cross," *Int* 25 (1970) 151–77.

Marshall, I. Howard. "The Christ-Hymn in Philippians," *TynBul* 19 (1969) 104–27.

Martin, Ralph P. *A Hymn of Christ.* Downers Grove, IL: InterVarsity Press, 1997.

Minear, Paul S. "Singing and Suffering in Philippi," in Robert Fortna and Beverly Roberts Gaventa, eds., *The Conversation Continues.* Nashville: Abingdon, 1990, 202–19.

Moule, C. F. D. "Further Reflection on Philippians 2:5-11," in W. Ward Gasque and Ralph P. Martin, eds., *Apostolic History and the Gospels.* Grand Rapids: Eerdmans, 1970, 264–76.

Perkins, Pheme. "Philippians: Theology for the Heavenly *Politeuma,*" in Jouette M. Bassler, ed., *Pauline Theology I.* Minneapolis: Fortress, 1991, 89–104.

Sanders, John A. "Dissenting Deities and Phil. 2:1-11," *JBL* 88 (1969) 279–90.

Stagg, Frank. "The Mind in Christ Jesus. Phil 1:27–2:18," *RevExp* 77 (1980) 337–47.

Steenburg, Dave. "The Case Against the Synonymity of *Morphē* and *Eikōn,*" *JSNT* 34 (1998) 77–86.

Talbert, Charles H. "The Problem of Pre-existence in Phil. 2:6-11," *JBL* 86 (1967) 141–53.

Watson, Duane F. "A Rhetorical Analysis of Philippians and Its Implications for the Unity Question," *NovT* 30 (1988) 57–88.

Wright, N. T. "*Harpagmos* and the Meaning of Philippians 2:5-11," *JTS* 37 (1986) 321–52.

Young, N. H. "An Aristophanic Contrast to Phil 2:6-7," *NTS* 45 (1999) 153–55.

Their Manner of Life (2:12-18)

12. Consequently, my beloved, as you always obeyed, not only as in my presence, but rather now more in my absence, work out your salvation with fear and trembling, 13. for God is the one working in/among you [both] to will and to work for the good. 14. You do everything without murmuring and questioning 15. in order that you might be blameless and pure, children of God without spot in the midst of a crooked and distorted generation, in which you shine as luminaries in [the] world, 16. holding forth [a] word of life, that I may boast on the day of Christ that I did not run in vain or labor in vain. 17. But even if I am poured out on the sacrifice and service [of] your faith, I rejoice, and rejoice with all of you. 18. And the same also, you [yourselves] rejoice and rejoice with me.

NOTES

12. *Consequently, my beloved, as you always obeyed:* The particle *hōste* ("consequently") draws its conclusion from what precedes it and so is the link to the Christ hymn. On the basis of the hymn, Paul now appeals to the Philippians, picking up the root imperative of 1:27: "live your life worthily of the gospel of Christ." As Christ was exalted by his obedience, so the Philippians are to be obedient. "Consequently . . . my beloved" echoes the affection of 1:8, and a similar phrase opens 4:1 (compare 1 Cor 10:14; 15:58; 2 Cor 7:1; Rom 12:19). The turn of phrase is emotionally rich and reveals Paul's deep affection for the Philippians. They are not only brethren *(adelphoi),* they are beloved *(agapētoi);* the root word is "love." The verb for "obeyed" *(hypēkousate)* is a compound word that literally means "listen for." (Compare the Latin *obedire,* which is *ob,* "toward" plus *audire,* "to hear.") It was used in parallel literature for answering a door because it meant to obey as a result of listening; one opens to the knock one hears. It is thus particularly apt here. As a result of "hearing" the hymn, the Philippians are to obey its message. The same verb is used in the context of obedience in 2 Cor 2:9; 7:15; 10:5. Recall, as well, that in Hebrew Scripture hearing implies obedience to what is heard.

    not only as in my presence, but rather now more in my absence: The collection of adverbs and relative pronouns in the Greek makes for an awkward English phrase (literally "but now by how much more"), but the sense is clear. The Philippians are to behave exactly the same way whether Paul is with them or away (compare Col 3:22, where slaves are not to render "eye service," *ophthalmodoulia,* work because someone is watching, but to work singleheartedly, "fearing the Lord"). The same idea was expressed at 1:27. The parallel construction hangs on the opposites of presence/absence, *parousia,* literally "being with," and *apousia,* literally "being away." *Parousia* can mean "coming" and thus allude to Paul's impending visit (1:25-26). *Apousia* (literally "the absence of coming") appears only here and is uncommon elsewhere. Ultimately the Philippians are to be obedient to God (who is always present), not to Paul who may or may not return (see 1:19-26).

work out your salvation with fear and trembling: Again the verb is a compound and therefore perfective, that is, "work out" implies continuing to work toward the conclusion of something already begun. "Your" in the Greek is an article and a plural pronoun *(tēn heautōn)* carrying the idea "you all" or "each one of you." Paul's concern is for their common life as they, together and individually, work out or live their salvation. The word "salvation" hearkens back to 1:28, where it is from God. The Philippians are not "earning" their salvation, but living into all it means and expects of them; they are completing something already begun. "Fear and trembling" occur together frequently in Hebrew Scripture (Gen 9:2; Exod 15:16; Isa 19:16), but here the sense of dread is missing and the sense of awe in God's presence, as in Psalm 2:11, is in view. (For Pauline uses of the phrase see 1 Cor 2:3; 2 Cor 7:15; Eph 6:5.) In 1:28 Paul has assured the Philippians that there is no reason for fear, and so in the context here the term must be related to humility, knowing one's place before God. Karl Barth coined the happy phrase "startled humility" to express the idea. The pair of words occurs elsewhere in the Pauline literature in 1 Cor 2:3; 2 Cor 7:15; Eph 6:5, in the last case in the context of the relationship between slave and master.

13. *for God is the one working in/among you:* For *(gar)* introduces how they will carry out the command to obedience. God is the primary agent of the Philippians' salvation as in 1:29 God was among them granting the gifts of faith and of suffering. Paul here places the command in v. 12 under the umbrella of God's prior action. "Working" carries the idea of effectual work, work with results. "You" is plural, and the preposition before it *(en)* can either be translated "in" (as in "within" the individual) or "among" (as in "in the midst of" the community). Either is correct, although in the context I favor the plural, communal connotation (compare 1:6; 2:5).

[both] to will and to work for the good: God desires the salvation of the Philippians and works in the world toward it. "Will" expresses desire for or determination. God does not desire the death of sinners, but their salvation (compare John 3:16-17 and 1 Tim 2:4). "Good" *(eudokia)* means "good pleasure" or "satisfaction" and was the word Paul used at 1:15 to describe the noble motive for preaching Christ. Verse 13 is of crucial importance. It is the link to God's activity in 2:9-11 and a reminder that salvation depends on God, not human effort (see 2 Cor 5:18 and Eph 2:8).

14. *You do everything without murmuring and questioning:* Verse 14 begins a sentence that continues through v. 16. Many commentators suggest it echoes and plays on Deut 32:4-5: "A faithful God, without deceit, just and upright is he; yet his degenerate children have dealt falsely with him, a perverse and crooked generation" *(NRSV)*. Perhaps we see "through" the verse, as it were, an image of the difficult relations within the Philippian church. Are the members grumbling against the leadership, the bishops and deacons of 1:1? If we are to take Rom 13:1-7 seriously, Paul understood human authority figures to be divinely ordained (compare 1 Tim 2:1-3 and Titus 3:1). The "you" is both plural and emphatic. The following two participles are also plural, stressing again that Paul is speaking to the whole community. "Murmuring" is used in Hebrew

Scripture to describe expressions of dissatisfaction with God's actions and commands; it is what the Hebrews did in the wilderness against Moses, Joshua, and God (see Exod 15:24; 16:2-12; Num 14:2-29; Josh 9:18, and compare 1 Cor 10:1-13). "Questioning" might also be translated "disputing." It implies internal skepticism, perhaps intellectual rebellion against God. The unusual English word "cavilling" carries the idea of raising trivial, frivolous objections, what are sometimes called "scruples." "Murmuring and questioning" are the outward expression of an inward rebellion against God, arguing with what God has ordained, and thus implicitly with God's right to rule and God's wisdom and judgment. The alternative to this has been described by Paul in 1:12-26 in his equanimity in the face of difficult circumstances, and will be emphasized again at 4:11-12 (and it was an attitude also taught by the Stoics). As *NJBC* suggests, Paul introduces the negative response as a contrast to the positive cooperation he expects from the Philippian Christians.

15. *in order that you might be blameless and pure:* The phrase begins a purpose clause. The words describing what Paul hopes for the Philippians, that they will be blameless, pure, and spotless, are all constructed with an "alpha privative," a strong Greek construction (which has appeared often in the letter's vocabulary) in which a substantive is negated by prefixing the alpha. "Blameless" *(amemptoi)* is found in medical writing for that which will not hurt, "harmless" substances. It is used of Paul's own character in 1 Thess 2:10. "Pure" *(akeraioi)* is found as an adjective in connection with wine and gold and means "unmixed" or "unadulterated." In Greek commercial writing the term describes the highest quality. The same terms appeared at 1:10 (compare Matt 10:16; Rom 16:19).

children of God without spot: That Christians are God's children is a common idea in Paul's writings (see, for example, Rom 8:6, 17, 21, especially 9:8; also Eph 3:6). The word for "without spot" *(amōma)* is also used in connection with sacrifices. The sacrifices offered to God must be "blemishless" (see Num 19:2; 28:3. Note that Moses uses this same language to criticize Israel in Deut 32:5 LXX). The term very subtly prefigures the idea that Paul is himself a sacrifice in vv. 17-18.

in the midst of a crooked and distorted generation: "Distorted" *(diestrammenēs)* literally means "twisted," but here is used to describe a moral condition. "Generation" is used figuratively for an era (compare Deut 32:5 LXX; Matt 12:39; 17:17). Perhaps understandably, Paul's view of the condition of his world is hardly positive! In every "generation" those who view the world from God's perspective have reason for alarm.

in which you shine as luminaries in [the] world: "Shine" is in the present indicative, indicating continual action; they "are shining" or "continually shine." Light and darkness are frequently used as moral terms in Scripture. For example, Isaiah speaks of those who live righteously as those from whom light breaks forth (see Isa 58:6-9, especially v. 8). There seems to be allusion here to the apocalyptic vision of Dan 12:1-4, especially v. 3. As opposed to "the Gentiles," whom Eph 4:17-18 describes as "darkened," Christians "shine." "Luminaries" *(phōstēres)* is often translated "lights" or "stars," since it is the word for "lights" in the creation account (Gen 1:14-18) and is used in parallel literature to describe the light given off by heavenly bodies. In English a "luminary" is a person of prominent achievement (a "star" in movie magazines) or something that gives light; both senses apply here. "World" *(kosmos)* means "created universe," but in view of the immediately previous phrase may refer to human society. Deuteronomy 32 provides an interesting gloss on this verse. In that chapter God suggests that the Israelites lost their identity because they became like the people around them. Christians are not to conform to the "twisted" or disordered world in which they live. They are "in" but not "of" the world (cf. John 17:15-16) and are to serve as the salt and light that transforms it (compare Matt 5:13-16). Both are images of smallness in proportion to the size of the task.

16. *holding forth [a] word of life:* "Holding forth" *(epechō)* can mean "hold fast," but here is used in the sense of "offering" as, for example, offering food or holding out light (compare 1 Tim 4:16). "Word of life" is a genitive construction meaning "word that brings life," and clearly implies the Gospel. The luminousness of Christians is derivative; it comes from the Gospel and so from Christ.

    that I may boast on the day of Christ: "Boast" is a favorite Pauline word (see Rom 2:17, 23; 1 Cor 1:31; 2 Cor 7:4; 10:17; 11:21; Gal 6:14). "Day of Christ" is used in Gal 3:23 and Eph 4:30 and perhaps suggests the eschatology of Dan 12:1-4 (see the Note on 1:6, and compare 4:5b). Paul apparently has "judgment day" in view. At this point he brings himself and his own circumstances back into the discussion.

    that I did not run in vain or labor in vain: The structure of the phrase is parallel. "To run" is a Pauline metaphor for the conduct of one's individual life (see 1 Cor 9:24, 26, and especially Gal 2:2). The metaphor is from the games in the stadium. Paul is like an athlete who knows his training has been worthwhile. (For other athletic metaphors see 1:8; 3:12-14.) "Labor" is what Paul did among them; it is thus a way of speaking of his public work and ministry. The character and activity of the Philippians are the measure of Paul's success.

17. *But even if I am poured out:* Verses 17-18 now explicitly recall Paul's own situation (1:12-26), the possibility that he will be killed for the faith. The major metaphor of vv. 17-18 is that of sacrifice, a practice known both in Judaism and in Hellenistic religions like those practiced in Philippi (compare Exod 29:38-41; Lev 23:12-13; Num 15:3-10). "Without spot" in v. 15 has already introduced the language of sacrifice. "Pour out" suggests libations, the drink offerings poured on the ground to honor a deity. Here Paul views his life as a libation to God. Interestingly, in Rom 15:15-16 he speaks of conducting his ministry so that the "Gentiles might become an offering acceptable to God."

    on the sacrifice and service [of] your faith: "Sacrifice" is fairly straightforward. Paul's sacrifice (like his joy) is reciprocated by the Philippians, and so 4:18 calls their gift to him a "sacrifice." But "service" *(leitourgia)* is the term from which "liturgy" derives. Marvin R. Vincent suggests it derives from an adjective meaning "belonging to the people," i.e., "work," what ordinary people do. It became a cultic word associated with sacrifice. It is found in 2 Cor 9:12 in the context of the collection. "Your faith" is an objective genitive; the sacrifice consists of their faith. Their faith has led them to be persecuted; the persecutions are "offered up" as sacrifices.

I rejoice, and rejoice with all of you: The dominant note of the Philippian letter is joy. Forms of the word occur four times in vv. 17-18. Here it is Paul's joy even at the thought of being sacrificed for the faith. This continues the sacrificial metaphor because the offering or pouring out of wine in the Old Testament signified joy, the joy of God's blessing on God's people, but it also is used as a metaphor for martyrdom (see Eph 3:13 for a parallel idea, and compare Mark 14:24). "Rejoice" *(sygchairō)* can also mean "congratulate," and if it is so translated eliminates the repetitiveness of the turn of phrase. Again, Paul's rejoicing is inclusive of *all* Christians in Philippi (cf. 3:2ff.).

18. *And the same also, you [yourselves] rejoice and rejoice with me:* And, likewise, the Philippians rejoice with Paul, who is imprisoned and unsure about the outcome of that imprisonment (see 1:12-26). Recall that at 1:18, 19 Paul rejoices even if the motives of those who preach Christ are not "pure," even in the face of his uncertain circumstances, and at 4:4 he commands rejoicing "always."At 1:19 he is able to rejoice because of the Philippians' prayers for him. Here that reciprocity of joy is emphasized. They are to rejoice in their own circumstances as well as in Paul's.

INTERPRETATION

As noted above, many scholars have seen a chiasm in 1:27–2:18 (A, 1:27–2:4; B, 2:5-11; A', 2:12-18). At the very least the Pauline imperatives to the Philippians form an inclusion around the Christ hymn, the model he wants them to emulate. In the Notes above the many parallels with 1:27-30 are highlighted. Indeed, instructions to the Philippian church (1:27–2:18; 3:1–4:1) frame examples of the behavior Paul wants them to exhibit (2:19-30). In the larger section instructions to the church alternate with examples (1:27–2:4, instruction; 2:5-11, example; 2:12-18, instruction; 2:19-30, examples; 3:1-3, instruction; 3:4-16, example; 3:17–4:1 instruction). We begin to see clearly at this point the alternation of instructions and personal examples that characterizes the body of the letter. Duane F. Watson's rhetorical analysis of the letter suggests that 2:1-18 is the second development of the proposition, most recently restated at 2:1-4. It seems clear that at this point Paul is returning to his initial appeal to the Philippians to live worthily of the Gospel they have received.

The passage is particularly complex due to its high degree of intertextuality (its reliance on images and ideas occurring elsewhere in Scripture and in this epistle) and metaphorical character. One wonders why Paul used so many Hebrew scriptural allusions in writing to a Gentile church. The answer is probably that they were the "furnishings" of his mind, the way he thought, just as, until recently, the Vulgate or the King James Bible informed the thinking of many. Be that as it may, the overall message of this text is clear. Paul calls upon the Philippian community (for the thrust of the passage is communal and not individual, *pace* several evangelical commentators) to continue to live in the light of their salvation (2:12-13). He knows the call is to do this in a hostile environment (2:15), but he is not reticent about using "emotional blackmail" to make his plea: he is, after all, in a "hostile environment," imprisoned for the faith, about to be poured out as a libation (2:17). Whether the appeal is to Jewish or Hellenistic sacrificial practice seems immaterial. The point is that Paul is making his appeal on the basis of what may be his own martyrdom: "make me proud of you as I go to my death." This is another indication of the close emotional ties between Paul and this community.

Verses 12 and 13 are sometimes taken as a theological conundrum, a statement of the "faith verses works" debate. Do we "work out our salvation" or receive it from God? But this oversimplification overlooks that, indeed, the verses are parallel, occur together, and thus reconcile Pelagians and Augustinians. The Philippians are called to "work out," that is, to bring to completion (v. 12) the salvation God has given them (v. 13, and see 1:28). The *kata* in "work out" in v. 12 is perfective; they are to finish something already begun, and begun by God in Jesus Christ. They have just been vividly reminded of the "something" in 2:6-11. It is "God's work," God's ongoing impetus toward deliverance of the human family, that the Philippians are "working out" in their awe-inspired life of obedience. That process is dependent on God, who gives even the desire for it. There is no salvation without God, but humans must accept and "work with" what God offers. Obedience is the happy response to salvation given. (A particularly helpful discussion of this point is found in Gordon Fee's commentary, pp. 230–40.)

The call here (v. 12) is clearly to obedience. But obedience to what? It is important to note that no list of rules and regulations is given. Obedience, "listening toward," is to the God who was revealed in the self-giving Christ. The call is to be obedient to the model that has just been given in 2:5-11, implied in Paul's own life (2:16-18) and about to be recapitulated in the lives of Timothy (2:19-24) and Epaphroditus (2:25-30). Practically, all of this is to be done without grumbling and complaining. This may seem mundane in the light of the high theology and biographical drama of the passage, but nothing undercuts group unity like "grousing." The "corporate culture" of the Philippian church is to be different from that around it, that "crooked and distorted" culture. If they are to live worthily, they must live in unity (1:27; 2:2) and love (2:1). The sweet temperedness of that unity and love will, indeed, be "light in the darkness,"as, indeed, it is today when we catch glimpses of it or experience it in a community.

As he has so frequently, and will again later in the letter, Paul returns here to the theme of joy. He rejoices in prison (1:18), in their prayers for him (1:19), in the presumption that they will "complete [his] joy" (2:2), and now even in the thought of his martyrdom (2:17). Joy of this sort is, by its nature, mutual and best when shared. The whole letter operates with an "abundance model": "There is more than enough salvation and love to go around, so let us celebrate it and share it with one another." Paul rejoices in the Philippians' movement toward perfection in the circumstances in which they find themselves, just as he knows they rejoice in the same process at work in him, in his dramatic circumstances. In fact, as members of a *religio illicita* both Paul and the Philippians live under the threat of persecution (and perhaps martyrdom) from outside the church, yet they, like other Christians before (and after!) them (see Acts 5:40-41), rejoiced not because of, but in spite of, such persecution. If ever there was a clear demarcation between ephemeral "happiness" and that God-given "joy," this passage reflects it.

For Reference and Further Study

Finlayson, S. K. "Lights, Stars or Beacons," *ExpTim* 77 (1966) 181.
Stagg, Frank. "The Mind in Christ Jesus. Phil 1:27–2:18," *RevExp* 77 (1980) 337–47.
Watson, Duane F. "A Rhetorical Analysis of Philippians, and Its Implications for the Unity Question," *NovT* 30 (1988) 57–88.

THE EXAMPLES OF TIMOTHY AND EPAPHRODITUS: 2:19-30

To facilitate clarity about the biographies of Paul's coworkers, the texts on Timothy and Epaphroditus are treated separately. The Interpretation of both follows, on pp. 105–107. Structurally, the examples of behavior Paul wants to encourage (2:19-30) follow instructions to the community (2:12-18) and precede further community instructions (3:1–4:1).

Timothy (2:19-24)

19. But I hope in [the] Lord Jesus shortly to send Timothy to you in order that I also might be glad when knowing the things concerning you. 20. For I have no one like-minded who genuinely will care for [the

things] concerning you. 21. For all seek the things of themselves, not the things of Jesus Christ. 22. But you know his character that, as a father, a child, he served with me in the gospel. 23. Therefore I hope to send this one as soon as I see the things about me. 24. I am persuaded in the Lord that I also will [myself] come shortly.

Notes

19. *But I hope in [the] Lord Jesus shortly to send Timothy to you:* At v. 19 we pick up the thread of the "narrative" left off after 1:26. Mention of rejoicing in v. 18 leads Paul to shift toward something he hopes will give the Philippians reason for joy, his dispatching Timothy and Epaphroditus to them. This recommendation for Timothy is marked off as an inclusion by the phrase "in the Lord" in vv. 19 and 24. Paul "hopes in the Lord Jesus" for this; that is, he will do it if it is the Lord's will (compare 2:5). The Lord is the sphere of his hope. The term "hope" appears with Paul's travel plans at Rom 15:24; 1 Cor 16:7; Phlm 22. In view of v. 24, "shortly" probably means "as soon as possible." It carries a sense of urgency.

    in order that I also might be glad: This phrase begins a passive expression of purpose that completes the sentence. "Be glad" *(eupsychō)* means "have courage" or "be encouraged." It is a rare word in Greek and is found in the papyri and on tombs in words of encouragement to the bereaved. It will make Paul glad both to give the Philippians joy and to receive word of them.

    when knowing the things concerning you: It will be an encouragement to Paul to know what the situation in Philippi really is. This is especially true in view of the difficulties there to which he has alluded (1:28-30) and which he is about to address in chapters 3 and 4. The verse expresses again Paul's real care and concern for the church.

20. *For I have no one like-minded:* Paul has appealed in 2:2-4 that the Philippians be like-minded and concerned for one another. In vv. 20-21 he reminds them that Timothy embodies these qualities. "For" suggests the reason why Paul is sending Timothy: Paul most trusts him with the care of the congregation. "Like-minded" is a rare Greek adjective and *hapax legomenon* that literally means "same-souled." Clearly it is related to the concept of *homothymadon* or one-mindedness in 2:2-4.

    who genuinely will care for [the things] concerning you: "Genuinely" is an adverb that has its root in a term meaning "legitimate birth," and so foreshadows the father/child metaphor in v. 22, but also alludes to Timothy's legitimate authority. "Care for" is a verb that literally means "give one's thought to" and so expresses deep concern. The idea at the root of the verse is that Paul and Timothy are so similar (*isopsychos,* "same-souled") that Paul's concern for the Philippians is also Timothy's. These verses are high praise for Timothy, but along with those that follow they reflect rather badly on Paul's other associates; they "damn with faint praise."

21. *For all seek the things of themselves, not the things of Jesus Christ:* "For" suggests another explanation is to follow. The first part of the sentence literally reads "for all seek after their own thing," a dramatic, 1960's turn of phrase! The article with the adjective *(hoi pantes)* excludes exceptions; *everybody* is self-concerned. One wonders where Paul is imprisoned and if this is a particularly unflattering portrait of the church there! It is more likely that what Paul means is that he has no one who exhibits the particular qualities Timothy has (as per the next verse). Throughout this letter what is important is "the things of Jesus Christ." That would include his example (set forth in 2:6-11) of how to live as individuals and as a community as well as the mission of the Gospel.

22. *But you know his character:* "Character" is a term used in parallel literature of the testing of precious metals and means "approved after being tested." Timothy has a "proven character." They "know" Timothy (forms of the word are used in vv. 20 and 22 and imply "know by experience" vs. intellectual knowledge only), as Acts 16 reports he was involved in the founding of the Philippian church. He is "tried and true" and known by the community, both strong points in his favor as Paul's representative.

    that, as a father, a child: Behind the phrase is the family structure of the Near East in which it is the child's fondest duty to care for the parent. Paul thinks of and refers to his converts as his children (see 1 Cor 4:15). In the Pastoral Epistles, Timothy is specifically referred to as Paul's child (1 Tim 1:18; 2 Tim 1:2; 2:1). The phrase communicates the deep and abiding relationship between the two men. *Teknon* emphasizes the relational aspect of sonship. But what is communicated, as the next phrase will make clear, is Timothy's childlike or son-like faithfulness to the Gospel. It is not so much Paul whom Timothy serves as a son (although he apparently does this), but the Gospel itself.

    he served with me in the gospel: The root of the verb "served" is the noun for "slave" that appeared in 1:1 as Paul announced to the Philippians that he and Timothy were "slaves of Christ Jesus." The two served together. There is no hierarchy of teacher/student or apostle/lesser believer; *together* the two men are slaves of the same Master, working together for the same end, the Gospel, which is here a metaphor for the mission of proclaiming Jesus Christ. (Compare 2:25 and 4:3 for other instances of working side by side.)

23. *Therefore I hope to send this one as soon as I see the things about me:* Paul repeats the phrase with which this section opened. He wants to send Timothy to Philippi, both for their sake and for his, but "hope" includes a note of tentativeness in face of the emphatic "therefore." "As soon as" *(hōs an)* also communicates temporal uncertainty. Paul is apparently waiting to know the outcome of his imprisonment before he sends Timothy. Secondarily, because Timothy is well known to the Philippians, he is an especially apt bearer of apostolic instruction.

24. *I am persuaded in the Lord that I also will [myself] come shortly:* Verse 24 exhibits a confidence that v. 23 does not. (Is Paul "whistling in the dark"?) "I am persuaded" is a strong verb and in the perfect, which tends to indicate certainty. Additionally, Paul's confidence is "in the Lord," thus echoing v. 19 and

completing the inclusion, and may indicate, as per John Calvin's commentary, that he has some word from Jesus about the outcome of his circumstances (although "in the Lord" may indicate content rather than agency). "Shortly" is also repeated from v. 19. This hope of Paul's impending visit (as carrot or stick?) was declared at 1:18 and alluded to at 1:27 and 2:12.

Epaphroditus (2:25-30)

25. But it was necessary to send to you Epaphroditus, my brother and fellow worker and fellow soldier and your apostle and minister of my needs, sent by you. 26. Because he was longing for you all and was distressed, because you heard that he was sick. 27. And he even ailed near to death, but God had mercy on him, and not only him, but also me that I should not have grief upon grief. 28. Therefore I send him with haste, that, seeing him again, you might rejoice, [and] I [myself] might be without grief. 29. Therefore welcome him in the Lord with all joy and hold such a one honored 30. because, on account of the work of Christ, he drew near death, risking life, in order that he might complete your lack of service toward me.

Notes

25. *But it was necessary to send to you Epaphroditus:* "But" suggests the turn of thought. Timothy's visit may be delayed, but there is no reason to delay Epaphroditus' visit and every reason to expedite it. "It was necessary" carries the connotation of something like compulsion, as opposed to the "possible" visit of Timothy. The opening Greek phrase indicates that on the basis of some recent past event Paul thought it necessary to send Epaphroditus. The reason is immediately forthcoming: Paul needs to send the letter, and Epaphroditus needs to go home.

my brother and fellow worker and fellow soldier: The language of the phrase is that of great collegiality. Paul frequently uses filial language for fellow believers (see "brother" for Timothy in 1 Thess 3:2 or "sister" for Phoebe in Rom 16:1). After the term "brother" there are two compound words formed by *syn* (with) and a substantive: "with-worker" and "with-soldier." "Coworker" is one of Paul's favorite terms for a fellow laborer. He uses it again in this letter for Euodia and Syntyche at 4:3 (and see Rom 16:3; 9:2; 2 Cor 1:24; 8:23; Phlm 1, 24, and Rom 16:21 and 1 Thess 3:2 where it is used of Timothy). The term also occurs in Pauline enjoinders to "work together" (1 Cor 16:16; 2 Cor 6:1). "Fellow soldier" is interesting because military metaphors are infrequent in the Pauline literature (see, for example, Phlm 2 or 2 Tim 2:3). Its use here probably suggests the struggles Paul and Epaphroditus had faced together. As was the case in v. 22, there is no hierarchy suggested here, but mutual ministry. "Fellow worker" or "coworker" describes the relationship between those who serve God together.

and your apostle and minister of my needs, sent by you: The lexical meaning of apostle as "one sent" is retained here (compare 2 Cor 8:23). Epaphroditus is not an "apostle" in the sense Paul uses the term of himself or as it describes an office in Acts 1:21-22. He is a courier or messenger. For Notes on "minister" *(leitourgos)* see 2:17 and 30. The term suggests that Epaphroditus performed some priestly service for Paul. Bear in mind that all the Romans provided for those in prison was the prison cell. All the needs of the prisoners had to be met by their family and friends. Having "ministers" to those in prison was crucial and, indeed, in the early church the ministry of serving the needs of those in prison continued into the fourth and fifth centuries as a special service of the order of widows. And recall Jesus' teachings about caring for the imprisoned in Matt 25:31-46 (especially vv. 36, 39, 43, 44).

26. *Because he was longing for you all and was distressed:* The Greek construction here suggests a constant or continued state and gives the reason for the action in v. 25. "Longing" (or "yearning") is the same word Paul used in reference to his own feeling for the Philippians in 1:8. It means something like "homesick for." "Distressed" is a strongly emotional word that implies "distraction" and was used by Mark at 14:33 for Jesus in Gethsemane. What the Greek words convey is Paul's sensitivity to the depths of Epaphroditus' emotional state.

because you heard that he was sick: Epaphroditus is not distracted because of his own illness, but because he knows his friends in Philippi will worry about it. He is looking not to his own interests, but to the interests of others (2:4). Additionally, as a Philippian, he would have been concerned about the situation alluded to in chapter 1 and about to be reported in chapter 3. The word for "sick" here is quite strong and literally means "without strength." The illness, as the next verse makes clear, was serious.

27. *And he even ailed near to death:* The opening words of the verse *(kai gar)* are emphatic and occur at other places in contexts where Paul is being persuasive (see 1 Thess 3:4 or 1 Cor 11:9). Paul wants the Philippians to know how ill Epaphroditus really was. The degree of his illness is an indication of the depths of his commitment to the Gospel.

but God had mercy on him: When Paul thinks of God as the one who has the power to heal the sick, he slips into Semitic idiom and adds the article *(ho theos)* before the noun for the deity (compare 1:3, 8 and 2:9). The point is clear; it is God who brings healing. Epaphroditus has been a special recipient of divine grace, perhaps the gifts of healing Paul describes in 1 Cor 12:9, 28, 30.

and not only him, but also me that I should not have grief upon grief: Just as Epaphroditus' illness brought suffering both to him and to the Philippians, his healing brings joy both to them and to Paul. Throughout Philippians the deep connectedness of Christians to one another is communicated; *koinōnia* is seen incarnate (compare 1 Cor 12:14-26, especially v. 26). "Grief" *(lypē)* is another term used in the description of Jesus at Gethsemane and continues the strong emotional language of the passage (see v. 26).

28. *Therefore I send him with haste, that, seeing him again, you might rejoice:* The opening of this verse parallels that of v. 25. Another translation of this phrase is "I am all the more eager, therefore, to send him." Having shared in concern for Epaphroditus, Paul wants the Philippians to share in the joy of his recovery.

[and] I [myself] might be without grief: Like Epaphroditus (v. 26), Paul will be less grieved when the Philippians' anxiety is assuaged. And because he is so close to the community, when they rejoice, he rejoices.

29. *Therefore welcome him in the Lord with all joy:* The word for "welcome" means "receive favorably." It is now clear that this is a note of commendation for Epaphroditus. Paul is providing letters of recommendation both for Timothy and for him. This explains, in part, the language of v. 25, where there are so many terms referring to Epaphroditus' work.

and hold such a one honored: Suffering for the Gospel is a mark of honor. The phrase recalls 1:12-26, Paul's apology for his imprisonment. It has been suggested that his phrase is inserted because, for some reason, the Philippians might *not* honor Epaphroditus. There *are* those who mistakenly think illness is a moral failure. It seems to me more likely, however, that Paul is following the literary conventions of a letter of commendation, not correcting some error in the Philippians' attitude.

30. *because, on account of the work of Christ:* What is in view is suffering for the Gospel, not just arbitrary suffering (compare Mark 8:34-38 and parallels). For more on this point see the Interpretation at 1:18b-26 above.

he drew near death, risking life: "He drew near" is an idiom in Greek: "as far as" death. "Risking" is a word that is found in parallel literature in descriptions of gambling. The word *paraboleusamenos* describes a game in which a stake was thrown to land in the ground; Epaphroditus was literally "throwing the stake." The idea is that of exposing oneself to danger. In the papyri the term is used for one who exposes himself to danger for the sake of friendship, so the word is an important one for those who understand the Philippian letter to be a classic example of the rhetoric of friendship. The idea here is that Epaphroditus gambled with his life for the sake of the Gospel.

in order that he might complete your lack of service toward me: My translation of this phrase, while literal, is awkward and demands explanation. It is not to be taken to mean that Paul is unhappy with the Philippians for some neglect. The whole tone of the letter militates against such a reading, as does Paul's own attitude in 4:11-12. (Other scholars suggest on the basis of 2 Cor 8:2 that the Philippians were heretofore too poor to assist Paul monetarily). The Greek word "complete" has as its root a term that means "fulfill" or "perfect" or "make complete" (compare 1:6 and 2:2). Epaphroditus completed the Philippians' service to Paul by delivering the gift they could not present in person. Or perhaps what Paul "lacks" is the consolation of the presence of his Philippian friends, a lack that Epaphroditus' presence does in fact "fill up" (compare the idea in 1 Cor 16:17). "Service" *(leitourgias)* is a fascinating and complex word choice. It normally means official and commissioned service of some sort. It is rare in the NT, but when it is used, it implies priestly service (Phil

2:17; Luke 1:23; Heb 8:6; 9:21) or is used in the context of monetary contributions (Rom 15:27 and 2 Cor 9:12) as well as in this text, where it seems to be connected to Epaphroditus' delivery of the Philippians' gift (see 4:10-20). Its connotation recalls the sacrificial language of v. 25. Epaphroditus will finish the service the Philippians have already offered Paul. Loh and Nida translate the phrase "in order to give me the help that you yourselves could not give" (*Translator's Handbook,* 85). The *RSV* suggests "risking his life to complete your service to me." In both cases what is in focus is not the Philippians' shortcomings, but Epaphroditus' service. The point is that he is to be esteemed for risking his life in Christ's work and for his service to Paul. He, like Timothy, is an example of one who has lived the kind of life Paul commends to the Philippians in 2:1-4.

Interpretation

Paul normally relates his travel plans and speaks of his coworkers at the end of epistles. This fact has led some commentators to suggest that 2:19-30 is the close of one of the Philippian letter fragments. (See the discussion of the unity of the letter in the opening essay on literary backgrounds.) But while 2:19-30 appears to be simply a recapitulation of his hopes to visit them and news about companions of Paul who are known to the Philippians, the verses are, in fact, integral to the appeal in this section of the letter, as each man mentioned exemplifies the qualitites Paul has commended in 2:1-4. The immediately preceding appeal to live blamelessly, 2:12-18, is followed by two examples of men who do so, who exhibit "the same mind that was in Christ Jesus" (2:5). There are many verbal echoes in this text to earlier material: 2:4-5 and 2:20-21; 2:7 and 2:22; 2:8 and 2:30. (R. Alan Culpepper's article listed below carefully charts these parallels.) Timothy and Epaphroditus are those whose lives set the standard for a unified church. As R. C. Swift has noted, every reference Paul makes to individuals in this letter is made in connection with that person's partnership in the Gospel and either his or her help or hindrance of *koinōnia,* common life. These men are, immediately or "shortly," to be dispatched to Philippi with Paul's apostolic authority. This will represent an effective counter to the false teachers to be introduced in chapter 3. I see no real evidence in this passage for the "fragment theory" of Philippians.

As pointed out in the notes above, the two passages are, in one sense, letters of commendation. Additionally, one frequently encounters in Paul's letters a combination of travel plans and promises to visit churches. This is sometimes called a "travelogue form." Robert Funk has made the interesting suggestion that 2:19-24 is an example of a particular form of Pauline composition he dubs the "apostolic *parousia*" and finds most clearly articulated here and in Rom 15:14-33 and of which 2:25-30 may also be an example. The paradigm includes a statement of Paul's purpose in writing and the basis of his relationship to the recipients of the letter. There follow the "implementation of the apostolic *parousia*" in expressions of Paul's eagerness and/or hope to see them, his hindrance and/or delay in doing so, and his dispatch of an emissary. Paul invokes divine approval for his visit and mentions the benefits that will accrue to himself and his recipients as the result of his visit. Many elements of the "form" are in evidence in this passage, although in my view its purpose is not so much to prepare for Paul's visit to the Philippians (which is uncertain) as to provide them with examples of the behavior he wants them to exhibit.

Timothy is frequently encountered in Paul's letters (1 Cor 4:17; 16:10-11; 2 Cor 1:1), co-authored several epistles (2 Corinthians; Philippians; Colossians; 1 Thessalonians; 2 Thessalonians), and generally served as Paul's right-hand man in the Greek churches. He was well known in those churches as one who had been tested by, and triumphed in the face of, persecution. When Paul wanted information about a church or wished to send one a word (positive or negative!), he often sent Timothy. Acts 16 and 17 note that he was with Paul when the Philippian church was founded. In this letter he is implicitly compared to Christ. He is described as a "slave" (1:1) like the Christ who assumed this role (2:7). He "served" the interests of others (2:22) like Jesus who did not "grasp at" his equality with God (2:6). If one is needed, 2:19-22 functions as a letter of commendation for Timothy to the Philippians. (Compare Rom 16:1-2. For more information see the entries on Timothy in *ABD* and *DPL*.)

Epaphroditus is a common name in Greek inscriptions. The name meant "charming" or "amiable," literally "honored by Aphrodite," a goddess (of love!) to whom his family may have been devoted. He is less well known than Timothy. Some have suggested that "Epaphras" in Col 4:12-13 is an abridgment of this name, although no evidence connects that person with Phil 2:25 or 4:18. The latter verse indicates that Epaphroditus was the Philippians' deliveryman and carried their gift to Paul. Perhaps their degree of worry about him includes not only concern for his personal welfare but also for their gift, and whether it had reached Paul, as, indeed, he understood (v. 26). It is not clear whether Epaphroditus fell ill when he reached Paul (in Rome or Ephesus?), or on the way there and presumably forged on and collapsed upon arrival. His illness was "near to death" (2:27, 30); the phrase in 2:30 is that used of Jesus in 2:8.

Although neither parallel is perfect, Epaphroditus, like Timothy, imitated the life of Christ. Because he was a respected person in Philippi, it was to Paul's advantage to send him home to help ward off the threats there of divisiveness from within and some sort of danger from without, which will be addressed in chapter 3. Additionally, the strong notes of commendation for Epaphroditus suggest he was to have been a permanent member of Paul's "staff." Paul does not want him to receive a negative reception because he has returned home. There is no honor lost because a worker becomes ill (2:29).

Some scholars have seen in this passage evidence for the geographical proximity of Paul to the Philippians; that is, support for the Ephesian provenance of the letter. But hopes for and promises of an early visit are just that: longing for a quick temporal reunion, not an indication of spatial nearness. What should not be overlooked is the insight this passage gives into Paul the man. He had a particular genius for friendship and cared deeply about those with whom he worked. This care is reflected in letters of commendation like this (and Rom 16:1-2) and in passages in which he speaks highly and respectfully of those with whom he works *side by side* (compare, for example, Romans 16 or Col 4:7-17). This text is an exceedingly clear portrait of the sympathy, courtesy, and tenderheartedness Paul showed toward his coworkers.

After the high theology that undergirds the pastoral issue in 2:1-18, this material may seem "merely" biographical, a sweet portrait of Paul and his friends Timothy and Epaphroditus. Such a conclusion, while on one level true, misses the point of its inclusion here. Timothy and Epaphroditus put flesh and blood on Paul's imperatives to the Philippians. Here are men already doing what he has commanded: looking to the affairs of others, giving up (or risking) "self," working for the Gospel. And in returning them to Philippi Paul is addressing the next major issue in Philippians, that of the "opponents" to whom he alludes in chapter 3. Paul's two coworkers in 2:19-30 serve as a "personified transition" in the letter, looking back to the matter of internal unity and forward to the danger of false teaching.

For Reference and Further Study

Black, David. "The Discourse Structure of Philippians," *NovT* 37 (1995) 16–49.

Buchanan, C. O. "Epaphroditus' Sickness and the Letter to the Philippians," *EvQ* 36 (1964) 157–66.

Culpepper, R. Alan. "Co-Workers in Suffering, Phil 2:19-30," *RevExp* 77 (1980) 349–58.

Funk, Robert W. "The Apostolic *Parousia:* Form and Significance," in William R. Farmer, C.F.D. Moule, and Richard R. Niebuhr, eds., *Christian History and Interpretation.* Cambridge: Cambridge University Press, 1967, 249–68.

Furnish, Victor R. "Fellow Workers in God's Service," *JBL* 80 (1961) 364–70.

Mackay, Barry S. "Further Thoughts on Philippians," *NTS* 7 (1960-61) 161–70.

Swift, R. C. "The Theme and Structure of Philippians," *BSac* 141 (1984) 257–75.

Excursus II

The "Break" at 3:1

In the introductory material "Literary Backgrounds for the Study of Philippians," it was suggested that the letter is not, as some have argued, a series of fragments, but one unified composition. This position requires that the apparent "break" between 3:1 and 3:2 be dealt with in more detail. As Jeffrey T. Reed has noted in his article on Phil 3:1, there is ". . . no other verse in Philippians with so many grammatical and lexical interpretative difficulties . . ." (p. 72). Chief among these difficulties are the opening "finally" *(to loipon)* and the dramatic shift in tone between 3:1 and 3:2.

All major modern translations of Philippians translate the beginning of Phil 3:1 "finally." The sense of the English word certainly indicates a drawing to a close. But this is by no means the only possible connotation for the Greek *to loipon.* In 1 Thess 4:1, for example, the term is used as a transitional phrase and is also followed by imperatives. Here "rejoice" *(chairete)* echoes 2:17-18 and has led several scholars to suggest that "in future" or "henceforth" is a more appropriate translation of *to loipon,* since it would indicate the last item in a sequence. As Loveday Alexander points out, in parallel letters it is used before the closing elements of a letter ("Hellenistic Letter-Forms," 96), and in other Pauline letters it is used both to indicate the last item in a sequence (2 Cor 13:11) and as a transitional device (1 Thess 4:1). In my view the note on this matter in Fritz Rienecker and Cleon Rogers' *Linguistic Key to the Greek New Testament* is helpful: "Paul probably intends to draw to a close the general admonitions and then takes up specific matters in the latter part of the letter" (p. 555).

Granting that *to loipon* might indicate, not the end of the letter, but the last of the issues in a sequence of things Paul is discussing, what of the tonal shift? The end of chapter 2 has lifted up two colleagues whom Paul commends and holds up as examples to the Philippians, Timothy (2:19-24) and Epaphroditus (2:25-30). They are part of his reason for commanding the Philippians to "rejoice" (3:1). But then what of the sharp warning against "dogs" *(kynas)*? This is the same word Jesus uses to address a Gentile woman in Mark 7:27 and, in spite of commentators' attempts to soften it, is a sharp, ugly term. It referred not to house pets but to feral creatures, scavengers who traveled in packs, preyed on livestock, and ate the garbage in the streets. Thus Jews used "dogs" as a term of contempt for Gentiles, whom they considered unclean. If Paul is warning against Judaizers (see Excursus III below), the term is a terribly insulting one.

Several commentators suggest that this shift in tone is understandable when seen in the overall context of the letter. Paul has been addressing the beloved Philippians for whom he cares so deeply, and he now thinks of those who are a threat to them. Little wonder he speaks harshly of the opponents! Furthermore, in his rhetorical analysis of the letter Duane F. Watson argues that the shift in tone between 3:1 and 3:2 is transitional to the third development of the proposition. B. S. MacKay notes that the change in tone at 3:2 is momentary and that Paul quickly resumes his more conciliatory mode. The apostle, he argues, is given to these "outbreaks" (see, for example Gal 3:1 or 4:21), and they seldom signal breaks in the text or multiple letter fragments.

While there is certainly a distinct shift in tone between 3:1 and 3:2, this in itself does not argue that 3:2 begins a new "fragment" of another letter. When viewing Philippians as one letter it is possible to see 1:27–2:18 and 3:2–4:1 as parallel. Each is focused on instructions to the Philippians, and each has a "personal example" at its core, Jesus in 2:5-11 and Paul in 3:4-11. T. E. Pollard, "The Integrity of Philippians," makes an interesting case that the common OT background of each passage is Isaiah 53. Jesus' "self-emptying" in chapter 2 is paralleled, though imperfectly, of course, by Paul's in chapter 3. Additionally, there seems to be a similar parallel between chapters 3 and 4. There is a "break" at the beginning of Chapter 3, then exhortation is followed by the example of Paul. There is also a "break" between 4:9 and 4:10. Both 3:2 and 4:10 begin with the imperative "rejoice." Again 4:4-9 is ethical exhortation, followed in 4:10-20 with the example of Paul himself (and compare Gal 6:1-10 and 6:11 or Col 4:2-6 and 4:7-9). So the rhetorical pattern of exhortation/Pauline example seems consistent in chapters 3 and 4.

Several commentators have suggested that sudden shifts in tone characterize personal letters. There are shifts between 1 Cor 15:57 and 58 and Gal 2:21 and 3:1, and these have not led to "multiple letter" theories. And Paul is certainly more relaxed in writing to the church at Philippi, where his authority has not been questioned and where the church is basically healthy, than he is in writing either to the church in Corinth where things are much messier or to Galatia where his gospel is being attacked. Could not the "shift" between chapters 2 and 3 of Philippians simply reflect the more informal and affectionate relations between Paul and that community?

Indeed, B. S. Mackay has suggested that Phil 3:4–4:9 follows the pattern of the testament of a dying father to his children. That pattern includes information about the moral life of the patriarch, an exhortation to avoid his faults or imitate his virtues, and a prediction of the destiny of his tribe. In the *Verbindungsbrief* of Philippians, Paul the patriarch who may be facing martyrdom (1:18-26) seeks to strengthen the family of the church by describing himself (3:4-14), exhorting the Philippians to follow his example (3:15-17 and, obliquely, 4:4-8, but especially v. 9a), and indicating their final destiny (3:20-21; 4:9b). Furthermore, Gordon Fee points out that the five sentences in 3:1-2 are asyndetic (without nuancing particles), which in Paul's writing indicates closeness to those so addressed (*Philippians*, 288). The content of this section of the letter is certainly consistent with the genre of a hortatory letter of friendship.

Jeffrey T. Reed has made a convincing case that 3:1 is a literary hesitation formula that serves as a transition in the discourse pattern of Philippians. In Hellenistic letters the hesitation formula uses some form of the verb *okneō* (to hesitate) or the adverbial form *aoknōs* (without hesitation) combined with a dependent clause using an infinitive form of *graphō* (write). The recipient of the letter is told that its sender does not hesitate with regard to some matter. The most common use of the formula is to request that the recipients of the letter not hesitate either to write the sender about their situation or to carry out a task mentioned in the letter. The parallels to Phil 3:1 are clear. Paul does not hesitate to write them (indeed, friendship encourages him to do so) to remind them that rejoicing is a cause of stability for them (thus the repeated use of forms of "rejoice" in the letter). Positive exhortations in chapter 2 are followed by negative warnings in chapter 3, and 3:1 provides the transition between them.

In view of all of the above it seems clear that while there is indeed a shift in emotional tone between 3:1 and 3:2, there is no necessary break in the rhetorical and thematic unity of the letter. Paul's attitude toward the Philippian Christians is consistent and his approach to instructing them remains constant.

For Reference and Further Study

Alexander, Loveday. "Hellenistic Letter-Forms and the Structure of Philippians," *JSNT* 37 (1989) 87–101.

Black, David A. "The Discourse Structure of Philippians: A Study in Text-Linguistics," *NovT* 37 (1995) 16–49.

Fee, Gordon D. *Paul's Letter to the Philippians.* Grand Rapids: Eerdmans, 1995. See especially pp. 285–92.

Furnish, Victor P. "The Place and Purpose of Phil. III," *NTS* 10 (1963–64) 80–88.

Mackay, B. S. "Further Thoughts on Philippians," *NTS* 7 (1960–61) 161–70.

Pollard, T. E. "The Integrity of Philippians," *NTS* 13 (1966–67) 57–66.

Reed, Jeffrey T. "Philippians 3:1 and the Epistolary Hesitation Formulas: The Literary Integrity of Philippians, Again," *JBL* 115 (1996) 63–90.

Rienecker, Fritz, and Cleon Rogers. *Linguistic Key to the New Testament.* Grand Rapids: Zondervan, 1980.

Watson, Duane F. "A Rhetorical Analysis of Philippians, and Its Implications for the Unity Question," *NovT* 30 (1988) 57–88.

INSTRUCTIONS TO THE PHILIPPIANS: 3:1–4:1

Many commentators take 3:2–4:1 to be a fragment of a polemical letter against Judaizers who have brought their message to Philippi. While in content I concur, as the preceding excursus indicates, I think 3:1 is a transitional verse between two sections of a single letter: 2:19-30 with the positive examples of Timothy and Epaphroditus, and 3:1–4:1 with its various negative warnings (against "dogs" 3:2 and "enemies" 3:18). The series of imperatives that began at 2:29 is resumed at 3:2. The overall structure of the section is self-evident: 3:1-3 is a warning against false teachers (who they are is the subject of Excursus III below); 3:4-16 lifts up the example of Paul, providing the Philippians with his "resumé" in 3:4-6, the transformation Christ effected in him in 3:7-11, and a cautionary note and challenge in 3:12-16. At the heart of 3:1–4:1 is 3:17, the implicit principle of the whole letter. The section warns the Philippians against "enemies" and contrasts those enemies (3:18-19) with Paul and the Philippian Christians (3:20-21).

Verses 3:1 and 4:1 are clearly transitional and mark off a unit of material that works on the basis of comparison between "us" and "them." Paul has just given the positive examples of Timothy and Epaphroditus and now warns against the negative influence of the "dogs" and "enemies." As was the case in 1:27–2:18, at the heart of this section of the letter is the example of one who has "emptied himself" or "humbled himself" (there Jesus in 2:5-11, here Paul in 3:4-11), precisely the attitude ("mind," 2:2, 5) that will advance the unity of the church. Paul insists that circumcision is not necessary for followers of Jesus Christ and that righteousness is based on faith in him. The pattern of the chapter follows one established earlier: Paul's situation leads to that of the Philippians. This material is the last segment in an *inclusio* formed by the repetition of the imperative "stand fast" in 1:27 and 4:1. Here Paul is returning to the Philippians' circumstances.

Warning about "Dogs" (3:1-4a)

> 1. As to the rest, my brothers and sisters, rejoice in the Lord. For me to write the same things to you [is] not troublesome but for your steadying. 2. Look to the dogs! Look to the evil-workers! Look to the mutilators! 3. For we ourselves are the circumcision, the ones worshiping by the spirit of God and boasting in Christ Jesus and not confident in flesh, 4a. even though I myself have confidence also in flesh.

Notes

1. *As to the rest, my brothers and sisters, rejoice in the Lord:* As indicated in Excursus II above, the opening phrase *to loipon,* which is usually translated "finally," does not necessarily indicate closure in Greek but may designate the last in a series or serve as a transitional phrase (compare, for example, 1 Thess 4:1). "Rejoice" is the characteristic word of the letter and also appears at major points of transition (see, for example, 1:19; 2:17-18; 4:1, 4, 10). In my view there is no real evidence for translating it "farewell," as some have suggested. All rejoicing is "in" the Lord Jesus. Certainly it is not dependent on external circumstances (here Paul's imprisonment or the trials of the Philippian church; cf. 2:18), and in the matter at hand it provides protection from false teaching. In Neh 8:10 the joy of the Lord is a source of strength (and compare Ps 32/31:11). Thus Paul commands them to rejoice.

   For me to write the same things to you [is] not troublesome: Placing the phrase "the same things" first is emphatic and would refer primarily to Paul's imperatives to this point and also allude to the warnings that are to follow. Some commentators have suggested that, following Polycarp's allusion to Paul's *letters* to Philippi, the reference here is to previous correspondence, but in my view this is purely speculative. "Troublesome" *(oknēron)* has two basic meanings when used adjectivally, "shrinking" or "timid" and "things that cause fear" or "fear-inducing." Both carry the connotation of reluctance. "It is no trouble for me to write these things to you," means Paul has no reluctance in doing so. The point is that Paul is not hesitant to say what he says here (as the following verses make manifestly clear!). This phrase serves to introduce what is to follow.

   but for your steadying: The phrase describes why Paul is not incommodated by writing; what he writes will help the Philippians. The word *asphales* has as its root a term meaning "to trip up" or "to overthrow," that is, to make unstable or unsteady. Paul is writing precisely to "steady" or to "strengthen" them (compare the LXX Prov 8:28; Wis 4:3; 7:23; 14:3). In other contexts the term describes clearly discernible facts, information that is specific and concrete, thus "for your certainty" (see Acts 25:26). Paul's purpose in this section of the letter is to stabilize the Philippian church.

2. *Look to the dogs! Look to the evil-workers! Look to the mutilators!:* Paul's first salvo is a dramatic triple warning. Apparently the same group (a circumcision party in the Philippian church? traveling Judaizers? Jews?) is here described in three wildly unflattering ways. This is invective of a high order and, as Morna Hooker points out, made more dramatic in the Greek by alliteration of the letters "b" and "k." The first meaning of the imperative verb *blepete,* "see" or "look," is generally taken in context to mean "beware" or "consider." G. D. Kilpatrick has suggested that it can only be translated "beware" when it appears in a clause with a negative aorist subjunctive or by *apo* with the genitive. Thus "consider" or "take note" would be the translation and what follows would be a "cautionary example." Such a reading, while grammatically correct, ignores the tone and content of what follows. Perhaps the best English

rendering would be the old British turn of phrase "mind" as in "mind your head" or "mind the step"; that is, "pay attention so as not to be harmed." "Dogs" *(kynas)* is an extremely negative term (see Excursus II above, and compare Isa 56:10-11 and Rev 22:15). Here the word is highly ironic. Judaizers who are trying to make Gentile men "clean" by circumcision have thus themselves become unclean animals. The emphasis in the word is on impurity. "Evil-workers" or "doers of evil" is particularly strong. "Workers" *(ergates)* is the usual term for agricultural workers (compare 2 Cor 11:13). Psalm 5:5 refers to those who do not follow the Law as "evil-workers." Perhaps it is stretching the meaning too far, but I wonder if Paul does not have the "works" versus "faith" matter in mind (see commentary above on 2:12-13). The word for "mutilators" (*katatomēn,* literally "cutting away" or "cutting to bits") is a pun on the word for circumcision (*peritomē,* literally "cutting around") in 3:3. Jews circumcise; pagans mutilate. The prophets of Baal slashed themselves (1 Kgs 18:28) and the followers of Cybele cut themselves in religious ecstasy (compare Lev 21:5). The Jewish religious rite of circumcision was viewed with horror by Greeks and Romans as defacing the body (perhaps something like the way we older people view body piercing today!). For Jews it was the mark of fidelity to the Torah. For Paul it has become an "external" matter, but one with serious consequences since what is at issue is whether Torah observance is necessary for fidelity to Christ. (Recall the importance of this issue in Galatians, and compare Acts 15.) Again there is irony here as the word suggests something is being destroyed (cut to bits). In fact, the whole verse is highly ironic as it applies to Judaizers terms *they* might use for outsiders, to the "pure" terms indicating impurity. The larger issue for Paul is that those who receive circumcision are "bound to keep the whole law" as he says in Gal 5:3, and are thus "severed from Christ" (Gal 5:4).

3. *For we ourselves are the circumcision:* The emphatic "ourselves" can be read as the "royal we," thus emphasizing Paul's view of himself, or as an inclusive pronoun ("you and I, Philippians") emphasizing the distinction between Paul and the Philippians and those just described in 3:2. The point is the contrast to those who are mere "mutilators" (compare Gal 5:12!). "The circumcision" is a way of speaking of Jews or "Israel" (see Gal 2:8; Rom 4:12). The phrase is a subtle indication that the "markers" of who is the "true Israel" have changed dramatically. (However, it should be remembered that even in Israel physical circumcision alone does not confer appropriate relationship to God. See Deut 10:16; 30:6; Jer 6:10. "Circumcision of the heart" pleases God: Jer 4:4; 9:24-25; Ezek 44:7.) Paul and the Philippian believers are the (singularity emphasized) circumcision (compare 2:14-16, and especially Rom 2:28-29).

   the ones worshiping by the spirit of God and boasting in Christ Jesus: The phrase explains that "the circumcision" are those who worship God by the Holy Spirit bestowed by Christ. "Worshiping" *(latreuontes)* comes from a word that means serving and ministering and is used in the LXX of service of divinity (especially of Levites in "service" in the Temple) and in the NT in worship contexts. It is the term Paul used at 2:25 to describe how Epaphroditus looked after his needs. It means "service" in the broadest sense of a people's devotion to God.

Here it contrasts with the "evil-workers" of v. 2 since *this* worship is "by God's spirit," reminding the Philippians that it is a gift (i.e., not "work"). Note the Trinitarian content of the phrase. To "boast" or "glory" is a common word in the Pauline corpus (some thirty-five uses). Here the context is positive rather than negative because the boasting, like the rejoicing in 3:1, is "in Christ Jesus." "Boast" is used negatively by Paul when it refers to one's own accomplishments (see, for example, its ironic use in 2 Cor 10:8-17 and 11:16–12:10), but positively when Christ is in view.

and not confident in flesh: The root word of "confident" is "persuaded." "Flesh" *(sarx)*, a negative term, is always used in Paul in contrast with "body" *(sōma)*, which is positive or neutral. Paul's point is certainly not that the physical body is evil. Indeed, the point of this passage is that God has eternal plans for the body (3:20-21). One might think of "flesh" as the person without animating spirit. The flesh is that which is corruptible, literally "meat." The human person is to be thought of as something more than a lump of meat that will rot. "Flesh" is that which is subject to decay, impermanent, as opposed to the "body," which is enduring (see Gal 3:2-3). If v. 2 gives three unflattering names for the troublemakers, v. 3 provides three reasons why Paul and believers in Philippi are the "true circumcision": they worship/serve by the Spirit of God; they boast/glory in Christ; and they do not trust in what is impermanent.

4a. *even though I myself have confidence also in flesh:* The last phrase is startling. The Philippians are warned against those with confidence in what is impermanent, and then Paul says he has confidence *also* (that is, in addition to something else, i.e., Jesus Christ) or *even* in flesh! What will follow will explain this oddity. Paul's reason for opposing the "dogs" comes from his own experience. If they want to play the game of "human accomplishments" (compare resumés!), Paul will win. "Myself" is emphatic. The participle here is present active, but its use is concessive, the sense being something like "I myself *continue to have* confidence." Three times in vv. 3 and 4 Paul repeats some form of "confidence (or trust) in flesh." It is clearly an important idea for him, and the following text (3:4-16, but especially vv. 4-6) demonstrates why.

Interpretation

At this point in the letter Paul returns to the matter of the Philippians' own circumstances (left off at 1:27–2:4), encourages continued rejoicing in Christ, and warns against false teachers in the community, probably itinerant Judaizers, Christians who insist one must become Jewish first in order to be fully Christian, but perhaps Jews seeking to win converts *from* Christianity, although this seems unlikely in non-Jewish Philippi. The reasons for Paul's opposition to this position are at the heart of his understanding of the Gospel and are deeply entwined in his own biography, the implications of which form the next section of the letter.

Paul warns in the strongest terms against "dogs" (a polemical way to show his contempt for the rival teachers), "evil-workers" (anyone who would be divisive in the community, and perhaps "super-doers" in general), and "mutilators of flesh" (those who advocate circumcision). The contrast in the passage is between those described in v. 2 and those in v. 3. Paul has frequently faced a Judaizing tendency in the churches (see 2 Corinthians 10–11 or Galatians, for example). These false teachers proclaimed that in order to be fully Christian one must first be fully a Jew, that is, men must submit to circumcision. One can understand the appeal of this message to former Gentiles who might well have been attracted to the ritual life of the Judaism that had produced and nurtured their recently accepted Lord Jesus Christ. Paul opposes such teaching (cf. 2 Cor 11:13-15), and thus circumcision, in the strongest terms because it brings people back under the law of Moses from which Jesus liberated people (compare Gal 4:1-7; 5:1). Paul understood that what God was doing in Jesus was *precisely* to include rather than to exclude (see Eph 1:9-10; 2:1-9, and especially 2:14-19). And if it was required to be "fully Christian," circumcision excluded half the human race, the very half among whom the Gospel first took root in Philippi! The real issue (as in Colossians) is the adequacy of God's grace in Jesus Christ. Paul has already established in this letter the sufficiency of God's act and gift in Christ (1:6, 28; 2:13). No other ritual act is necessary.

This is why v. 3 is the theological focal point and so important to what follows. It reminds the Philippians that the true mark of "inclusion" is that one has received the spirit of God and worships in "*the* God's" spirit. As Paul writes so eloquently in Rom 2:28-29: "For a person is not a Jew who is one outwardly, nor is true circumcision something external and physical. Rather, a person is a Jew who is one inwardly, and real circumcision is a matter of the heart—it is spiritual and not literal" *(NRSV).* One does not receive the gift of God's spirit, of inclusion in God's family, by means of a "cut," or by "work," but from accepting what God has done in Christ Jesus. One's trust should be in him and only in him, not in any "perishable" thing (i.e., "flesh"; compare Gal 5:2-6). However, in perhaps the only place in Philippians where he asserts authority, Paul goes on to say: "if you are looking for accomplishments, I have more than these troublesome teachers have," and he proceeds to enumerate the features of his Jewish "pedigree" in 3:4b-6 before announcing the real point: that all of it is so much "rubbish." Before we examine Paul's "resumé," a brief excursus on the identity of the "opposers" is in order.

For Reference and Further Study

Furnish, Victor P. "The Place and Purpose of Phil. III," *NTS* 10 (1963–64) 80–88.

Kilpatrick, G. D. "*Blepete,* Philippians 3:2," in Matthew Black and Georg Fohrer, eds., *In Memoriam Paul Kahle.* BZAW 103. Berlin: Topelmann, 1968, 146–48.

Pohill, John B. "Twin Obstacles in the Christian Path: Philippians 3," *RevExp* 77 (1980) 359–72.

Reed, Jeffrey T. "Philippians 3:1 and the Epistolary Hesitation Formulas: The Literary Integrity of Philippians, Again," *JBL* 115 (1996) 63–90.

Excursus III

Paul's Opponents in Philippi

The startling polemic at the outset of 3:2–4:1 raises the question of the identity of Paul's opponents in Philippi. This question is one of the most intriguing puzzles connected with the Philippian letter. While I will not be able to "solve" the puzzle here, I hope at least to present some of its pieces clearly.

At least four times in the epistle Paul alludes to or addresses "opponents" or "enemies" of some kind: 1:15-18; 1:28-30; 3:2-3; 3:18-19. Who are they, and what is their relationship to the apostle and to the Philippian church? One must begin with the most honest answer: "we cannot know for sure." In reading Philippians we are, as it were, listening in on one side of the conversation in which the speaker and those he addresses share information we do not have. Paul and the Philippians know to whom Paul is alluding in chapters 1 and 3, and thus the apostle does not need to "name names" or be explicit. We are left to construct the identity of these opponents on the basis of hints and glimpses given in the text itself; the text sets the limits of what we can know. Speculative reconstructions can be utterly fascinating, but they are just that, speculative.

Jerry Sumney has done important work in setting up methodological principles for determining the identity of Pauline opponents. He notes that in the places where Paul mentions opponents there are three kinds of material: explicit statements, allusions, and affirmations (of a teaching or a doctrine). These statements are not equally reliable, and the fact that Paul says something about an opponent does not mean that it is literally true since, rhetorically, Paul's job is to refute the opponents (and usually their interpretation of the Gospel), not to present a clear picture of their identity or a fair description of their positions. The aim of invective and polemic, for example, is not to describe opponents but to insult them, to vilify their positions. That being the case, Paul's polemical attacks on his opponents are the least reliable sources of information about them, his apologetic statements are likely to have less distortion, and his didactic remarks are most likely to be reliable. Using these principles provides some help in discerning the identity of the opponents in the Philippian letter, although one must rely on the important material in 3:2, which is clearly polemical.

First, in Philippians it is reasonably clear that there are different groups of opponents. The first to be encountered are the "rival preachers" in 1:15-18. They seem to be located where Paul is imprisoned. Paul is apparently reporting their activity to the Philippians. These badly motivated preachers use Paul's imprisonment to their advantage. They proclaim their version of the Gospel, knowing he is imprisoned and cannot refute it; this is the thrust of "[they] from selfishness preach the Christ, not purely, imagining to raise tribulation for my bonds" (1:17). Paul dismisses them with a "so what?" The most important thing is that the Gospel is preached; the motivation of the preachers is secondary. These opponents do not, in his view, present a serious or credible threat (see the commentary on 1:15-18 above).

The second group of opponents is located in Philippi. Paul alludes to them in 1:28 when he encourages the Philippians not to be frightened of them. The Philippians' lack of fear in the face of these opponents will be an "omen" to them of their "destruction." Whoever they are, they seem, first, to be a group from outside the Christian community and, second, to pose a serious threat to the Philippian church in the short term, but in the long term they are destined for "destruction" as are the "enemies of the cross" in 3:18-19. The lexical repetition of "destruction" and "suffer" in 1:28-30 and 3:18-19 has suggested to some students of Philippians that the same group of opponents is in view. Insofar as at 1:30 Paul is drawing parallels between his situation and that of the Philippians it is possible that the opponents in 1:28-30 are more likely to be Romans or perhaps Philippian civil authorities, so that the Philippian Christians would be facing persecution from the authorities, as Paul was, because of their adherence to an illegal religion. The text does not give a definite word on the matter.

Chapter 3, with its sharp invective, has been the scholarly focus of the "opponents question" in Philippians. Are those addressed in 3:2-3 the same group as those in 3:18-19? And what is their position? Here is what Paul says about them: they are "dogs" and "evil-workers" who "mutilate the flesh" (3:2). They live "as enemies of the cross of Christ" (3:18). Their "god" is the belly; they glory in their shame; their minds are set on earthly things (3:19). Their "end" is "destruction" (3:19). On the basis of this list some scholars have suggested that Paul is facing *two* sets of opponents in Philippi: Jewish legalists (Jews or Jewish Christians?) who insist on male circumcision and Torah adherence (3:2), and Gentile antinomians who live as "libertines" (3:19) (perhaps Gnostics or "divine-man missionaries"?).

Those who view the opponents as Gentiles advance several theories about their identity. Some point out that the opponents have a realized eschatology (seen most clearly in 3:9), which Paul combats by showing that completion (or "fullness") has yet to occur (see 3:12-16, 20-21). Other scholars suggest the opponents are "libertines" who scorn the moral elements of Paul's gospel. Again this suggestion depends on 3:19. Still others argue Paul is confronting the same "Gnostics" who were active in Galatia and Corinth, an argument that assumes that, at this early date, there *were* Gnostics in those places, a fact that is far from certain.

While it is quite possible that there were at least these two groups of opponents in Philippi (Jewish legalists *and* Gentile antinomians), it is also possible to reconcile the textual evidence around a hypothesis that the opponents in chapter 3 are Judaizers of the same sort Paul has met elsewhere in his ministry. Certainly that seems to be the identity of the opponents in 3:2, a verse with which those who support Gentile opponents struggle. It has been noted that "belly" (*koilia*, 3:19) can mean intestinal tract or sexual organs. While commentators have observed that focus on these "appetites" is characteristic of Gentile libertines, "their god is their belly" (3:19) can also imply either undue focus on what is eaten (i.e., Jewish food laws) or on the male sexual organ (i.e., circumcision). Jerome Murphy-O'Connor has noted that the relationship between stomach and diet is clear; "that between shame and circumcision becomes evident . . . when it is recalled that Greeks and Romans heaped scorn and ridicule on circumcision, and that out of shame some Jews underwent an operation to restore the foreskin" (*Paul*, 229). Certainly Judaizers are "enemies of the cross of Christ" (3:18) if they deny its sufficiency by their preaching the necessity for various other observances.

Perhaps the strongest argument for the Jewish identity of the opponents throughout chapter 3 is Paul's use of himself as a corrective example. What would be the point of detailing the very important achievements of his own Jewish background to non-Jews? The example in 3:4-11 "works" precisely because Paul had previously *held* the position of the Judaizers. That he would call his privileged background "garbage" in comparison to "knowing Christ" (3:8) would only be convincing (and, in this case, rhetorically startling) to those who either *were* Jews or who were being encouraged to become Jews by circumcision. Paul has "suffered the loss" of these things and says so precisely because he wants to make clear that he now understands them to be unimportant and unnecessary. Paul's own experience as a Jew is his strongest case against these opponents.

If the opponents in view in chapter 3 are Judaizers (and the *if* here is genuine and not rhetorical), the question might be raised: "why would Gentile Christians be attracted by Judaism?" At best, Jews were a tolerated minority. A simple answer might be that becoming Jewish was understood as a way to draw closer to the Lord Jesus Christ who was, unquestionably, a Jew. Might a Gentile Christian be drawn to the ritual and moral and theological origins of his or her Lord? A more nuanced answer is suggested by Mikael Tellbe's study of sociological factors behind the Philippian letter.

Tellbe assumes the opponents are traveling Jewish-Christian missionaries who have brought to Philippi some version of the message they preached elsewhere. The root issue is what is required for membership in the genuine people of God. Tellbe points out that the social identity of first-century Christians was precarious. Formerly Gentile Christians were no longer able to participate in the civic cults, and formerly Jewish Christians were no longer members of the synagogue. Both groups had lost a clear social identity. In particular, Philippi was a proud Roman colony. It must have been costly to "opt out" of its civic practices and especially of expressions of the imperial cult. To take on Judaism was, at the very least, to become part of a *religio licita,* a legal religion. If that did not confer social standing either because Jews were not well thought of or because there were few Jews in Philippi, at least it freed one from certain social and political obligations and from participation in the imperial cult.

To accept circumcision and thus the Law, however, indicates lack of comprehension of Paul's preaching of the Gospel. The whole Philippian letter suggests that suffering for Christ characterizes Christian experience. Jesus himself suffered (2:5-11). Paul is suffering in prison for the Gospel (1:12-26; 4:14). Epaphroditus risked his life for it (2:25-30). The Philippian Christians are themselves persecuted (1:17-30). To take on a Jewish social identity might circumvent some of that suffering, but it would betray the very meaning of the cross. This is why Paul says the opponents "live as enemies of the cross of Christ" (3:18). They do not understand its meaning and effect. Furthermore, "emptying" oneself of status and self-interest is what characterizes the lives of those Paul holds up to the Philippians as examples: Jesus (2:5-11), Timothy (2:19-24), Epaphroditus (2:25-30), and Paul (3:4-11). To seek to gain or preserve status is to miss the mark.

It would appear that the Philippians are facing the same danger that Paul's church at Galatia faced, the influx of Judaizing preaching and a rivalry for converts. After Paul left Philippi these other preachers came in declaring a "better way." In Philippi such preaching has not yet taken root. While in Galatians Paul appeals to Scripture to refute the Judaizers (the example of Abraham and of the children of Sarah and Hagar), here he appeals to his own experience precisely because Hebrew Scripture is unfamiliar. But the facts of his own life are not. What he has done is the model for the Philippian Christians; 3:17, then, is one of the principles of Paul's appeal in the letter. His tone here is calmer toward the Philippians (though not toward the rivals!) because they have not yet embraced the false teaching. Paul's attack is not on Judaism *per se,* but on an inadequate Jewish Christian understanding of the Gospel. Paul was, and remained, a Jew, but one who belonged to Jesus the Messiah.

At the very least the text indicates that the Philippian opponents advocate adherence to Torah, attach little importance to the cross, and live for what is impermanent ("belly" or "earthly things"). All of this is "putting confidence in the flesh" and, whoever the opponents were, that fact in itself was enough to raise Paul's ire.

For Reference and Further Study

Holladay, Carl R. "Paul's Opponents in Philippians 3," *ResQ* 12 (1969) 77–90.

Jewett, Robert. "Conflicting Movements in the Early Church as Reflected in Philippians," *NovT* 19 (1970) 362–90.

Klijn, A. F. J. "Paul's Opponents in Philippians iii," *NovT* 7 (1965) 278–84.

Koester, Helmut. "The Purpose of the Polemic of a Pauline Fragment, Philippians III," *NTS* 8 (1961–62) 317–32.

Mearns, C. L. "The Identity of Paul's Opponents at Philippi," *NTS* 33 (1987) 194–204.

Murphy-O'Connor, Jerome. *Paul: A Critical Life.* Oxford: Clarendon Press, 1996.

Schmithals, Walter. "The False Teachers of the Epistle to the Philippians," in idem, *Paul and the Gnostics.* Trans. John E. Steely. Nashville: Abingdon, 1972, 65–122.

Sumney, Jerry. *Identifying Paul's Opponents.* JSNTSup 40. Sheffield: JSOT Press, 1990.

________. *'Servants of Satan,' 'False Brothers,' and Other Opponents of Paul.* JSNTSup 188. Sheffield: Sheffield Academic Press, 1999.

Tellbe, B. Mikael. "The Sociological Factors Behind Philippians 3:1-11 and the Conflict at Philippi," *JSNT* 55 (1994) 97–121.

The Example of Paul (3:4b-14)

4b. If any other supposes to trust in the flesh, I am more: 5. with respect to circumcision, the eighth day; of race, Israel; of tribe, Benjamin; [a] Hebrew from Hebrews; according to law, [a] Pharisee; 6. according to zeal, persecuting the church; according to righteousness in law, having become blameless. 7. But what things were profit to me, these I have reckoned loss on account of the Christ. 8. But more than that, also I reckon all to be loss in order to know the surpassing greatness of Christ Jesus, my Lord, on account of whom I suffered loss of all things, and I reckon [them] refuse, in order that I might gain Christ 9. and might be found in him, not having my own righteousness from law, but through faith of Christ, the righteousness of God [based] upon the faith, 10. to know him and the power of his resurrection and the fellowship of his suffering, taking the same form as his death, 11. if somehow I might attain to the resurrection from the dead. 12. Not that I already received or already have been perfected, but I pursue if I may also lay hold of that for which I was laid hold of by Christ Jesus. 13. Brethren, I myself do not claim to have hold, but one thing I do, forgetting [what is] behind, stretching forward to the things that are before, 14. according to a goal, I pursue the prize, the high calling of the God in Christ Jesus.

Notes

4b. *If any other supposes to trust in the flesh:* The phrase "trust in the flesh" occurs three times in vv. 3-4 and links these two sections of the letter. The phrase also serves as an oblique reference to the opponents or "enemies" (see Excursus III above). "Trust" implies having been persuaded and therefore being confident. On "flesh" see the Note on 3:3 above. The verb for "supposes" *(dokeō)* can also be translated "thinks," but the speculative connotation of "suppose" fits this context well, as "to suppose" implies an assumption that might or might not be correct.

I am more: The Greek phrase is literally "I much more." That is, Paul is more confident. He does not "suppose" his superiority; he knows it, as his "resumé," which follows, immediately indicates. First he introduces what is his by birth (v. 5), then what is his by choice or volition, his own "theological positioning" (vv. 5b-6); (compare the list Paul gives at 2 Cor 11:22).

5. *with respect to circumcision, the eighth day:* Recall that it is precisely circumcision that has been at issue in 3:2-3. Prescriptions for this rite, which was normally performed on the eighth day of a male infant's life, are found in Gen 17:9-14 and Lev 12:3. During the Hellenistic period circumcision was a key issue for Jews as well as new Christians. Jewish men who wished to assimilate to Greek culture avoided it or sought to have its "mark" removed (see 1 Macc 1:15; Josephus, *Ant.* 12.5.1). In the Jewish community the circumcision of an infant boy was a joyous and celebrative occasion, welcoming a new "citizen" of Israel, a new "son of the promise."

of race, Israel: "Race" *(genos)* here means "family group" or "bloodline." "Israel" is a collective name for the twelve tribes descended from Jacob. However, the name may first have been used for the first tribes to inhabit the land, the tribes of Ephraim, Manasseh, and Benjamin, this last Paul's own family. Paul's point is that he is not a convert to Judaism, but was "born to it." (For a discussion of the meaning of Israel in Paul see William S. Campbell, "Israel," *DPL* 441–46.)

of tribe, Benjamin: Not only was he a "cradle Jew," Paul was born into one of Israel's most distinguished "families" or tribes, one known for bravery. "Benjamin," of course, literally means "son of the right hand" and thus "son of the promise," a particularly interesting etymology in this context. Jacob, we are told, "preferred Benjamin" (Gen 35:18) as the only son born in the "promised land." While small, the house of Benjamin was the house of Saul (the first king of Israel, thus a royal house) and the only tribe that remained loyal to Judah (1 Kgs 12:21). As Benjamin was known for resisting pagan influences, Paul may be quietly asserting his purity.

[a] Hebrew from Hebrews: "Hebrew" is an ethnic or national designation for descendants of Abraham. It is used in the Old Testament when those descendants are juxtaposed with other peoples, for example the Egyptians (see, e.g., Gen 43:32; Exod 2:11). It is the way Israelites refer to themselves. In the New Testament "Hebrew" is used for persons who maintain the Jewish heritage (ethnic and linguistic). Again, Paul's point is that he is not a convert or from a "mixed marriage" or "Hellenized." Both his parents were Jews before him, and he is proud of that cultural and linguistic heritage.

according to law, [a] Pharisee: The previous "advantages" Paul was born into. Now he enumerates those he chose for himself. Judaism in the Second Temple Period was far from monolithic. There were many groups and "parties." Paul belonged to the Pharisees, an observant, learned, and influential party (see Acts 23:6-9; 26:5; Gal 1:14). Christians tend to think negatively of Pharisees because in the gospels they are seen as interlocutors and rivals of Jesus, but they were pious and observant students of Torah who wanted to help their fellow Jews understand and live the Law, in short, "good guys." Pharisees are described both in rabbinic literature and in Josephus' writings. Both sources suggest they were scholars of Torah who accepted both written and oral law and were especially interested in ritual observance (purity, food laws, Sabbath), just the sorts of things Paul alludes to later in this passage. As such, they were moral and religious authority figures in their communities, and some sources suggest they were politically influential as well. (For a helpful discussion of the Pharisees see Stephen Westerholm, "Pharisees" in Joel B. Green, et. al., eds., *Dictionary of Jesus and the Gospels* [Downers Grove, IL: InterVarsity Press, 1992] 609–14).

6. *according to zeal, persecuting the church:* Paul was not a "marginal Jew"; he was zealous, a particular characteristic of the Pharisees (1 Macc 2:24-29). Zeal for God is considered praiseworthy in the OT (Num 25:11, 13; 1 Kgs 19:10, 14). And his zealous energy was expended in "pursuing" or "persecuting" those he understood to be challenging the Law, that is, the church or Christians. "Pursuing" implies hunting down a quarry, hunting down animals. This is a particularly strong point in this list of Paul's "fleshly accomplishments." He had vigorously opposed those among whom he now numbered himself. Indeed, he had sought to snuff out the very light he now bears (compare 1 Cor 15:9; Gal 1:13; and Acts 8:3; 9:1-2; 22:45; 26:9-11).

according to righteousness in law, having become blameless: Another translation of the phrase would be "according to righteousness, which is in the law, having become faultless." "Righteousness" resides in the Law, not in those who are called to conform to it. Paul emphasizes the validity of the Law, which is the larger point at issue in this section of the letter. But while valid, the Law does not make right relationship with God possible. This, too, is a stunning claim and clearly the capstone of the list. Paul asserts his absolute legal rectitude. Precisely by following the Law he had become "blameless." The word is particularly strong and means "innocent," literally "without fault." Paul asserts that his Torah observance was faultless, *not* that he was sinless. It is a subtle but important distinction.

7. *But what things were profit to me:* At v. 7 Paul begins to describe his transformation in Christ and how he came to set aside what he had previously found of most value. "But" serves rhetorically to cancel out everything that came before it. With Paul's conversion, from which this change of thought arises, this verse is a great "hinge" of Scripture, as so much turns on Paul's changed understanding. The "things" previously valued are the items just enumerated in vv. 5-6. "Profit" or "gain" is a commercial term: "what was on the plus side of the balance sheet." The dominant metaphors of vv. 7-8 are commercial, from accounting.

   these I have reckoned loss on account of the Christ: The form of the verb (perfect middle indicative) indicates completed past action, the results of which continue into the present. It can also be translated "consider," but "reckoned" continues the accounting metaphor that is also evident in "loss," the negative side of the balance sheet. The verse's drama comes from the opposites "profit/loss." The connotation is that of deliberate judgment. Karl Barth's comment on the phrase is wonderful: "the heights on which [Paul] stood were *abysmal*" (*Philippians*, 97). Again, to translate *dia* as "on account of" perpetuates the dominant metaphor of accounting. Here is the reason for Paul's transformation. The point of the verse is that Paul has transferred everything on the "assets" side of his balance sheet to the "loss" column "because of" or "for the sake of" the Christ. It is a stunning transfer.

8. *But more than that, also I reckon all to be loss:* Verse 8 repeats and extends what has just been said and introduces the subject that follows. If this transfer of assets to losses is not startling enough, there is "more." *Everything* is "loss" in comparison to knowing Christ. The "more" is detailed in vv. 8-11, which are one long sentence in the Greek with many emphatic participial phrases. The accounting metaphor of v. 7 continues in the repetition of the terms "reckon" and "loss." Here the verb tense changes to the present.

   in order to know the surpassing greatness of Christ Jesus, my Lord: The phrase is in apposition to the preceding clause. Here Paul provides the reason *why* all his "assets" now appear to him losses. "To know" is an important term. "Knowledge" is a key word in pagan religions and refers to the revealed knowledge received in the Mysteries and to communion with the deity. "Know" is used in the Greek world with regard to an object. In the LXX the verb is used for profound, intimate knowledge: Adam "knew" Eve. In Hebrew thought the same word implies deep personal knowledge and relationship. In Hebrew Scripture such knowledge only comes because of God's self-revelation. "Surpassing" *(hyperechon)* is a particularly strong word meaning literally "above having," thus "excelling." The meaning of "Lord" has been discussed several times in this commentary (see the Notes on 2:11). Here Paul carefully speaks of "his" Lord. This is not some abstract power, but the one to whom Paul owes personal fealty (see Gal 2:20).

   on account of whom I suffered loss of all things: Paul's loss is not random or coincidental but purposive. It is because of his Lord that Paul has suffered loss, not just in general or partially, but "of all things." "All" is repeated for emphasis. To render the point in contemporary slang, "On account of Christ I became a loser." Paul has chosen to empty himself of familial, theological, and religious status for the sake of knowing the Christ.

and I reckon [them] refuse: "Reckon" continues the commercial metaphor. "Refuse" *(skybala)* is a vulgar and shocking word, and all its connotations would elicit the emotional response of disgust. It literally means "excrement" and is used for rubbish or garbage, the scrapings left over from a feast, what is thrown out in the street for the dogs (see the Note on 3:2). The implication is that the very things the Judaizers prided themselves on were so much filth.

in order that I might gain Christ: "Gain" continues the accounting metaphor; it is a cognate of the noun for "profit" in v. 7 and is the opposite of "loss." To gain Christ more than compensates for what Paul has "lost," but to gain him Paul must empty himself of that in which he previously "gloried." The subtle implication is that Paul has modeled his behavior on that of his Lord (see 2:6-8).

9. *and might be found in him:* Verse 9 is a classic and concise statement of the Pauline gospel and the key verse in this section of the letter. Paul finds himself transferred "into" Christ. "Found" is in the passive voice; it is a divine passive that indicates God is the actor (compare 1:21 and Gal 2:20). The prepositional phrase "in Christ" is used frequently by Paul to describe the "context" or matrix of the life of believers (compare 2:21; Gal 2:20).

not having my own righteousness from law: The latter part of v. 9 is a concise statement of the Pauline doctrine of justification by faith. (For fuller treatments see Romans and Galatians.) The structure of the verse sets up a comparison between righteousness from law and righteousness from faith. "Righteousness" is a heavily theological word with strong relational connotations. It means being in proper relationship with God. The phrase negates Paul's "claim to fame" in the latter half of v. 6. Paul has come to understand that what has put him in right relationship with God is not law and not something belonging to him by birth or something he has done ("my own"). It is not "achieved," but "accepted," and law alone cannot achieve it (compare Rom 4:13-15; Gal 2:15-16; and see *NJBC,* "Pauline Theology" 82:68–70). "Law" refers most obviously to the Law of Moses, the Torah, of which Paul in principle approved (Rom 7:12).

but through faith of Christ: The phrase is much debated because of the closing prepositional phrase. Is it faith *in* Christ (Paul's faith) or faith *of* Christ (Christ's faith)? In view of the context I think it is Christ's faith (subjective genitive) that is in view here. Paul's righteousness comes as a gift by means of Christ's faithfulness (another possible translation of *pistis*), his obedient sacrifice (for another view see Fee, *Philippians,* 324–26). The whole point of this passage is repudiation of human (even theological or spiritual) accomplishment. What Christ did makes personal relationship with God possible.

the righteousness of God [based] upon the faith: All righteousness belongs to God, who is the source of Christ's atonement. It is offered to human beings via Christ, but must be accepted by faith. The gift is not a gift if it is not opened and accepted with gratitude (see Rom 8:3).

10. *to know him:* Verses 10-11 are a purpose clause that modifies the preceding verses, although in Greek the structural relationship is less than clear. At v. 10 Paul begins to describe his new aspiration, which in essence, is to follow the pattern set by Jesus in 2:6-11. On "know" see the Notes on 3:8 above. Here the verb is an infinitive of purpose. As the *NJBC* so succinctly states, "to 'know Christ' means to experience him as 'life-giving Spirit' (1 Cor 15:45; 2 Cor 3:17)" (p. 796).

    and the power of his resurrection: "Power" *(dynamis)* is usually God's, the God who raised Jesus from the dead (compare Acts 2:22-24, 32). The implication of the phrase is that Christ's resurrection had an effect that went well beyond the restoration of his own life. When God raised Jesus from the dead a great, benevolent power was set loose in the universe, and with it the assurance that things that have not yet occurred will indeed happen.

    and the fellowship of his suffering, taking the same form as his death: Suffering has been a theme of the letter to this point. Paul audaciously desires not only the positive power of Christ's resurrection, but the honor of sharing in the sufferings of Christ, that is, the suffering of crucifixion. "Fellowship" is a key term in the letter (1:5, 7; 2:1; 4:14, 15). This phrase is clearly to be understood in the light cast by 2:6-8. The root "form" *(morphē)* is repeated from 2:6, 7 (see discussion of the meaning of the term there). The suffering in view is the hideous suffering of crucifixion. Paul literally asks to be "conformed" *(symmorphizomenos)* to the suffering and death of Christ. This may be what is behind Paul's earlier remark that he desires to "depart and be with Christ" (1:23, and compare Rom 8:17).

11. *if somehow I might attain to the resurrection from the dead:* By now it is clear that what Paul aspires to, he cannot do for himself. The uncertainty here is not of doubt but, as Marvin R. Vincent pointed out so long ago, "an expression of humility and self distrust" (*Philippians and Philemon,* 106). Resurrection is tied to "conforming to his death." "Attain" carries the sense of "reach the destination of." The term for resurrection here *(exanastasin)* is a double compound and a *hapax legomenon*. Perhaps Paul chose it for dramatic emphasis. Paul's point is that he *will* attain resurrection, although he has not *yet*. Paul's assertion here is to be read in light of his earlier remarks in 1:12-14, 19-26. Verses 10 and 11 constitute an *inclusio* that mirrors the pattern of Christ's (and Paul's? and the Philippians'?) life. It is framed by reference to the resurrection: resurrection (v. 10), suffering (v. 10), death (v. 10), resurrection (v. 11). As an historical aside, it is probably worth noting that there was apparently in Philippi a tradition of false teachers who misunderstood the resurrection. They may have had a realized eschatology, that is, taught that the resurrection had already occurred. Later, Polycarp reports that false prophets taught "there is neither resurrection nor judgment" (*Pol. Phil.* 7).

12. *Not that I already received:* Although the language of v. 11 indicates that what Paul desires he cannot get by means of his own accomplishments, he wants to make sure that fact is crystal clear. Additionally, he wants to stress that he has not reached this goal, but is still striving toward it. These points he makes in vv. 12-14, which are dominated by the metaphor of a race. The secret of

obtaining the "goal," Paul asserts, is to forget the past and press on to what is ahead (God/Christ; see 1:21-23). "Not that" is an idiom that qualifies what has just been said. What Paul aspires to, he "receives" *(elabon)*. He does not "earn" or "accomplish" it, but receives it as gift (as per vv. 9-11). The language here echoes that of v. 9.

or already have been perfected: "Perfected"or "completed" *(teteleiōmai)* is a word found in the writings of the mystery religions as a description of the highest state of religious attainment. It implies reaching a goal. It is in the perfect tense, making a delicious grammatical pun: the perfect form of the word for perfection! It is a *hapax legomenon* in Paul's writing, suggesting to some scholars that he is here quoting his opponents.

but I pursue: The verb "pursue" *(diōkō)* is the same used in v. 6 with the connotation of hunting. Here the sense is that of a runner in the homestretch and straining forward toward the finish line. Paul used to chase Christians; now he has a nobler quarry. The verb means "straining toward" (or "pressing on"), and is the word Paul used at 1:8 for his longing for the Philippians.

if I may also lay hold of that for which I was laid hold of by Christ Jesus: An alternative translation would be "if I may also grasp that for which I was grasped." While the translation of the Greek is awkward, the meaning is clear: Paul has not reached the perfection he seeks, but he is striving toward it. Two forms of the verb *katalambanō*, which means "obtain," "make one's own," "take aggressively," occur here, once in the active voice and once in the passive. Paul is the subject of each; he strives to attain, and he has been obtained. Paul is acted upon by Christ. Certainly the reference is to the Damascus Road experience (Gal 1:12; Acts 9:1-25), and the point is that the prior "work" is Christ's.

13. *Brethren, I myself do not claim to have hold:* Paul insists emphatically that he does not claim to have obtained what he seeks. It is not clear precisely what that is, as the object of the verb (repeated from the previous verse) is uncertain. The point is that Paul has not yet "arrived."

but one thing I do: The phrase is literally "but one thing." Paul has a one-minded, one-pointed focus in his striving. He does the one necessary thing: here it is to aim for the "prize" before him (compare Luke 10:41-42).

forgetting [what is] behind: That is, not just putting behind him, but forgetting completely the life described in vv. 7-9. Paul not only leaves the past behind, he utterly forgets that it ever existed.

stretching forward to the things that are before: The image is that of a runner stretching toward the finish line. The idea is that what is past must be left behind in order to obtain the promise of the future. In this context Paul is leaving behind the achievements of the past (3:4-6) for the promises of the future (compare 1 Cor 9:26). The construction of v. 13 is *"men/de."* On the one hand he does not have what he strives for; on the other hand he is stretching toward it. Loh and Nida aptly remark on this verse, "the runner has lost when he turns back to see what is behind him" (*Translator's Handbook,* 111).

14. *according to a goal:* Paul's forward striving is not undirected; it is "according to" or "toward" a goal. The word *skopos* is a *hapax legomenon* in the NT, but in

parallel literature it is a mark on the finishing post at the race track on which the runner concentrates as he runs toward it.

I pursue the prize, the high calling of God in Christ Jesus: "Pursue" is the same verb used in vv. 6 and 12. Although the "prize" is not defined, it is probably Christ himself (as per v. 8). What may be in the back of Paul's mind here is the award ceremony in which the winning runner is called to the dais to receive a prize. The adverb "high" here can also be translated "above." Both senses work. God's call (subjective genitive) is "high," and it is also to what is "above" as opposed to the "earthly things" to which the enemies aspire (see 3:18-19). God does the calling, but again the call is "in Christ Jesus."

Interpretation

In 3:2-4a Paul has warned the Philippians against false teachers. As Jerome Murphy-O'Connor has pointed out, Paul views them as an imminent danger. Part of their mistaken attitude is apparently a false confidence in their own accomplishments, what accrues to them because of circumcision. Paul counters that he and the Philippian believers are "the true circumcision" and that putting "confidence in the flesh" is in error. However, if that is the game the opponents are playing, Paul knows he can win it. This text first gives his reasons for "confidence in the flesh" and then his reasons for repudiating them.

The structure of the passage is clear. Paul begins with his opponents in view. At least in vv. 2-14 they seem to be Judaizers of some sort (see Excursus III above). Verses 4-6 are Paul's resumé, the sociological, and in this instance religious, factors that indicate his status. Then in vv. 7-11 Paul describes the change Christ effected in him; vv. 7-9 describe his transformation in Christ and vv. 10-11 Paul's ultimate in hope in him. Apparently Paul either thinks he has gone too far or is refuting the realized eschatology of the opponents, and so in vv. 12-14 he points out that he has not achieved perfection but is striving toward it.

In vv. 4-6 Paul reflects on his qualifications as a Jew. As in Galatians 1–2 and 2 Cor 11:16-30 (which may be the closest parallels to this passage), Paul does not write autobiography for its own sake. He is pointing out that if qualifications are the issue, he is overqualified. But as the issue here is the adequacy of grace offered by God through Jesus Christ (the same issue that underlies the Colossian letter), Paul hastens to assert in vv. 7-9 that these qualifications pale, indeed become garbage, in comparison to knowing, that is, having profound personal acquaintance with Christ. Verse 9 is the theological center of the passage, a reminder (since Paul has already made the point variously in 1:6, 28; 2:13) that righteousness is God's. The "good work" done among the Philippians has divine origin. "Righteousness" is such a weighty theological word that it is easy to forget that what lies behind it is relational. The issue is how to be related to God. What opens the door to fellowship with God? It is not, Paul asserts, one's family inheritance, or one's own qualifications or achievements, or even the Law, but faith, understood in this case as a verb, "believing in," not a noun, "the faith" (a body of doctrine). The object of the verb "faith" is "Jesus Christ."

In any age these verses cut close to home. The human tendency is always to establish status by means of personal accomplishment. One of the most radical features of Christianity is its utter repudiation of this. Instead of a hierarchical, status-oriented community, the church offers only one "status," that of slave (1:1; compare Mark 9:35; 10:42-45). Every Christian, from bishop to theology professor to laborer, is a slave of Jesus Christ. We are all redeemed sinners, and thus the only relational pattern among Christians should be that of siblings, "brethren" and "beloved" (1:12; 2:12; 3:1). Everyone is a child of the same divine parent.

Verses 10-11, then, are a clear statement of Paul's "post-Law" aspirations. They indicate that spiritual maturity has to do with appetite, with what one desires (see, for example, Ps 42:1-2). Paul understands that we are formed in the image of what we desire. These verses are a clear statement of the five spiritual desires of the apostle: (1) to know Christ (not *about* Christ, but the Savior himself); (2) to know the power of his resurrection (which, of course, is God, the divine self); (3) to have the fellowship of his suffering (that is, to share the life that Christ had); (4) to become like him in his death (to share martyrdom); and (5) to attain resurrection. In short, what Paul desires is exactly the self-emptying and divine elevation set out in 2:6-11 as characteristic of the life of Jesus Christ.

We do well to remember that the context of these desires is Paul's imprisonment and uncertainty about his immediate future (1:12-26). Paul takes it for granted that Christians live in what Barnabas Ahern calls "a climate of suffering" ("Fellowship of Sufferings," 2). Jesus himself said, "in this world you will have trouble" (John 16:33b). It is a divine promise! For Paul, whose theological categories were thoroughly Jewish, these sufferings were probably understood as sharing in the trials of the "last days." But on a much deeper, personal level suffering is an entry into the life of Christ himself, albeit imperfect, a way of sharing his experience. While one does not enjoy suffering, it is possible to discover in it a profound fellowship with Christ who suffered. After the cross, no one need suffer alone. (For a very full and helpful treatment of suffering in Philippians see the work of L. G. Bloomquist, *The Function of Suffering in Philippians.*)

Some scholars have worried about the note of uncertainty in v. 11, the "if somehow" or "if only." They point out that the problem is a perceived hesitation on Paul's part. Does *ei pōs* imply conditionality about resurrection itself? Almost everyone concludes, "no." Randall E. Otto has made a convincing case that Paul is firm on the *object* of his hope (resurrection), but conditional on his *subjective* apprehension of it. What Otto suggests is in view is Paul's doubt in the face of what may be his impending martyrdom. Certainly martyrs in the Jewish tradition were afforded special status (see, e.g., Wis 3:1-9 or 2 Macc 6:18–7:42). Paul wonders if he will maintain his confession in the face of martyrdom. I find it difficult to imagine that one who had the physical courage to endure forty lashes five times, three beatings with rods, a stoning, and three shipwrecks (2 Cor 11:25) doubts his physical courage. But as Otto points out, it is one thing to die suddenly as a martyr and quite another to languish in prison awaiting a decision. (The parallel to the intolerable circumstances of modern death row inmates is self-evident.) Paul's question seems to be about his present situation. It is this situation of persecution because he is a Christian that Paul shares with the Philippians (1:28-30) and in which he wishes to encourage them (1:24).

The turn at v. 12, then, is completely logical. In the nearly intolerable circumstances of indefinite imprisonment awaiting a verdict and sentencing, Paul says "if only I could be resurrected instead of enduring *this*." Then he quickly goes on to assure the Philippians that he does not view himself as "having arrived." While the power of Christ's resurrection calls for an interior "death" to some aspects of the human person, the Christian is not "complete" or "perfect" until the final goal is attained. In order to realize this perfection at least two things are necessary. First, one must forget what is behind one, let go of the past, especially the past failures that discourage, the personal equivalents of Paul's persecuting the church. One cannot help but recall Lot's wife, whose desire to look back is so understandable and so devastating (see Gen 19:15-26, especially vv. 17, 26; and Luke 17:30-35, especially v. 32). Second, one must "strain toward" what is ahead. One can lose the "prize" not only by looking back, but also by forgetting that the goal is "the high calling of God in Christ Jesus." It is a goal Paul has not yet attained.

Verses 4b-14 present an important description of the transformation of the human person in Christ Jesus, a transformation that all must accept and that each Christian either cooperates with or hinders. Verses 12-14 make clear the "already/not yet" quality of that transformation. In view of the suffering Paul faces, the Philippians face, and all Christians can expect, this passage, along with Rom 8:28-29, is not only of theological importance (and a frequently overlooked source in dealing biblically with the problem of theodicy), but also of pastoral centrality. As was the case at the outset of the letter, here Paul's own story provides the model for the Philippians to follow. The very personal appeal gives force to what Paul wants the Philippians to do: "press on." A close analysis of this passage, while intellectually clarifying, can lose sight of its deep fervor. It is a moving expression of what the apostle Paul holds most dear in his own life and finds most essential for other Christians to understand. The reader is now challenged to go back and re-read this passage with an openness to its confessional depth.

For Reference and Further Study

Ahern, Barnabas M. "The Fellowship of Sufferings: Phil. 3:10," *CBQ* 22 (1960) 1–32.
Becker, Jürgen. *Paul: Apostle to the Gentiles.* Louisville: Westminster John Knox, 1993.
Bloomquist, L. G. *The Function of Suffering in Philippians.* JSNTSup 78. Sheffield: JSOT Press, 1993.
Doughty, D. J. "Citizens of Heaven: Phil. 3:2-21," *NTS* 41 (1996) 102–22.
Forestell, J. Terence. "Christian Perfection and Gnosis in Philippians 3:7-16," *CBQ* 18 (1956) 123–36.
Loh, I-Jin, and Eugene A. Nida. *A Translator's Handbook on Paul's Letter to the Philippians.* Stuttgart: United Bible Societies, 1977.
Murphy-O'Connor, Jerome. *Paul: A Critical Life.* Oxford: Clarendon Press, 1996.
Otto, Randall E. "'If Possible I May Obtain Resurrection From the Dead' (Phil. 3:11)," *CBQ* 57 (1995) 324–40.
Pfitzner, Victor C. *Paul and the Agon Motif.* Leiden: Brill, 1967.
Pohill, John B. "Twin Obstacles in the Christian Path: Philippians 3," *RevExp* 77 (1980) 359–72.

Warning about "Enemies" (3:15–4:1)

15. Therefore, as many as [are] perfect, let us think thus, and if you think anything different, even this God will reveal to you. 16. In summary, let us walk by what we have attained. 17. Be fellow imitators of me, brethren, and observe those walking thus, just as you have us [as an] example. 18. For, as I said to you often, and now again I say weeping, many walk [as] enemies of the cross of Christ, 19. whose end [is] destruction, whose God [is] the belly and [who] glory in their shame, thinking on earthly things. 20. But our citizenship exists in heavens from where also we await a savior, [the] Lord Jesus Christ, 21. who will change our humble body conforming to his glorious body according to the power working in him, even to subdue all things to himself. 4:1. Therefore,

brethren, beloved and longed for, my joy and crown, in this way stand firm in [the] Lord, beloved.

Notes

15. *Therefore, as many as [are] perfect, let us think thus:* Both the transitional word "therefore" *(oun)* and the shift to first person plural here indicate the opening of a new section of the letter. Following the pattern established in the epistle, instructions to the Philippians follow the presentation of Paul as an example. "As many as" or "those who" is inclusive; it might be rendered in English "those of us who." Paul is including himself. "Perfect" echoes v. 12. Is Paul now commending what he has just argued against? Or is the remark ironic or "tongue in cheek"? Or is he calling even those whose teaching he rejects to agree with him? "Perfect" here is to be read in light of v. 16; it suggests "mature" in the sense of "doing what has been attained." The implication for the Philippians is that those who are working *toward* perfection, which Paul has just asserted he, at least, does not yet have, should think or "be minded" as the familiar word suggests (2:2, 5), as he has just explained in vv. 12-14. The echo of *phroneō* ("think") from the earlier material reminds the recipients that, as before, inaccurate teaching leads to wrong action. As one is "minded," as one thinks, so one will act (compare Matt 5:21-48).

    and if you think anything different, even this God will reveal to you: The Greek construction implies a plausible situation. If there are differences of opinion between Paul and the Philippian Christians, they should not be matters for dissension, but for awaiting further revelation from God. Again *phroneite* implies a general disposition. "Even this" implies that God has already revealed other things. "Reveal" *(apokalypsei)* is the future form of the verb meaning to "make known," "manifest," "reveal," with the implication of revealing what is hidden. Paul uses the term for God's revelation of what otherwise would be unknown (Gal 1:16; Eph 3:5). The attitude suggested here is the same as that at 1:18. The phrase seems a surprising turn, but is consistent with the rhetoric of friendship. Friends do not always have to agree. They are called to listen to each other and, in this case, to listen together to the God they both call "Father." Such "joint listening" preserves the sort of unity Paul commends in Philippians.

16. *In summary, let us live by what we have attained:* The phrase is awkward in Greek and would read literally "nevertheless to what we arrived, [by the same] to walk." In other words, Paul encourages the Philippian Christians to live by what they *do* know, in the maturity they *have* achieved. "In summary" *(plēn)* is literally "nevertheless," but is used to summarize a section. "Attained" is from the verb *phthanō,* meaning "to come" or "to arrive at." Paul urges the Philippians to keep living as they have been. "Live" renders a root infinitive sometimes translated "walk" *(stoichein).* It is related to a word used in Colossians, *stoicheia,* meaning "first principles" or "the alphabet," that is, what is "lined up first." Here used in an imperative sense, the verb means "walk in a

line" or "march" as for battle. The Roman phalanx was nearly impregnable because the soldiers lined up shoulder to shoulder and moved forward together. The implication is of walking together toward a goal, and so Paul's goal of strengthening unity in the Philippian church is clearly in view.

17. *Be fellow imitators of me, brethren:* The word for "imitate" here is prefixed by *syn*, "with," thus "with-imitators" (compare 1 Cor 4:16; 1 Thess 1:6). "Imitate me" is a Hellenistic pedagogical principle. Teachers were expected to live out the message they taught, and if they did not do so observably, their teaching was undermined. (For more see Werner Jaeger, *Early Christianity and Greek Paideia* [New York: Oxford University Press, 1961].) In Jewish tradition as well, one indicated mastery of an idea or a teaching by putting it into practice (or, as my mother used to admonish us as children, "if you know better, you do better"). A helpful gloss on Paul's "pedagogy" is provided by 1 Cor 11:1: "Be imitators of me, as I am of Christ."

and observe those walking thus, just as you have us [as an] example: To "observe" is to be attentive to, to look carefully at, to focus on. The verb *skopeite* has the same root as "goal" *(skopos)* in v. 14. "Walking" is a favorite Pauline metaphor for the way of conducting one's life (Rom 6:4; 8:1; 1 Cor 3:3; Gal 5:16; and see Ps 1:1). It is a different form from the word for "walk" in v. 16., but both reflect the popular notion that human life is a journey. The word for example *(typos)* means "formed by an impression." It implies "example" in the sense of a pattern to follow, a "model," or what we now call a "paradigm." Certainly Paul is referring here to Timothy and Epaphroditus (2:19-30) as well as himself (and perhaps to others known to the Philippians?). Paul is making the point that there is need for community in order to mature in the Christian life. We learn the Christian life by walking it (as the "discipleship journey" sections of Mark and Luke suggest) and by imitating others who "walk it" well.

18. *For, as I said to you often, and now again I say weeping:* Verses 18-19 provide the reason for the imperative in v. 17. The opening phrase is highly emotional. "Weeping" *(klaion)* means crying aloud and connoted a loud expression of grief; perhaps "keening"carries the idea (see 2 Cor 2:4, where Paul also writes in tears over difficulties in a community). What Paul has in view here, he frequently has warned them about before. It is not a new threat.

many walk [as] enemies of the cross of Christ: The problem is serious, since "many" conduct themselves as enemies. "Many" suggests Paul has in mind persons *outside* the Philippian church; otherwise he could have used a second-person pronoun. "Walk" here is the same word as in v. 17 and means "behave" or "conduct oneself." Unfortunately, many conduct their lives as active opponents of the cross. "Cross" is for Paul both *the* cross of Jesus and a shorthand way of speaking of God's whole plan of redemption in Christ. In view of 3:1-14, perhaps the particular enemies in view are those who hold to the necessity for Torah observance (Judaizers), which of course negates the cross. To deny the sufficiency of the cross is to be its "enemy." Other scholars have suggested that "enemies of the cross" are those who omit the importance of the cross in Christian preaching and, as a result, claim they are *already* mature or perfected. Paul faced a similar threat in Corinth. Certainly in 3:12–4:1 Paul asserts *he* is not already perfect. Or perhaps "enemies of the cross" are those who deny the reality of (even need for?) suffering in Christian life. Whoever the enemies are, Paul weeps over the division they cause in the community. The exact nature of the division is unclear, but it seems to be the result of some in the church following the false teaching alluded to in 3:2 and again here.

19. *whose end [is] destruction:* Verse 19 is made up of a series of clauses, each of which characterizes the enemies in some way. Rendered literally, the Greek of this phrase is "of whom the end, destruction." "End" *(telos)* suggests "last judgment." "Destruction" *(apōleia)* means "utter ruin" and is Paul's term for the opposite of "salvation," what the *NJBC* calls "eschatological ruin" (compare 1:28; 1 Cor 1:18; 2 Cor 2:15).

    whose god [is] the belly: "Belly" *(koilia)* is literally "stomach," but is also a Pauline metaphor for bodily life (see Rom 16:18). Thus the enemies of the cross whom Paul has in view have made their appetites a god. It is a stark accusation. Alternatively *koilia* can mean "womb" (Gal 1:15) or "navel," suggesting that self-absorption is the failing ("navel gazing"). The phrase appears in Euripides' *Cyclops* (316-340), and the word *koiliodaimon* ("one who makes a god of the belly") appears in Greek poetry, so the idea may have been familiar to the Philippians. The point is that the "enemies" have deified themselves and their appetites.

    and [who] glory in their shame: "Glory" is a word Scripture normally associates only with God. Here the enemies are so degenerate that they exult in or boast of what they should be ashamed of. Some commentators read the phrase as suggesting sexual immorality, but the language itself gives scant evidence for such a reading. The context is wider than sexuality, and thus more important and potentially damning.

    thinking on earthly things: The word for "thinking" has, as in 2:2-5 and 3:15, the root "minded." The enemies' habitual attitude is directed toward what is of the earth *(epigeia)*, not the "upward call" commended in v. 14. The point, once again, is not that creation is bad, but that it is impermanent. The enemies are living for what passes away (or in the case of *koilia*, what passes through!) rather than for what is enduring. The enemies are not focused on the model of Christ. A most helpful gloss on this phrase appears in Rom 8:5-11.

20. *But our citizenship exists in heavens:* The emphasis falls on the plural pronoun "our," as the phrase is in clear contrast to the immediately preceding verses. Paul contrasts "us and them," the earthly and the heavenly. The enemies of the cross are "earth-focused"; "we" are "heaven-focused." "Citizenship" *(politeuma)* is a *hapax legomenon* and yet a key term in the letter. That it is a relatively rare word outside the NT suggests it is a technical term of some sort. Hellenistic writers used it in relationship to some form of government or in regard to obligation to an external principle of order. For Philo it connoted allegiance to heavenly order. A similar word in Acts 23:1 implies Paul's allegiance to divine will. Paul has apparently chosen it here to recall 1:27 and the high status of Philippi as governed by Roman law. At the time of Paul a *politeuma* was a group of foreigners living abroad who were allowed to form a separate community with their own leaders and laws. (This was not unlike

the position of Jews in the empire as members of a *religio licita.*) Paul is suggesting that Christians belong to such a community. They are "in" but not "of" Philippi and the Roman empire (compare Eph 2:19). "Exists" *(hyparchei)* is present tense; the believer is a citizen of heaven now, actually. "Heavens," plural, is a Semitism and reflects the context of Paul's thought. The verse cuts at least two ways. To those who hold a realized eschatology (who think they have "arrived") it says, "our home is elsewhere; we are not there yet." To those who are proud of earthly privileges (Jewish attainments like those in 3:4-6, or Philippian citizenship) it says "our country is not this one; our ultimate loyalty belongs elsewhere." The believers' "belonging" is with God.

from where also we await a savior, [the] Lord Jesus Christ: "Await" implies "expect anxiously," "eagerly await," or "look forward to" (compare Gal 5:5 and Rom 8:19-25). One does not await what one has. Again, the phrase attacks a realized eschatology. The verse as a whole expresses the "already/not yet" character of Christian life that is a keynote of the letter. "Savior" is a term that is used infrequently in the NT as a title. It is found most frequently in the Pastoral Epistles (1 and 2 Timothy and Titus), which may be significantly later than Paul's time. Recall that there were many "saviors" in Hellenistic times (see 1 Cor 5:8). Has Paul chosen the term here because the Philippians would know "savior" was a title for the Caesar? Certainly the term is in the emphatic position. "Lord Jesus Christ" reflects the fullness of Pauline christology and is the church's earliest creed. But its use is rare in the Pauline corpus. Here it echoes the thought of 2:11.

21. *who will change our humble body conforming to his glorious body:* Verse 21 reveals an important purpose of the savior's coming; he effects human transformation. Again, Paul, his exemplary associates, and the Philippians cannot transform their *own* bodies; only Christ can do that. The language of v. 21 echoes that of 2:6-7. Here it demonstrates what the savior will do. "Change" *(metaschēmatizō)* has as its root the term "likeness" *(schēma),* which was of such importance in 2:7. It means to change the outward form or the appearance of something. As noted above, God has eternal plans for the "body," the *sōma* as opposed to the flesh *(sarx),* which for Paul implies the whole person. He has used both terms previously in 1:20-26, where he makes a concession to live in the flesh, knowing that the body continues whether in life or death. The body exists in at least two forms, the "lowly body" (*tapeinōsis,* which has as its root "humble"), which means "earthly existence," and the "glorious body" that belongs to the risen Christ, and Christians and will share in the "commonwealth of heaven." Only the savior can change one to the other. "Change" *(symmorphos)* involves both the inward and outward substance and is the same root as the word in 2:6 (and recall 3:10). The point, which has been made frequently in this commentary, is not that human flesh is evil, but that it is impermanent, subject to illness, disease, dissolution. The action of Jesus has transfigured flesh (made of it a *sōma*?) because by him its enemy, death, has been destroyed. Anything that harms the body is harming God's property (see 1 Cor 6:19-20). Note, again, that Christ *will* at some future time change the humble body; it has not yet happened. (For more on the transformation Christ will affect see 1 Cor 15:35-57, especially vv. 42-44, 49, 52-53 and Rom 8:18-23.)

according to the power working in him: The power working in Jesus Christ is God's power, the power that in 2:9-11 raised and exalted Christ. The term for "power" *(energeia)* is used in the NT only of supernatural power.

even to subdue all things to himself: Suddenly the context changes from the individual to the cosmic. The phrase indicates the extent of Christ's power; it can place all things under him. Paul probably expects the letter's recipients to remember the last phrases of the Christ hymn, 2:10-11. (For more on these parallels see the Interpretation below.)

4:1 *Therefore, brethren, beloved and longed for, my joy and crown:* "Therefore" can also be translated "so then" or "accordingly," and may be used either as an introductory or a concluding formula. A similar phrase, "therefore, my beloved" (2:12), serves to conclude the other large section of instructions to the Philippians, 1:27–2:18. This verse is the concluding exhortation of the section 3:1–4:1, which begins and ends with "brethren." Karl Barth calls it "an adjuratory conclusion to chapter 3" (p. 117). Because of what Paul has explained to the Philippians in this section of the letter, he issues this closing admonition couched in the language of friendship. The greeting clearly indicates the depth of Paul's relationship to the Philippians; they are not only his "siblings" ("brethren"), but his "beloved." "Longed for" is a verbal adjective, a *hapax legomenon,* but the idea is similar to that in 1:8. "Joy" is the leitmotif of the letter and marks the transition between all its major sections (see 1:3-4, 19; 2:2, 18, 29; 3:1; 4:4, 10). The Philippians *are* Paul's joy; he expresses pride in them, even a slight sense of ownership of their achievements. "Crown" *(stephanos)* is the crown of the victor in the athletic games (see the metaphor in 2:12-14, and compare *2 Clem.* 7:3) or that given to the guest at a banquet. The Philippian believers are Paul's "crown," his mark of "having won" (compare 1 Thess 2:19-20; 3:9). They are, so to speak, his "trophies."

in this way stand firm in [the] Lord, beloved: "Stand" *(stēkete)* implies "stand firm" and is the same verb used in 1:27 and 3:16. The ability to "stand firm," to be resolute against opponents or enemies, is "in the Lord." The power of God alluded to in 3:21 makes that possible. The final imperative of this section of the letter closes on a strong note of affection.

Interpretation

In 3:15-16 Paul invites the Philippians to join him in stretching toward perfection. This section of the letter both suggests how this will come about and warns against those who have abandoned the "race." If 3:15-17 is a summons to perfection, 3:18-21 is a setting forth of the "two ways," the "do" and the "don't." Verse 17 provides the ethical principle for the whole letter: imitate those who are doing the right thing. Paul explicitly invites the Philippians to imitate him (3:17) as he had earlier invited them to imitate Jesus (2:5-11) and more obliquely to imitate Timothy and Epaphroditus (2:19-30). Certainly Gentile converts to Christianity needed models to follow, but not, as 3:1-3 makes clear, more "rules." The Philippian believers are specifically warned against "enemies" in vv. 18-19 to whom they are compared in vv. 20-21, verses that reflect on the fullness of life in Christ and echo 2:6-11. Verses 15-16 and 20-21 are first person plural and frame the warning in vv. 18-19, which is in the first person singular. The effect of the pronoun shift is one of strong comparison; 4:1 is a summary exhortation delivered in highly emotional and affectionate language.

In light of what he has shared of his own biography in 3:6-14 (which in her article "Philippians: Theology for the Heavenly Politeuma," 99, Pheme Perkins calls "apologetic autobiography"), Paul urges Philippians who, like himself, are "mature" to continue to do as they are doing, to hold fast to the level of maturity they have attained. That he can use his biography in this way is evidence that his authority has not been challenged in Philippi. The context is, of course, the opponents alluded to in 3:2-3, 18-19. Whether or not these are the same opponents/enemies or different groups is a scholarly conundrum. In 3:2-3 they seem to be Judaizers of some sort who insist on circumcision and Torah observance. Could these same persons exhibit the libertinism alluded to in v. 19? Many scholars think not and suggest the church is attacked on two fronts: Judaizers who insist on the Law, and libertines or "antinomians." The identity of the enemies cannot be definitively established on the basis of the text alone. (For a balanced evaluation of the textual evidence see Fee, *Philippians*, 367–70.) Whoever they are, they make a god of appetite, glory in what they should be ashamed of, are attentive to earthly things, and are under divine judgment. What is clear is that Paul wants Philippian believers to hold onto what *he* taught them, indeed to imitate him (3:17) and his close associates (2:19-30).

In my view 3:17 provides the key to the structure of the Philippian letter. Paul alternates personal examples (both himself and others) of whom he approves with instructions to the Philippians about their own behavior. (See the section on "Form and Structure of Philippians" in "Literary Backgrounds for the Study of Philippians" in the Introduction, and compare Paul's similar approach in 1 Cor 10:23–11:1.) The contrast in 3:15-21 is between the Philippians who are trying to follow "good examples" and the "enemies of the cross of Christ" described in vv. 18-19. "Enemies of the cross" is a particularly damning epithet for Paul, for whom the cross is central in his preaching. "Christ died for our sins" is the starting point of Pauline christology (see Rom 5:6-8 or 1 Cor 15:3, for example). That act is also the cornerstone of Paul's ethical thought. Christians are, likewise, to give their lives for one another (here see 2:1-4). As Joseph Plevnik noted in his article "The Center of Pauline Theology," ". . . in the apostle's theology, the twofold event, Christ's death and resurrection, seen in its saving significance, is a primary notion with respect to justification by faith or participation in Christ" (p. 476). Both Paul's teaching on justification by faith and what has been called his "Christ mysticism" begin with the cross.

In this section of Philippians the "enemies of the cross," whose lives are focused "on earthly things" (v. 19), are contrasted with the "citizens of heaven" in vv. 20-21, verses of particular interest because it has been suggested that they are a hymn fragment. Certainly their vocabulary echoes that of 2:6-11. Perhaps the strongest case that 3:20-21 is a hymn fragment is made by John Reumann in "Philippians 3:20-21—A Hymnic Fragment?" (See Excursus I above on early Christian hymns.) Reumann, who assumes that Philippians is a composite of three letters, notes that there is no introductory formula at 3:20 to introduce the "hymn." In terms of style it shares with other NT hymns the use of participial phrases, a rhythmic style, and simple syntax. Lexically it exhibits the use of the relative pronoun *hos* ("who"), which is found in many hymns, and an unusual vocabulary for Paul that is both liturgical and exalted. In content, like many hymns, vv. 20-21 reflect early creedal formulas, a presentation of the basic truths of salvation history, and an acclamation of Jesus' lordship. On the basis of its structure and apocalyptic thought framework, Reumann offers the tentative conclusion that this is a hymn fragment that both the Philippians and Paul knew and that supports Paul's position here. That is, this fragment is used much as the hymn in 2:6-11 was.

Whether or not 3:20-21 is a hymn fragment, the many parallels to 2:6-11 have frequently been noted. In 1956 Neal Flanagan succinctly outlined the literary and doctrinal parallels between the two. Exact phrases or words containing the same lexical roots that occur in both places include the following: heavens (2:10; 3:20), exists/is (2:6; 3:20), Lord Jesus Christ (2:11; 3:20), appearance (2:7; 3:21), humility (2:8; 3:21), form (2:6, 7; 3:21), and glory (2:11; 3:21). Even the most careful scholar can suppose that in 3:20-21 Paul is consciously using the same vocabulary that appeared in the Christ hymn. Paul wants those hearing the letter read aloud to be put in mind of the hymn, and this for at least two reasons.

First, in chapter 2 Paul had presented the pattern of Christ's life as the model to be followed (2:5), just as here he presents himself and his associates as models to be followed (2:17). He is using these passages to refute false assumptions. Second, the theological point of 2:6-11, that Jesus emptied himself of status and thus was raised up by God, is precisely the matter at hand in 3:1–4:1. Paul is attempting to combat those who elevate themselves. His point is that if the Philippians follow the proper models, God will "raise them up." Flanagan's comment is worth citing in its entirety: ". . . God became man to make men God. This doctrine, as applied to the *soul* of the Christian, is found at every turn in the writings of

St. Paul. It must also be applied to the *body.* The glorious body . . . which Christ did not demand at the time of His incarnation will be given to us. What Christ, in His humility, did not insist upon for himself at birth, He will bestow on us" (p. 9).

Verses 20-21, then, serve as a clear summary of Paul's argument in this section of the letter. First, that they are to receive a "new body" reminds the Philippians that, while they have attained some maturity, they have not attained perfection. That is yet to come. Realized eschatology and personal triumphalism are both ruled out. Second, the verses reflect Paul's understanding that resurrection is not resuscitation of the flesh, but something else in which the "resurrection body" will have some continuity with, but be different from, the "earthly body" (compare Paul's reasoning in 1 Corinthians 15 and Mary of Magdala's encounter with the risen Christ in John 20).

In *Paul: A Critical Life* Jerome Murphy-O'Connor has pointed out the many important parallels between this section of Philippians and the Galatian letter. The autobiographical material in 3:4-8 is echoed in Galatians 1. Righteousness earned from obedience to the Law and righteousness given by God through faith in Christ appears both here and in Galatians 3–4 (compare, for example Phil 3:9 and Gal 2:16). That salvation is a continual stretching toward a goal summarizes Paul's teaching in Galatians 5–6. In Gal 6:17 Paul bears Jesus' stigmata and in Phil 3:10 yearns to share his sufferings. And the call to imitate Paul in 3:17 echoes Gal 4:12. Murphy-O'Connor's observations serve as an important reminder that Philippians 3 is a major, if often neglected, source of Pauline theology.

It is worth highlighting that one of several comparisons in 3:15–4:1 is between earthly and heavenly citizenship. The issue is really that of ultimate loyalty. The Philippians were proud citizens of a city governed by Roman law. Paul must remind them that their *real* citizenship is heavenly; their final loyalty is not to Rome, or even to him, but to the enthroned Christ (2:10-11). This is a particularly important word for citizens of the proud and mighty nations in our own day. No matter how good one's earthly citizenship is, the Christians' ultimate citizenship is in heaven, and they must live under its laws and mandates and no other, lesser ones (no matter how good they may seem) should be allowed to take precedence. In Paul's view Christian communities are, in fact, outposts of heaven and their citizens bow the knee only to Christ.

Another point well worth pondering is that God has an eternal purpose for the human body. This means it is important how one treats, uses, and cares for it now. Paul here reminds the Philippians of the eternal destiny of the human body. It will be transfigured to become like the Lord's body. The enemy of the body, death, has been destroyed by Jesus Christ. Whatever harms the body is not only transgressing against God's property; it is ignoring the body's astonishing potential and end. (Paul expounds on these ideas in Rom 8:1-17 and 1 Corinthians 5; 6:12-20; 15:35-58, and compare 1 John 3:2.)

A final theological note: Many scholars have noted that 3:1–4:1 presents all the features of Paul's understanding of salvation. Loosely following the schema set out in Marvin R. Vincent's commentary (pp. 121–22), this would include: (1) a "prior life," vv. 4-6, (2) a recognition of its incompleteness, vv. 7-8, (3) an act of faith in Christ, justification through faith, vv. 8-9, (4) that results in a deep spiritual union with Christ's life, vv. 10-11; also (5) that life is not perfect, but involves striving toward the goal of Christ, vv. 12-14, (6) with the promise of final transformation into the likeness of Christ, vv. 20-21. While the pattern is clearly that of individual transformation, it happens in the context of a community, a "commonwealth" whose citizens are "brethren," siblings striving together and supporting each other in the journey, the "walk" toward the same goal. In the context of Paul's understanding of Christian development, 3:15–4:1 reflects on the fullness of life with and in Christ that is promised to Christians.

For Reference and Further Study

Becker, Jürgen. "Erwägungen zu Phil. 3:20-21," *ThZ* 27 (1971) 16–29.

________. *Paul, Apostle to the Gentiles.* Louisville: Westminster John Knox, 1993, 322–31.

Doughty, D. J. "Citizens of Heaven: Phil. 3:2-21," *NTS* 41 (1995) 102–22.

Flanagan, Neal. "A Note on Philippians 3,20-21," *CBQ* 18 (1956) 8–9.

Käsemann, Ernst. "Pauline Theology of the Cross," *Int* 24 (1970) 151–77.

Klijn, A. F. J. "Paul's Opponents in Philippians iii," *NovT* 7 (1965) 278–84.

Murphy-O'Connor, Jerome. *Paul: A Critical Life.* Oxford: Clarendon Press, 1996, 223–30.

Parrent, A. H. "Dual Citizens, Not Resident Aliens," *Sewanee Theological Review* 44 (2000) 44–49.

Perkins, Pheme. "Philippians: Theology for the Heavenly Politeuma," in Jouette M. Bassler, ed., *Pauline Theology I.* Minneapolis: Fortress, 1991, 89–104.

Plevnik, Joseph. "The Center of Pauline Theology," *CBQ* 51 (1989) 461–78.

Reumann, John. "Philippians 3:20-21—A Hymnic Fragment?" *NTS* 30 (1984) 593–609.

THE EXAMPLE OF EUODIA AND SYNTYCHE: 4:2-3

2. I entreat Euodia and I entreat Syntyche to think the same things in the Lord. 3. Yes, I also ask you, true yokefellow, assist them who struggled with me in the gospel, also with Clement and the rest of my fellow workers, whose names [are] in [the] Book of Life.

Notes

2. *I entreat Euodia and I entreat Syntyche:* "Entreat" *(parakalō)* is from a word that literally means "call alongside" and has as a first definition "beg," with implications of both "encouraging" and "consoling." It carries a sense of urgency, but not necessarily of censure. We do not know who Euodia and Syntyche were. Clearly they were women leaders in the church in Philippi, a church that was founded among women (see Acts 16) and that, historically, had prominent women leaders. (See the section on women in Philippi in the Introduction, and Tarn's *Hellenistic Civilization.*) The meaning of their names is intriguing. "Euodia" means "good journey" or "pleasant." (Some have made the omicron an omega, *euōdia*, and thus "sweet smelling" as per 4:18.) "Syntyche" has as its root *tychē*, Greek for the Latin *Fortuna*, the goddess of good luck. The name (like that of Epaphroditus) may mean its bearer was formerly a pagan. The prefix *syn* meaning "with" implies unity (see the Note on 3:3). Both are attested names. By repeating the verb with each name Paul gives the women equal prominence, declining to take sides linguistically in their disagreement, and thus intensifies his entreaty.

   to think the same things in the Lord: "To think" *(phronein)* is another appearance of that important term in Philippians, "to be minded," "to have an habitual attitude." Its use here recalls the important issue of unity raised at 2:1-5, especially v. 2, which uses the same phrase, and v. 5 where forms of the word appear. Spatially closer in the letter are the imperatives of 3:15-16, where the mature are to be like-minded, and if they are not, to wait for God's revelation. The term itself is a call for one-mindedness and links an individual case with the general appeal of the letter that the Philippians maintain their unity. "The same things" gives no clue about the nature of the conflict or disagreement between these two women leaders. That it is "in the Lord," however, implies it is not a petty personality conflict, but has to do with the mission of the Gospel in Philippi, their role as *leaders,* not their gender as women. It simply indicates a disagreement that can be resolved "in the Lord," a motive to which Paul has appealed before in this epistle (see 2:5).

3. *Yes, I also ask you, true yokefellow:* The word *nai* ("yes") is a particle of confirmation or assent. Here the verb changes from the more energetic "entreat" to the quieter form "ask" *(erōtō)*. "You" is singular; someone is being addressed. There is a question about the word *syzyge*, here translated by the word "yokefellow." Is this a proper name, *Syzygus* (as per *NJB*), or a general description of an unknown person (as per *KJV, NAS, NIV, NAB*)? Some argue the noun in the vocative masculine singular should be read as a proper name and thus some-

one Paul is singling out to help the women reconcile. But to my knowledge there is no evidence of the existence of this name at the time. The image behind the term is that of being "yoked together," like beasts of burden pulling a load together. The adjective for "true" *(gēneios)* appeared at 2:20. Apparently Paul appeals to a third fellow worker to help reconcile the two women leaders. The person is unknown, although several scholars have made a case for Epaphroditus whom we know from 2:25-30 Paul is sending home (for more see Fee, *Philippians,* 393–96).

assist them who struggled with me in the gospel: The verb for "assist" *(syllambanou)* is a compound opening with *sy[n]* ("together") that literally means "bring together." It is a word used in the Gospel of Luke for fishermen pulling in the nets together (Luke 5:7). "Struggled" *(synēthlēsan)* means "fought alongside of" (compare 1:27-28). Paul and these women have labored side by side, not, note, the *apostle* Paul over them as "authority" or "leader" but side by side; the description is important. Whoever these women were, Paul views them as his fellow "athletes" on behalf of the Gospel, another point in the case against Paul the misogynist. His care is not only for the unity of the Philippian church, but for two individuals who are his friends in it. Note, as well, that Paul speaks of these women much as he did of Timothy (1:1; 2:19-24) and Epaphroditus (2:25-30, especially v. 25).

also with Clement and the rest of my fellow workers: The women are on a par with "Clement" (also otherwise unknown, but apparently a Philippian Christian and almost certainly not Clement of Rome) and others whom Paul calls "fellow workers" *(synergoi).* The term appears at 2:25 and elsewhere in the NT for itinerant workers who are equal to each other (compare 1:27) and is used in parallel literature for those fighting together in a war or working together on a team in the athletic arena (see "struggled" above).

whose names [are] in [the] Book of Life: The phrase literally reads "of whom the names in Book of Life." "Book of Life" echoes the eschatology of 3:20-21 and reflects several interesting trajectories of thought. In Hellenistic cities registers were kept of the names of the citizens of the city. Thus the phrase may connect with 1:27 and 3:19 with their "citizenship" metaphors. (Recall that Roman citizenship was also recorded.) In the OT the phrase is used for the record of the covenant (Exod 32:32; Ps 69:28; Dan 12:1; Isa 4:3; Ezek 13:9) and in the rest of the NT for those who will inherit the life to come (Luke 10:20; Rev 3:5; 18:8; 20:12), which, again, ties in nicely with the end of chapter 3, especially vv. 20-21. To be listed in the Book of Life is to be a citizen of God's commonwealth (3:20). Verse 3 is dominated by words with the prefix *sy* or *syn* (four words) meaning "with" or "together." Apparently Paul has chosen these terms for effect and to emphasize what he is asking, that the church be drawn together rather than torn apart.

Interpretation

Paul's letters often close with greetings and instructions to specifically named persons. Here 4:2-3 picks up the theme of unity, the issue that seems to have precipitated the letter. It represents a case in point of the general concern the apostle has for the Philippian church. The language here echoes that of 2:1-5, which introduced the Christ hymn of 2:6-11, an example of the life on which Christian unity is modeled. Indeed, Boyd Luter asserts that 4:2-3 parallels 2:2-4 ("Partnership in the Gospel," 412). If so, it is a "reverse image," the negative side of Paul's positive injunction.

Apparently two prominent women in the Philippian community are having a disagreement, the subject of which is not specified. This presents yet another challenge to the unity of the church. Paul almost never mentions his opponents by name. That he does here reinforces the perception that these women are his friends. That they are mentioned by name is a mark of their importance. According to John Chrysostom, "it appears . . . that these women were heads of the church at Philippi" (*Nicene and Post Nicene Fathers* [Grand Rapids: Eerdmans, 1979] 13:244). David Garland suggests that the primary purpose of Philippians was to diffuse the controversy between these two women ("Composition and Unity"). Spiritual leadership, even spiritual maturity, does not, alas, prevent such manifestations of "the flesh." Paul's approach to the problem substantially follows that outlined in Matt 18:15-20; he asks a fellow Christian, one who has apparently worked with the women before and thus would know them well, to adjudicate the disagreement.

Although brief, this is an important text for the wider issue of Paul's position vis-à-vis women in the church. Here there is no restriction on the role of women. In fact, Veronica Koperski ("Feminist Concerns") argues that Gal 3:28 is most evidently realized at Philippi. Recall that, according to Acts 16, the church in Philippi was founded among women and that Macedonian women were noted for their competence in public venues. (The evidence for the prominence of women in the Philippian church is marshaled in the article by Boyd Luter, "Partnership in the Gospel.") Paul assumes their leadership; what is in question is their disagreement. The witness of these strong women is diluted if they disagree. More to the point, the unity of the church itself will be jeopardized. Paul's expressions of confidence in recipients of a letter are designed to reinforce the purpose of the letter and to gain the confidence of those addressed. That strategy is at work here as he compliments the women before making a direct request of them and the "true yokefellow." But of course, in accordance with the conventions of friendship, the request is implied rather than directly stated.

The spiritual issues here are important ones. First, leadership in the Christian community presumes that leaders will transcend their private preferences and differences for the good of the whole community. Second, when there is dissension in a community, the community itself is to help in the healing, not "take sides" and widen the rifts.

For Reference and Further Study

Note: For a fuller bibliography of the place of women in Philippi see "The Place of Women in the Philippian Church" in the Introduction.

Ellis, E. Earle. "Paul and His Co-Workers," *NTS* 17 (1971) 437–52.
Ezell, Douglas. "The Sufficiency of Christ: Philippians 4," *RevExp* 77 (1980) 373–81.
Furnish, Victor P. "Fellow Workers in God's Service," *JBL* 80 (1961) 364–70.
Garland, David E. "The Composition and Unity of Philippians," *NovT* 27 (1985) 141–73.
Koperski, Veronica. "Feminist Concerns and the Authorial Readers in Philippians," *Louvain Studies* 17 (1992) 269–92.
Luter, Boyd. "Partnership in the Gospel: The Role of Women in the Church at Philippi," *JETS* 39 (1996) 411–20.
Murray, George W. "Paul's Corporate Witness in Philippians," *BibSac* 155 (1998) 316–26.
Olson, Stanley N. "Pauline Expressions of Confidence in His Addressees," *CBQ* 47 (1985) 282–95.
Russell, Ronald. "Pauline Letter Structure in Philippians," *JETS* 25 (1982) 295–306.

INSTRUCTIONS TO THE PHILIPPIANS: 4:4-9

Toward the end of the body of Paul's letters one normally finds several kinds of material, which may include epistolary *topoi* (self-contained teachings on a single subject with only loose connection to the context), *paraenesis* (closing ethical exhortation), the sending and receiving of greetings, travel plans, and general autobiographical statements. The body of Philippians draws to a close with final instructions to the Philippians, first an entreaty to two members of the community (4:2-3), then a *topos* on prayer (4:4-7), and finally *paraenesis*, a closing exhortation in the form of a virtue list (4:8-9). In style these verses resemble similar short, pithy imperatives that close 1 and 2 Corinthians and 1 Thess 5:12-22. To highlight the different literary forms I have separated the *topoi* from the virtue list in the translation and notes. The single interpretation section (as in 2:19-30) indicates their relatedness.

On Prayer (4:4-7)

4. Rejoice in the Lord always. Again I say, rejoice. 5. [Let] your forbearance be known [to] all persons. The Lord is at hand. 6. Be anxious in nothing, but in everything, by prayer and supplication with thanksgiving, let your requests be known to the God. 7. And the peace of God surpassing all understanding will guard your hearts and your minds in Christ Jesus.

Notes

4. *Rejoice in the Lord always. Again I say, rejoice: Chairete* can also be translated "farewell," but as "joy" is a leitmotif of the letter (1:4, 18, 19; 2:2, 17, 18, 29; 3:1; 4:1), that seems an unwarranted rendering of the word. "Rejoicing" is the key emotional note of the letter (forms of the word occur sixteen times), and its appearance in the imperative often marks transitions between sections (see 3:1). The question has been raised whether this is an imperative or an optative, a mood used to express a wish; that is, "may you always be joyful." "Always" means "in whatever circumstances," present or future, in positive circumstances or in trial. The command takes on special poignancy in light of Paul's circumstances (1:12-26) and the Philippian church's difficulties (1:27-30; 3:2-3). Consistent with other occurrences in the epistle, here all rejoicing is "in the Lord," and Christians should find their satisfaction in him (compare 1:21). The source and end of Christian joy is the hope Christ offers in one's personal relationship with him. Repetition of the imperative "rejoice" gives emphasis and is an indication of how strongly Paul feels about the matter. The second person plural suggests the corporate or communal aspect of Christian piety that, again, characterizes this letter.

5. *[Let] your forbearance be known [to] all persons:* The word here rendered "forbearance" (*epieikes,* sometimes translated "moderation") is difficult to translate. In the LXX it is used for a quality of God (see Ps 85:5). Luther suggests this translation: "Let your lenity *(Lindigkeit)* be made known." It means reasonableness in judging as well as an attitude that does not seek retaliation. Douglas Ezell suggests it implies "meeting a person half way" ("The Sufficiency of Christ," 376; compare its nominal use in 2 Cor 10:1). It implies both self-discipline and courtesy and respect for the dignity of others. Barth's commentary notes that Johannes Bengel saw a connection between joy and "lenience": "joy in the Lord begets true equity" (quoted in Barth, *Philippians,* 121). Perhaps the word came to Paul's mind in light of the situation presented in 4:2-3. Forbearance is exactly the attitude the two women need if church unity is to be maintained. The Philippian Christians are to be reasonable in all circumstances so that everyone, not just fellow Christians, will take note. Paul is frequently concerned with what outsiders will see of Christians and therefore conclude about Christianity (compare, for example, Romans 13).

The Lord is at hand: Paul's imperatives are interrupted by this statement of fact. Gordon Fee suggests that Ps 145:18 may have been "between" 5a and 5b. "At hand" or "near" *(eggys)* can be used both spatially and temporally. One could argue, then, that the imperative is a reminder of the Lord's ever-nearness, a mystical concept, or of the nearness of the "Day of the Lord," an eschatological statement. Paul refers to the "day of the Lord" or the "day of Christ" earlier in the letter (1:6; 2:16), and the end of chapter 3 (3:20-21) and 4:3 ("Book of Life") both have eschatological overtones. Whether this reflects the expectation of a temporally imminent return of Christ is unclear. What is clear is Paul's deep, existential understanding of the implications of "Emmanuel," God with us, as a motive for action.

6. *Be anxious in nothing, but in everything:* The phrase plays on the tension between the opposites "nothing" and "everything." These are the two options: anxiety or prayer. "Anxious" *(merimnate)* implies both anxiety and trouble (what one "frets over" or "broods on") and was used at 2:20 in the context of concern for another's welfare. Paul's command is made in the context of any number of things they might well be anxious about: persecution, opponents, divisiveness, and enemies. Certainly Paul has spoken of the Philippians' anxiety about him (1:12-26; 2:17–3:1).

by prayer and supplication with thanksgiving: The phrase, which reads in Greek "by *the* prayer and *the* supplication" (italics mine), is a constellation of words, each describing a category of prayer. "Prayer" *(proseuchē)* has as its root verb *euchomai,* which means both "to pray to God" and "to wish." It is found exclusively in the context of addressing the deity. In parallel literature the word is used for prayer addressed to God and has the derived meaning of a place *for* prayer. Interestingly, this latter usage is found in Acts 16:13 for the place of prayer where Paul found Lydia and her companions when he came to Philippi. The Vulgate translates the noun *oratio.* "Supplication" *(deēsis)* is used for petitions addressed both to God and to human beings. The verbal form derives from *deō,* "want" or "need." In classical usage it denotes "asking," "wanting," and "needing," so suggests an expression of personal need, what might now be termed "petitionary prayer." The Vulgate translates the verb *deprecatio.* The phrase "prayer and supplication" is frequent in the NT and the terms are nearly interchangeable, although the first is used for prayer in general and the second of specific requests. "With thanksgiving" *(eucharistia)* suggests that thanksgiving or gratitude is the attitude that should accompany and characterize all prayer. That it appears without the definite article ("the") underscores its generality. Every request made to God is made in the context of gratitude for what God has already done and given. (For a wonderful study on this important idea see David Steindl-Rast, *Gratefulness, The Heart of Prayer* [New York: Paulist, 1984].)

let your requests be known to the God: The point is subtle; one makes *requests (aitēmata)* of God; one does not command or demand. The object of prayer is "the God," the One God and Father of Jesus Christ, not any of the deities of the Greco-Roman world. Paul apparently introduces the Semitism here for clarity's sake.

7. *And the peace of God:* The coordinating conjunction "and" indicates that what follows is a result of what preceded. If v. 6 is the charge, v. 7 is the result. The phrase "the peace of God" appears only here in the NT. God's peace is never, in the Bible, the absence of conflict, but something much deeper. That God is the source of peace is a Pauline assumption (Rom 15:33; 16:20).

surpassing all understanding: "Surpassing" *(hyperexousa)* means "to rise above" or "to be superior to." "Understanding" *(nous)* means "mind," the faculty of human intelligence. What is being offered in Christ is above what the human intellect can achieve or comprehend (compare Eph 3:18-19, part of a prayer for human understanding of a divine attribute). The phrase serves as a subtle reminder to us not to be prisoners of the Enlightenment, not to assume rationality is the only way of knowing. That mistake stunts the possibility of many kinds of growth in the interior life.

will guard your hearts and your minds in Christ Jesus: "Guard" is a military term. Behind it is the idea of a garrison keeping watch. The old translation "keep" was a good one insofar as the "keep" was the place at the center of the castle where valuables (and people) were put for safety. Note the distinction between "heart," in biblical anthropology the core of the person, the center of willing, feeling, and thinking, and thus of personality, and "mind," Paul's term for the rational, thinking self. Both, and thus the whole of the person, are guarded or protected in Christ Jesus (compare Prov 4:23). The verse has three separate but related ideas: (1) the peace of God that cannot be humanly/rationally explained, (2) the military metaphor of "keeping" or "protecting" the heart, (3) the idea that all of this is "in Christ," within the sphere of Christ's concern and influence. A very similar exhortation is found in 1 Pet 5:7.

Virtue List and Final Exhortation (4:8-9)

8. Finally, brethren, whatever is true, whatever noble, whatever just, whatever pure, whatever acceptable, whatever praiseworthy, if any virtue and if any praise, consider these things. 9. And what things you learned and received and heard and saw in me, do these, and the God of peace will be with you.

Notes

8. *Finally, brethren, whatever is true:* In v. 8 there are six plural adjectives preceded by *hosa* ("whatever") and two singular nouns preceded by *ei tis.* The verse is a Greco-Roman virtue list, a teaching technique probably borrowed from the Stoics that lists virtues (and in the case of vice and virtue lists, the vices) a teacher wishes his students to exhibit (or shun). None here is specifically Christian; all were highly commended in Greek philosophy. (For more on

Paul's use of such lists see Ralph Martin, NCBC *Philippians,* 157–58; and for a particularly helpful reading see Fee, NICNT *Philippians,* 413–21.) "Finally" *(to loipon)* was discussed at length at 3:1. Here it seems to mark the end of a unit of material. "Brethren" *(adelphoi),* used so frequently in this epistle, is a familial term. Paul is speaking to his siblings in Christ. "Truth" is one of the highest virtues in the Greco-Roman pantheon of virtues and thus opens the list.

whatever noble: "Noble" *(semna)* means "worthy of respect," "awe-inspiring," "dignified," thus "noble." The now antiquated term "venerable" might catch the sense of moral excellence that is implied.

whatever just: "Just" *(dikaia)* is at the root of the term "righteousness." It is a relational term and suggests the communal nature of virtue. It might have echoed the language of 3:9 and served as a reminder that justice, too, is ultimately from God. Justice is a key virtue for peaceful communal life.

whatever pure: "Pure" *(hagna)* is formed with an alpha privative, so it is a particularly strong word. It implies moral purity, although it is the word the LXX uses for the ceremonially pure (compare Acts 21:24; 24:18). It is applied to Christ in 1 John 3:3.

whatever acceptable: The word *prosphilē* is a compound, literally "toward lovely," thus "pleasing," "lovely," or "attractive." It is a *hapax legomenon* implying things whose grace attracts. It points toward the value of aesthetic beauty in the moral and spiritual life. The connotation of the word has evangelistic implications in that Paul commands the Philippians to live in ways that will be attractive to others.

whatever praiseworthy: Also a *hapax, euphēma* means "well-sounding," thus "praiseworthy" or "appealing." Again the appeal is to the reputation of Christians (and thus Christianity) in the larger community (see the Note on 4:5).

if any virtue, and if any praise: Here the construction changes from the plural adjective to an abstract pronoun *(tis).* The shift is from the six specific virtues just enumerated to comprehensive ones. "Virtue" *(aretē)* was one of the most important terms in Hellenistic philosophy. It does not appear elsewhere in Paul, but is found in 1 Pet 2:9 and 2 Pet 1:3, 5. In Greek moral thinking it is the comprehensive term for moral excellence of any kind, so it serves as a summary idea here. The construction in Greek implies the positive answer (compare 2:1). There *is* virtue, and praise. Paul has just been praising them.

consider these things: Here the verb is not *phroneō* ("to be minded"), which has appeared so frequently heretofore. "Consider" or "think on" *(logizesthe)* means "meditate on" or "mull over" and was used at 3:13. The invitation/ command is literally to fill the mind with these virtues. Paul is an astute psychologist and knows that the greatest area of sin is that of thought, and so he gives "alternatives" to sinful or even useless or trivial or petty thoughts (compare the Note on the first phrase of 3:15). As the Sermon on the Mount makes clear, a Christian must be as careful in thought as in action (Matt 5:21-48).

9. *And what things you learned and received and heard and saw in me, do these:* Verse 9 might be called a catalogue of Hellenistic "learning styles." It echoes 3:17, albeit in more detail. It not only enumerates the ways Paul taught, but

suggests something of the sources of his teaching. The verse opens with four verbs preceded by "and." *Manthanō* is the ordinary verb for "learn." "Received" *(paralabete)*, however, is a technical term for what is handed down and received in tradition. It is the term Paul uses at 1 Cor 11:23 for his reception of the words of institution of Jesus at the Last Supper and at 1 Cor 15:3 for the *kērygma*. "Hearing and seeing" represent two ways one learns from a teacher. One hears his or her words and then sees whether or not they are lived out in the teacher's life (compare Jas 1:22, and see the Notes on 3:17 above). "Do these" carries the idea of continuous action or repetition. "Practice these virtues" is Paul's command.

and the God of peace will be with you: The phrase "the God of peace" appears only in Paul (Rom 15:33; 16:20; 1 Thess 5:23) and in Heb 13:20. Note again "the God" from v. 6 as well as the repetition of the first phrase of v. 7. The two parts of v. 9 reflect the command/result pattern just seen in vv. 6, 7; "if you do x, y will result." The source of true peace is restored relationship to God, which for Paul comes through Jesus Christ.

Interpretation

In many ways 4:2-20 reflects aspects of the closing of other Pauline letters. At the end of the body of a letter Paul characteristically greets friends, gives news about himself and his plans, gives instructions, and speaks of his prayers for the letter's recipients. Certainly 4:4-9 continues the pattern in Philippians of alternating blocks of material that present personal examples, both positive and negative (1:12-16; 2:19-20; 4:2-3), and offer instructions to the Philippians (1:27–2:18; 3:1–4:1; 4:4-9). Here the instructions deal with two matters, prayer in 4:4-7 and attitudes or "mental dispositions" in 4:8-9. The verses address both the interior life and the exterior action that grows from it. Both result in particular actions that Paul commends.

Although his language and cast of mind are frequently prayerful, there are few examples of prayer texts in Paul's letters and few passages in which he gives explicit teaching about prayer. Philippians, however, has many references to Paul's prayers (1:4, 9) and to the Philippians' prayers for him (1:19). Philippians 4:4-7, especially vv. 6-7, is an explicit instruction on the life of prayer. That the Philippians should rejoice no matter what the external circumstances is Paul's most pervasive "advice" in this letter. It characterizes his own approach to life, an approach they are to imitate (3:17; 4:9). This attitude of joy, even in the face of difficulty, is itself an example of the forbearance or reasonableness v. 5 commends.

But Paul is a realist and knows human nature. People worry. And this worry or "anxiety," as v. 6 describes it, can be sinful because it is an "outward and visible sign" of the inward condition of not trusting God and

God's provident care. Paul suggests that the alternative to anxious fretting is prayer, in fact three forms of prayer: prayer for ourselves, prayer for others, and, most potently, thanksgiving. People worry and are anxious because they try to carry burdens that are too large for them. Paul's remedy for this common malady is to suggest what Ps 55:22 also urges: transfer the load to One who can bear it and still sustain. Perhaps the greatest antidote to anxiety is gratitude, "counting our blessings" in common parlance. Prayer and supplication are always made in the context of gratitude for what God has already done and given.

If anxiety is one of the sufferings we inflict upon ourselves, peace is a gift that God is ready to give to all comers. Verse 7 describes the practical result of a life of prayer. The one who prays will be a peaceful person. She or he will receive the peace of God that is unaffected by the external events of life, the peace that "passes understanding." Indeed, those who exhibit such peace are living conundrums in the world in which we live. How can they be so serene in the face of such turmoil, injustice, and suffering? The answer is: not because of anything they do, but because of the One *in whom* they live, the One who "keeps" or "guards" them. Prayer continues the process of transformation Paul described in 3:7-16 in part because it transfers the heart and mind (the life of affect and will and intellect) to the realm of Jesus Christ. The quality of life Paul is commending here is precisely what Jesus described in the Sermon on the Mount in Matt 6:25-34 (compare Luke 12:22-34).

As Douglas Ezell suggests, 4:8-9 describes how those who know the peace of God are to live in the world, what they are to "think" (v. 8) and "do" (v. 9) ("The Sufficiency of Christ," 377). Since the way we think determines how we live, in 4:8 Paul gives principles to determine the conduct of the mind. Verse 8 lists recommended "contents" for the "heart and mind" in a typical virtue list. Paul borrowed the genre of vice and virtue lists from Hellenistic pedagogy. It has been suggested that the use of the form was common before Paul, who then made use of an "approved" teaching method. Certainly vice and virtue lists are common in the early church and appear in Paul's writings, 1 Peter, James, and later in the *Didache*, *Barnabas*, and the Qumran *Manual of Discipline*, and catalogues of virtues were widely used by the Stoics in their teaching. The form of such teaching is as follows: an imperative verb is followed by a list of either vices to be avoided or virtues to be practiced. In 4:8-9 Paul reverses the pattern and lists the virtues first and then the imperative, "think about them." In Paul's letters vice and virtue lists are often linked with eschatological passages or thought (see, for example, Gal 5:21; 1 Cor 6:9). Here the virtue list is loosely in the context of such thought (4:3, "book of life," and 4:4, "the Lord is at hand"). None of the virtues commended is specifically Christian; all are highly esteemed in Greco-Roman writing. The six specific virtues (all neuter plural adjectives in Greek) are summarized by the last two (nouns) in the list by "excellence" and "worthy of praise." Paul is suggesting that the Christians of Philippi, citizens of heaven though they are (3:20), act in ways that are approved of in their earthly community.

If v. 8 borrows a Hellenistic teaching technique, v. 9 reflects Paul's understanding of what and how people learn (see the Notes on v. 9 above). Some lessons are "received"; they are "handed on" by the tradition. Some are learned by listening to and, more importantly, watching a teacher. The old saw "actions speak louder than words" applies here. One of the teaching principles of the whole epistle is to present clear, personal examples (Jesus Christ, Timothy, Epaphroditus, Clement, himself) of what Paul wants the Philippians to do so they can "see" what they are to "do." Together 3:17 and 4:9 provide what in my view is the structural key to the whole letter (Colossians 3:1-3 provides an excellent gloss).

Two related elements are noteworthy. First, in this closing exhortation Paul does not reject outright the culture of the Philippian converts. In fact, he specifically uses language and forms of literature they would recognize. Moreover, v. 8 commends attitudes and actions the culture would laud. Rather than condemn aspects of culture he opposes, Paul lifts up what is commensurate with the Christian Way. Second, his concern for the moral well being of his friends reflects what was commonly understood as a requirement of friendship. Not only hospitality and reciprocity characterized friendship; concern for the moral well being of one's friends was expected. Friends did not let friends run wild (see Aristotle, *Nicomachean Ethics* chs. 8–9). In a hortatory letter of friendship, which many scholars take Philippians to be, a passage of this nature is *de rigueur*. Such explicit use of the conventions of friendship prepares the reader/hearer for 4:10-20, which follows.

Note that both sections of this text close with references to the peace of God. If the Philippians are people of prayer and if they "think about" virtues and thus "become them," they will be open and disposed to receive the gift of God's peace. It is as the prophet Isaiah said, "Thou wilt keep him in perfect peace, whose mind is stayed on thee, because he trusteth in thee" (26:3, *KJV*). Philippians 4:4-9 sets forth the model of Christian life, which is to be joyful, prayerful, moderate, and peaceful. It can be so because it is protected, "kept" by God. As Karl Barth noted, "The peace of God is the order and security of the kingdom of Christ among those that are his" (*Philippians,* 123).

The body of the Philippian letter comes to a close on a note of joy and peace. Neither exists independently of suffering or persecution, but in the midst of both. One who seeks to live as Christ lived enters into the source of his own joy and peace, the inner life of God.

For Reference and Further Study

Bradley, David G. "The *Topos* as a Form in the Pauline Paraenesis," *JBL* 72 (1953) 238–46.

Cannon, George E. *The Use of Traditional Materials in Colossians.* Macon, GA: Mercer University Press, 1983. Chapter 3 deals with vice and virtue lists.

Easton, B. S. "New Testament Ethical Lists," *JBL* 51 (1932) 1–12.

Ezell, Douglas. "The Sufficiency of Christ: Philippians 4," *RevExp* 77 (1980) 373–81.

Murphy-O'Connor, Jerome. *Paul the Letter Writer.* Collegeville: Liturgical Press, 1995.

Reumann, John H. P. "Philippians and the Culture of Friendship," *Trinity Seminary Review* 19 (1997) 69–83.

Russell, Ronald. "Pauline Letter Structure in Philippians," *JETS* 25 (1982) 295–306.

Stendahl, Krister. "Paul at Prayer," *Int* 34 (1980) 240–49.

Witherington, Ben III. *Friendship and Finances in Philippi.* Valley Forge, PA: Trinity Press International, 1994.

THANK YOU: 4:10-20

10. So I have rejoiced in [the] Lord greatly because now at last your thinking on my behalf sprouts again, upon whom you were thinking, but
without opportunity [to show it]. 11. Not that I am speaking from lack,
for I myself learned in what I am to be content. 12. And I know [how] to
be made low, and I know [how] to abound. In everything, and in all
things, I have been initiated both to be filled and to hunger, both to
abound and to fall short. 13. I can do all things in the One empowering
me. 14. Nevertheless you did well sharing my suffering. 15. And also
you, yourselves, know, Philippians, that in the beginning of the gospel,
when I went out from Macedonia, not one church shared with me in
giving and receiving except you only 16. because also in Thessalonica,
both once and twice, you sent to my need. 17. Not that I am seeking the
gift, but I am seeking the fruit increasing into your account. 18. But I have
all things, and I abound; I have been filled, receiving from Epaphroditus
the things from you, an odor of sweet smell, an acceptable sacrifice,
pleasing to God. 19. And my God will fill every need of yours according
to his riches in glory in Christ Jesus. 20. Now to the God and our Father
[be] the glory unto the ages of ages. Amen.

Notes

10. *So I have rejoiced in [the] Lord greatly:* "So" (the particle *de*) marks the opening of a new unit of thought. Here the familiar word "rejoice" is in the aorist passive. It is an epistolary aorist and so is often rendered in the present tense, "I am rejoicing." As in 3:1, 4; 4:4 this rejoicing is "in the Lord," the source of Paul's joy. Here it is intense; he rejoices "greatly." In the face of his own uncertain circumstances and knowing his friends' difficulties, Paul still rejoices.

because now at last your thinking on my behalf sprouts again: "Now at last" represents an English rendering of a Greek idiom, *ēdē pote*. The word for "thinking" in this verse reflects the familiar (nine times in the letter) and important verb *phroneō*, "to be minded," "to have as a habitual attitude" (see, e.g., 1:7; 2:2; 4:2). To use "sprouts" in this context sounds odd in English, but reflects the Greek verb *anathallō*, "to shoot up," "to sprout again," which has a gardening or growth connotation (as plants). It is a botanical metaphor meaning "bloom again," and thus refers to doing again something previously done. The prepositional prefix *ana* has a causative force. After some lapse of time Paul knows the Philippians are once more considering him.

upon whom you were thinking, but without opportunity [to show it]: Perhaps realizing that the last phrase sounds harsh or ungrateful, Paul hastens to soothe the letter's recipients by saying he knows they were thinking about him, but that they had had no opportunity to show it. The form of *phroneō* here is imperfect active indicative, indicating continuous past action. The Philippians were thinking of Paul all along; "without opportunity" means they had had no chance to show their concern.

11. *Not that I am speaking from lack:* "Not that" signals a qualification to prevent misunderstanding (compare 2 Cor 1:24; 3:5). The word for "lack" here *(hysteresis)* is the same one used of the widow's poverty in Mark 12:44. Paul wants to assure the Philippians that he is not in need, and thus the letter is not an appeal for support of some sort. Seneca, for example, wrote that mentioning a need could be understood as a request for help. Paul is not "soliciting" the Philippians for anything.

for I myself learned in what I am to be content: "Learned" may be a punctiliar aorist; at some point in time this idea "dawned on" Paul. He did not develop it through practice. "In what I am" renders the Greek literally. To do so extends the meaning of Paul's thought. It is not only that Paul has learned by experience to be content in whatever circumstances he finds himself, which he has done. He has also come to be content in "who he is"; he has made peace with himself. "To be content in which things I am" is not just about external gifts or needs, but reflects a profound and mature self-knowledge and peace in self-acceptance. "Content" *(autarkēs)* is a *hapax legomenon* meaning "self-sufficient." The word is found in Stoic ethical texts for the state of mind of a person independent of all things and people. It is one of the attributes of the wise person in Stoic teaching. When asked who was the wealthiest person, Socrates is said to have replied "the one who is content with least, for contentment is nature's well." Seneca wrote "the happy man is content with his present lot, no matter what it is, and is reconciled to his circumstances" (*De Vita Beata* 6.2). The word "serene" might describe the sort of person in view here. As in 4:8 Paul commends, or here practices, behavior of which the Philippian culture approved.

12. *And I know [how] to be made low, and I know [how] to abound:* Verse 12 is rhythmical and evinces antithetic parallelism similar to that found in Hebrew poetry. The verse fleshes out the meaning of the word "content" in v. 11. The verb for "know" here *(oida)* implies to know by experience as opposed to intellectual or theoretical knowledge. "To be made low" is the same root word *(tapeinos)* that appeared in 2:8 to describe Jesus; "he *humbled* himself," made himself "low." Humility was hardly a positive Stoic virtue or commended by Greco-Roman moralists. Its use here signals an important shift in thought (see the comments on 2:3 and 8). One cannot be made low if one has chosen the humility of the Christ. "Abound" literally means "overflow."

    In everything, and in all things, I have been initiated: The opening two prepositional phrases are intended to convey the comprehensive extent of Paul's attitude. "I have been initiated" *(memuēmai)* is from a verb used to describe the act of initiation into the mystery cults. Its use would have been striking to the Philippians, who might well have known it from its religious context. It suggests that what Paul "knows," he had to be "taught" or initiated into by someone else. The implication is that he learned it from the model of Christ (2:6-11). Again, what Paul knows, he knows by experience, not "in theory."

    both to be filled and to hunger, both to abound and to fall short: The phrase is built of two pairs of infinitives that express opposite ideas, continuing the antithetic parallelism. To "be full" *(chortazesthai)* is a word used of fattening up animals (for slaughter?). Paul has learned to be satiated and to be in hunger, to have more than enough and to suffer need, and all with equanimity. The whole verse works on the basis of the tension between opposites (compare 1:15-27).

13. *I can do all things in the One empowering me:* Verses 11 and 12 clearly depict Paul as a Stoic wise man. At this point a transformation is made explicit because, unlike the case of such a person, the source of Paul's wisdom and "contentment" is not his own achievement. It is "empowered" (*endynamounti,* which has as its root *dynamis,* power, a stronger word in English than "strengthened") by Christ. By himself Paul is powerless, but he can do all things with Christ (compare 1:21; 2:13, and recall that in Acts 18:18 Luke reports that Paul had his hair cut after his trip through Macedonia as a symbol of his complete dependence on God).

14. *Nevertheless you did well sharing my suffering:* As at 3:16 "nevertheless" *(plēn)* signals a shift in thought; Paul interrupts himself to prevent a misunderstanding (as he also did at 3:12 and 4:11a). Even though Paul is "content," the Philippians have done a good thing for him, which he wants to acknowledge. The word for "sharing" has as its root *koinōnia;* its nominal form *(sygkoinōnous)* appeared at 1:7, where Paul described the Philippians as "fellow sharers with me in my bonds." The word for suffering here *(thlipsis)* is used in Mark 13:19 for the suffering of the end times and occurs in a similar context in Paul at

2 Thess 1:6. The reference is to real tribulation (of the "deliver us from the time of trial" sort), not simple inconvenience. An important aspect of Christian fellowship, then, is always the fellowship of suffering. Christians are not to be "fair weather friends" to one another. Paul says the Philippians not only stood by him in his suffering, but *shared* it with him.

15. *And also you, yourselves, know, Philippians:* Verses 15-16 are replete with the vocabulary of Greco-Roman friendship and rehearse the history of Philippian support for Paul, using commercial language to express a relationship of social reciprocity. The verses commend the Philippians' behavior. Again, as in 4:12, the verb for "know" means "know by experience." The reflexive pronoun and the noun of direct address add dramatic effect. Paul is not imparting new information, but highlighting something well known.

that in the beginning of the gospel, when I went out from Macedonia: Paul's reference to "the beginning of the gospel" is apparently to the beginning of his mission in what we now call "Europe." According to Luke in Acts 16, Paul landed first in Macedonia and went directly to Philippi where, he reports in 1 Thess 2:1-2 (and suggests in 2 Cor 7:5), he was mistreated, as indeed Acts 16 records.

not one church shared with me in giving and receiving except you only: "Shared," again, has as its root *koinōnia*. "Giving and receiving" begins the use of a commercial metaphor that continues in vv. 16-18. Here it suggests payment into an account. Interpreters must be careful not to take the metaphor too far; this is a letter of friendship, not a business document. The phrase also reflects the mutuality that was always at the core of Paul's thinking about giving, what we now call "stewardship" (see, for example, 2 Corinthians 8–9, especially 8:1-14). Paul here singles out the Philippian church as being in a special relationship with him. They had entered into partnership with him at the outset of his European mission, and that partnership included financial support of Paul.

16. *because also in Thessalonica, both once and twice, you sent to my need:* "Both once and twice" reflects a Greek idiom that might more smoothly be rendered in English "more than once" (compare 1 Thess 2:18, and see Leon Morris, *"kai hapax kai dis,"* for a study of this *hapax*). The point is that the Philippians have sent aid to Paul on several occasions (as 2 Corinthians 8–9 bears out). The phrase is a subtle indication that Paul's relationship of friendship with them is quite different from that with Christians in Thessalonica (compare 2 Thess 3:7-10). The circumstances Paul described in vv. 15-16 are corroborated by remarks in 2 Corinthians in which Paul explains that he preached the Gospel "without cost" there: "I robbed other churches by accepting support from them in order to serve you. And when I was with you and was in want, I did not burden any one, for my needs were supplied by the brethren who came from Macedonia" (2 Cor 11:7-9). These Macedonians who supported Paul were themselves "in a severe test of affliction," and yet "their abundance of joy and their extreme poverty have overflowed in a wealth of liberality on their part" (2 Cor 8:2). They gave to Paul "beyond their means, of their own free will" (2 Cor 8:3). One of the reasons Paul is so fond of the Philippians is precisely that they supported him in their own crisis and from their own

meager circumstances. Although Gal 6:6 makes clear that a teacher might expect payment from students, here Paul cancels any such debt the Philippians might have.

17. *Not that I am seeking the gift:* This verse repeats the idea expressed at the outset of v. 11 and opens with the same phrase (see the Notes on v. 11 above). Paul is not seeking support from the Philippians. "Gift" *(doma)* is "what is given," not something earned as payment for services rendered (compare Eph 4:8). "Seek the gift" is considered by some scholars a technical term for payment of interest. If so, it continues the commercial metaphor from v. 15.

    but I am seeking the fruit increasing into your account: "Increasing into your account" certainly continues the commercial metaphor begun at v. 15 (and recall 3:7-8). It is a business term for paying into an account, rather like making a deposit in a savings account today. Here it is an earthly investment with heavenly dividends! Paul is not seeking something from the Philippians for his own sake, but in accepting their generosity, he allows them to exercise that important virtue. Paul's joy is not because his need is supplied, but because the Philippians are doing the right thing, that is, not in the gift itself, but in its "fruit" in their lives.

18. *But I have all things, and I abound:* But *(de)* is a connective to what preceded, coordinating and not adversative. As was implied in v. 11, here Paul makes clear that he has everything he needs not only materially, but also spiritually, in the interior life. "I have all things" *(apexō)* means having in full or having received in full. It is found in commercial documents of the period for having received a sum and being given a receipt for it. Paul is "paid in full" for their debt to him, which was the Gospel he brought them.

    I have been filled, receiving from Epaphroditus the things from you: "I have been filled" has as its root *plērōma,* a term of importance in the Pauline letters to the Colossians and Ephesians. It means not only spatially complete (as a full cup, for example), but perfected, matured. Paul's completion would have been impossible apart from the gift he received from the Philippians, which was carried by Epaphroditus (see 2:25-30). It is a subtle but clear picture of the sort of mutuality Paul commends throughout his dealings with his churches and, finally, an explicit reference to their gift to him, their support of his work. This verse is as close to an explicit "thank you" as Paul comes in the letter.

    an odor of sweet smell, an acceptable sacrifice, pleasing to God: The metaphor of commerce (vv. 15-17) now shifts to that of sacrifice, the "sweet savor" offerings made in the Temple, thanksgiving offerings (compare 2:17; Eph 5:2; and Gen 8:21 LXX; Exod 29:18; Ezek 20:41). The "gifts" from the Philippians are "sacrifices," suggesting they came at some cost to the givers (see 2 Corinthians 8). Paul can offer the Philippians no higher praise or thanks than to liken their gift to him with sacrifice to God. Thus not only is Paul gratified, but God is pleased: "God loves a cheerful giver" (2 Cor 9:7). In the OT financial generosity is praiseworthy. Proverbs 19:17, for example, uses language similar to that found here. Spiritual sacrifice was a common notion in Paul's time and is reflected in the NT by Heb 13:16. Paul's thanks for their gifts to him come subtly in an allusion to the thanksgiving offerings of sacrifice.

19. *And my God will fill every need of yours:* The focus in this passage now shifts from Paul's response to the Philippians' gifts in vv. 10-18a to God's response to them in vv. 18b-20. Verse 19 asserts for the Philippian church what Paul asserted for himself in v. 13: God supplies what is needed. Paul has already explained in 4:13 that his self- sufficiency is not his own doing; it comes from another. Now he reminds the Philippians that the One Who empowers him will also "fill" (again as in v. 18 *plērōsei,* complete or perfect or mature) their needs: not, note, their "wants," which is quite another thing. Spiritual maturity makes a clear distinction between what is needed and what is wanted, what is really required and what is "icing."

   according to his riches in glory in Christ Jesus: The causal clause reminds the Philippians of how God fills needs: in Christ Jesus (compare 3:21). "Riches in glory" is language found again in Ephesians 2 and 3 (and compare 1 Tim 6:17). The whole verse introduces the language of reciprocity that characterizes Paul's thinking about giving.

20. *Now to the God and our Father [be] the glory unto the ages of ages. Amen:* Having explained that God will meet every need, Paul has nowhere to "go" but to doxology. When one realizes how everything one needs, one has in God, one can only praise. When one is given a glimpse of God's glory, one can only glorify God! Even in writing to a Gentile church, Paul's devotional life is thoroughly Jewish. He gives glory to *the* God. "Unto the ages of ages" is a Semitism (see Gal 1:5). Paul breaks into doxology, closing with the Hebrew affirmation "Amen," "so be it" (compare Rom 16:27; Eph 3:21; 1 Tim 1:17; Rev 4:21-23).

Interpretation

At the very end of the epistle Paul finally concludes the "thank you note" he apparently began as early as 1:3-5, which some commentators think is the primary reason for the letter. Paul acknowledges the gift brought by Epaphroditus (2:25-30). Several scholars have noted many parallels between 1:3-11 and 4:10-20 (see, for example, Gerald W. Peterman, *Paul's Gift from Philippi*) and suggest the two passages form an inclusion around the body of the letter. But it is an odd "thank you" insofar as the words are never explicitly spoken, although gratitude is implied at both 1:3-7 and 2:25 (a very different interpretation of this passage from the one suggested here is given by Jerome Murphy-O'Connor in *Paul: A Critical Life*).

Paul opens another autobiographical passage in 4:10-13 (compare 1:12-26). He then rehearses the history of his relationship with the Philippian church (4:14-18) and closes with an affirmation of God's care for them (4:19) and a doxology (4:20). The opening is clearly signaled by the now characteristic "joy formula" (1:19; 3:1; 4:4). Gordon Fee points to a pattern in which acknowledgment of a gift (vv. 10, 14) is qualified (vv. 10, 15-16) by a "not that" clause (vv. 11-13, 17) (*Philippians,* 424). This suggests another way to see the structure of the passage: vv. 10-18a describe Paul's response to the Philippians' gift, with two qualifications in vv. 11 and 17; then vv. 18b-20 shift the focus to God's response to it.

In vv. 10-13 Paul turns to his autobiography as a way of teaching the Philippians. As noted earlier, Paul never speaks of his own life simply to be "autobiographical"; he does so to be instructive. In the Pauline letters autobiography is always pedagogical or didactic; Paul uses his life experience to exemplify some point he wants to make. (Perhaps he realizes that our own lives are never as interesting to others as they are to us!) In effect Paul here reprises 1:12-26 in a different key. He reiterates that, although he has been in difficult circumstances, it is ultimately for the good. Moreover, he depicts himself as the Stoic wise man who is unaffected by external circumstances. This being the case, he does not really *need* gifts from the Philippians because he is strengthened by Jesus Christ. And it is that strengthening that, in fact, makes him very different indeed from the Stoics.

Nevertheless, Paul understands that their gifts to him are the way in which the Philippians participate in the Gospel mission. Verses 14-18 make clear that Paul is grateful that the Philippian church has assisted him, not so much because of his need as because it is spiritually good for them to be generous. The ideal of reciprocity behind these verses is more clearly and expansively presented in 2 Corinthians 8–9 (see especially 8:13-14), which also corroborates the history of his relationship with the church in Macedonia (see 2 Cor 8:1-5; 9:1-5). The point is that Paul is in a unique relationship of reciprocity vis-à-vis the Gospel with the Philippian church. The communal ideal of virtue here, as L. Michael White suggests, is an adaptation of the Hellenistic moral paradigm of *philia,* the love of brothers and sisters.

Still, the problem posed by this "thank you note" remains. First, why does it come at the end of a letter that ostensibly began in order to thank its recipients? Second, why does Paul continually "pull back" (4:11, 17) and never, in fact, say "thank you"? The answer to the first question presumes that Philippians is a single letter and not a series of fragments. Thus 4:10-20 is not a letter fragment, but an integral part of this letter. In his analysis of the discourse structure of the letter David Black suggests it is a second unit of *narratio* that obliquely expresses gratitude for their gift and recalls their earlier pattern of support. If, Black argues, the primary appeal of the letter is for unity grounded in the mind of Christ, then the need for self-denial and sacrificial giving is integral to that unity ("The Discourse Structure of Philippians"). This is why, for example, this section of the letter moves toward the language of sacrifice (v. 18).

In my view Paul uses the closing "thank you" to summarize the major ideas in the letter: common life in Christ, imitation of Jesus (and other exemplary Christian figures), the need for reciprocity in work for the Gospel, and Paul's genuine love for the Philippians. Because Pauline expressions of confidence in those to whom he writes are part of his effort to secure a positive hearing for what he proposes, closing the letter on a note of gratitude shores up the appeal he has made for unity. When the letter is read aloud, the last thing the Philippians hear is Paul's gratitude. And they hear it in the context of the other major issues that were raised in the body of the letter.

Second, one must keep firmly in mind the genre of the Philippian letter. It was suggested in the Introduction that Philippians is a hortatory letter of friendship. In such letters there are several conventions. Care for each other's morality and reciprocity in the matter of giving and receiving are only two. It is important to understand that the conventions of friendship were different in the Greco-Roman world than they are today. Friendship was taken much more seriously. In relationships of social reciprocity, friends expected to give and to receive from each other. Gratitude was expressed by means of return rather than by "saying thank you" which, as the Note on v. 11 suggests, could be construed as a request for something.

Paul indicated at the outset of the letter that he viewed the Philippians as "partners in the gospel" (1:5). While this may not be, as J. Paul Sampley suggests, a full blown example of Roman consensual *societas* (a legally binding, reciprocal partnership built around a common goal), it is certainly a partnership in the Gospel. The reciprocal nature of the relationship means that the financial language in the passage is to be understood as metaphorical; the metaphors express their common filial relationship in Christ. As a friend and social equal of the Philippians, Paul had the "right" to expect assistance from them. Effusive verbal thanks would indicate a dependence on them not characteristic of the nature of their relationship. Such an expression of thanks would effectively put Paul in the "client" position relative to the "patron" Philippians.

Moreover, as their friend and equal, Paul was responsible for the Philippians' welfare. His "thank you note," then, has a didactic purpose: teaching the Philippians the meaning, the spiritual significance, of their gifts to him. He wants them to understand their gift in spiritual terms, not in terms of the economic conventions of their society. So he reminds the Philippians that their gift pleases God and gives God glory. The relationship here is based not on need but on reciprocity, as *both* Paul and the Philippians are servants of the Gospel. As Fee's commentary points out, the commendation of their mutual partnership in the Gospel is the last thing the recipients of the letter "hear" when it is read in the community.

The letter closes on the note of joy and commendation with which it opened and is a subtle reminder of the "heavenly citizenship" of believers, as contrasted with the Roman citizenship with its various economic conventions. Its final note is doxology. As Fee remarks in his article "To What End Exegesis?" "True theology is expressed in doxology, and doxology is always the proper response to God, even . . . in response to God's prompting friends to minister to friends" (p. 86).

Several points in the passage bear reflection. First, the matter of money is always delicate in the church. While the "worker deserves his pay," it is awkward to give the appearance of profiting financially from the Gospel. The story is told of a Protestant pastoral search committee who prayed for a "poor, humble shepherd." "God," they prayed, "you keep him humble, and we'll keep him poor." Paul here strikes a healthy balance between impoverishment and venality. Second, money, and the power it represents, is as much a temptation today as it was in the first century. By seeing giving and receiving as reciprocal, Paul disarms the weapon of wealth. Third, the passage makes clear that in regard to monetary relations (giving and receiving), Christians are not to relate to one another in terms of the economic conventions of the society. Christian *koinōnia* means that believers are responsible for each other financially as well as in myriad other ways. After the very early days of the Jerusalem church's experiment with communal property (Acts 2–4), this has gone by the board except in monastic and religious communities and some experiments in radical Protestantism. Alas.

For Reference and Further Study

Black, David A. "The Discourse Structure of Philippians: A Study in Text-Linguistics," *NovT* 37 (1995) 16–49.

Capper, Brian J. "Understanding Paul's Argument in Phil 1–2 from His Thanksgiving in 4:10-20," *ThZ* 49 (1993) 193–214.

Ezell, Douglas. "The Sufficiency of Christ: Philippians 4," *RevExp* 77 (1980) 373–81.

Fee, Gordon D. "To What End Exegesis? Reflections on Exegesis and Spirituality in Philippians 4:10-20," *BBR* 8 (1998) 75–88.

Fitzgerald, John T., ed. *Friendship, Flattery and Frankness of Speech: Studies on Friendship in the New Testament World*. NovTSup 82. Leiden: Brill, 1996.

Fowl, Stephen. "Know Your Context: Giving and Receiving Money in Philippians," *Int* 56 (2002) 45–58.

Morris, Leon. *"kai hapax kai dis,"* *NovT* 1 (1956) 205–208.

Murphy-O'Connor, Jerome. *Paul: A Critical Life*. Oxford: Clarendon Press, 1996, especially "An Ambivalent Expression of Gratitude," 216–18.

Olson, Stanley N. "Pauline Expressions of Confidence in His Addressees," *CBQ* 47 (1985) 282–95.

Perkins, Pheme. "Philippians: Theology for the Heavenly Politeuma," in Jouette M. Bassler, ed., *Pauline Theology I*. Minneapolis: Fortress, 1991, 89–101.

Peterman, Gerald W. *Paul's Gift from Philippi*. Cambridge: Cambridge University Press, 1997.

________. "'Thankless Thanks': The Epistolary Social Convention in Philippians 4:10-20," *TynBul* 42 (1991) 261–70.

Reumann, John H. P. "Philippians and the Culture of Friendship," *Trinity Seminary Review* 19 (1997) 69–83.

Sampley, J. Paul. *Pauline Partnership in Christ. Christian Community and Commitment in Light of Roman Law*. Philadelphia: Fortress, 1980.

White, L. Michael. "Morality Between Two Worlds: A Paradigm of Friendship in Philippians," in David L. Balch et al., eds., *Greeks, Romans and Christians*. Minneapolis: Fortress, 1990, 201–15.

Witherington, Ben III. *Friendship and Finances in Philippi*. Valley Forge, PA: Trinity Press International, 1994.

FINAL GREETINGS: 4:21-23

21. Greet all the saints in Christ Jesus. The brethren with me greet you.
22. All the saints greet you, but especially those from the house of Caesar.
23. The grace [of] the Lord Jesus Christ [be] with your spirit.

Notes

21. *Greet all the saints in Christ Jesus:* The "greeting form" in a Pauline letter includes a greeting verb (usually, as here, *aspazomai*) and mention of who is doing the greeting. Paul is sending a "blanket greeting" to those in the Philippian church (compare 2 Cor 13:13). The Greek word for "greet" is the aorist middle imperative of the most common form of the word "to greet" or "to give greetings." "Saints" is literally "holy ones," that is, those set apart by God for the Gospel. The reference is to each of God's people in Philippi (compare the Notes on 1:1); the word does not have a moral connotation. The believers in Philippi are "holy" insofar as they are "in Christ Jesus," (i.e., because of Christ) that short but crucially important prepositional phrase (see, for example, 1:14; 3:1; 4:4). The final greeting, then, echoes almost exactly the opening greeting at 1:1b. By greeting the whole church Paul makes a subtle final appeal for unity, thus reinforcing one of the two primary reasons for the letter, to say "thank you" and to encourage unity.

    The brethren with me greet you: The circle widens and greetings are now extended to the Philippians by Paul's associates at the place of his imprisonment. As at earlier places in this letter, *adelphoi* is here translated "brethren" in an inclusive sense. The named "brethren" with Paul are Timothy and Epaphroditus (1:1; 2:19-30). But would believers from the praetorian guard (1:13), believers who have been emboldened to speak because of Paul's imprisonment (1:14), all those alluded to at the outset of the letter be included here as they seem to be in v. 22a?—even those who did not have the Philippians' or Paul's interests at heart (2:20-21)?

22. *All the saints greet you:* The circle now reaches its greatest extent as the greeting includes "all the saints." Again Paul repeats the fact that the greeting is not just his own, but from the believers where he is. "All" is understood by some commentators to suggest a sizable group. Again the word translated "saints" is, as in v. 21, "holy ones."

but especially those from the house of Caesar: The phrase alludes back to 1:12-26 and Paul's report of his imprisonment. The "house of Caesar" probably did not mean the imperial family itself, but would include the praetorian guard of 1:13, freedmen, servants, slaves, and retainers. For some scholars the phrase, along with 1:13, reinforces the likelihood of an imprisonment in Rome, although a "household of Caesar" could be found in any Roman administrative center. Wherever Paul is imprisoned, that a "Caesar's household" would send greetings to the church in Philippi gives a glimpse of the startling extent of Christian *koinōnia*. Immense distances are bridged as believers in the imperial household, those who represent the Roman establishment that may well be the source of the Philippians' suffering (1:7, 28-30) and are certainly behind Paul's own imprisonment, are considered "saints" alongside those in Philippi. Perhaps for this reason Paul calls attention to them with the word "especially" *(malista),* which Marvin R. Vincent speculates may suggest persons with previous acquaintance with the Philippians.

23. *The grace [of] the Lord Jesus Christ [be] with your spirit:* The central element of the Pauline benedictions is the "grace" *(charis)* wish (see 1 Cor 16:23; Gal 6:18; 1 Thess 5:28; 2 Thess 3:18; Phlm 25). "Of the Lord Jesus Christ" is a genitive of origin; that is, the grace comes from Jesus. This was made especially clear in Philippians with its vivid depiction of how God made Jesus "Lord" (2:9-11). The phrase is probably of confessional or liturgical origin. "Your spirit" is communal, meaning the entire "person" (which Paul wants to be "one-minded") of the Philippian church. The letter ends as it began at 1:2 on a "grace note." (Some strong manuscript traditions, including 𝔓[46], Sinaiticus, and others, include "Amen.")

Interpretation

Letters of the period usually close with a farewell and a luck wish. Adapting the conventions of the Greco-Roman letter, Paul's epistles close with greetings and final blessings. Harry Gamble has suggested that the closing of a letter follows the pattern of hortatory remarks, wish of peace, greetings, and a grace benediction. In fact, according to this schema the closing of Philippians is shorter than usual, including only greetings (which in the imperative might be considered "hortatory") and the grace benediction. For some scholars this is evidence of the fragmentary character of the epistle, but it should be noted that the normal pattern in Paul's letters is greeting followed by grace benediction. Furthermore, the letter has just offered a promise (4:19) and doxology (4:20), and, in any case, Paul's friendship with the Philippians precludes the need for extensive greetings as it precluded the need to say explicitly "thank you" for their gifts to him. The letter's bearer, Epaphroditus, would also, of course, verbally bring Paul's various greetings.

Greetings in Pauline letters are used to cement these bonds of friendship. They are of three types: first person, in which the writer greets someone (here v. 21a); second person, in which the writer tells the addressees to greet someone for him; third person, in which the writer gives the greetings of others to those addressed in the letter (here vv. 21b and 22). Jerome Murphy-O'Connor speaks of the "reserve" in the Philippian greeting, which seems to him odd in light of Paul's closeness to that church, and which he attributes to Paul's unease about the gift of money (4:10-20) (*Paul the Letter Writer,* especially 102–107). But, as indicated, it is precisely the conventions of friendship that account for both. In writing about the closing greetings, some scholars have suggested that a clear distinction should be made between "the brethren," who represent a limited group of workers who were associated with the Pauline mission, and "the saints," including all believers. This seems unlikely in a letter that is written, in part, to encourage church unity and "one-mindedness." In Pauline letters the concluding blessing often echoes the opening greeting. The basic form of the blessing is "grace be with you," and the source of the grace is Jesus Christ.

Paul's specific reference to Caesar's household is noteworthy. In effect he is reminding the Philippians that some, at least, of his captors were also his "brethren," "fellow saints and members of the household of God." One wonders at what risk such persons became Christian. It leads one to ponder the extent to which one might be able to remain faithful to Christ in the face of loss of job or status. Additionally, it may well have been Roman officials who were persecuting the Philippian Christians. If so, Paul is drawing the circle of inclusion very widely indeed by reminding the Philippians that they are bound to at least *some* Roman officials in the "bonds of Christ." Again one is led to ponder the fate of Christians today who are still persecuted for their faith, or the degree to which rich and powerful Christians in the "first world" are implicated in the structures that oppress their "brethren" elsewhere.

The overall impression given by the closing formula of Philippians is of the importance of unity in the church. Christians are bound together "in Christ" across geographical distances, cultural divides, and even when "in the world" they might well be in adversarial relationship to one another. This emphasis on fellowship and unity, especially in the work of spreading the Gospel, is one of the major emphases of the letter, and it is fitting that Paul's "last word" should echo these themes, and the grace of God, given in Jesus Christ, that makes Christian unity possible.

For Reference and Further Study

Ezell, Douglas. "The Sufficiency of Christ: Philippians 4," *RevExp* 77 (1980) 373–81.

Gamble, Harry. *The Textual History of the Letter to the Romans*. Grand Rapids: Eerdmans, 1977.

Mullins, Terence Y. "Greeting as a New Testament Form," *JBL* 87 (1968) 418–26.

Murphy-O'Connor, Jerome. *Paul the Letter Writer*. Collegeville: Liturgical Press, 1995.

Murray, G. W. "Paul's Corporate Witness in Philippians," *BSac* 155 (1998) 316–26.

Russell, Ronald. "Pauline Letter Structure in Philippians," *JETS* 25 (1982) 295–306.

Philemon

Judith M. Ryan

AUTHOR'S PREFACE AND ACKNOWLEDGMENTS

Brief as it may be, Paul's correspondence with Philemon merits its position within the canon of undisputed letters. This is especially evident when Philemon is recognized as a pastoral letter on par with the rest, one that seeks to illustrate and bring into being a more practical and concrete way of living out what it means to stand under the lordship of Jesus Christ. Paul writes not to a slaveowner to whom he is sending back a runaway slave, but to the host and leader of a Christian community who is also a beloved friend, coworker, and even spiritual son whom he trusts, with every confidence of receiving a positive response. Paul demonstrates exquisite rhetorical skill in combining the Gospel imperative with a friendly persuasion for Philemon to partner with Paul in eliciting the support of his community to graciously welcome Onesimus back home, not as a returning slave but as a brother and even an honored guest—in fact, as Paul himself. Nothing short of a radical reversal of the norm (and expectation) is requested here, as a slaveowner is to warmly receive the runaway slave back into his household and house church. Such action may be the only way for the community to fully comprehend the reality of his conversion and baptism into Christ, with the new status it creates for Onesimus as "brother" and equal within the faithful community. In light of the history of this brief yet powerful letter, which has so often been misused and abused to support the opposite of its original intent, it is my hope that this commentary can contribute in some significant way to a fuller understanding of the radical nature of the Gospel that creates equality and always works to raise the dignity of each and every human person.

In keeping with the Sacra Pagina format, this commentary includes my own translation of the Greek text, Notes that include a linguistic and grammatical analysis of the text, and an Interpretation that seeks to incorporate all the literary, historical and social approaches and methodologies currently available. More recent interest in this letter has led me into a joyful engagement with the works of numerous scholars and commentators, some of whom I wish to thank here. Commentators to whom I am indebted include Peter O'Brien, Eduard Lohse, Murray Harris, John Koenig,

N. T. Wright, and especially Joseph Fitzmyer for his most recent and meticulous commentary on Philemon. I wish also to thank Norman Peterson and John Paul Heil, who led me to attend to some of the finer nuances of the letter, and Marion Soards, J. Louis Martyn, Gerhard Lohfink, Richard Horsley, and John Ziesler, whose many insights have inspired me throughout the writing of this commentary.

I wish to express my gratitude to many students and seminarians for their feedback and encouragement throughout this process. I want to thank friends and colleagues, especially Ray Rafferty, Richard Dillon, Eileen Fagan, Dan Doherty, Mike Barre, Dan Moore, Corbin Eddy, Honora Werner, and John Donahue for their friendship and encouragement throughout. I especially wish to express my gratitude to Daniel Harrington, who carefully read my manuscript and made many helpful suggestions, and to Linda Maloney for all of her help, encouragement, and support throughout this project. Most especially, I want to thank Bonnie Thurston for inviting me to join her in this joyful collaboration. Finally, my deepest love and gratitude go to my family, Betty and Jim, Barbara and Jerry, for a lifetime of loving kindness, encouragement, and support.

JUDITH M. RYAN
Trinity Sunday, 2004

PHILEMON

INTRODUCTION

Unique in its largely singular appeal to Philemon, who is a leader in a house church he hosts, this pastoral letter also includes the entire community Paul hopes to bring to a more faithful following of the Lord Jesus Christ. For the center of the letter not only states the Gospel imperative that Philemon receive Onesimus back as a "beloved brother" in Christ (v. 16), it also issues the invitation for Philemon to collaborate with Paul in encouraging his own community to welcome this returning slave as they would the apostle himself (v. 17).

While the news of Onesimus' baptism (v. 10) already implies a change in relations and status due to his "new creation" in Christ, the low regard for and inferior status of slaves may have necessitated Paul's call for a radical reversal of expectations as the slaveowner graciously receives his returning slave as an honored guest. Perhaps nothing less than a total reversal of status (with the master serving the slave) could make the community recognize this runaway slave as their own brother in Christ. To better appreciate the radical nature of Paul's request, this introduction begins with a brief look at the situation of slavery in the ancient world.

Slavery in the Greco-Roman World

Classical scholars who for centuries so highly praised the many accomplishments of ancient Greek and Roman civilizations all too often overlooked the fact that they were also societies that, for their own benefit, brutally exploited whole populations of people (Horsley, "Slave Systems," 19–22). Military campaigns to expand the sphere of Roman rule from the third century B.C.E. onward generated what Moses Finley called the largest "slave society" in the ancient world (*Slavery in Classical Antiquity*, 45–49). More recently, Orlando Patterson aptly described it as "systematic violence" institutionalized by the Roman imperial state (*Slavery and Social Death*, 5; see also his "Paul, Slavery and Freedom," 263–79).

The overwhelming majority of slaves were prisoners of war, captives and others who were kidnapped and separated from their families, their homeland, and even other countrymen and -women so that they would be less likely to unite and rebel. This slave-based economy provided honor and status to conquerors and ruling classes who, because of their status and power, considered themselves due the tribute and loyalty of slaves in exchange for preserving their lives and providing further protection. Therefore in ancient times slavery was viewed as exclusively linked to revenue and not specifically to race (Tacitus, *Ann.* 13.21; see Finley, *Ancient Economy,* 72, and Lyall, *Slaves, Citizens and Sons,* 28). However, while even Romans could find themselves in bond or debt slavery, the majority of slaves were not citizens, but foreigners, regarded as property (chattel slavery) and having few if any human rights and little access to justice (cf. Aristotle, *Politics* 1.2, cited in Fitzmyer, *Philemon,* 26; Lyall, *Slaves, Citizens and Sons,* 35). While there were discussions and debates concerning the treatment of slaves (Seneca, *Moral Epistles,* 47), no genuine legislation protecting slaves apparently existed (Lyall, *Slaves, Citizens and Sons,* 35; Finley, *Slavery in Classical Antiquity,* 53–58). Owners had exclusive rights over slaves, which meant that the owners who were responsible for protecting their slaves also had the legal right to inflict punishment and even death (Bradley, *Slaves and Masters,* 15–16). Therefore the condition of a slave's life depended to a great extent upon his or her owner as well as the kind of service he or she could provide.

While there may have been a fortunate few who served and perhaps even managed the estates of wealthy and influential owners as well as those who enjoyed meaningful labor, perhaps in law, medicine, teaching, etc., the vast majority worked in as many varieties of employment and circumstances as one can imagine (Martin, *Slavery as Salvation,* 11–22). This could range from hard labor in ships' galleys, mines, refineries, fields, and mills to what could be all kinds of domestic and clerical work in and around the house, similar perhaps to the position Onesimus had within the household of Philemon (Brown, *Introduction to the New Testament,* 503–505). It appears that all who could afford to own a slave did, from the more typical few to as many as hundreds and even thousands (Tacitus, *Ann.* 14.43.4, cited by Bradley, *Slaves and Masters,* 15–16). It is estimated that in some places the slave population was more than half the total population. Even conservative estimates place the number of slaves around thirty percent (see Fitzmyer, *Philemon,* 26).

Ancient writings also show that slaves were stereotyped as useless, lazy, and even criminal. The apostle's reference to Onesimus' former service as "useless" (v. 11) may well reflect the prevailing mindset as well as the situation that led him to seek Paul. Seneca's personal disdain for slaves was evident when he wrote that "There are as many enemies as there are slaves" (*Ep. Mor.* 47; see Bradley, *Slaves and Masters,* 27–29, 38). Even philosophers who spoke of the "brotherhood of all humanity" appear to have been indifferent to slaves and to the dire circumstances they faced (Finley, *Slavery in Classical Antiquity,* 52). Many times slaves had to pay for the right to marry and raise families. Even then, there was no guarantee that their children would not be sold when the financial need of the owner so dictated (Bradley, *Slaves and Masters,* 79–80).

The strength and resolve of Roman imperial forces were such that every early effort on the part of slaves to revolt against the system was immediately quashed. Even the powerful and organized effort of gladiators led by Spartacus (ca. 73–71 B.C.E.) met with defeat, and with it went every hope of liberation (Callahan, *Slave Resistance,* 144–47). Sadly, slaves would even socialize their children not to resist their slave status in order to protect them (Scott, *Domination and the Arts of Resistance,* 24). In fact, slaves were expected to be loyal to their owners. They would only be released for military conscription in times of warfare (Finley, *Slavery in Classical Antiquity,* 65). Since in a number of places Paul alludes to his mission as a "campaign" (2 Cor 10:4) and to himself as "a soldier" (1 Cor 9:7), yet not in a worldly or violent sense of the term (2 Cor 10:3), it may be that in describing Archippus as "fellow soldier" (v. 2) he is hinting at Onesimus' release to serve the Gospel alongside him (cf. vv. 13-14).

Generally, however, flight was the only way for a slave to secure freedom. Subsequently laws were enacted that made running away a serious crime that could label the offender a fugitive who, when found, would be returned to the owner to face severe punishment and even death. Anyone who harbored such a fugitive could also be charged with theft. A slave could, however, reasonably seek asylum from an abusive owner or could seek mediation from an owner's friend *(amicus domini)* who could legally provide temporary refuge but might still be responsible for any financial loss to the slaveowner (Watson, *Roman Slave Law,* 49–60). This seems the most likely scenario in the case of Onesimus, as Paul does assume responsibility for any financial losses and yet does not mention or even hint at any possible illegality.

There was only one ray of hope offered to slaves, and that was the possibility of manumission. Yet even this was only another means to exploit and regulate the behavior of slaves with the possibility of a reward after a lifetime of hard service. Manumission itself was not the equivalent of liberation, or what in modern times has been called emancipation or abolition. Manumission was more of a limited freedom that still kept the freedman or freedwoman *(libertus, liberta)* legally bound to the former owner. The freedperson was still obliged to provide services, loyalty, honor, and gratitude to the previous owner (Finley, *Slavery in Classical Antiquity,* 135–37, 142–44). Tacitus wrote that the freedman who failed to show grateful deference to his former owner should be punished (*Ann.* 13.26; Wallace-Hadrill, *Patronage in Ancient Society,* 33). There was also little change in status for the freedperson, who was still considered a slave. Apparently several generations might pass before his or her descendants would be considered equals within society (Bradley, *Slaves and Masters,* 17–18). In a letter that is often cited as the closest parallel to Paul's letter to Philemon, Pliny the Younger writes to his friend, slaveowner Sabinianus (*Ep.* 9.21, ca. 61–112 C.E.), in an appeal on behalf of his freedman who has done something to anger his former owner and fears serious repercussion. Pliny's request for mercy and his emphasis on the freedman's contrition speaks volumes about the subservient conditions under which even freedpersons continued to live (DeVos, "Once a Slave," 100–101).

Actually, the freedperson's situation could be even worse than that of the slave. She or he could lose the owner's protection, as often happened in the event of the owner's death, and could face even worse poverty and other hardships. One former slave, Epictetus, who appears to be in a better situation than most, laments the hardship and the precarious state of the freedman (*Diss.* 4.1.35-37). In many ways manumission served to benefit the owner more than it did the slave, as it promised reward for a lifetime of hard work after which the owner was freed from the obligation to provide for and to protect elderly slaves (Barclay, "Paul, Philemon, and the Dilemma of Christian Slave Ownership," 168–69; Hopkins, *Conquerors and Slaves,* 117–18, 128–32). The one advantage, however, was that the freedman had a voice in society that the slave apparently never did. Even in Paul's letter the voice of Onesimus is silent—that is, at least until he is sent with the letter as Paul's representative and is entrusted with explaining its content, hopes, and expectations.

While at times it may have been possible for slaves to purchase their own manumission, it is not likely that many would have been able to pay amounts that ranged between four and eight years of wages (Bradley, *Slaves and Masters,* 105–106). But even though manumission meant little change in status, evidence from its special emphasis on burial inscriptions suggests its value to slaves and their families (cf. DeVos, "Once a Slave," 89–105). While manumission seems to have been a frequent occurrence, it was limited at times, especially as the numbers of foreign slaves who became citizens of Rome began to outnumber the original inhabitants. One decree by Augustus required a minimum of thirty years of servitude before one could be granted freedom (Suetonius, *Aug.* 21.2; cf. Bradley, *Slaves and Masters,* 84, 86 n. 19). How extensive such restrictions were and what, if any, local strictures also existed as Paul wrote to Philemon could have affected both his request and its response. In any case, it shows just how exceptional was Paul's hope for Onesimus' return to join him in the Gospel mission.

Slavery in Israel

Ancient Israel also had slaves, and while it considered slavery cruel and inhumane (Isa 14:3, 4; 47:6; Ezra 9:9) still, in practice, slaves were viewed as inferiors who were required to honor their masters (Mal 1:6). Some of Israel's rulers, most notably Solomon, used forced labor to build palace and Temple (1 Kgs 9:15, 20, 21; 12:4). And yet Israel stands apart from other nations, especially ancient Greece and Rome, in having many laws that restricted the punishment and abuse of slaves.

Israel is well known for its Torah-inspired and enlightened stance that sought genuine protection and relief for all the poor and oppressed, including slaves, Israelites in particular, but also foreign slaves. Israel's own formative memory and yearly Passover remembrance still celebrate God's ongoing deliverance of this people from slavery, and as covenant partner with a good and gracious, compassionate and liberating God, Israel is obliged to do the same (Isa 61:1; cf. Isa 1:17; Jer 7:1; 22:3; Fretheim, *Exodus,* 16–22). This self-understanding resulted in far more humane treatment of slaves, both foreign and Israelite (Exod 21:2-11, 20-21, 26-27; cf. Jer 7:6; 22:3; 34:8-17; Sir 33:24-33). Israel was reminded not to despise the resident alien but to remember that they once were slaves in Egypt when "the Lord your God ransomed you from there" (Deut 24:18). Ideally, Israelite slaves were to be redeemed from resident foreigners because they were called to be God's servants or slaves (Lev 25:55).

An inspired expansion of the Sabbath practice that gave all people, including slaves, a day off to worship God in freedom (Exod 20:10) was to become a regular observance of a sabbatical year (Exod 23:10-11; Deut 15:1-18; cf. also the Jubilee year, Lev 25:1-55). The Law's intent was to provide a way to ensure that poverty, homelessness, and even slavery would not become a permanent condition within Israel (Hoppe, "Torah Responds to the Poor," 277–82). Accordingly, every seventh or sabbatical year Israelites who had become indentured slaves were to be granted their freedom and their needs provided for abundantly (Deut 15:11-18). The motivation in Deuteronomy not only promises God's blessing on the nation but reminds Israelites that they are members of one family and should care for one another as brothers and sisters (Deut 15:1-18). Other texts also recall Israel's own ancestral journey as wanderers and strangers in foreign lands who had depended on others for survival and support (Lev 25:23; Deut 26:5). All this was the ideal. Biblical evidence suggests that the sabbatical year was indeed practiced by *some* in Israel (Neh 10:32; 1 Macc 6:49, 53). Josephus records that the Essenes did not even permit slavery in their community (*Ant.*18.1.5; Fitzmyer, *Philemon,* 31).

While chattel slavery was allowed in Israel (Lev 25:44-46), slavery did not develop to the extent it did in the slave-dependent economies of

Greece and Rome. Unlike the wealthy nations that overpowered Palestine, Israel had numerous laws that offered unique protection to both Israelite and foreign slaves, including a prohibition against kidnapping (Exod 20:15) and regulations concerning the taking of captives in war (Deut 21:10-14; cf. Exod 21:16; Deut 24:7). Even foreign slaves in Israel were, according to the Law, to be treated with dignity as human beings, who also had rights (Deut 24:17-18) and were to be treated with justice (Job 31:13-15).

Freedom and Slavery in Paul's Letters

It seems clear, especially from language that speaks of salvation as "redemption," that the suffering of slaves in the ancient world had a huge impact on the biblical understanding of and hope for God's action in human history (cf. 1 Cor 6:20). The prophetic view of Israel's sin as a return to enslavement finds in the reality of human bondage an adequate symbol for all that opposes God's will and plan for creation, human persons in particular (see, e.g., Jer 2:14, 19-20). Standing within this tradition, Paul also uses slavery as a metaphor to describe the hopelessness of the human situation prior to the redemption that was brought by Christ. He continues to remind Christians that Christ died to free people from their sins so that they might serve God in the new life of the Spirit (Rom 6:22; 7:6) and that they are no longer captive to sin (Rom 7:6), but are now under grace (Rom 6:14).

In Pauline theology those who belong to Christ have been moved by his Holy Spirit from the sphere of captivity to sin and into the new realm of grace. Thus, given a spirit of adoption (Rom 8:15; cf. 2 Cor 3:17) to become the children of God (Rom 8:21; Gal 4:5-9), one is liberated from all that holds human beings in bondage, including the anxious management of one's own life, which one now lives to and for God (Rom 8:23; 1 Cor 1:30). It is from this perspective that Paul can offer pastoral advice for slaves not to be anxious over their status (1 Cor 7:21), as he affirms their equal standing before God and in the body of Christ where "a slave is a freedman of the Lord" and the free are "slaves of Christ" (1 Cor 7:22; cf. 1 Cor 9:19; 2 Cor 4:5). This is not a freedom to do whatever one pleases, but a freedom to seek God's reign in the present circumstances (Rom 8:14-29; for a synoptic parallel see Dillon, "Ravens, Lilies and the Kingdom of God," 605–27; see also Ziesler, *Pauline Christianity,* 70, 80–82).

This is also a freedom that overcomes all powers that seek to dominate and oppress human beings, powers Paul describes as "elemental spirits of the universe" (Gal 4:3) that divide human beings, Jew and Greek, male and female, slave and free (Gal 3:28; Horsley, *Paul and Empire,* 176–77).

The movement from slavery to freedom, for Paul, involves a shift to standing under the lordship of Jesus Christ, which in this instance can only mean that Christ, and not Philemon, has a claim on Onesimus' honor and obedience (cf. Rom 6:16-22). This is a freedom that is also offered to Philemon, "not to be conformed to the present world but transformed by the renewal of your minds," so to make visible God's will and its realization in the present (Rom 12:2; Gaventa, *From Darkness to Light*, 44–45). While the fullness of freedom awaits Christ's second coming (Rom 11:25-32; 1 Cor 15:24, 51-57), it is nevertheless also already present in the new sphere of grace that Christ has made available (Wilson, "From Jesus to Paul," 10; Donfried, *Paul, Thessalonica and Early Christianity*, 233–52; deBoer, "Paul, Theologian," 33).

Slavery is nowhere sanctioned by Paul (Felder, "Philemon," 886) as he exhorts the Christian not to become anyone's slave (1 Cor 7:23; Stuhlmacher, *Philemon*, 43–46; see also Bartchy, *First Century Slavery*). Following Jewish precedent, Paul boasts that he and his companions are "slaves of Christ Jesus" (Phil 1:1, cf. Rom 1:1), and here even "prisoner of Christ Jesus" (Phlm 1, 9; cf. v. 23). "In Christ Jesus" an imprisoned Paul is still free to boldly proclaim the Gospel (v. 8), and to empower both Onesimus (vv. 10-11) and Philemon (vv. 16-17) to share in that freedom (cf. Eph 6:19-20; Wis 5:1-2). Paul's message and action are also prophetic as they announce God's freedom to do something new and to offer hope to those most in need of it.

For Paul, this world with all its oppression and injustice is passing away, and its struggle to survive is itself a sign of its temporary nature (Keck, *Paul and His Letters*, 98). In its midst a new world is being created by God. Even in the present, in this sphere of God's activity, the slave's lowly status has already been reversed as her or his true identity as a child of God who is destined for eternal life and freedom in God is revealed. While Paul does nothing to directly oppose or generate a conflict with Roman or other authorities (cf. Rom 13:1-7), he and early Christians came to be regarded as a threat to imperial rule. The early claim of Jesus as Lord could easily be seen as counter-imperial, as was perhaps the view of the apostles as royal ambassadors who proclaim or herald God's reign on earth. Some of the military imagery Paul uses (e.g., "fellow-soldier," v. 2) also fits the apocalyptic mindset that saw the old world passing away to be replaced by the new one (Wright, "Paul's Gospel," 161–62; Downing, *Cynics, Paul, and the Pauline Churches*, 165; deBoer, "Apocalyptic Eschatology," 169–90; Martyn, *Theological Issues*, 257–65).

Paul's understanding of baptism also directly challenges the status quo as, in this letter in particular, he makes no accommodation to the societal pressures that do appear to influence the later Deutero-Pauline letters, which could reflect a backlash against the radical nature of Paul's request (Eph 6:5-9; Col 3:22–4:1). The almost total accommodation seen in the Pastorals seems to suggest that these NT writers are not so aware of the Gospel's life-transforming claim (1 Tim 6:1-2; Titus 2:9-10).

"The only way to imagine a society without slavery would have been to imagine a different society" (Horsley, "Slave Systems," 59). This is precisely what Paul is doing with his appeal to move Philemon's community to stand more authentically under the lordship of Christ and to live more visibly as God's new creation in the midst of the old world. Paul's daring request may well have set the precedent that led to the early church's concern for slaves and its subsequent action to gain manumission for enslaved Christians.

Given the *parousia* expectation that this world would soon be passing away (1 Thess 4:15-17), Paul's primary focus was not on the institution of slavery but on the possibilities for transformed relations, as Philemon demonstrates. His concern centers on the power of the Gospel to effect salvation and so to transform the lives of believers even now, in the present (Preiss, *Life in Christ*, 32–42). In reality, to work for the abolition of slavery might not only have placed the lives of slaves in grave danger but would have been "like tinkering with the engine of a sinking ship" (so Ziesler, *Pauline Christianity*, 120; see also Westermann, *Slave Systems*, 150). Also there is no suggestion that either Paul or his companions had any access to power or even knew of anyone who had the influence or ability to effect such structural change in Greco-Roman society.

Yet far from tolerating such evil, what Paul did was to provide a foundation and set in motion what would eventually lead to its rejection and decline, planting "seeds for its destruction when he identifies Onesimus as Philemon's brother in the Lord" (Matera, *Strategies for Preaching Paul*, 160). While there is no way of knowing the actual impact of Philemon's response to the appeal, it apparently led to the alleviation of the suffering of some slaves as Paul placed pastoral focus on the household, where slavery was most commonly found (Schnackenburg, *Moral Teaching*, 259–60). The apparent freedom Onesimus has to travel with Tychicus (Col 4:7-9) and the fact that the letter to Philemon was given canonical status suggest that Paul's partner granted his request and did "even more" as Paul had anticipated (v. 21). There is no question that Christianity did much to lighten the burden of slaves in these ancient times (Davis, *Problem of Slavery*, 89).

Philemon in the Pauline Letter Tradition

Philemon stands in a unique position within the collection of Paul's seven undisputed letters in being the briefest communication and in expressing a singular concern within a predominantly one-to-one appeal throughout most of the letter. Yet even as Paul directs his address to his friend Philemon, the opening salutation, request for prayers, and final exchange of greetings clearly open the letter to the wider Christian community. Thus Paul's inclusion of the community, along with a content that expresses both his theological and pastoral concerns, serve to place a uniquely personal letter solidly alongside the rest of the apostle's correspondence.

Paul's letter to Philemon has often been linked with the Deutero-Pauline letter to the Colossians because of the similarity of names that appear in both of the letters. Yet this connection seems related more to a common destination in the Lycus Valley, somewhere near or in Colossae, rather than to any corresponding or similar content. In fact, in terms of theological content and pastoral concern Philemon has much more in common with the Philippian correspondence, another prison letter (or letters; see above on Philippians) that could possibly have been written during the same imprisonment. If this is true, then Philemon, with its expectation of an imminent release (v. 22), would have been written after the Philippian letter, in which Paul still faces an uncertain and even life-threatening outcome (Phil 1:19-20).

These two prison letters are among the friendliest in the apostle's correspondence and testify to the intimate bond Paul shares with those who are considered his true companions and even partners in ministry. The word Paul uses for expressing this shared participation in faith, *koinōnia,* in both letters refers to the close collaboration between the apostle and such "partners" (Phlm 6, 17; Phil 1:5, 7), who are apparently the only Christians from whom Paul will accept personal aid and support (Phlm 13-14, Phil 4:15). Numerous points of contact between the two letters include corresponding themes and theological terms such as the apostle's emphasis on "love" and expressions related to it (Phlm 1, 5, 7, 9, 16; Phil 1:9, 16; 2:1, 2, 12; 4:1), "joy" (Phlm 7; Phil 1:4, 18, 19, 25; 2:2, 18, 29; 4:1), "good deeds" and the extension of such goodness (Phlm 6, 14; Phil 1:6). Terms and expressions found only in the two prison letters include the relatively rare use of a Greek term for "knowledge" (*epignōsis,* Phlm 6; Phil 1:9; see Notes), the description of Paul's imprisonment using an alternative Greek word, *desmos* (Phlm 10, 13; Phil 1:13, 14, 17), the description of Archippus (Phlm 2) and Epaphroditus (Phil 2:25) as "fellow-soldier" *(systratiōtēs),* Paul's request for prayers for his release from prison, voiced early in the Philippian letter (1:19) and at the closing in Philemon along with his promise of a personal visit (Phlm 22; Phil 2:24). And, considering Paul's own stated purpose in writing, it appears that Philemon is at the threshold of a new partnership with Paul that is similar to the kind of committed partnership he has shared for some time with the Philippians, a community that kept flourishing into the next century (Polycarp, *Phil.* 1.2).

Like the church at Philippi, Philemon and his community are also called to be "lights in the world" amidst a "crooked and perverse generation" (Phil 2:15) as they respond to an appeal that calls them into a reciprocal partnership with this "prisoner of Christ Jesus" (Phlm 1; Phil 4:15) and may well involve some suffering and persecution (Phil 1:29-30; 4:14).

People, Places, and Possible Journey

Just as in the Philippian letter, Timothy joins Paul as sole co-sender of the letter to Philemon (cf. 2 Cor 1:1). Perhaps Paul's most trusted and valued partner (see Phil 2:19-23 and the Notes there), Timothy may also be well known throughout this region, especially to those who are personally named. Philemon, who is addressed in cordial terms as "our beloved friend and coworker" (v. 1), is also presented as host to the community that gathers in his home (v. 3). As the person Paul singularly engages throughout most of the letter, Philemon is the one to whom the appeal is made, an appeal that invites him to join Paul in exhorting his community to welcome Onesimus as they would welcome the apostle himself. As the appeal concludes with closing remarks concerning indebtedness and mutual reciprocity, the recipient of the letter and subsequent listeners/readers are either reminded or made aware of the bond Paul shares with Philemon who, like Onesimus, was also brought to faith in Christ Jesus by the apostle himself (v. 19).

Also likely to be known to both Paul and Timothy, who may have brought them to faith as well, are the letter's other named recipients, Apphia and Archippus (v. 2). Apphia, the only woman to be greeted personally in an extant opening salutation, is identified as "the sister," in terms similar to Timothy, "the brother," which would suggest that she functioned in a leadership capacity. Archippus, like Epaphroditus, the messenger sent by the Philippians to minister to Paul in prison, is also given special distinction as "fellow-soldier" (Phil 2:25), although the reason remains unspecified. Both Apphia and Archippus could have served in the Gospel mission as coworkers with the apostle and Timothy. Whether or not they were also related to Philemon as spouse and son, as traditionally suggested, cannot be known with any certainty.

The list of companions who send greetings, including Mark, Aristarchus, Demas, Luke, and Paul's fellow prisoner Epaphras (Phlm 23-24), are all mentioned in the Colossian letter along with Onesimus and Archippus, which suggests that Philemon's house is somewhere within the Lycus Valley. While most scholars seem to take for granted that this house church was in Colossae, some lack of agreement between the two letters makes it best not to specify the exact location to more than the surrounding region. Even John Chrysostom specifies this location only as Phrygia (Homily on

Phlm 2.1; *MPG* 62.708). It is even less likely that both letters could have been written at the same time or by the same author. Nowhere are Philemon and Apphia mentioned in the Colossian letter, nor is Tychicus, who is traveling with Onesimus, mentioned in Philemon. Even more curious are the differing names of Paul's fellow-prisoners. Epaphras, who is Paul's companion in prison as he writes Philemon, is not in prison at the time the Colossian letter is sent (Col 1:7; 4:12-13), whereas Aristarchus, apparently free as Paul writes to Philemon, is described as in prison with the apostle in the Deutero-Pauline correspondence (Col 4:10). Mention of Onesimus as a Colossian ("one of yourselves," Col 4:3) also proves nothing, as slaves were often taken from their place of birth to serve in another location. And the fact that Onesimus is described in the Colossian letter as traveling with Tychicus (Col 4:7-9) would seem to suggest that he had already been set free by Philemon to join Paul in the mission. Even the admonishment of Archippus at the end of the letter, which seems almost an afterthought (Col 4:17), fails to correspond in any way with the commendation he receives in Philemon. And given the likelihood that Paul did visit Philemon's house church as promised, yet not the Colossian community (Col 2:1), it seems that while they may be near one another they are not in the same location. It is entirely possible that if Colossians was written some fifteen years after Philemon (Fitzmyer, *Philemon,* 22; Stowers, *Letter Writing,* 160), the community at Colossae had not even been founded when Philemon was sent. Finally, it is hard to reconcile Paul's radical appeal in Philemon with what is written in Colossians concerning the relationship between masters and slaves (Col 3:22–4:1), which is not much different from the recommendation of just treatment for slaves that is found in the Hebrew Scriptures (Exod 20:10; Lev 25:43, etc.; see also MacDonald, *Colossians,* 148, 159).

Among the three sites proposed as the place from which Paul wrote to Philemon, Rome (ca. 61–63) claims traditional support, as it is historically known to be the place of the apostle's final imprisonment and subsequent martyrdom (Bruce, Caird, Lightfoot, Moule, Müller, and Vincent). Caesarea Maritima (ca. 58–60), the place according to Acts where Paul was imprisoned for two years while en route from Jerusalem to Rome (Acts 23:33–24:32), has found some support from scholars, such as Lohmeyer, Greeven, and Dibelius. But the proposal for Caesarea shares the same difficulty as the Roman hypothesis in having to explain why Paul asks his friend to keep a room ready for his arrival, given the lengthy journey from either Rome or Caesarea to Asia Minor, some seven hundred to one thousand miles away. Also, Acts does not mention Timothy as accompanying Paul beyond Troas to Caesarea (Acts 20:4-5).

Hence the third proposal of an Ephesian imprisonment (ca. 54–56) has gained the greatest support, especially in light of the shorter distance between Ephesus in western Asia Minor and the likely location of Philemon's house in the Lycus Valley, only some one hundred and twenty miles southeast (so Brown, Fitzmyer, Gnilka, Knox, Lohse, Martin, Marxsen, Michaelis, Deissmann, and O'Brien; the last concurs but holds on to Rome as a possible location).

Although an Ephesian imprisonment is nowhere mentioned in the New Testament, Paul's ministry in Ephesus is itself well documented. In writing of Ephesus, Paul speaks of "a wide door for effective work" that has opened up to him although "there are many adversaries" as well (1 Cor 16:8-9; cf. Acts 18:22). Paul is thought to have spent up to four years in this capital of Asia, a place that may also have been a strategically important center for the spread of the Gentile mission throughout Asia (cf. Acts 19:22; Patzia, *Emergence of the Church,* 127–28). Paul's reference to his "many imprisonments" prior to his fateful journey to Jerusalem with the collection for the saints (2 Cor 6:5; 11:23; cf. Rom 15:25-27) could easily refer to an Ephesian imprisonment, for it is in this location that Paul describes opposition from "wild beasts at Ephesus" (1 Cor 15:32; Malherbe, "The Beasts of Ephesus," 71–80) who threatened his life and those of his companions (2 Cor 1:8-10; cf. Acts 19:23-40), and which may have included the death sentence he faced in the Philippian letter (Phil 1:20). Ephesus could well be the place where Paul wrote most of his extant letters, including one or more of his letters to Corinth (1 Cor 16:19) and possibly Galatians, as well as Philippians and Philemon.

The later Christian tradition distinguished Ephesus as the site of Mary's assumption, as the place where the Fourth Gospel was written, and as a location closely associated with the names of Luke, Mary Magdalene, Philip, and Timothy, who is called bishop of Ephesus (Eusebius, *Hist. eccl.* 3.4.5). Historically Ephesus was the location of the third Ecumenical Council (431 C.E.), where the union of Jesus' full humanity and full divinity was affirmed and where Mary was given the title God-bearer *(Theotokos)* or Mother of God (Koester, "Ephesos," 119–40; Arnold, "Ephesus," *DPL* 249–53).

And yet what is especially interesting and even ironic in connection with Philemon is that while writing in Ephesus, which was at this time a major slave trade capital of the Roman empire, Paul produces a letter that effectively eliminates all distinction between master and slave as he reunites them as brothers, "both in the flesh and in the Lord" (v. 16). This clearly demonstrates the apostle's understanding of how God's powerful word makes itself tangibly present right in the midst of a violently oppressive, unjust, and cruel world (Horsley, "Slave Systems," 40; Patzia, *Emergence of the Church,* 127–28).

The Ephesian hypothesis also provides the most likely scenario to explain Paul's journey after his release from prison. Once refreshed by his partner, Philemon, and given further cause for joy in Christ (vv. 20, 22), Paul then travels through Macedonia for a promised visit to his close friends and partners at Philippi (2:24), taking up the collection as he travels through these regions until he finally reaches Corinth, where he writes to the Romans of his plans and asks their assistance in a westward campaign to Spain once he brings the collection to Jerusalem (Rom 15:24-29; Brown, *Introduction to the New Testament,* 496).

The Occasion of the Letter

The precise details surrounding the circumstance of Onesimus' departure and how he came to be with the apostle are likely to remain uncertain. The traditional view, which presumes that Onesimus had run away from Philemon's household, is still held by the majority of scholars (including Brown, Fitzmyer, Getty, Glancy, Harrison, Lightfoot, Martin, Peterson, Soards, Suhl, and Stuhlmacher). Growing in popularity, however, is the suggestion that the letter falls into a particular category: a friendly appeal to a slaveowner on behalf of a freedman or slave from a friend of the master *(amicus domini)* to whom the slave or former slave has fled for help and mediation. Peter Lampe's proposal that Onesimus would not, in this case, be considered a legal "fugitive" has sparked some new discussion of the issue. This receives some support from the letter itself, which does not suggest that the apostle was under any compulsion to send Onesimus back to Philemon (*pace* Lohse, *Philemon,* 187) as Paul states his own decision to do so (v. 12; Lampe, "Keine 'Sklavenflucht,'" 137; Rapske, "Prisoner Paul," 187, 195–96, 201–203; Nordling, "Onesimus Fugitivus," 99, 109–10).

While commentators often consider that Onesimus must have done something to get himself into trouble, was a thief, or had at least absconded with some funds to support his journey (Caird, Lightfoot, Moule, Stuhlmacher), there is nothing in the letter itself to suggest that he was a thief or a criminal (Felder, "Philemon," 885). In fact, the question of some injury or wrong being done by Onesimus to Philemon is presented as only a possibility and not a certainty (v. 18), and it is likely to refer simply to service that was lost during his temporary absence. Thus mention of Onesimus' prior "useless" service (v. 11) may have less to do with any possible character flaw and more to do with his inability as a non-Christian to serve fully within a Christian household that also functioned as a house church (v. 2). Verse 11 might also offer the best clue as to why Onesimus had left his household to seek the one who brought Philemon, and perhaps others, such as Apphia and Archippus, to faith in Christ Jesus. And Paul, no doubt, would often have been remembered with great love and affection by his spiritual children (so Lohse, *Philemon,* 187;

O'Brien, *Philemon,* 266). Alternative suggestions that Philemon had sent Onesimus to Paul with a message or gift (so Knox; see also Winter, "Paul's Letter," 13) and he had failed to return in due time (so Bruce, *Paul,* 400) seem untenable, as it would be unlikely that Philemon would send a "useless" servant to Paul (Barclay, "Paul, Philemon," 164). Even if Philemon had sent Onesimus to Paul, the letter itself provides nothing to confirm or deny such a suggestion.

Movement of the Letter

The letter begins with an epistolary salutation (vv. 1-3) that is typically Pauline except for Paul's unique self-description as a "prisoner of Christ Jesus." Paul's singular reference to "your house" also provides the first hint that what follows will be a unique one-to-one address to Philemon. However, the extended greetings to the wider congregation and the theological content that follows make it clear that what Paul asks of his primary addressee is also intended to be heard by the entire local community as well.

The focused address opens in the thanksgiving section (vv. 4-7), where Paul also provides the essential theological content and all the foundation that is needed to support his appeal. Introduced here are a number of theological terms and expressions that will resurface at key points throughout the letter. An emphasis on Philemon's love and faith that reverses the usual ordering of these virtues (1 Cor 13:13) together with a chiasmus in v. 5 and a chiastic pattern that runs throughout vv. 5-7 (see the Notes) serves to give a priority to love *(agapē),* which will be the basis for the letter's appeal (v. 9) and primary goal (vv. 16-17). Love's own grounding in faith (v. 5) returns as Paul expresses his confidence in Philemon's "obedience," which is a visible expression of that faith (v. 21).

The apostle's use of theologically rich and weighty terms in this section calls attention to the pastoral nature of the appeal as it introduces, in general terms, themes that will take on greater focus and particularity as the letter unfolds. Paul's prayer for an effective realization of his "participation" or "partnership" *(koinōnia)* in faith receives greater specificity as Paul invites Philemon to "partner" *(koinōnon)* him in carrying out this appeal within his own community. Similarly, "realization of all the good that is ours in Christ" (v. 6) moves toward concrete expression in Philemon's "goodness" (v. 14) in sending Onesimus back to Paul for "useful" service of the Gospel (vv. 11, 13-14). Paul's prayer for their "knowledge" *(epignōsis)* or "realization of all the good that is ours in Christ" (v. 6) is given greater clarity as Paul's discernment of God's will (v. 15) prepares for the appeal (vv. 16-17) whose response will make his prayer and God's purposes come to fruition. The thanksgiving period includes a transitional sentence that reemphasizes Philemon's love as it introduces (v. 7) and later concludes (v. 20) the appeal on what is a joyful and encouraging note.

Paul starts the body of the letter (vv. 8-20) by providing the rationale behind his appeal to love (vv. 8-9) as he emphasizes the importance, even necessity, of its response and of his decision to base this appeal on love rather than on any form of coercion. Both emphases are supported by the fact that, as Christ's ambassador and now also prisoner (vv. 8-9), Paul's request reflects both the seriousness of the appeal and the desire to keep Philemon's free decision intact, especially as he invites his friend to "partner" him in eliciting the essential response from his community (v. 17).

The thanksgiving section has already set the stage for the joyful announcement of Onesimus' conversion by Paul (v. 10), his current "useful" service (v. 11), and the close personal bond they have come to share. The contrast and comparison between his previous "useless" service and his present contribution, with its pun on Onesimus' name (which means "profitable" or "useful"), could serve to lighten what might be a tense reminder of the reason why this slave left his household in the first place. While the benefit to Paul is easy to understand, what profit there is for Philemon will only make sense when Paul expresses his desire to have kept Onesimus "that he might serve on your behalf during my imprisonment for the Gospel" (v. 13). No sooner does Paul state his decision to send Onesimus back to Philemon (v. 12) than he expresses his desire (and implied personal request) to keep him nearby instead (vv. 13-14).

Verses 13-14 also appear to be pivotal, as the focus shifts from the intimate relationship Paul shares with Onesimus (vv. 10-12), one that also includes a working relationship with Philemon (vv. 13-14), to the personal, filial bond they all, especially Philemon and Onesimus, share in the Lord (v. 16). From here the letter progresses rapidly into the appeal as Paul begins by placing it within the larger context of divine plans that are just beginning to unfold as Philemon meets his newly-found brother in Christ for the first time. Verse 15 brings the discussion to a whole new level in the decisive shift from Paul's actions in converting Onesimus and sending him back (vv. 10-12), to divine activity (v. 15) that thrusts the letter toward "what is necessary" in the Gospel imperative that Philemon recognize Onesimus "no longer as a slave, but much more than a slave, a beloved brother . . . both in the flesh and in the Lord" (v. 16). The "indicative" of Onesimus' baptism in Christ leads to this "imperative" that Paul, as Christ's representative, makes clear. Paul now moves to the appeal that will invite Philemon to partner him in exhorting his own community to welcome Onesimus as they would welcome the apostle himself, that is, as an honored guest. This is no small request in a society that condoned and promoted slavery, viewed slaves as inferior both in literature and popular culture, and provided them with little to no access to legal rights and justice.

As Paul situates the appeal within the familiar cultural context of indebtedness and reciprocity (vv. 18-19), he anticipates any impediment that could stand in the way of a full response to his appeal. As father to Onesimus, Paul assumes any debt he may have incurred while also ameliorating any dishonor that may have affected Philemon (v. 18). However, no sooner does Paul state this than, in a surprising reversal of indebtedness, he gently reminds Philemon of the debt he owes the apostle for his own Christian life. Now that Philemon is shown to be indebted to Paul, he is thereby obliged to grant his request.

The concluding statement, "Yes, brother, I want some benefit from you in the Lord. Refresh my heart in Christ" (v. 20), brings the appeal full circle to where Paul first prepared for it by repeating in reverse order its sentiment and expression (v. 7). "Yes" appropriately concludes the letter's affirmative character and the confidence Paul has in his friend and partner (v. 21), while the repetition of the vocative "brother" serves to reemphasize the critical relationship at the heart of the appeal. Paul's final request for some "benefit" (v. 20) seems to pick up on the earlier, lighthearted pun on Onesimus' name (v. 11) with "even more" (v. 21), serving to remind Philemon of the earlier implied request for Onesimus' return to the Gospel mission (vv. 13-14).

This letter concludes in a manner similar to Paul's other letters, with final greetings (vv. 23-24) and a concluding blessing (v. 25). A similar request for prayers for his release from prison (v. 22) is mentioned earlier in the Philippian correspondence (1:19), and a promised plan to visit, found here in Philemon (v. 22), also appears in another location in Philippians (1:26).

The Dual Appeal of Philemon

The literary structure and movement of the appeal suggest that Paul has two goals in view, a first and central one that reflects a more broadly pastoral goal (vv. 16-17), and a second that includes Paul's own personal need and desire (vv. 13-14). The first goal (vv. 16-17), whose "necessity" is already made clear at the outset (v. 8), is driven by the flow and movement of the letter itself, which begins with the announcement of Onesimus' conversion, the Gospel indicative that presses toward the imperative that Philemon and his community welcome Onesimus back home as the brother he now is, and not as the slave he was (v. 16). (For the question whether Paul expected manumission for Onesimus, see the discussion at the end of the next section.) The appeal itself immediately follows, as Paul invites Philemon into a partnership that goes even further with the request that he receive Onesimus as he would the apostle himself (v. 17). Paul's early declaration of being "bold enough" (v. 8) already anticipates the bold nature of a request that expects Philemon to encourage and exhort his own community to welcome back the returning runaway with the dignity and esteem of an honored guest.

What is the hinge, or even the pivotal center of the letter, in vv. 13-14, provides the second goal as Paul implies that Philemon should send Onesimus back to Paul to continue his "useful" (v. 11) work in the Gospel mission. These verses appear to be the center of an overall chiastic pattern that runs throughout the entire letter (for specific details see Heil, "Chiastic Structure," 178–206). Just after the apostle has spoken of the affectionate bond he shares with his new convert he expresses his own personal wish (and implied request) for Onesimus to serve on Philemon's behalf (v. 13) as he sent him back (v. 12) for the benefit of his friend (v. 14; cf. 15-16). Two further hints to this request resurface in the letter's concluding remarks, as Paul asks for some "benefit" from his friend (v. 20, a light-hearted reminder of the earlier pun on Onesimus' name in v. 11), and in his expectation of "even more," as the appropriate response to sending Onesimus back home to Philemon would be for him to reciprocate the favor (cf. vv. 12, 19). In studying and comparing the narrative or story behind the letter, Peterson *(Rediscovering Paul)* has convincingly demonstrated the letter's emphasis on indebtedness and mutual reciprocity. It appears that Paul is concerned with establishing the same fruitful collaboration and partnership with Philemon and his community that he has shared for some time with the Philippians.

Theological Significance of Paul's Appeal

The imperative of love, which rests on Philemon's faith and includes his obedience to Christ and to his Gospel (vv. 5, 6, 21), requires that he receive Onesimus back as the "beloved brother" he now is and not "as a slave" (v. 16). Onesimus cannot be both a "brother" and a "slave," for these two modes of relating are mutually exclusive. Moreover, even as "in the Lord" should be taken as extending into every sphere of one's existence, Paul's decisive addition of "in the flesh" ensures that the fraternal relationship is to be realized not only within the context of the Christian community, but also within the secular realm of everyday life.

But the apostle goes so far as to request that Onesimus be received not only as a "beloved brother," but also as an honored guest, even as Paul himself (v. 17). And in this letter Paul goes out of his way to present this appeal not as his friend, apostle, or spiritual parent (cf. v. 19), but as Christ's ambassador and prisoner (v. 9), that is, as an appeal that comes from the Lord himself. The theological perspective found in Paul's other letters will provide some helpful insight, but it is also important to note that perhaps the only way a formerly "useless," and especially a runaway, slave could be reintroduced as a "beloved brother" and new creation in Christ would be for Paul to take concrete measures to effectively reverse his former status. This could explain why Paul goes out of his way to specifically ask that Onesimus be received "as me" (v. 17), that is, with the dignity of one who comes even as Christ's ambassador. Nothing other than a radical reversal of the master-slave relationship could work to drive home the radical nature of the new relations that have been established in Christ. In requesting so honorable a welcome Paul has gone beyond even the glowing recommendations he usually provides for those companions and coworkers he entrusts with the Gospel message (Rom 16:1-2; 1 Cor 16:10-11; Phil 2:19-24, 28-30).

This is a reception that serves to recognize and promote the genuinely equal and loving relations that exist among members of the Christian community. This is highlighted in other letters in which Paul sought to promote equality among diverse members of the community regardless of status or standing in the world. In his first letter to the Corinthians, Paul spoke eloquently of Christians being united as one body in Christ whose members, though many and diverse, are one body. "As a body is one though it has many parts, and all the parts of the body, though many, are one body, so also Christ. For in one Spirit we were all baptized into one body, whether Jews or Greeks, slaves or free persons" (1 Cor 12:12-13). Paul continues to describe how such equality is achieved as he writes, "Indeed, the parts of the body that seem to be weaker are all the more necessary, and those parts of the body that we consider less honorable we surround with greater honor. . . . But God has so constructed the body as to give greater honor to a part that is without it, so that there may be no division in the body, but that the parts may have the same concern for one another . . . if one part is honored, all the parts share its joy" (1 Cor 12:20-26). It is likely to be around the same time when Paul describes slaves as "freedmen in the Lord" and free persons as "slaves in Christ" (1 Cor 7:22), which fits well an appeal for such a dramatic reversal of roles. This theological perspective easily explains the radical nature of Paul's request and the need for status reversal as the former master, Philemon, graciously extends an honorable welcome and so serves the one who was formerly his slave. While Paul obviously needed to spell all of this out for the immature Corinthians (cf. 1 Cor 11:17-21), he has no need to do so for Philemon, the community leader and host, who is now drawn into a deeper partnership with the apostle.

All the theological foundation Paul needs to ground his appeal is briefly stated in the theologically-rich thanksgiving period (vv. 4-7), where all essential terms and expressions introduced here are repeated in key locations throughout the letter (so Soards, "Neglected Dimensions," 209–19; Brown, *Introduction to the New Testament*, 503; Harrington, *Philemon*,

22). Paul includes only what is needed to make his case, as much of what is central to his theology often remains unstated in his letters (Achtemeier, "Finding the Way," 30–33). This is especially the case in this letter, where Paul writes to a beloved friend who is also his colleague and spiritual son (cf. v. 19) and requires no elaborate theological exposition.

However, rather than simply exhort his friend and the community to do what the Gospel requires, Paul chooses instead to approach Philemon with a more respectful, even honorable appeal as he presents the request as "ambassador and prisoner of Christ Jesus" (v. 9). Thus instead of introducing the more typical apostolic exhortation Paul presents an appeal that elicits a partnership to be freely accepted. This primary goal makes this more diplomatic approach all the more understandable. Yet even as the appeal works to bolster Philemon's own honor and authority within his own community, it also shows Paul's care to assert at the outset "what is necessary" as it leads to the Gospel imperative that stands behind this appeal, for his making this appeal as Christ's representative assures that it comes not only from Paul but is the demand and claim of the Lord himself (Ziesler, *Pauline Christianity*, 62; *pace* Wickert, *Philemonbrief*, 230–38).

"Ambassador" is a term Paul also used to foster his ministry of reconciliation with the Corinthian church, with whom he had difficult and painful relations at times (2 Cor 5:20). In the ancient world, as today, such emissaries wielded no enforceable authority, but they did have enormous persuasive power and influence (Cassidy, *Paul in Chains*, 99). The unlikely combination of "ambassador" and "prisoner," the former a position of esteem, the latter one regarded as lowly and even despised by the world's standards, takes on a new and transformed meaning in connection with "Christ Jesus" (v. 9). Like the cross and human weakness (2 Cor 12:9-10), "prisoner of Christ Jesus" seems to belong to what has been called a "language of affliction" (Plank, *Paul and the Irony*, 73–75) that Paul uses to creatively reinterpret the meaning of human life and suffering as it is transformed by God's powerful, loving presence. Such world-estranging language is deliberate and aims at transforming the world's values as it provides an opening for the newness the Gospel brings.

"Prisoner of Christ Jesus" is also given further clarification in the other prison correspondence, where Paul finds joy in an imprisonment that works to promote the Gospel and to effect conversions (Phil 1:12-14; 4:22). A similar cause for rejoicing in the baptism of Onesimus (v. 10) appears to provide the basis for Paul's appeal to Philemon. Thus in declaring that he is a "prisoner of Christ Jesus" (v. 1) Paul is not simply notifying Philemon of his imprisonment for the sake of the Gospel (as in v. 13), but may be announcing himself as Christ's prisoner and that his imprisonment serves Christ, the only one to whom he is truly bound. For even his imprisonment serves God's purposes (vv. 10-11, 13-14, 15) as it also testifies to the fact that he is bound by the love of Christ (2 Cor 5:14) and that he lives no longer for himself, but for Christ "who has loved me, and given himself up for me" (Gal 2:20). Considering his appeal for his friend's partnership, such a self-description may well include the suggestion that, in partnering with Paul, Philemon may also come to share in his suffering, as did his Philippian partners (Phil 1:29-30; 3:10; 4:14; cf. Rom 8:17; 1 Cor 4:9-13; 2 Cor 1:5-7; Gal 6:17). It is certainly reasonable to suggest that Paul is "engineering a crisis for his fellow worker" (Peterson, *Rediscovering Paul*, 99; also 269–70, 288) which could involve a loss of reputation and honor within his own community and the wider society as well.

It is precisely this kind of appeal that explains Paul's emphasis on Philemon's love (vv. 5, 7, 9), his goodness (vv. 6, 14), and his obedience of faith (vv. 5, 6, 21). All Christians, and especially Paul's partners, are to share with each other the joys and sufferings that such a close following of Christ will bring in a world that both accepts and rejects God's rule (Hultgren, *Christ and His Benefits*, 140). Throughout the letter Paul relates to Philemon as more of a trusted friend and partner who, as leader of his own community, needs no further instruction or guidance. What is noticed throughout Paul's letters is the genuine collegial nature of a ministry that works to empower others for leadership within their own communities so that he and his coworkers can move on to other places where Christ had not yet been preached (cf. Rom 15:19-20).

The indicative of Onesimus' baptism (v. 10), which makes him "a new creation" in Christ (2 Cor 5:17; cf. Gal 6:15; Käsemann, "Worship in Everyday Life," 193) necessarily leads to the imperative that he be welcomed as such, that is, as a "beloved brother" in the Lord (v. 16). This single fact of Onesimus' transformation in Christ drives and informs the whole letter, which, more emphatically than any other, focuses on such familial relations throughout. As the letter opens, "sister" and "brother" serve to introduce Apphia (v. 2) and Timothy (v. 1), who is elsewhere described differently as Paul's co-writer. Emphatically bracketing both ends of the appeal is the vocative singular, "brother" (vv. 7, 20), that not only focuses all the attention on Philemon but also points to what is at the heart of Paul's argument as he discerns the divine plan for Philemon to have Onesimus back forever as his " beloved brother" (vv. 15-16). This fraternal relationship takes precedence over, and even replaces, their previous relation as master and slave (White, *Apostle of God*, 166; Schnackenburg, *Moral Teaching*, 259; Peterson, *Rediscovering Paul*, 204–16). It is God's action in Christ that makes possible this transformed human existence that offers the hope of a new life that never existed before (Martyn, *Theological Issues*, 283; also Hodgson, "Christ Incarnate," 231–64).

It appears that Paul is careful to avoid any expression of status distinction even in inviting Philemon to partnership and deepened mutual relations. The conditional nature of this partnership rests on Philemon's gracious reception of Onesimus "as me" (v. 17), that is, as Paul's emissary or personal representative. While this might seem radical in the slave society of Paul's time, as mentioned earlier, it is not so radical a proposal given the apostolic exhortation for Christians to treat each other with esteem and even regard one another as better than oneself (Phil 2:3-4), which in this situation may be the only way to reverse the status of a lowly and even despised slave. The community that stands under the lordship of Jesus Christ is to transcend all divisions of race, gender, and class (Gal 3:28). This is what makes Christian hospitality distinctive in a world that could not survive without it.

The appeal for such a hospitable welcome for Onesimus from his own house church now explains Paul's prayer for an effective *koinōnia* (v. 6) or "ekklesial communion" (so Lohfink, *Jesus and Community,* 99–102) that realizes God's creation of the new family formed in Christ, a transformation into the household of God that transcends by far the traditional *paterfamilias* (Malherbe, *Social Aspects,* 68–69; Meeks, *First Urban Christians,* 72–73; Theissen, *Social Setting,* 69–119; Banks, *Paul's Idea of Community,* 45, 53–60; Bartchy, "Undermining Patriarchy," 68–78).

Koinōnia, a term that Aristotle simply defined as "friendship" (Stowers, "Friends and Enemies," 107, 110–11, 121; also Schroeder, "Friendship in Aristotle"), takes on rich and varied expressions in the Pauline writings that are all joined to a participation in God's Spirit (Phil 2:1). And this Spirit continues to inspire and instigate growth and movement toward the actualization of God's rule on earth (see Dillon, "Spirit as Taskmaster," 682–702; Käsemann, "Cry for Liberty," 127–37). The communion that *koinōnia* intends seeks to include all those whom the world often fails to consider or even notice as it also divides people into exclusive categories such as slave and free, rich and poor, male and female, Jew and Gentile, categories that work to separate and even alienate people from one another (e.g., Rom 15:25-27; 1 Cor 11:17-34; 12:13; Gal 3:28; Fiddes, *Participation in God,* 270; Moltmann, *Spirit of Life,* 183). The very nature of this "friendship" is such that the mutual affection it engenders also establishes equality where it did not initially exist (Vacek, *Love, Human and Divine,* 280–318; see especially Schneiders, "A Community of Friends," 162–79). It is what Paul expects such an appeal to love will effect, both for Onesimus as he returns home as "brother" within his own household and also for Philemon, who is invited to share mutual relations with Paul as an equal partner (Stowers, "Friends and Enemies," 111; Hooker, "A Partner in the Gospel," 83–100).

The settling of debts (vv. 18-19) that follows the central request (vv. 16-17) has the effect of situating the appeal within the culturally acceptable context of indebtedness and reciprocity, which could work to mitigate any dishonor Philemon either faced (through his slave's departure) or could face (in granting Paul's request). It is here that Paul makes an unassailable case that it is Philemon who actually owes an inestimable debt to Paul and therefore can do nothing other than grant his request. Thus with the subsequent cancellation of any additional financial debt Paul's signature would be less of a promissory note or I.O.U. (as Lohse, O'Brien, *et al.*, suggest) and more of a certification that it is the apostle himself who is actually making this appeal and not Onesimus, who is the letter's likely carrier. This would perhaps be all the more necessary if Onesimus were also Paul's amanuensis (so Cassidy, *Paul in Chains*, 161 n. 5).

Paul is not looking to establish new patron-client relations between himself and Philemon, but is seeking to establish a new criterion that transcends the Greco-Roman patronage system with entirely new relations made possible through Christ. Thus in Christ an entirely new basis for reciprocity and indebtedness is being established. Originating in the love of God manifest in Christ, the only debt that Christians are to owe is the debt "to love one another" (Rom 13:8; cf. 12:9-13). Unlike the patron-client or master-slave relation that maintains and solidifies existing inequalities (Malina, *New Testament World*, 90–116), relations among Christians are to foster equality, especially where none had previously existed, as they help to bring the community together in a mutually beneficial reciprocity that readily exchanges spiritual gifts for material goods (Rom 15:27; 1 Cor 9:11; cf. also Phil 4:15).

The apostle's prayer for "all the good that is ours in Christ" (v. 6) is not solely limited to the central appeal, as Paul has already made known his wish to have retained Onesimus to serve by his side and on behalf of Philemon (vv. 13-14). The social requirement for mutual reciprocity, especially between partners and friends, almost demands that Philemon return Paul's favor and send Onesimus back where his services are needed and desired. While "all the good" certainly presses toward its eschatological fulfillment, here, as elsewhere (1 Cor 8:1), it generally refers to a concrete demonstration of love that builds up the community (Furnish, "Inside Looking Out," 110–11). In Romans, Paul's advice to "hold fast to what is good" is joined with the encouragement to love one another with a familial affection and even to "outdo one another in showing honor," a reminder that corresponds perfectly with this appeal (Rom 12:9-10; cf. 1 Cor 14:1; Phil 2:1-4).

Given the fact that Paul had consistently refused any offer of support from communities he did not consider to be mature in faith (1 Cor 9:12; 2 Cor 11:9; 12:13), this implied request for personal support (vv. 13-14), together with an explicit appeal for collaboration (v. 17), makes it clear that Philemon is considered a mature partner who, like the Philippians, is invited to share mutually reciprocal relations with the apostle (Phil 1:5, 7;

4:14-16). It is possible that Onesimus, like Epaphroditus, the emissary sent by the Philippians (Phil 2:25-30), assisted the apostle during the final stage of his imprisonment in Ephesus. In providing such assistance for Paul, Philemon appears to be only beginning a mutual relationship the Philippians have already shared with Paul, who expressed his gratitude to them with the statement, "I have received full payment, and more; I am filled, having received from Epaphroditus the gifts you sent, a fragrant offering, a sacrifice acceptable and pleasing to God" (Phil 4:18).

While the narrative structure points to the letter's denouement or resolution in vv. 18-19 with the expectation of reciprocity, the focus of letter's overall chiastic pattern also points back to Paul's personal appeal (vv. 13-14). Twice more, in the appeal and in the letter's summary statements, Paul reminds Philemon that he wants "some benefit" (v. 20) from him, with a repeated pun on Onesimus' name (v. 11), and "even more" (v. 21), taking his request beyond the central demand. The interplay of structural and rhetorical strategies has enabled Paul to express both the Gospel's demand (vv. 16-17) and his own personal request for assistance (vv. 13-14).

What still remains is the debate over whether Paul was actually asking Philemon to set his slave free, that is, legally manumit Onesimus, making him, in Greco-Roman terms, a freedman. While some scholars view the request for manumission as self-evident (so Winter, "Paul's Letter," 11; Peterson, *Rediscovering Paul,* 97), or a likely consequence of Paul's request (O'Brien, *Philemon,* 305; Bruce, *Paul, Apostle of the Heart Set Free,* 206; Harrison, "Onesimus and Philemon," 276–80; Houlden, *Philemon,* 232; Knox, *Philemon,* 24–26; Lohmeyer, *Philemon,* 188; Marshall, "Philemon," 175–91; Wiles, *Paul's Intercessory Prayers,* 216–21), still others do not see the freedom Paul seeks for Onesimus as necessarily requiring manumission (Perkins, *Abraham's Divided Children,* 75; Betz, *2 Corinthians,* 193–95). Peter Stuhlmacher rightly notes that Onesimus could be sent back to serve on Philemon's behalf either as a slave or as a freedman (*Philemon,* 40–41). This seems more likely since, for Paul, either way Onesimus is already free in the sense that he has been given the essential freedom to serve Christ and his Gospel (1 Cor 7:20-24; O'Brien, *Philemon,* 270; Thomas, *Reading the Letters,* 75).

And yet even if manumission stands in the background, Paul's intent was not simply to secure a legal procedure that did little to appreciably affect or change the slave's unequal status (Theissen, *Social Reality,* 196). The freedman was still obligated to his former owner to provide services as well as lifelong gratitude, honor, and allegiance (Finley, *Slavery in Classical Antiquity,* 135–37, 142–44; Barclay, "Paul, Philemon," 165–70). Another consideration was that manumission could be limited by decrees and other local restrictions that may or may not have been in effect when

Paul wrote this letter (Bradley, *Slaves and Masters*, 84–86). While his apparent freedom to travel with Tychicus does suggest that Onesimus had been manumitted at some point (Col 4:7-9), still what Paul expected in terms of Onesimus' new status as "beloved brother," welcome guest, and even distinguished envoy went far beyond anything manumission could ever offer. What is true and genuine freedom for Paul is the freedom that both he, as prisoner, and Onesimus, as slave, have already received in Christ. Everything else, including his freedom to continue "useful service" with Paul and possibly manumission, seems to be only part of an all-encompassing freedom Christ has gained for all humanity, whether one is free or still a slave.

Commentators have often cited the letter of Pliny the Younger (*Ep.* 9. 21), who writes to Sabinianus on behalf of his freedman, as an ancient correlate to Paul's letter to Philemon. The suggestion is that like Pliny, Paul writes as an *amicus domini,* that is, as a friend of the master in a somewhat accepted practice that mediated benefit to both parties involved. Aside from some shared rhetorical strategies that appeal to the friend's loving and virtuous nature, however, Paul's letter on behalf of Onesimus differs vastly from Pliny's plea for mercy for the unnamed yet repentant freedman. What the comparison does point out, however, is the limited advantage manumission offered, as this freedman was still legally subject to his former owner's anger and punishment. Manumission falls far short of the freedom that emancipation and abolition will come to mean in later centuries, but even more important to this study is that, in comparison with Pliny's letter, Paul's appeal stands apart as all the more radical in its demand for new and equal relations, not to mention its unprecedented hospitality that included no mention of repentance, forgiveness, or even a petition for leniency in punishment. Paul's request goes far beyond reconciliation and restoring relations between a master and slave as it seeks to establish entirely new relations that are intended to replace the old ones and effectively dismantle all former ones. Paul writes not just as an *amicus domini* but as Christ's ambassador and prisoner who also invites Philemon and his community into a more committed following of the Lord, and what has been called by scholars a test case of Gal 3:28 and all that baptism in Christ intends to effect (Wright, *Colossians and Philemon,* 166; Wenham, *Paul: Follower of Jesus,* 235; Martyn, *Theological Issues,* 109; Furnish, *Love Command,* 97).

Supportive Rhetorical Strategy

Despite its brevity, this "masterpiece of persuasion" (Havener, *Philemon,* 1169; also Gorman, *Cruciformity,* 259) makes full use of ancient rhetoric including all three elements of *ethos, pathos,* and *logos* together with what has been described as a rhetoric of politeness (Wilson, "Pragmatics of Politeness," 107–19), which demonstrates the apostle's concern not to dishonor Philemon in any way, but rather to build up his authority within his own community.

Ethos ("character") is found in the thanksgiving section with an expression of Paul's gratitude for Philemon's loving and generous character (vv. 4-7) and his concern for extending such goodness in the present situation (vv. 13-14). Even though in Greco-Roman culture the expression of gratitude was itself sufficient to elicit further benefit (so Mott, "Power of Giving and Receiving," 60–71), Paul seeks to establish reciprocal relations through a more involved partnership (v. 17). Paul can count on Philemon as his friend and partner to do "what is necessary" (vv. 8, 16) and also to encourage and exhort the appropriate response from his community (v. 17).

Pathos ("emotion") is the cornerstone of the appeal (v. 9) that seeks to elicit fraternal and loving relations between Philemon and Onesimus (v. 16; Olbricht, "Pathos as Proof"). While familial language is used throughout, Paul also emphasizes the close bond he shares with Philemon as "beloved" friend and coworker (v. 1) and especially with his convert, Onesimus, who is described by Paul as "my own child" (v. 10). In sending Onesimus back to Philemon, Paul continues to clarify that he is sending his "own heart" (v. 12) who is to be welcomed as the apostle himself ("as me," v. 17), as he also tells his partner to charge any debt Onesimus may have incurred "to me" (v. 18).

The classical persuasive element of *logos* ("reason") stands behind Paul's appeal to love, which is verified as he makes this appeal as Christ's ambassador (v. 9). This means that while he announces the powerful claim of Christ, he brings it without any authority of his own to force or compel a response. It is truly an appeal that has the effect of honoring its recipient and bolstering his authority even as the necessity of his response is made clear. This kind of an appeal (as Christ's ambassador) rather than the more typical apostolic exhortation makes sense in a letter that seeks what may be a costly partnership, especially as Philemon's response is likely to meet with some resistance and opposition from without and possibly even within his own community.

It is also reasonable that, as Paul's partner, Philemon could be asked to send Onesimus back to assist Paul in what has already been presented as "useful" service (vv. 11, 13-14). But perhaps Paul's logical rhetoric is used to greatest effect where he downplays Onesimus' temporary absence as he effectively places the entire appeal within the context of God's providential plan that he "have him back forever" (v. 15), which flows directly into the central appeal itself (vv. 16-17). And it is the logic and basis of partnership to expect some contribution from each of the participants to their mutual benefit (Mitchell, "New Testament Envoys," 641–62).

Another powerfully persuasive move comes at the end of the appeal with the surprising shift in indebtedness. Immediately after assuming personal responsibility for any and all debts Onesimus might owe Philemon (v. 18), Paul, as unobtrusively as rhetorically possible, reminds his friend that he owes him his very life (v. 19). The close friendship Paul shares with Philemon is especially evident as he freely exclaims, "Yes, brother, I want some benefit from you in the Lord! Refresh my heart in Christ!" (v. 20), with a directness and repeated humor (pun on Onesimus' name, v. 11) that could only work between friends. One final affirmation of confidence in his friend's love and fidelity perfectly rounds out the persuasive appeal that brings the reader back to where Paul had started (vv. 1, 4-7). The "even more" expresses Paul's confidence that his friend has heard, in vv. 13-14, even his implied request for some personal help (Marxsen, *New Testament Foundations,* 221).

Function of the Letter and Its Importance in the Canon

Scholars have pointed out the various connections between Philemon and contemporary letters of recommendation or reconciliation and even friendly private correspondence, given its brevity and largely singular address (Doty, *Letters in Primitive Christianity,* 22; White, *Light from Ancient Letters,* 19–20, 218–20; Schubert, *Form and Function,* 365–77). Yet even as Philemon has many of the characteristic elements found in recommendations (cf. Rom 16:1-2; 2 Cor 3:1-3; Kim, *Form and Structure,* 123–27), and in letters that seek reconciliation (Mitchell, *Rhetoric of Reconciliation,* 65–183), it goes far beyond either of the two in what it actually seeks to accomplish.

Philemon is even unique in presenting less of an apostolic exhortation and more of an appeal that is friendly and yet somewhat diplomatically official, in making what John Koenig has aptly described as a "graceful persuasion to justice" (*Philemon,* 186–91). Paul comes as Christ's emissary as he invites his partner, Philemon, to elicit the necessary response from his community, who are to graciously welcome Onesimus back home as their "beloved brother."

Perhaps a reasonable scenario that recognizes the special nature of the appeal and takes into account the circumstances involved can imagine Onesimus, who is sent back with the letter, delivering it first to Philemon (and perhaps Apphia and Archippus), who will then make all the necessary preparations for it to be read aloud within the gathered community, perhaps in a way that will ensure that the congregation is ready to grasp and accept all the implications involved (cf. 1 Cor 14:16; 1 Thess 5:27; also Acts 9:2; Cox, "Reading of the Personal Letters," 74–91).

Questions as to how so brief a letter actually made it into the canon generally have circled around the speculation that Onesimus, who treasured his so-called "charter of liberty" (Bruce, *Paul: Apostle of the Heart Set Free,* 406), was the same person Ignatius referred to as bishop of Ephesus some fifty years later, and that he was instrumental in guaranteeing its placement among the Pauline collection (*Ign. Eph.* 1.3; Knox, Houlden). And while it has been posited that its canonical stature must mean that Onesimus was granted his freedom to accompany Paul (so O'Brien, *Philemon;* Wright, *Colossians and Philemon,* 170), it seems more likely that the letter to Philemon stands on its own merits, given its radical, even groundbreaking appeal, testifying to the uncompromising nature of the Gospel and continuing to challenge all who belong to Christ to live in a way that is a clear indication of God's reign on earth.

Although in the Roman Catholic lectionary it is read only once every three years on the Twenty-third Sunday in Ordinary Time (Phlm 9-10, 12-17; Cycle C) and once every two years on a weekday (Phlm 7-20; 32d week, Year II), both readings are paired with selections from the Gospel of Luke (Luke 14:25-33 and Luke 17:20-25). These combinations are interesting insofar as they support the interpretation that is given here. In both readings Jesus meets suffering and opposition when he breaks through socially accepted relationships to establish new ones in a world that opposes the coming of God's reign.

Early Christianity and Its Response to Slavery

Although in Pauline circles some thought was apparently given to the better treatment of slaves, not all churches seemed to grasp what Paul saw as the Gospel imperative to regard Christian slaves as brothers and sisters and "no longer as slaves" (v. 16). While the Deutero-Pauline letters remind slaveholders that they, like their slaves, also have one Master in the Lord Jesus Christ (Col 3:22–4:1; Eph 6:5-9), later Christian letters exhort slaves to honor their masters but do not voice the earlier and corresponding admonitions to their owners (cf. 1 Tim 6:1-2; Titus 2:9-10).

Still, Paul's daring request and its likely outcome in Onesimus' release may well have set the precedent for future practice in the early church in gaining freedom for Christian slaves. A letter from Ignatius, bishop of Syrian Antioch, to Polycarp, bishop of Smyrna, provides evidence that money needed for the manumission of slaves was being taken out of church funds (Ign. *Pol.* 4.3; cf. *Smyrn.* 6.2; *Phld.* 6.3; Herm. *Mand.* 8.10; Herm. *Sim.* 1.8; Osiek, "Ransom of Captives," 373–74; Rupprecht, "Attitudes on Slavery," 262). It is thought that when Ignatius writes that slaves should not demand such funds he is not stating any opposition to manumission but only that these funds be first distributed to those who need it the most, such as the hungry, homeless, and imprisoned, especially those abused and condemned for their faith (Harrill, *Manumission of Slaves,*

194–95; cf. *Apostolic Constitutions* 4.9, 12; 5.1). The early Christians were also known to become bond slaves to ransom prisoners and to feed the hungry (*1 Clem.* 55:2; 59.4; Osiek, "Ransom of Captives," 369; Harrill, *Manumission of Slaves,* 30 n. 70), a practice that was also attested by Justin Martyr (*Apol.* 67.6; Osiek, "Ransom of Captives," 372–73; eadem, *Philemon*).

Throughout the first century Christian writers continued to speak of the harsh lives of slaves, yet few seemed to realize or act on the radical implications of baptism or the significance of Paul's appeal. Perhaps no one spoke out in favor of slaves and the obligation of Christians to teach them to be self-supporting and subsequently to grant them their freedom more than John Chrysostom (ca. 347–407), who favored Paul and his letters. Fully aware of the opposition he faced, he writes, "I know I am annoying my hearers, but what am I to do? For this purpose I am appointed. I will not cease speaking so" (Homily 40 on 1 Cor 10; Maxwell, *Slavery and the Catholic Church,* 38–39; Rupprecht, "Attitudes on Slavery," 273, 275–76).

Those who did speak out on behalf of slaves were often people who had contact with slaves and knew of their situation. Yet still, much as in the Old Testament, directives had to be provided, such as the right of slaves to be free to worship on Sundays and holy days (*Apostolic Constitutions* 33) and legislation that prevented the breakup of slave families (*Theodosian Code* 2.25.1). Under Constantine manumission was officially sanctioned by the church (cf. Augustine [*Sermons* 21, 6] who refers to a manumission ceremony; Finley, *Slavery in Classical Antiquity,* 144).

Still, the impact of Greek philosophers such as Plato and Aristotle, who regarded slaves as inferior and slavery as completely natural, continued to be enormously influential. And when coupled with the view of slavery as a consequence of sin this assumption made it difficult to overturn prejudices against slaves or to elicit concern for their plight. The tendency toward spiritualizing poverty and glorifying suffering in itself made it even more difficult for people to appreciate the good news for the oppressed that Christ had already effected or to recognize and oppose the injustice of slavery that, for the most part, went unchallenged for the next fifteen hundred years. It was only in the last few centuries that large-scale abolition movements arose to seek social justice and freedom for people on a widespread, even universal, scale. Still, much remains to be done as slavery continues to exist wherever the poor and powerless continue to be exploited in every country of the world.

Various attempts to secure freedom for slaves dot the centuries and a study of the numerous efforts of Christians throughout history goes beyond the scope of this study. However, in the Roman Catholic tradition what has been described as the first abolition text is a letter written by a Benedictine monk to Louis the Pious in an effort to keep prisoners of war alive and obtain freedom for slaves, dated around 830 C.E. (Maxwell,

Slavery and the Catholic Church, 42–43). Also notable was the decision of Irish bishops to set the English free at the council at Armagh in 1117 C.E. Sadly, however, there is also the history of slavery employed as an ecclesiastical penalty, imposed by some local councils and popes from 633–1535 C.E. And yet from 1537 onward there were both papal and conciliar denunciations of slave trade in the Americas in response to the plight of the American Indians; by 1839 Pope Gregory XVI condemned African slave trading. By the sixteenth century numerous individuals and groups protested the evils of slavery (Maxwell, *Slavery and the Catholic Church,* 68). Prior to the eighteenth century no one thought to question the morality or legality of slavery as an institution (ibid. 10; Brett, *Slavery and the Catholic Tradition,* 212–19). The Second Vatican Council (1962–1965) spoke of slavery as an affront to God the creator and as poison within society whose institutions are to serve the purpose of promoting human dignity (*Gaudium et Spes* 27, 29).

The detrimental interpretation of the curse of Ham by the Alexandrians had already been given another interpretation a century earlier by Justin Martyr who interpreted the curse of Genesis 7 to show that slaves and free would, someday, be one in Christ (*Apol.* 1.27; Rupprecht, "Attitudes on Slavery," 263). Tragically, this was lost on those who used the curse in Genesis to serve their own agendas in the American slave debates that also abused the Pauline texts to legimate slavery (Horsley, "Paul and Slavery," 153–54). Even taking Philemon 12 out of context to suggest that Paul sent a slave back to his owner completely ignores his primary intent to have Philemon embrace him no longer as a slave, but as a "beloved brother," within both the household and the community (v. 16), and to ensure that he will be greeted with the same welcome as Paul would receive, that is, as an honored guest and ambassador of Christ (v. 17). Also important is the fact that Paul is writing not merely to a slaveowning friend, but to his own beloved son in Christ (v. 19), who is also his friend, coworker, leader, and host of the community, and even a partner Paul trusts to grant his request and even release Onesimus to work alongside the apostle, with or without manumission (vv. 21, 13-14).

A positive outcome also remains, however, in the witness to the promise and power the Gospel can convey to those who are poor and powerless, captive and enslaved in what Vincent Wimbush has called "A Meeting of Worlds" (190–97), where he describes the amazing embrace of the slaveowners' Gospel by African-American slaves who, perhaps like slaves in the first century, heard themselves addressed in it and by it and came to experience its hope, its consolation, and its enormous power to transform their lives and their future for the betterment and hope of all humanity.

GENERAL BIBLIOGRAPHY

A. *Commentaries*

Barclay, J. M. G. *Colossians and Philemon.* Sheffield: Sheffield Academic Press, 1997.

Barth, Marcus, and Helmut Blanke. *The Letter to Philemon: A New Translation with Notes and Commentary.* Grand Rapids and Cambridge: Eerdmans, 2000.

Bruce, F. F. *The Epistles to the Colossians, to Philemon, and to the Ephesians.* Grand Rapids: Eerdmans, 1984.

Caird, G. B. *Paul's Letters from Prison (Ephesians, Philippians, Colossians, Philemon) in the Revised Standard Version: Introduction and Commentary.* Oxford: Oxford University Press, 1976; reprint 1981.

Dibelius, Martin. *An die Kolosser, Epheser, an Philemon.* 3rd ed. Tübingen: J. C. B. Mohr (Paul Siebeck), 1953.

Dunn, James D. G. *The Epistles to the Colossians and to Philemon: A Commentary on the Greek Text.* Carlisle: Paternoster; Grand Rapids: Eerdmans, 1996.

Fitzmyer, Joseph A. *The Letter to Philemon.* New York: Doubleday, 2000.

Getty, Mary Ann. *Philippians and Philemon.* Wilmington: Michael Glazier, 1980.

Gnilka, Joachim. *Der Philemonbrief.* HTKNT 10.4. Freiburg: Herder, 1982.

Harrington, Daniel J. *Paul's Prison Letters: Spiritual Commentaries on Paul's Letters to Philemon, the Philippians, and the Colossians.* Hyde Park, NY: New City Press, 1997.

Harris, Murray J. *Colossians & Philemon.* Grand Rapids: Eerdmans, 1991.

Havener, Ivan. *First Thessalonians, Philippians, Philemon, Second Thessalonians, Colossians, Ephesians.* Collegeville: Liturgical Press, 1983.

Houlden, J. L. *Paul's Letters from Prison: Philippians, Colossians, Philemon and Ephesians.* Philadelphia: Westminster, 1970; reprint 1977.

Koenig, John. *Galatians, Philippians, Philemon, Thessalonians,* in Edgar Krentz, John Koenig, and Donald H. Juel, eds., *Augsburg Commentary on the New Testament.* Minneapolis: Augsburg, 1985.

Knox, John. *Philemon Among the Letters of Paul: A New View of its Place and Importance.* Chicago: University of Chicago Press; New York and Nashville: Abingdon, 1939; rev. ed. 1959.

Lightfoot, J. B. *St. Paul's Epistles to the Colossians and to Philemon.* London and New York: Macmillan; Grand Rapids: Zondervan, 1879; reprint 1978.

Lohmeyer, Ernst. *Die Briefe an die Philipper, an die Kolosser und an Philemon übersetzt und erklärt.* KEK 9. 13th ed. Göttingen: Vandenhoeck & Ruprecht, 1964; reprint 1974.

Lohse, Eduard. *A Commentary on the Epistles to the Colossians and to Philemon.* Hermeneia. Philadelphia: Fortress, 1971.

Martin, Ralph P. *Ephesians, Colossians, and Philemon.* Atlanta: John Knox, 1991.

Moule, C. F. D. *The Epistles of Paul the Apostle to the Colossians and to Philemon.* Cambridge: Cambridge University Press, 1958.

Müller, J. J. *The Epistles of Paul to the Philippians and to Philemon.* Grand Rapids: Eerdmans, 1955.

O'Brien, Peter T. *Colossians, Philemon.* Waco, TX: Word Books, 1982.

Osiek, Carolyn. *Philippians, Philemon.* Nashville: Abingdon, 2000.

Stuhlmacher, Peter. *Der Brief an Philemon.* EKKNT 18. 2nd ed. Zürich: Benziger Verlag; Neukirchen-Vluyn: Neukirchener Verlag, 1981.

Suhl, Alfred. *Der Brief an Philemon.* Zürcher Bibelkommentare: NT 13. Zürich: Theologischer Verlag, 1981.

Vincent, M. R. *A Critical and Exegetical Commentary on the Epistles to the Philippians and to Philemon.* ICC. New York: Scribner's; Edinburgh: T & T Clark, 1895; 5th ed. 1955.

Wright, N. T. *The Epistles of Paul to the Colossians and to Philemon: An Introduction and Commentary.* Grand Rapids: Eerdmans, 1986.

B. *Studies*

Achtemeier, Paul J. "Finding the Way to Paul's Theology: A Response to J. Christiaan Beker," in Jouette M. Bassler, ed., *Pauline Theology.* Vol. 1. *Thessalonians, Philippians, Galatians, Philemon.* Minneapolis: Fortress, 1991, 25–36.

Aune, David E. *The New Testament in Its Literary Environment.* Philadelphia: Westminster, 1985.

Bahr, Gordon J. "Subscriptions in the Pauline Letters," *JBL* 87 (1968) 27–41.

Balch, David L., and Carolyn Osiek, eds. *Early Christian Families in Context: An Interdisciplinary Dialogue.* Grand Rapids: Eerdmans, 2003.

Banks, Robert. *Paul's Idea of Community.* Grand Rapids: Eerdmans, 1980.

Barclay, J. M. G. "Paul, Philemon and the Dilemma of Christian Slave Ownership," *JSNT* 37 (1991) 161–86.

Bartchy, S. Scott. *First Century Slavery and the Interpretation of 1 Corinthians 7:21.* Missoula: Scholars, 1973.

________. "Undermining Ancient Patriarchy: The Apostle Paul's Vision of a Society of Siblings," *BTB* 29 (1999) 68–78.

Bassler, Jouette M. "Grace Probing the Limits," *Int* 57 (2003) 24–33.

Beker, J. Christiaan. "Recasting Pauline Theology: The Coherence Contingency Scheme as Interpretative Model," in Jouette M. Bassler, ed., *Pauline Theology.* Vol. 1. *Thessalonians, Philippians, Galatians, Philemon.* Philadelphia: Fortress, 1991, 15–24.

Best, Ernst. "Paul's Apostolic Authority — ?" *JSNT* 27 (1986) 3–25.

Betz, Hans Dieter. *2 Corinthians 8 and 9: A Commentary on Two Administrative Letters of the Apostle Paul.* 2d ed. Philadelphia: Fortress, 1985.

Boer, Martinus C. de. "Paul and Jewish Apocalyptic Eschatology," in Joel Marcus and Marion L. Soards, eds., *Apocalyptic and the New Testament: Essays in Honor of J. Louis Martyn.* Sheffield: JSOT Press, 1989, 169–90.

________. "Paul, Theologian of God's Apocalypse," *Int* 56 (2002) 21–33.

Boers, Hendrikus. "Ἀγάπη and Χάρις in Paul's Thought," *CBQ* 59 (1997) 693–713.

Bradley, Keith R. *Slaves and Masters in the Roman Empire: A Study in Social Control.* New York: Oxford University Press, 1987; paperback ed. 1998.

Branick, Vincent. *The House Church in the Writings of Paul.* Wilmington: Michael Glazier, 1989.

Brett, Stephen F. *Slavery and the Catholic Tradition: Rights in the Balance.* New York: Peter Lang, 1994.

Brown, Raymond E. *An Introduction to the New Testament.* New York: Doubleday, 1997.

Bruce, F. F. *Paul, Apostle of the Heart Set Free.* Grand Rapids: Eerdmans, 1997.

Brueggemann, Walter. *Peace.* St. Louis: Chalice, 2001.

Bultmann, Rudolf. *Theology of the New Testament.* Vol. 1. London: S.C.M., 1952.

Callahan, Allan D. *Embassy of Onesimus: The Letter of Paul to Philemon.* Valley Forge, PA: Trinity Press International, 1997.

________, and Richard A. Horsley. "Slave Resistance in Classical Antiquity," *Semeia* 83/84 (1998) 133–51.

Campbell, John Y. "'*Koinonia.*' Its Cognates in the New Testament," in idem, *Three New Testament Studies.* Leiden: Brill, 1965, 1–28.

Cassidy, Richard J. "Roman Imprisonment and Paul's Letter to Philemon," in Anthony J. Tambasco, ed., *The Bible on Suffering: Social and Political Implications.* New York, NY, and Mahwah, NJ: Paulist, 2001, 144–64.

________. *Paul in Chains. Roman Imprisonment and the Letters of Paul.* New York: Crossroad, 2001.

Collins, Raymond F. *First Corinthians.* Collegeville: Liturgical Press, 1999.

Conzelmann, Hans. *An Outline of the Theology of the New Testament.* New York: Harper & Row, 1969.

Cousar, Charles B. *The Letters of Paul. Conversations in Context.* 4th ed. Nashville: Abingdon, 1998.

Cox, Claude E. "The Reading of the Personal Letters as the Background for the Reading of the Scriptures in the Early Church," in Abraham J. Malherbe, Frederick W. Norris, and James W. Thompson, eds., *The Early Church in its Context: Essays in Honor of Everett Ferguson.* Leiden and Boston: Brill, 1998, 74–91.

Cranfield, C. E. B. *A Critical and Exegetical Commentary on the Epistle to the Romans.* 6th ed. Edinburgh: T & T Clark, 1975–1979.

Davis, David Brion. *The Problem of Slavery in Western Culture.* Ithaca, NY: Cornell University Press, 1966.

Deissmann, Adolf. *Light from the Ancient East.* London: Hodder & Stoughton, 1910, 227–42.

DeVos, Craig S. "Once a Slave, Always a Slave? Slavery, Manumission and Relational Patterns in Paul's Letter to Philemon," *JSNT* 82 (2001) 89–105.

Dillon, Richard J. "Ravens, Lilies, and the Kingdom of God (Matthew 6:25-33// Luke 12:22-31)," *CBQ* 53 (1991) 605–27.

________. "The Spirit as Taskmaster and Troublemaker in Romans 8," *CBQ* 60 (1998) 682–702.

Donfried, Karl P. *Paul, Thessalonica and Early Christianity.* London: T & T Clark, 2002.

Doty, William G. *Letters in Primitive Christianity.* Philadelphia: Fortress, 1973.

Downing, F. Gerald. *Cynics, Paul and the Pauline Churches.* New York: Routledge, 1998.

Durham, John I. "שׁלום and the Presence of God," in John I. Durham and Joshua Roy Porter, eds., *Proclamation and Presence: Essays in Honour of Gwynne Henton Davies.* London: S.C.M., 1970, 272–93.

Felder, Cain Hope. "The Letter to Philemon," *The New Interpreter's Bible.* Nashville: Abingdon, 2000, 881–905.

Fiddes, Paul S. *Participation in God. A Pastoral Doctrine of the Trinity.* Louisville: Westminster John Knox, 2001.

Finley, Moses I. *Slavery in Classical Antiquity: Views and Controversies.* London: Lowe and Brydone, Ltd., 1964.

________. *The Ancient Economy.* Berkeley: University of California Press, 1985.

Fretheim, Terence E. *Exodus.* Louisville: John Knox, 1991.

Funk, Robert R. "The Apostolic Parousia: Form and Significance," in William R. Farmer, C. F. D. Moule, and Richard R. Niebuhr, eds., *Christian History and Interpretation: Studies Presented to John Knox.* Cambridge: Cambridge University Press, 1967, 249–68.

Furnish, Victor Paul. *The Love Command in the New Testament.* Nashville: Abingdon, 1972.

________. "Inside Looking Out: Some Pauline Views of the Unbelieving Public," in Janice Capel Anderson, Philip Sellew, and Claudia Setzer, eds., *Pauline Conversations in Context: Essays in Honor of Calvin J. Roetzel.* Sheffield: Sheffield Academic Press, 2002, 104–24.

Gaventa, Beverly R. *From Darkness to Light: Aspects of Conversion in the New Testament.* Philadelphia: Fortress, 1986.

Gillman, Florence M. *Women Who Knew Paul.* Collegeville: Liturgical Press, 1992.

Glancy, Jennifer A. *Slavery in Early Christianity.* Oxford and New York: Oxford University Press, 2002.

Gorman, Michael J. *Cruciformity: Paul's Narrative Spirituality of the Cross.* Grand Rapids: Eerdmans, 2001.

Greeven, Heinrich. "Prüfung der Thesen von J. Knox zum Philemonbrief," *TLZ* 79 (1954) 373–78.

Harrill, J. Albert. *The Manumission of Slaves in Early Christianity.* Tübingen: J. C. B. Mohr (Paul Siebeck), 1995.

Harrington, Daniel J. *The Church According to the New Testament. What the Wisdom and Witness of Early Christianity Teach Us Today.* Franklin, WI: Sheed and Ward, 2001.

________. "Love as the Primary Virtue," in Daniel J. Harrington and James F. Keenan, eds., *Jesus and Virtue Ethics: Building Bridges Between New Testament Studies and Moral Theology.* Lanham, MD: Sheed and Ward, 2002.

Harrison, P. N. "Onesimus and Philemon," *ATR* 32 (1950) 268–94.

Heil, John P. "The Chiastic Structure and Meaning of Paul's Letter to Philemon," *Bib* 82 (2001) 178–206.

Hodgson, Peter C. "Christ Incarnate: The Shape of Redemptive Love," in idem, *Winds of the Spirit: A Constructive Christian Theology.* Louisville: Westminster John Knox, 1994, 231–64.

Hooker, Morna D. "*Pistis Christou*," in eadem, *From Adam to Christ: Essays on Paul.* New York and Cambridge: Cambridge University Press, 1990, 165–86.

________. "A Partner in the Gospel: Paul's Understanding of His Ministry," in Eugene H. Lovering, Jr., and Jerry L. Sumney, eds., *Theology and Ethics in Paul and His Interpreters: Essays in Honor of Victor Paul Furnish.* Nashville: Abingdon, 1996, 83–100.

Hopkins, Keith. *Conquerors and Slaves.* Cambridge: Cambridge University Press, 1978.

Hoppe, Leslie J. "The Torah Responds to the Poor," *TBT* 32 (1994) 277–82.

Horsley, Richard A., ed., *Paul and Empire: Religion and Power in Roman Imperial Society.* Harrisburg, PA: Trinity Press International, 1997.

________. "The Slave Systems of Classical Antiquity and Their Reluctant Recognition by Modern Scholars," *Semeia* 83/84 (1998) 19–66.

________. "Paul and Slavery: A Critical Alternative to Recent Readings," *Semeia* 83/84 (1998) 153–200.

Hultgren, Arland. *Christ and His Benefits: Christology and Redemption in the New Testament.* Philadelphia: Fortress, 1987.

Johnson, Elizabeth A. *She Who Is: The Mystery of God in Feminist Theological Discourse.* New York: Crossroad, 1992; reprint 2002.

Käsemann, Ernst. "Worship in Everyday Life," in idem, *New Testament Questions of Today.* Trans. W. J. Montague. Philadelphia: Fortress, 1969, 188–95.

________. "The Cry for Liberty in the Worship of the Church," in idem, *Perspectives on Paul.* Trans. Margaret Kohl. Philadelphia: Fortress, 1971, 122–37.

Keck, Leander. *Paul and His Letters.* Philadelphia: Fortress, 1979, 94–95.

Kim, Chan-Hie. *Form and Structure of the Familiar Greek Letter of Recommendation.* SBLDS 4. Missoula: Society of Biblical Literature, 1972.

Koester, Helmut. "Ephesos in Early Christian Literature," in idem, ed., *Ephesos. Metropolis of Asia: An Interdisciplinary Approach to its Archaeology, Religion, and Culture.* Harvard Theological Studies 41. Valley Forge, PA: Trinity Press International, 1995.

Lampe, Peter. "Keine 'Sklavenflucht' des Onesimus," *ZNW* 76 (1985) 135–37.

Lapsley, Jacqueline E. "Feeling Our Way: Love for God in Deuteronomy," *CBQ* 65 (2003) 350–69.

LaVerdiere, Eugene. *Eucharist in the New Testament and the Early Church.* Collegeville: Liturgical Press, 1996.

Lewis, Lloyd. A. "An African-American Appraisal of the Philemon-Paul-Onesimus Triangle," in Cain Hope Felder, ed., *Stony the Road We Trod: African American Biblical Interpretation.* Minneapolis: Fortress, 1991, 232–46.

Lohfink, Gerhard. *Jesus and Community: The Social Dimension of Christian Faith.* Trans. John P. Galvin. Philadelphia: Fortress; New York, NY, and Mahwah, NJ: Paulist, 1984.

Lyall, Francis. *Slaves, Citizens and Sons. Legal Metaphors in the Epistles.* Grand Rapids: Zondervan, 1984.

MacDonald, Margaret Y. "Reading Real Women Through the Undisputed Letters of Paul," in Ross S. Kraemer and Mary Rose D'Angelo, eds., *Women and Christian Origins.* New York and Oxford: Oxford University Press, 1999, 199–220.

________. *Colossians and Ephesians.* Collegeville: Liturgical Press, 2000.

Malherbe, Abraham J. "The Beasts of Ephesus," *JBL* 87 (1968) 71–80.

________. *Social Aspects of Early Christianity.* Philadelphia: Fortress, 1983.

Malina, Bruce J. *The New Testament World: Insights from Cultural Anthropology.* Louisville: Westminster John Knox, rev. ed. 1993.

Marrow, Stanley B. *Speaking the Word Fearlessly: Boldness in the New Testament.* New York, NY, and Ramsey, NJ: Paulist, 1982.

Marshall, I. Howard. "The Theology of Philemon," in Karl P. Donfried and I. Howard Marshall, eds., *The Theology of the Shorter Pauline Letters.* New York: Cambridge University Press, 1993, 175–91.

Martin, Clarice J. "The Rhetorical Function of Commercial Language in Paul's Letter to Philemon (Verse 18)," in Duane F. Watson, ed., *Persuasive Artistry: Studies in New Testament Rhetoric in Honor of George A. Kennedy.* Sheffield: Sheffield Academic Press, 1991, 321–37.

Martin, Dale. *Slavery as Salvation: The Metaphor of Slavery in Pauline Christianity.* New Haven and London: Yale University Press, 1990.

Martyn, J. Louis. *Theological Issues in the Letters of Paul.* Nashville: Abingdon, 1997.

Marxsen, Willi. *New Testament Foundations for Christian Ethics.* Trans. O. C. Dean. Minneapolis: Fortress, 1993.

Matera, Frank, J. *Strategies for Preaching Paul.* Collegeville: Liturgical Press, 2001.

Maxwell, John F. *Slavery and the Catholic Church: The History of Catholic Teaching Concerning the Moral Legitimacy of the Institution of Slavery.* Chichester and London: Barry Rose Publishers, 1975.

Meeks, Wayne A. *The First Urban Christians: The Social World of the Apostle Paul.* 2d ed. New Haven and London: Yale University Press, 2003.

Michaelis, Wilhelm. *Einleitung in das Neue Testament.* 2d ed. Bern: B. Haller, 1954.

Miller, James C. *The Obedience of Faith, the Eschatological People of God, and the Purpose of Romans.* SBLDS 177. Atlanta: Society of Biblical Literature, 2000.

Mitchell, Margaret M. *Paul and the Rhetoric of Reconciliation: An Exegetical Investigation of the Language and Composition of 1 Corinthians.* Louisville: Westminster John Knox, 1991.

________. "New Testament Envoys in the Context of Greco-Roman Diplomatic and Epistolary Conventions: The Example of Timothy and Titus," *JBL* 111 (1992) 641–62.

________. "John Chrysostom on Philemon: A Second Look," *HTR* 88 (1995) 135–48.

Moltmann, Jürgen. *The Spirit of Life: A Universal Affirmation.* Trans. Margaret Kohl. Minneapolis: Fortress, 2001.

Mott, Stephen Charles. "The Power of Giving and Receiving: Reciprocity in Hellenistic Benevolence," in Gerald F. Hawthorne, ed., *Current Issues in Biblical and Patristic Interpretation.* Grand Rapids: Eerdmans, 1975, 60–72.

Moule, C. F. D. *An Idiom Book of New Testament Greek.* 2d ed. Cambridge: Cambridge University Press, 1959; reprint 1990.

Moulton, James H., and George Milligan. *The Vocabulary of the Greek New Testament Illustrated from the Papyri and other Non-Literary Sources.* London: Hodder & Stoughton, 1930; reprint 1957.

Mullins, Terence Y. "Greetings as New Testament Form," *JBL* 87 (1968) 418–26.

________. "Visit Talk in New Testament Letters," *CBQ* 35 (1973) 350–58.

________. "The Thanksgivings of Philemon and Colossians," *NTS* 30 (1984) 288–93.

Nordling, J. G. "Onesimus Fugitivus: A Defence of the Runaway Slave Hypothesis in Philemon," *JSNT* 41 (1991) 97–119.

Olbricht, Thomas H. "Pathos as Proof in Greco-Roman Rhetoric," in Thomas H. Olbricht and Jerry L. Sumney, eds., *Paul and Pathos*. Atlanta: Society of Biblical Literature, 2001.

Ollrog, Wolf-Henning. *Paulus und seine Mitarbeiter: Untersuchungen zu Theorie und Praxis der paulinishen Mission*. Neukirchen-Vluyn: Neukirchener Verlag, 1979.

Olson, Stanley N. "Pauline Expressions of Confidence in His Addressees," *CBQ* 47 (1985) 282–95.

Osiek, Carolyn. "The Ransom of Captives: Evolution of a Tradition," *HTR* 74 (1981) 365–86.

________, and David L. Balch. *Families in the New Testament World: Households and House Churches*. Louisville: Westminster John Knox, 1997.

Panikulam, George. *Koinōnia in the New Testament: A Dynamic Expression of Christian Life*. Rome: Biblical Institute Press, 1979.

Pao, David W. *Thanksgiving: An Investigation of a Pauline Theme*. Downers Grove, IL: InterVarsity Press, 2002.

Patterson, Orlando. "Paul, Slavery and Freedom: Personal and Socio-Historical Reflections," *Semeia* 83/84 (1998) 263–79.

________. *Slavery and Social Death: A Comparative Study*. Cambridge: Harvard University Press, 1982.

Patzia, Arthur, G. *The Emergence of the Church: Context, Growth, Leadership and Worship*. Downers Grove, IL: InterVarsity Press, 2001.

Peperzak, Adriaan. "Giving," in Jean-Joseph Goux, Edith Wyschogrod, and Eric Boynton, eds., *The Enigma of Gift and Sacrifice*. New York: Fordham University Press, 2002, 161–75.

Perdue, Leo G. "The Household, Old Testament Theology and Contemporary Hermeneutics," in Carol Meyers, Joseph Blenkinsopp, John J. Collins, and Leo G. Perdue, *Families in Ancient Israel*. Louisville: Westminster John Knox, 1997, 223–57.

Perkins, Pheme. *Abraham's Divided Children: Galatians and the Politics of Faith*. Harrisburg, PA: Trinity Press International, 2001.

Peterson, Norman R. *Rediscovering Paul: Philemon and the Sociology of Paul's Narrative World*. Philadelphia: Fortress, 1985.

Plank, Karl A. *Paul and the Irony of Affliction*. Atlanta: Scholars, 1987.

Plevnik, Joseph. "The Understanding of God at the Basis of Pauline Theology," *CBQ* 65 (2003) 554–67.

Post, Stephen G. *A Theory of Agapē: On the Meaning of Christian Love*. Lewisburg, PA: Bucknell University Press; Cranberry, NJ: Associated University Presses, 1990.

Preiss, Théo. *Life in Christ*. Trans. Harold Knight. London: S.C.M., 1954.

Radl, Walter. "Kult und Evangelium bei Paulus," *BZ* 31 (1987) 58–75.

Rapske, Brian M. "The Prisoner Paul in the Eyes of Onesimus," *NTS* 37 (1991) 187–203.

Riesenfeld, Harold. "Faith and Love Promoting Hope. An Interpretation of Philemon v. 6," in Morna D. Hooker and S. G. Wilson, eds., *Paul and Paulinism: Essays in Honor of C. K. Barrett*. London: S.P.C.K. 1982.

Roetzel, Calvin J. *The Letters of Paul: Conversations in Context*. Atlanta: John Knox, 1975; reprint 1985.

———. *The World that Shaped the New Testament.* Atlanta: John Knox, 1985.

Rupprecht, Arthur A. "Attitudes on Slavery Among the Church Fathers," in Richard N. Longenecker and Merrill C. Tenney, eds., *New Dimensions in New Testament Study.* Grand Rapids: Zondervan, 1974, 261–77.

Sakenfeld, Katherine Doob. "Loyalty and Love: The Language of Human Interconnections in the Hebrew Bible," in Michael. P. O'Connor and David Noel Freedman, eds., *Backgrounds for the Bible.* Winona Lake, IN: Eisenbrauns, 1987, 215–29.

Sampley, J. Paul. *Pauline Partnership in Christ: Christian Community and Commitment in Light of Roman Law.* Philadelphia: Fortress, 1980.

Sanders, Jack T. "The Transition from Opening Epistolary Thanksgivings to the Body of the Letters of the Pauline Corpus," *JBL* 81 (1962) 348–62.

Schnackenburg, Rudolf. *The Moral Teaching of the New Testament.* New York: Herder & Herder, 1965.

Schneiders, Sandra M. "A Community of Friends (John 13:1-20)," in eadem, *Written That You May Believe: Encountering Jesus in the Fourth Gospel.* New York: Crossroad, 1999, 162–79.

Schroeder, Frederic M. "Friendship in Aristotle and Some Peripatetic Philosophers," in John T. Fitzgerald, ed., *Greco-Roman Perspectives on Friendship.* Atlanta: Scholars, 1997.

Schubert, Paul. *Form and Function of the Pauline Thanksgivings.* Berlin: Töpelmann, 1939.

Schüssler Fiorenza, Elisabeth. *In Memory of Her: A Feminist Theological Reconstruction of Christian Origins.* New York: Crossroad, 1983.

———. "The Praxis of Coequal Discipleship," in Richard A. Horsley, ed., *Paul and Empire: Religion and Power in Roman Imperial Society.* Harrisburg, PA: Trinity Press International, 1997, 224–41.

Schütz, John Howard. *Paul and the Anatomy of Apostolic Authority.* Cambridge: Cambridge University Press, 1975.

Scott, James C. *Domination and the Arts of Resistance: Hidden Transcripts.* New Haven: Yale University Press, 1990.

Soards, Marion L. "Some Neglected Theological Dimensions of Paul's Letter to Philemon," *PRS* 17 (1990) 209–19.

Stambaugh, John E., and David L. Balch. *The New Testament in Its Social Environment.* Philadelphia: Westminster, 1986.

Stowers, Stanley K. *Letter Writing in Greco-Roman Antiquity.* Philadelphia: Westminster, 1986.

———. "Friends and Enemies in the Politics of Heaven: Reading Theology in Philippians," in Jouette M. Bassler, ed., *Pauline Theology.* Vol. 1. *Thessalonians, Philippians, Galatians, Philemon.* Minneapolis: Fortress, 1991, 105–21.

———. "Paul and Slavery: A Response," *Semeia* 83/84 (1998) 295–311.

Taylor, N. H. "Onesimus: A Case Study of Slave Conversion in Early Christianity," *Religion and Theology* 3 (1996) 259–81.

Theissen, Gerd. *The Social Setting of Pauline Christianity: Essays on Corinth.* Edited and translated by John H. Schütz. Philadelphia: Fortress, 1982.

———. *Social Reality and the Early Christians: Theology, Ethics and the World of the New Testament.* Trans. Margaret Kohl. Minneapolis: Fortress, 1992.

Thomas, Carolyn. *Reading the Letters of Saint Paul.* New York, NY, and Mahwah, NJ: Paulist, 2002.

Thurston, Bonnie Bowman. *Women in the New Testament: Questions and Commentary.* New York: Crossroad, 1998.

Unnik, W. C. van. "The Christian's Freedom of Speech in the New Testament," *BJRL* 44 (1962) 466–88.

Vacek, Edward Collins. *Love, Human and Divine: The Heart of Christian Ethics.* Washington, DC: Georgetown University Press, 1994.

Wallace-Hadrill, Andrew, ed. *Patronage in Ancient Society.* London: Routledge, 1989.

Watson, Alan. *Roman Slave Law.* Baltimore, MD: Johns Hopkins University Press, 1987.

Wedderburn, A. J. M. "Some Observations on Paul's Use of the Phrases 'in Christ' and 'with Christ,'" *JSNT* 25 (1985) 83–97.

Weima, Jeffrey A. *Neglected Endings: The Significance of the Pauline Letter Closings.* JSNTSup 101. Sheffield: JSOT Press, 1994.

Wenham, Davis. *Paul: Follower of Jesus or Founder of Christianity?* Grand Rapids: Eerdmans, 1995.

Westermann, William L. *The Slave Systems of Greek and Roman Antiquity.* Philadelphia: American Philosophical Society, 1955.

White, John L. *The Form and Function of the Body of the Greek Letter: A Study of the Letter-Body in the Non-literary Papyri and in Paul the Apostle.* SBLDS 2. Missoula: Scholars, 1972.

________. *Light from Ancient Letters.* Philadelphia: Fortress, 1986

________. *Apostle of God: Paul and the Promise of Abraham.* Peabody, MA: Hendrickson, 1999.

Wickert, Ulrich. "Der Philemonbrief: Privatbrief oder Apostolisches Schreiben?" *ZNW* 52 (1961) 230–38.

Wiles, Gordon P. *Paul's Intercessory Prayers: The Significance of the Intercessory Prayer Passages in the Letters of St. Paul.* Cambridge: Cambridge University Press, 1974.

Wilson, Andrew. "The Pragmatics of Politeness and Pauline Epistolography: A Case Study of the Letter to Philemon," *JSNT* 48 (1992) 107–19.

Wilson, Stephen G. "From Jesus to Paul: The Contours and Consequences of a Debate," in Peter Richardson and John C. Hurd, eds., *From Jesus to Paul.* Waterloo: Wilfred Laurier University Press, 1984, 1–21.

Wimbush, Vincent. "A Meeting of Worlds: African Americans and the Bible," in Fernando F. Segovia and Mary Ann Tolbert, eds., *Teaching the Bible. The Discourses and Politics of Biblical Pedagogy.* Maryknoll: Orbis, 1998, 190–99.

Winter, Sara C. "Paul's Letter to Philemon," *NTS* 33 (1987) 1–15.

Witherup, Ronald D. *Conversion in the New Testament.* Collegeville: Liturgical Press, 1994.

Wright, N. T. "*Christos* as Messiah in Paul: Philemon 6," in idem, *The Climax of the Covenant: Christ and Law in Pauline Theology.* Edinburgh: T & T Clark, 1991, 41–55.

________. "Paul's Gospel and Caesar's Empire," in Richard A. Horsley, ed., *Paul and Politics: Ekklesia, Israel, Imperium, Interpretation: Essays in Honor of Krister Stendahl.* Harrisburg, PA: Trinity Press International, 2000.

Zerwick, Max. *A Grammatical Analysis of the Greek New Testament.* Translated, revised, and adapted by Mary Grosvenor. Rome: Biblical Institute Press, 1981.

Ziesler, John A. *Pauline Christianity.* New York and Oxford: Oxford University Press, 1983.

TRANSLATION, NOTES, INTERPRETATION

1. *Formal Epistolary Opening and Salutation* (1-3)

1. Paul, a prisoner of Christ Jesus, and Timothy our brother. To Philemon our beloved friend and coworker 2. and Apphia our sister and Archippus our fellow soldier, and to the church at your house: 3. Grace to you and peace from God our Father and the Lord Jesus Christ.

Notes

1. *Paul:* As in every apostolic letter, Paul employs his Greco-Roman name, *Paulos.* It is only in Luke's companion volume of Acts that we hear of the Semitic cognomen, "Saul" (*Saulos,* Acts 7:58; 9:4; 13:2). Yet even here the evangelist shifts to an exclusive use of *Paulos* for this apostle to the Gentiles as he begins his extensive, worldwide mission (Acts 13:9; 15:12; 21:39; 26:1; Fitzmyer, *Philemon,* 83). Even if Paul had previously used his Jewish appellation, one might expect the apostle to use his Greek name in writing to Greek-speaking congregations. There is no indication that Paul ever used the Latin *Paulus* (Collins, *First Corinthians,* 50).

   a prisoner of Christ Jesus: desmios, lit. "prisoner," provides the first notice of Paul's imprisonment. Punctual reminders throughout the letter (vv. 9, 10, 13, 23) point clearly to an actual imprisonment. Its unique emphasis becomes apparent with the realization that it is the only time in any of the letters that Paul uses such a self-designation, including his other undisputed prison correspondence to the Philippians and the Deutero-Pauline letters to the Colossians and Ephesians (MacDonald, *Colossians, Ephesians,* 4). Missing are some of his more customary self-descriptions, such as *apostolos* ("apostle," Romans; 1 Corinthians; 2 Corinthians; Galatians) as there is no need for Paul to legitimate his authority to his own beloved child in Christ (see v. 19), and the Pauline favorite, *doulos* ("slave/servant," Romans; Philippians), with its rich biblical precedent (see "servants of God" in Exod 14:31; 1 Sam 3:10; 1 Kgs 8:66; Job 1:8; Ps. 31:16; Isa 43:10; 53:11; Jer 33:21; Ezek 34:24; Zech. 3:8, etc.), which may have seemed inappropriate in an appeal written on behalf of a runaway slave. Variant readings that replace "prisoner" (*desmios*, D) with "apostle" *(apostolos)* or add "apostle" to it (minuscule 629), as well as minuscules that replace "prisoner" with "slave"(323, 945) are all poorly supported in the manuscript tradition and represent a likely assimilation to other letters. Joseph Fitzmyer (*Philemon,* 7) also calls attention to the remarkable absence of significant variant readings in this letter (only ten in seven verses). As with all his other self-designations, *doulos Christou Iesou* or *apostolos Christou Iesou,* here too Paul describes himself in relation to the Lord, qualifying "prisoner" with the addition "of/for Christ Jesus" *(desmios Christou Iesou).* While the traditional reading "prisoner for Christ Jesus" finds support in the text itself, where Paul speaks of his "imprisonment for the gospel" (v. 13), Peter O'Brien (*Colossians, Philemon,* 271–72) rightly notes its additional meaning as a possessive genitive, as a prisoner "of Christ Jesus," to convey the sense of belonging to Christ. Marion Soards argues convincingly for such an interpretation because it emphasizes God's initiative, involvement, and sovereign claim on those who belong to Christ ("Some Neglected Theological Perspectives," 213). G. B. Caird (*Paul's Letters from Prison,* 218), J. L. Houlden (*Paul's Letters,* 228), Norman Peterson (*Rediscovering Paul,* 188), and Marcus Barth and Helmut Blanke (*Philemon,* 245–47) are among an increasing number of scholars who have come to include the subjective genitive meaning in their understanding of this expression. The name of Jesus and its messianic equivalent, Christ (Messiah, Anointed One), are joined together very early in the Christian tradition, with "Jesus Christ" being the full name of the crucified and risen Lord, which Paul prefers to reverse as "Christ Jesus" (see Fitzmyer, *Philemon,* 84, for a full list of citations). This titular placement of "Christ" may serve to emphasize the fulfillment of God's promises to Israel in sending Jesus, the promised Messiah. Such a thoroughgoing theological emphasis can be found in Romans, where Paul takes up the issue of God's fidelity to Israel (Rom 4:21; 9:5; 10:4).

and Timothy our brother: Timothy is mentioned as co-sender in four of the seven letters (2 Corinthians; Philippians; 1 Thessalonians; Philemon; cf. Colossians; 2 Thessalonians). That co-sender could also mean co-writer would be unlikely in this instance, as Paul will address Philemon in the first person singular throughout most of the letter. It is more probable that by "co-sender" Paul intends to include Timothy as a partner who is in agreement with his statements and appeal. In the second letter to the Corinthians, as here, Timothy is described as *ho adelphos* ("the brother," cf. 1 Thess 3:2). *Adelphos* occurs 113 times in the seven authentic letters of Paul, almost a third of all 343 occurrences within the NT. In Paul's usage of this familial term, as for much of its figurative NT usage, *adelphos* can refer to one's own countryman or –woman (Rom 9:3; cf. Heb 8:11; Jer 38:34 LXX; Helmer Ringgren, *adelphos, TDNT* 1:188–93), one's fellow Christian (Phlm 16; Rom 8:29; 1 Cor 15:58; Phil 4:1; 1 Thess 1:4) and one's friend and coworker, which is found in most of the Pauline prescripts and final greetings (Johannes Beutler, *adelphos, EDNT* 1:28–30). One of the best known of Paul's missionary companions, Timothy, having participated in much of Paul's mission (see Acts 16:1-5; 18:5; 19:22; 20:4) and having also shared in the sufferings endured for the sake of the Gospel (2 Cor 1:8-9; cf. Heb 13:23), is mentioned in every one of the apostle's letters except Galatians.

Like Onesimus (v. 10) and Philemon (v. 19), Timothy is also Paul's "beloved and faithful child in the Lord" (1 Cor 4:17) who is spoken of as "a son with a father" working with Paul for the sake of the Gospel (Phil 2:19). Paul writes that as a coworker Timothy shows concern for the church unmatched by anyone (Phil 2:19-22). Serving as the apostle's personal emissary, Timothy was entrusted at times with the task of securing the faith of a newly founded and fledgling community (1 Thess 3:2, 6), on other occasions with a mission to comfort and encourage Paul's partners (Phil 2:23-24), and even to settle disputes and mediate conflicts between the apostle and his own communities (1 Cor 16:10-11). Personally addressed in two Pastoral letters, Timothy is certainly favored and remembered by the early tradition as one of the apostle's closest and trusted missionary companions.

To Philemon our beloved friend and coworker: Philemon is Paul's sole dialogue partner throughout the entire letter, apart from the apostle's initial greeting to the community (v. 3), concluding remarks that request their prayers for his release (v. 22), and his final blessing (v. 25). While Timothy remains a beloved colleague and friend, all attention is focused in this letter on Paul's relationship with the letter's principal addressee, Philemon, and Onesimus, the one on whose behalf Paul writes and the only other person besides Philemon to be called "beloved" (v. 16). That Philemon, like Onesimus (v. 10), is also understood to be Paul's own convert (cf. v. 19) only serves to strengthen more deeply the fraternal bonds that Paul will emphasize later (v. 16). Throughout his letters Paul uses *agapētos,* most often translated as "beloved/dear friend," for his own converts (Rom 16:5), friends (Rom 16:8-9), coworkers (Rom 16:12), and entire communities known for the love and faith that are to identify those who belong to Christ (Rom 1:7; 1 Cor 10:14; 15:58; 2 Cor 7:1; 12:19; Phil 2:12; 4:1; 1 Thess 8:8). Manuscript D adds "brother" *(adelphos)* to "beloved," probably an assimilation to v. 16. The plural possessive pronoun *hēmōn* ("our") qualifies both *agapētos* and *synergos* ("coworker," BDAG 969). *Synergos* could suggest that Philemon had, at one time, worked together with Paul and Timothy. The apostle's coworkers included a host of women and men who labored side by side with him in proclaiming and teaching the Gospel, especially in cities and along major trade routes where they could encounter as many people as possible. In other letters Paul would also speak of his service as a "priestly ministry" (Rom 15:16) and a "ministry of reconciliation" (2 Cor 5:18), an understanding that is especially pertinent to this letter. Since "coworker" implies an active preaching ministry (Ollrog, *Paulus und seine Mitarbeiter,* 67), perhaps Philemon, like other coworkers (cf. Rom 16:3-4), might also have returned home to establish the community he hosts (v. 3). Whether or not this Philemon is the same person later mentioned in the tradition as a bishop of Colossae (*Apostolic Constitutions* 7.46) cannot be known with any certainty. There seems no doubt, however, that Philemon had made a significant contribution to the growth and maturation of the earliest Christian churches. Given the letter's acceptance within the undisputed Pauline canon, together with the apostle's own assurance that his friend and partner will do "even more" than he requests (v. 21), it is almost certain that Philemon gave his spiritual father every reason to rejoice. The apparent freedom of Onesimus in accompanying

Tychicus in carrying the Deutero-Pauline letter to the Colossians can be taken to substantiate such optimism (Col 4:9).

2. *and Apphia our sister:* Apphia is an easily identifiable Phrygian name (*MM*, 73) found on many ancient and local inscriptions (Lightfoot, *Epistles*, 306–308). She, like "the brother" Timothy (v. 1) is similarly introduced as *tȩ̄ adelphȩ̄* ("the sister"), best translated as "our sister" as it is modified by the possessive pronoun *hēmōn* ("our") that also modifies "our fellow soldier." Traditional opinion has long considered Apphia to be Philemon's wife, but no explicit reference to any relationship is made within the letter. Even if Apphia had been Philemon's wife with management over the household, the use of *tȩ̄ adelphȩ̄* could serve to focus attention on Apphia's role as a Christian of influence within the local church that is to welcome Onesimus back home. Deliberate placement of "the sister" in tandem with "the brother" for Timothy could suggest some parity with respect to importance and/or influence within the community. Like Phoebe, who is also described as *adelphē* (Rom 16:1), Apphia is thought to be among Paul's coworkers (Johannes Beutler, *adelphos, EDNT* 1:30; cf. Rom 16:15; 1 Cor 7:15; 9:5; Jas 2:15; 2 John 13). A few manuscripts, such as D, and a number of minuscules either replace "sister" with "beloved" or, like ms. 629, add "beloved" to "sister" *(adelphȩ̄ tȩ̄ agapētȩ̄).* Such changes could reflect assimilation to "beloved" in the previous verse (so Fitzmyer, *Philemon*, 87). "Brother" and "sister" are the forms of expression Paul normally employs to describe both his own coworkers and Christians in general (e.g., Rom 8:29; 1 Cor 3:1). With already existing roots in the OT tradition (Deut 15:3) and especially given Jesus' own emphasis (Mark 3:34 *parr.*), such familial terms are likely to be the earliest ones used by Christians in distinguishing themselves as followers of Jesus Christ. This is certainly a traditional understanding Paul builds upon in forming such close-knit communities (Rom 8:14-16; Gal 4:5-7).

and Archippus our fellow soldier: Although Theodore of Mopsuestia (ca. 350–428 C.E.; *MPG* 66.950) thought that Archippus was the son of Apphia and Philemon, little is actually known of the person Paul characterizes as *tō̧ sustratiōtȩ̄ hēmōn* ("our fellow soldier"). Also translated as "comrade-in-arms," this Greek term denotes the highest military honor (BDAG 979; Zerwick, *Analysis*, 653; cf. Col 4:7). In this context it is expressive of dedicated service to the Gospel, the same sense found in Paul's use of the cognate form of the verb, *stratēuomai*, in describing his own mission in "serving as a soldier" (1 Cor 9:17) and in "waging a war" (2 Cor 10:3) for Christ, and in speaking of his own mission as a *stratēia* or "campaign" (1 Cor 10:4). Aside from Archippus, only Epaphroditus, the beloved "messenger and minister" who is sent by the Philippians to assist Paul in prison, receives this special distinction as "fellow soldier" (Phil 2:25). While it remains uncertain whether the person who is admonished in the Deutero-Pauline letter is the same person who is praised here (Col 4:17), the list of corresponding names both here and in the Colossian letter, including Epaphras, Mark, Aristarchus, Demas, and Luke (Col 4:10, 13-14; Phlm 23-24), Onesimus (Col 4:9; Phlm 10), and Timothy (Col 1:1; Phlm 1), would seem to indicate that Philemon's house church may be located somewhere in the region of the Lycus Valley, either near or within Colossae. Like Philemon, later tradition also records someone named Archippus as bishop of Colossae, succeeding Epaphras (Jerome, *In Ep. ad Philemonem* 1 [*MPL* 26. 642] and as bishop of Laodicea (*Apostolic Constitutions* 7.46; Fitzmyer, *Philemon,* 88). Whether or not this is the same person is impossible to determine.

and to the church at your house: As Paul extends his greetings to the entire community, he also specifies its location at Philemon's home. *Kat'oikon sou* ("at your house") employs the second person singular *sou* ("your") that refers back to the first-named addressee, Philemon, and gives the first notice of the singular address that will continue throughout the thanksgiving and the body of the letter (vv. 4-20). But even here the personal request made to Philemon includes greetings to the congregation along with the pastoral concern that the entire community welcome Onesimus as a returning brother. As leader and host to the gathered community, Philemon has the responsibility to set the stage for the hospitality Paul seeks for Onesimus. During the earliest centuries of Christianity most Christians gathered for fellowship, catechesis, and worship within private dwellings that are referred to as house churches (*tę̄ kat'oikon . . . ekklēsią:* Rom 16:3, 5; 1 Cor 16:19; cf. Col 4:15). *Kat'oikon sou* represents the elided *kata* joining the accusative *oikon* and possessive pronoun *sou,* meaning "in your house" (BDAG 695). *Tę̄ ekklēsią* or "church," which literally refers to a people who are "called out" (*ek-kaleō;* see Harrington, *Church According to the New Testament,* 49–55; Banks, *Paul's Idea of Community,* 45), expresses the self-understanding of Christians who, like the people Israel, are also called together by God as one community. In the LXX *ekklēsia* was a frequent translation of the Hebrew *qāhāl,* the term for an assembly of people, from the gathering of an army (1 Sam 17:47) to the solemn assembly of God's covenanted people *(ekklēsia Kyriou)* gathered together to hear God's word (e.g., Deut 4:10; 23:2-9; cf. Josephus, *Ant.* 4.45 §309; *Bell.* 1.4 §654). It is through the Lord Jesus Christ that this communion is made possible for Christians. Used most frequently by Paul (62x), *ekklēsia* is also found in the Acts of the Apostles (23x), Revelation (20x), the non-Pauline letters (6x), and the Gospel of Matthew (3x; O'Brien, *ekklēsia, DPL* 124). While still accepting the possibility that the early Jewish Christians chose *ekklēsia* to avoid confusion with *synagōgē,* another synonym for assembly, others are currently arguing for a closer association with the Hellenistic political assembly in that, in the Christian *ekklēsia,* God was providing a lifegiving alternative to the dominant Greco-Roman political forms (Horsley, *Paul and Empire,* 208–11).

3. *Grace to you and peace*: This greeting of grace and peace, found in every one of the undisputed letters, joins *charis* ("grace") in replacing the typical and similar sounding Hellenistic *chairein* ("greetings," Jas 1:1; Acts 15:23; 23:26), with *eirēnē* ("peace"), the customary Jewish greeting (in Hebrew *šālōm,* Ezra 4:17; 5:7). The expression stands alone and requires no verb in Greek (cf. John 20:21). "Grace" is a biblical term rich in theological meaning, sharing the same Hebrew root *(ḥnn)* as the word to express God's "favor" (*ḥēn;* cf. 2 Cor 8:4) and is also used to translate חסד *(ḥesed),* which refers to God's "steadfast, covenant love." As God's own self-disclosure as a gracious God (Exod 34:6) it is often linked with mercy and salvation (Num 14:18; Pss 86:15; 103:8; 145:8-9; Jonah 4:2; Joel 2:13). As a testament to God's action on their behalf it became central

to Israel's confession of faith in God as "gracious and merciful" (Num 14:18; Pss 77:9-10; 86:15; 103:8; 145:8; Joel 2:13; Jonah 4:2; Neh 9:17; Kselman, "Grace," *ABD* 2:1084–86; Conzelmann, *charis*, *TDNT* 9:393–98). As an assurance of divine loving presence it is often coupled with peace, God's "covenant of peace" (Ezek 34:25; 37:26; Isa 54:10, 13; 55:12; Ps 29:11) that envisions the divine shepherding of Israel toward a future that God promises to bring to fruition (Brueggemann, *Peace*, 5–6; Durham, "שָׁלוֹם and the Presence of God," 277). It expresses the power of God's gracious presence to effect an abundance of life in relationship with God and other people that embraces justice as its essential element (Isa 32:17; Ps 85:10; Zech 8:16-19). Prophetic visions of God's peaceable kingdom (Isaiah 11) ruled by the Prince of Peace (Isaiah 9) include images of peace flowing like a river (Isa 48:18; 66:12). God is known experientially to be continually faithful in recreating and restoring new life to Israel (Jer 32:18-22). Similar pairings occur as "mercy and peace" (*2 Bar.* 78:2; Tob 7:12 [Codex Sinaiticus]), and elsewhere in Paul's letters, as "Father of mercies and God of peace" (2 Cor 1:3) and as "peace and mercy" (Gal 6:16). Paul personally experienced this grace in the gift and task of his own apostolic call and commission from God (Rom 1:1, 5; 15:15-16; cf. 2 Cor 12:9; Gal 1:1, 11-12; Bultmann, *Theology of the New Testament*, 290–91). As Paul stresses the gifted, unmerited character of grace (Rom 3:24; 5:15; 6:23; 11:5-6, 29) he also exhorts believers to be open to its lifegiving and transformative power (Rom 1:16-17). The blessing that joins grace with peace has precedent in the ancient poem and priestly blessing: "The Lord bless you and keep you. The Lord let his face shine upon you, and be gracious to you. The Lord look upon you kindly and give you peace" (Num 6:24-26; Durham, "שָׁלוֹם and the Presence of God," 284). This pronouncement of peace confers the fullness of divine blessing that bestows a perfection of well-being and wholeness, the fulfillment of which only God can accomplish (Ps 29:11; cf. Isa 52:7). God's promise of peace is vividly pictured as the establishment of God's new creation, a new heaven and a new earth that divine rule will bring (Isa 11:4-5, 9; cf. Isa 9:5; 45:7-8; 60:17; 66:12, 22; Joseph P. Healey, "Peace," *ABD* 5:206). Paul finds its most definitive and fullest expression in the salvific act of God in Christ Jesus, who effects this peace and reconciliation between God and the world (Rom 3:24-25). Thus, for Paul, God's eschatological promise of *šālōm* has already been initiated through Jesus Christ, and Paul's own prophetic vision includes a future that far surpasses all possible human comprehension or imagining (1 Cor 2:9). Early Christian use of *šālōm* may have been influenced by earlier reminiscences of the word of "peace" spoken by Jesus to his friends and disciples after his resurrection (John 20:19, 21; cf. Luke 24:36-39), a word that is linked with the gift of the Holy Spirit to empower this new and life-transforming existence within the church.

from God our Father and the Lord Jesus Christ: The understanding of God as Father of the people Israel (Deut 32:6; Isa 63:16; 64:8; Jer 3:4, 19; 31:9; Mal 2:10; Sir 51:10) originates in Israel's own self-understanding as God's "sons" and "daughters" (Hos 11:1; Sir 4:10; *PsSol* 17:30; *Jub* 1:24-25). Drawing upon the best images of God in the OT, the even more intimate use of *Abba*, which Jesus taught his disciples to use (the Aramaic *ʾabbāʾ*, which Paul preserves in Rom

8:15; Gal 4:6), is similarly characterized by compassion and gentleness, an unconditional love that reverences and cares equally for all. As in all of the Pauline prescripts, *patēr* is used in Judaism to address God in prayer (e.g., Wis 14:3) and occasionally God is also spoken of as "my Father" (Sir 51:10; Kuhn, *abba, EDNT* 1:1-2). *Apo* ("from") specifies grace and peace as coming from both "God our Father" *(theou patros hēmōn)* and "the Lord Jesus Christ" *(kyriou Iēsou Christou).* Paul's fullest expansion of this combination appears in his letter to the Corinthians, "yet for us there is one God, the Father, from whom are all things and for whom we exist, and one Lord Jesus Christ, through whom are all things and through whom we exist" (1 Cor 8:6). Although in secular usage "lord" can refer to a human master, Paul draws on biblical usage, which replaces the sacred name of God, YHWH, with the Hebrew *ʾādōn (ʾădônai,* "my Lord"), in the LXX translated as *kyrios.* Therefore in using the confessional *kyrios* almost exclusively for Jesus, NT proclamation could not have given Jesus a more reverential and exalted title; it places him on par with God the Father while at the same time declaring his risen status (Rom 1:4; 10:9; 1 Cor 15:1-11; Fitzmyer, *Philemon,* 91). Old Testament texts that clearly pertain to YHWH's lordship over creation, humanity, and history are used to express God's action in Jesus Christ (Rom 10:13 [Joel 2:32]; 1 Cor 10:26 [Ps 50:12]; Werner Foerster, *kyrios, EDNT* 3:88–92). As C. F. D. Moule (*Colossians and Philemon,* 150) contends, this move, especially for a monotheistic Pharisee, was nothing short of astounding (cf. 1 Cor 8:6). As Jesus invoked God as *Abba,* so the earliest Christians called Jesus "Lord" in an Aramaic expression that Paul preserves in the appeal *maranatha,* "Lord, come! (from the Aramaic *māryā,* meaning "Lord"; 1 Cor 16:22). Calling Jesus "Lord" announces his sovereign and exclusive claim. And as *kyrios* was also a term widely used for the Roman emperor, one can readily appreciate how the Gospel proclamation, "Jesus is Lord," endangered the lives of its proponents who were living and preaching within the Roman empire (Roetzel, *World that Shaped the New Testament,* 75–76). So closely associated with the name of Jesus, *Christos* became part of the official name early on. Paul's favored reversal of this name, as "Christ Jesus" (Phlm 1, 9, 23), would seem to give prominence to Jesus' messianic role as "the Christ" ("Anointed One" or "Messiah"), especially significant to Paul and to the first Christians, who were all Jewish.

INTERPRETATION

Philemon as Similar and Yet Unique in the Pauline Letter Tradition. Paul begins what is the shortest of his extant letters in a manner similar to all the rest, using standard Hellenistic epistolary convention (Jas 1:1; Acts 15:23; 23:26; Dan 3:31; 4:1; Doty, *Letters in Primitive Christianity,* 25). He first names the senders and recipients and includes an opening salutation that he adapts to both his Christian audience and his Gospel proclamation. In some ways the brevity of this correspondence and its sustained singular address (see the Notes) place it closer than any of Paul's other letters to the private Greco-Roman letter. And yet, unlike this popular mode of contemporary exchange, a careful look at the letter to Philemon shows that while it presents a highly personal appeal it is, nevertheless, not private correspondence, but a letter that is intended to be read in public (cf. 1 Thess 5:27; Col 4:16). Even as Paul engages in a lengthy personal conversation with Philemon (with, of course, only Paul's side of that exchange in our possession), his prescript includes a co-sender, Timothy, the addition of Apphia and Archippus along with Philemon as named recipients, and an introductory greeting that includes the whole congregation. Paul's closing follows suit with his request for the prayers of the community for his release from prison (v. 22), the inclusion of final greetings from nearby coworkers (vv. 23-24) and a final blessing for all (v. 25). It is the apostle's hope to secure a genuinely warm and hospitable welcome for Onesimus from the entire community. Yet what most clearly sets the Pauline prescript apart from the contemporary Hellenistic one is his familiar and perhaps even signature apostolic blessing of "Grace to you and peace from God our Father and the Lord Jesus Christ," found in all of Paul's authentic letters (with only slight variation in the earliest Thessalonian correspondence).

Another distinctive feature of this letter, one that even sets it apart from the other Pauline letters, is his unique self-description as "a prisoner for Christ Jesus." Such early notice of what is obviously an actual imprisonment does not appear in Paul's other prison correspondence (Philippians) or in the Deutero-Pauline prison letters (Colossians and Ephesians). The novel nature of this self-designation, joined with punctual reminders of Paul's imprisonment throughout the letter (vv. 9, 10, 13, 22-23), have prompted scholars such as N. T. Wright to speak of his imprisonment as a significant "sub-theme" of the letter (*Colossians and Philemon,* 172). Others, focusing more on the phrase's qualifying modifier, *Christou Iēsou,* have also suggested the addition of yet another layer of meaning. If, as Marion Soards suggests, *Christou Iēsou* is to be taken as a possessive genitive (a prisoner "of Christ Jesus"), then Paul is not simply stressing or informing the recipients of his situation but is also declaring himself "Christ's prisoner." This would make Christ's prior and lasting claim on him stand over and against any apparent control his Roman custodians may appear to have in this temporary captivity (Soards, "Neglected Dimensions," 213; O'Brien, *Colossians, Philemon,* 271–72; Kittel, *desmios, TDNT* 2:43).

Timothy, one of Paul's closest companions and a longstanding partner in the Gospel mission, is named as co-sender of the letter (as also in 2 Corinthians; Philippians; 1 and 2 Thessalonians; Colossians). Here Timothy is given the rather succinct description "brother" in contrast to the often lengthy and glowing accounts and recommendations found elsewhere (see especially Phil 2:19-22; also 1 Cor 16:10-11; 1 Thess 3:2). Paul's descriptions of Philemon as "coworker," Apphia as "sister" (identical to Timothy's description as "brother"), and Archippus as "fellow-soldier" place all of them within the circle of the apostle's missionary companions who need no further introduction to Timothy who, like Paul, would be well known, especially to the named recipients. This simple reference to Timothy as "brother" could also serve to focus attention on what is the nexus of Paul's appeal, that is, to concretize the filial relationship that now exists between Onesimus and Philemon as the letter builds to this wholehearted acknowledgment (vv. 16-17). Once Philemon accepts Onesimus as his "brother, beloved in the Lord" (v. 16), Paul will have the desired response to his request for a hospitable homecoming guaranteed (v. 17). The importance of these filial relations is affirmed by repeated emphasis on them at key points throughout the letter (vv. 7, 16, 20).

The Intended Audience. Like Timothy (1 Cor 4:17; Phil 2:19-22) and Onesimus (Phlm 10), Philemon was also brought to faith in Jesus Christ by the apostle (v. 19). It is likely that Apphia and Archippus, as probable Pauline coworkers linked with Philemon (perhaps even as family members), may have also been converted by Paul. In that case all five persons introduced in the letter's prescript are joined together in a deeply spiritual and loving bond. The close nature of Paul's relationship with Philemon is expressed within the letter itself, both in the affectionate care and concern that looks to his friend's virtue and benefit (vv. 14-15) and in the unequivocal trust in his compliant response (v. 21). Paul writes to Philemon as to one whose own personal knowledge and experience of conversion make it possible for him to appreciate the genuine transformation it effects in one's identity and relation with others, especially other Christians. Thus Paul can be assured that the significance and relevance of Onesimus' conversion and baptism in the Lord Jesus would not be lost on his own beloved child in Christ.

But Paul does not simply address Philemon as his friend; he writes to him in his capacity as host and pastoral leader of the local congregation that gathers in his home. It is important to realize that, unlike similar Greco-Roman letters in which a slaveowner's friend writes to recommend leniency for a returning slave or freedman, Paul is writing to Philemon who is also a coworker entrusted with and sharing the same pastoral task of guiding the community toward an ever more faithful response to their call to be the Lord's disciples and followers. In his request for Philemon's compliance in the matter of Onesimus' welcome (for which the apostle has full confidence, v. 21) and in the implied appeal for Onesimus' return to assist him in mission (vv. 13-14), Paul is calling Philemon into a more concretely realized partnership (v. 17). From his other correspondence it is known that Paul rarely accepts such support and, when he does, it is only from those he trusts as mature partners in faith, such as the Philippians, who are known to have sent Epaphroditus to assist Paul during what appears to have been a lengthy prison stay (Phil 2:25-30; 4:18; cf. 2 Cor 11:7-9; 12:13-14).

Besides Philemon, Apphia and Archippus are also likely to have an important influence within the local community. Apphia, the only woman to be personally mentioned in the prescript of any NT letter, shares a description ("sister") similar to that of Timothy ("brother") that would place her among Paul's missionary associates (Johannes Beutler, *adelphos, EDNT* 1:30; MacDonald, "Reading Real Women," 206). Apphia also shares this description with Phoebe, a leader *(diakonos)* in her own local church (Rom 16:1) who also, as Paul's personal envoy and bearer of the letter to the Romans, is sent to proclaim and interpret the Gospel and so to prepare the mission base Paul will need to begin his westward journey to Spain (cf. Rom 15:24 and 16:2). New and recent studies are just beginning to recover and appreciate the essential positions and contributions many women made within the early Christian mission (see Gillman, *Women Who Knew Paul,* 43–58; Schüssler Fiorenza, *In Memory of Her,* 43–95).

The greeting that names Archippus as "fellow soldier" would seem to distinguish him as a colleague who may have participated in some common struggle or even endured personal suffering, as did Epaphroditus, the only other person to be called a "fellow soldier" by Paul (Phil 2:25). As a military image, "soldier" serves to remind the letter's interpreter of the battle the apostle sees himself, and the early church, as waging against all the forces that oppose Christ's rule in the world. Not only does it place what seems so private a correspondence in a wider, even apocalyptic context, it also seems to enlist Archippus as someone who is ready to hear and attend to orders such as the Gospel imperative that Paul will present. And given the societal norm and expectation that supports, and even legally sanctions, the slaveowner's right to harshly punish runaway slaves, Philemon may well have needed the support of Apphia and Archippus to secure the unheard-of hospitality for Onesimus that Paul deems so necessary (see v. 8) and essential to the livelihood of the Christian community (cf. Gal 3:26-28).

Paul always writes to Christian communities that he, along with others, either founded or intended to visit (v. 22; Rom 15:23-24, 32). Most often Paul is writing to local churches or *ekklēsiai,* even as they belong to a larger body and more extensive network of house churches that make missionary work possible (Rom 15:19, 24; Malherbe, *Social Aspects,* 61). While no doubt influenced by five centuries of Greco-Roman usage, the employment of *ekklēsia* by Christians meant far more than its secular sense as an assembly of people. The Christian understanding of *ekklēsia* seems to be deeply influenced by the biblical meaning, which differentiated the assembly of God as a people who gather together to hear and respond to God's word (cf. Deut 23:2-9). It is in this sense that the early Christians and Paul (1 Cor 10:32; 11:18, 20) appear to appropriate the expression for themselves as the new people of God who exist under the lordship of Jesus Christ instead of that of the Roman emperors, whose proclamation of *pax Romana* is a false one (Lohfink, *Jesus and Community*, 77; Meeks, *First Urban Christians*, 108, 230 n. 166; Branick, *House Church*, 30 n. 9).

While the connection with a "house" or household could also recall Israel's self-expression as *oikos Israel*, "the house of Israel" (Jer 38:33; Amos 5:25; cf. also 1QS 1:9; 3:20; 4:5, etc.), a closer and more important connection is found to exist between Jesus' own ministry, lived out within the homes of people he told stories to and taught, people with whom he shared meals and friendship, whom he also healed (Mark 1:29; 2:1, 15; 3:20; 6:34-44; 7:14-27; 8:1-10; 10:2-12; Matt 13:36; Luke 5:29; 7:36-50; 9:53; 10:38; 12:37; 14:1). Like Paul, Luke also writes of the early Christians breaking bread "at home" (*kat'oikon:* Acts 2:46; 5:42; also Acts 12:12). Paul's own letters supply evidence of the numerous house churches spread throughout the empire with hosts, like Philemon (Rom 16:3-5, 13, 23; 1 Cor 16:19), who provide the perfect setting for God's creation of a new family that transcended the older boundaries of the traditional *paterfamilias*. In these early communities entirely new relations were created that completely eliminated the prejudiced distinctions that had set apart Jews from Gentiles, males from females, and slaves from free persons (Gal 3:27-28). The household, which has been described as a microcosm of Greco-Roman society that would have included slaves along with family members, provided a natural setting to initiate and nurture this new family of God in uniting all as sisters and brothers to Jesus Christ and to each other. These local house churches would also have functioned as places that provided the respite and material support the early missionaries would have needed in order to survive (Rom 8:14-17; Gal 4:4-5; 6:15; 1 Thess 1:10; Meeks, *First Urban Christians*, 72–73; Theissen, *Social Setting*, 69–119; Banks, *Paul's Idea of Community* 45, 53–60; Malherbe, *Social Aspects*, 68-69).

The Pauline Signature Blessing. Paul's formal blessing, "Grace to you and peace from God our Father and the Lord Jesus Christ" may represent the apostle's own creative use and combination of the biblical and weighty theological words "grace and peace," a phrase with its origin in what seems a formal and confessional statement of faith in God as Father and in Jesus Christ as Lord. It appears that Paul combined the similar sounding *charis* ("grace"), as a modified form of the secular *chairein* ("greetings"), with another rich biblical word that also functions as the common Jewish salutation of *šālōm* or "peace" to greet the new communities that have come to include both Gentiles and Jews (Wiles, *Intercessory Prayers*,

108–13). For Paul, grace epitomizes the sum of all the blessings God bestows in Christ, whose abiding presence promises to bring to completion the fullness of justice, joy, and peace that will characterize God's rule on earth (Rom 14:7). Israel's thoroughgoing experience of God's boundless graciousness, especially toward the poor, vulnerable, and suffering people in this world, finds new expression in the early church as it also experiences this grace in the midst of present hardship and persecution. Paul incorporates this fundamental understanding of grace and peace in what becomes a deeply Christian expression of faith that unites the apostle with those who share his faith in God the Father and the Lord Jesus Christ as the origin and source of all these gifts. It both proclaims and invokes the continued blessing of God's loving presence upon those who are "in Christ" and who have already received this blessing of the Spirit that enables one to cry out to God as *Abba* (Rom 8:15; Gal 4:6) and to acknowledge Jesus as Lord (1 Cor 12:3; cf. 1 Cor 8:6; 2 Cor 4:5; Phil 2:11).

Paul's own experience of grace and peace was decisively shaped by his encounter with the crucified and risen Lord and continues in his present sharing in the suffering of Christ. This also continues in the Christian's participation in the divine action that gives birth to the church and to a new creation and a whole new history of grace and peace (Bassler, "Grace Probing the Limits," 24–33). God's overflowing graciousness is given eloquent expression as Paul speaks of the love of God that "has been poured into our hearts through the Holy Spirit" (Rom 5:5) so as to enable all "in Christ" to partner God in accomplishing God's will at the present time (cf. Rom 12:6-8; 1 Cor 3:9-10). It is with Philemon and his community in mind, a community already gifted by God to bring about the reconciliation, reception, and fruitful relations he seeks, that Paul writes this.

The combination of "God the Father and the Lord Jesus Christ" (cf. 2 Cor 1:3), perhaps already functioning in prayers, liturgical expressions, and creedal statements, is found in every one of the Pauline prescripts. Even as Jesus continued the OT usage of referring to God as "our Father" (as here with the Greek, *patēr*), in teaching his followers to call God "Abba" Jesus invited unparalleled intimacy with God by including his disciples in his own personal relationship with God (Mark 14:36 *parr.*). Far from imaging a patriarchal figure that exercises dominance or control, Jesus' Abba, like many of the images of God in the OT, is a loving parent whose presence and care include the best of maternal and paternal images that act to nurture to full maturity and to empower partnership that moves towards an ever-deepening and mutually loving friendship (Johnson, *She Who Is*, 80–81). By inviting his disciples to call God "Abba," Jesus creates a new family that transcends every barrier of race, class, and gender as it forges a new identity for believers that affects every dimension of life (2 Cor 5:17; cf. 1 Cor 6:15). Because Paul is a faithful disciple, all that he says and does works to promote this vision and understanding of God's plan and promise, especially within the communities that belong to Christ.

For Reference and Further Study

Balch, David L., and Carolyn Osiek, eds. *Early Christian Families in Context: An Interdisciplinary Dialogue.* Grand Rapids: Eerdmans, 2003.

Cousar, Charles B. *The Letters of Paul.* Nashville: Abingdon, 1996.

Doty, William G. *Letters in Primitive Christianity.* Philadelphia: Fortress, 1973.

Fitzmyer, Joseph A. "Introduction to the New Testament Epistles," and "Paul," in Raymond E. Brown, Joseph A. Fitzmyer, and Roland E. Murphy, eds., *The New Jerome Biblical Commentary.* Englewood Cliffs, NJ: Prentice Hall, 1990.

Harrington, Daniel J. *The Church According to the New Testament. What the Wisdom and Witness of Early Christianity Teach Us Today.* Franklin, WI, and Chicago: Sheed & Ward, 2001.

Lieu, Judith M. "Grace to you and Peace: The Apostolic Greeting," *BJRL* 68 (1985) 161–78.

Perdue, Leo G. "The Household, Old Testament Theology and Contemporary Hermeneutics," in Carol Meyers, Joseph Blenkinsopp, John J. Collins, and Leo G. Perdue, *Families in Ancient Israel.* Louisville: Westminster John Knox, 1997, 223–57.

Roetzel, Calvin J. *The Letters of Paul: Conversations in Context.* 4th ed. Louisville: Westminster John Knox, 1998.

Soards, Marion L. *The Apostle Paul: An Introduction to His Writings and Teachings.* New York, NY, and Mahwah, NJ: Paulist, 1987.

Stambaugh, John E., and David L. Balch. *The New Testament in its Social Environment.* Philadelphia: Westminster, 1986.

Stowers, Stanley K. *Letter Writing in Greco-Roman Antiquity.* Philadelphia: Westminster, 1986.

Thurston, Bonnie B. *Women in the New Testament: Questions and Commentary.* New York: Crossroad, 1998.

White, John L. "Saint Paul and the Apostolic Letter Tradition," *CBQ* 45 (1983) 433–44.

2. *Thanksgiving Prayer and Theological Basis for the Appeal* (4-7)

4. I give thanks to my God always as I remember you in my prayers, 5. because I hear of your love and the faith that you have toward the Lord Jesus and all the holy ones, 6. and I pray that your partnership in faith may be effective in realizing all the good that is ours in Christ. 7. For I have experienced much joy and encouragement from your love because the hearts of the holy ones have been refreshed through you, brother.

Notes

4. *I give thanks to my God always:* Formal greetings (vv. 1-3) proceed directly into the Pauline thanksgiving, introduced by its most characteristic verb, *eucharistein* (Rom 1:8; 1 Cor 1:4; Phil 1:3; 1 Thess 1:2), an important early Christian word that also figures centrally in the assembly of the community for fellowship and worship (LaVerdiere, *Eucharist in the New Testament,* 175). Paul speaks for himself as he expresses thanks to God with the first person singular form of *eucharistō,* "I give thanks," that also includes blessing and praise (BDAG 416; *ZBG* 124). Expressing thanks to "my God" (Rom 1:8; 1 Cor 1:4; Phil 1:3) echoes the personal prayer of God's people throughout history, from common usage in OT prayer (Exod 6:7; 15:2; Pss 5:3; 7:1; 13:4; 22:2, etc.) through the narrative gospels (Matt 12:50; John 20:28) and Paul (2 Cor 12:21; Phil 4:19), as it also testifies to the personal nature of relationship with God. The apostle's thanksgiving to God as well as his prayers for Philemon are ongoing and accentuated by the temporal adverb *pantote,* "always" (Rom 1:10; 1 Cor 1:4; Phil 1:4; 1 Thess 1:2; cf. Col 1:3; 2 Thess 1:3). Both the connecting phrase, "as I remember you in my prayers," and the context (vv. 5-7) help to convey the sense that whenever Paul is mindful of Philemon in prayer it is always with gratitude to God.

   as I remember you in my prayers: Paul typically employs the classical Greek expression *mneian poioumenos* for remembering someone in prayer. Combining the abstract noun, *mneian* ("remembrance") with the middle voice of *poiein,* to mean literally "to make mention," the expression is translated periphrastically "to remember" (cf. Rom 1:9; 1 Thess 1:2; BDF §310; *ZBG* 227). The genitive singular *sou* ("you") yet again (v. 2) points to Philemon as sole addressee, as the singular *mou* ("my") in "in my prayers" *(epi tōn proseuchōn mou)* also identifies Paul as the only writer in this unique one-to-one correspondence. Even here, however, Paul has the wider church in mind as he moves the discussion to concern for *koinōnia* (v. 6) and "all the holy ones" (vv. 5, 7). *Epi* with the genitive has the same sense as *en* with the dative. Further discussion of the content of Paul's present prayer (v. 6) follows the statement of the cause for this thanksgiving in the next verse.

5. *because I hear of your love and the faith that you have toward the Lord Jesus and all the holy ones:* The proximate motive for thanking God is provided by the causal phrase that begins with *akouōn,* "as I hear," that as a present participle conveys the sense of continuing action (Lohse, *Philemon,* 192–93; Harris, *Philemon,* 248). While the details concerning what Paul has heard remain unspecified, the

general description of Philemon's love and faith will provide the theological basis for both the appeal of the letter (v. 9) and the course of action taken (v. 12). Both here and throughout the letter *agapē* ("love") is placed first and in emphatic position as it prepares for the letter's appeal "on the basis of love" (v. 9). That this love expresses, as it also originates from, God's gift of faith in Jesus is best brought out by the chiastic (criss-cross) pattern within this sentence that places "faith in the Lord Jesus" in the central position. Scholars have noted the ABB'A' arrangement in this verse, with "love" (A) and "faith" (B) corresponding in reverse order to "toward the Lord Jesus" (B') and "all the holy ones" (A'). The remaining verses provide further support as each verse continues to unpack the meaning of each pair: v. 6 in linking "faith" (B) with "Christ" (B') and v. 7 in joining "love" (A) with "all the holy ones" (A'). Thus while *agapē,* the basis for the appeal, has the foremost position, "the faith" *(hēn pistin)* "that you have in the Lord Jesus" is also centrally placed and shown to be the origin of that love. This is apparently the way Paul's successors had taken the apostle's meaning, as they use the same sentence in the Deutero-Pauline thanksgiving (Col 1:4) but transpose it non-chiastically: "because we have heard of your faith in Christ Jesus and of the love which you have for all the holy ones" *(akousantes tēn pistin hymōn en Christǭ Iēsou kai tēn agapēn hēn echete eis pantas tous hagious).* The second person singular verb with its relative pronoun "that you have" *(hēn echeis)* specifies this as Philemon's faith. Use of the pronoun *pros* instead of *eis* for faith "in the Lord Jesus" *(pros ton kyrion Iēsoun)* is found only here in the NT with the likely nuance of a "leaning toward" or "dependence upon" the Lord (so *MM* 68; Moule, *Idiom Book,* 54, 68–69). Joseph Fitzmyer (*Philemon,* 96) notes that in several places the apostle combines *pros* with *pistin* and *eis* with *agapē* (see Rom 5:8; 2 Cor 2:8; 1 Thess 1:8; 3:12). Standing behind this gracious stance toward *pantas* ("all") "the holy ones" might be the confident expectation that this inclusive *pantas* will also come to include the gracious reception of the runaway slave for whom Paul writes this appeal. The adjective *tous hagious,* "holy," is substantive for "the holy ones" or "saints" (BDF §477.2).

6. *and I pray that your partnership in faith may be effective in realizing all the good that is ours in Christ:* This final clause of the lengthy periodic sentence provides the general content of the prayer first mentioned in the opening verse (v. 4). The absence of a main verb since v. 4 makes it dependent on that verse, as indicated by the many translations that insert "and I pray." This verse has been variously translated and its difficulties noted (Martin, *Philemon,* 162; Riesenfeld, "Faith and Love," 251–57). Part of the problem is that the specific content of Paul's prayer awaits fuller disclosure in the body of the letter. The expression *hē koinōnia tēs pisteos sou* has been translated in any number of ways including "your partnership in the faith" (Zerwick, *Analysis,* 652; Bultmann, *ginōskō, TDNT* 1:708; Stuhlmacher, *Philemon,* 33) and as "the sharing in your faith" (Fitzmyer, *Philemon,* 96–97; Riesenfeld, "Faith and Love," 251–57) with interpreters having the grammatical option of placing *sou* ("your") with either *koinōnia* ("partnership") or *pisteōs* ("faith"). *Koinōnia* belongs to a word group that includes translations such as fellowship, communion, partnership, participation or sharing, all of which express mutual relations (BDAG 552–53).

The sense of participation, even to the extent of partnership in Paul's ministry that is stated explicitly in v. 17 (also vv. 13-14), informs the translation chosen here (cf. Phil 1:5; Josef Hainz, *koinōnia, EDNT* 2:303–305). *Hopōs* ("so that") with the aorist middle subjunctive *genētai* ("may become") indicates purpose. Taken together with the adjective *energēs* ("effective"), the phrase indicates that Paul has some specific action in view, the realization of some goal that he hopes his letter will accomplish (so Friedrich Hauck, *koinōnos, TDNT* 3:805). *Epignōsis,* which can be translated as knowledge or recognition, governs the genitive "of all the good" *(pantos agathou).* The appositional relative pronoun *tou* ("that") is in agreement with *agathou* and further qualifies "all the good" as that which comes through Christ as its origin and constant source. The concept of "goodness," whether it be "the good," "doing good deeds," or divine "goodness" permeates the Scriptures from the revelation of the goodness of God's creation (Gen 1:4, 10, 12, etc.) to the divine goodness that redeems and effects goodness within persons (Phil 2:13). "Knowledge of the good" is essentially connected with the experiential knowledge of God as the source and future guarantor of that goodness (Rom 11:25-32; cf. 15:14). Since for Paul "all the good" always relates to God's action in Christ, "supreme good" means "knowing Christ," which is to experience "the power of his resurrection, to share in his suffering and become like him in his death, in the hope that I myself may be raised from death to life" (Phil 3:7-11; Käsemann, "Worship in Everyday Life," 189). Thus in praying for this "knowledge" Paul prays that his hearers will also seek to conform their way of perceiving and living to that of Christ. "All the good" makes best sense with the plural pronoun *hēmin* ("our") instead of the variant reading *hymin* ("yours") that seems to be an assimilation to the preceding use of the second person singular. "Ours" also keeps the focus on the relational aspect that began this verse *(hē koinōnia)* and lies behind Paul's goal to secure a welcome for Onesimus from the entire community (cf. Gal 5:6; BDF §205). As the *hopōs* clause begins to express all the goodness that derives from faith in Christ, it also expresses the content of Paul's prayer, which hopes for an increase in that goodness. In comparison with *gnōsis, epignōsis* is relatively rare in the OT, where it is used to refer to the knowledge of God's will (Prov 2:5; Hos 4:1). Several scholars take it as a technical term used by Paul for the knowledge of God that comes through faith in Jesus Christ (cf. Phil 1:9; Rom 2:18; 15:14; Bultmann, *ginōskō, TDNT* 1:707; Houlden, *Philemon,* 153). "Every good" also prepares for "the good" that Paul hopes to receive through his friend's loving concern for both the apostle and the Christian mission (v. 14). Together with "love" (vv. 5, 7, 9), "faith" (vv. 5, 6, and v. 21 the "obedience" of faith, cf. Rom 1:5), "partnership" (vv. 6, 17), "the good" (vv. 6, 14) and "prayer" (vv. 4, 22), Paul already provides a constellation of key theological terms that link the formal thanksgiving section together with the rest of the letter. Use of the preposition *eis* for "in Christ," instead of yet another repetition of the more common equivalent *en,* adds stylistic variation as it provides for an accusative ending to the sentence with *Christon* (cf. Gal 5:6; 2 Cor 1:21; 11:3). As either a name or title or both, *Christos* occurs in eight of eleven total references to Jesus Christ. This favored appellation appears twice in its fullest form as "Lord Jesus Christ" that begins and ends this letter (vv. 3, 25), three times as "Christ

Jesus," in every instance in connection with Paul's imprisonment (vv. 1, 9, 23), and as here, *Christos,* also in the verses that open and close the body of the letter (vv. 8, 20). When not referring to Christians as "brothers and sisters," (his favored usage), or God's beloved or holy ones (e.g., Rom 1:7), Paul refers to Christians as those who are "in Christ" to signify the essential transformation that has taken place, that enables the believer to call God "Father" and acknowledge Jesus as Lord. Because he is Lord, Jesus' claim extends into every aspect of the believer's life. Most especially that claim includes the call to belong to a new family, the community or *koinōnia* that God has made possible in and through Christ.

7. *For I have experienced much joy and encouragement from your love because the hearts of the holy ones have been refreshed through you, brother:* The addition of v. 7 extends the thanksgiving section beyond its formal necessity (similarly, e.g., Rom 1:8-9, 10 [15]; 1 Cor 1:4-7 [9]; Phil 1:3-8 [11]; 1 Thess 1:2-5 [10]). However, it remains part of this section in that, like v. 6 (in unpacking "faith in the Lord Jesus," v. 5), it also serves to clarify the meaning behind the initial mention (also in v. 5) of Philemon's love for all the holy ones. The postpositive conjunction *gar* ("for") is used by Paul as a transition to the body of his letters (Rom 1:18). Here it has the dual function of expressing cause for thanks and of providing the explanation as to why Paul will appeal to love (*agapē,* v. 9; BDAG 6–7) rather than simply exhort his friend to do what he should. "Joy" *(chara),* which follows "love" as a fruit of the Spirit (Gal 5:22; cf. Rom 14:17; 15:13; 1 Thess 1:6; Conzelmann, *chairō, TDNT* 9:369–70), joins *paraklēsin* ("encouragement") in letting Philemon know the personal significance his goodness holds for the apostle. More typically Paul uses the cognate verb, *parakalein,* to exhort Christians to walk more closely with Christ in their new life of faith (cf. Rom 12:8; 1 Cor 14:31; Phil 1:14; 1 Thess 3:2; 4:18; 5:11, 14). The rich meaning of *paraklēsin,* that also includes "comfort" and "consolation" (BDAG 764–65; cf. Rom 15:4; 1 Cor 14:3; 2 Cor 7:13; 8:4; Phil 2:1), is given special emphasis in the LXX as that which only comes from God (Otto Schmitz, *parakaleō, TDNT* 5:797–99). Modifying both *charis* and *paraklēsin, pollēn* ("much") strengthens the emotive impact deriving from Philemon's previous good deeds (the aorist verb, *eschon,* "has had," denotes past action). "From your love" *(epi tę̄ agapę̄ sou)* employs the preposition *epi,* commonly used after verbs that express emotion (BDAG 365). *Sou* ("you," as in vv. 4, 5, and 6) continues to identify Philemon as the beneficent giver. The causal *hoti* ("because," cf. Rom 1:8-9; 1 Cor 1:4-7; 1 Thess 2:13) places the final emphasis on the wider pastoral concern that is indeed Paul's own special call and task. In order to stress the importance of this concern, and since *agapē* is its driving force, Paul uses the most powerful word available, *splagchna,* which is best translated as "heart" (repeated in vv. 12 and 20), as it is considered the seat of deepest human emotion (Helmut Koester, *splagchnon, TDNT* 7:555). The adjective *hagioi* is taken as a substantive and is translated by "saints" or "holy ones." Stemming from OT usage, as the adjective *qādôš* or the substantive *qōdeš,* holiness could be ascribed to any person, place, or item that belonged to or was consecrated to God and is holy only by virtue of relation to God, who alone is the Holy One (Exod 15:11; 19:6; Lev 19:2; Isa 6:3; 29:23; 43:3, etc.; Otto Procksch, *hagios,*

TDNT 1:88–97). The holiness of God's Elect could express God's claim as well as the covenanted people's anticipated response to that claim (Lev 11:44; Ps 33:9; Hos 11:12). While Paul continues to speak of the "holy root" of Israel (Rom 11:16), it is only in relation to the holy and living God that Christians are called "holy ones" (Rom 8:9-11; 1 Cor 12:27; 2 Cor 6:16). Paul makes frequent use of this expression in addressing recipients of his letters (Rom 1:7; 1 Cor 1:2; 2 Cor 1:1; 13:12; 16:15; 1 Thess 3:13), his closest companions (Phil 4:21-22), as well as the poor in Jerusalem (Rom 15:26) and those who will judge the world (1 Cor 6:2). In Pauline usage it is an eschatological expression that appears to have its roots in biblical apocalyptic (cf. Dan 7:21), as do its contemporary parallels (cf. Tob 8:15; 12:15; 1 Macc 1:46; 1QSb 1:5; 1QM 6:6; see Horst Balz, *hagios, EDNT* 1:18–20). For Paul "the saints" refers to the baptized, those who constitute the eschatological people of God (cf. Rom 8:9-11; 2 Cor 6:16; Lohfink, *Jesus and Community,* 77). The perfect tense of the verb *anapepautai* ("to refresh," cf. Rom 15:32; 1 Cor 16:18) only highlights the enduring impact of this friend's kind deeds. *Dia sou* ("through you") adds further emphasis to Paul's direct address of Philemon as *adelphe* ("brother"), as one of only two occasions (here, and in v. 20) where the apostle Paul uses the vocative singular (Dunn, *Colossians and Philemon,* 320).

Interpretation

Theological Basis for an Appeal Based on Love: What begins as a characteristically Pauline thanksgiving that replaces the Hellenistic *proskynēma* formula, with its prayers and accompanying wishes for health and well-being (White, *Form and Function,* 8–9), turns out to be a tightly composed and carefully designed introduction that prepares for the letter's specific appeal. More recently, scholars have brought attention to its function in providing the theological foundation needed to support Paul's appeal (see especially Soards, "Neglected Dimensions," 209–19; Brown, *Introduction to the New Testament,* 503; Harrington, *Philemon,* 22). As Paul moves from expressing gratitude to God and appreciation for Philemon's Christ-like character and activity on behalf of other Christians, he prays for the continuing expression of this participation in love and faith as it impacts upon the particular appeal he is about to make. This section's concluding remarks set a joyful and anticipatory tone that the apostle invites and hopes his friend and colleague will share.

All the necessary elements that are found in a formal epistolary thanksgiving are present in vv. 4-6. This includes Paul's typical expression of gratitude, "I give thanks to God" (v. 4), the cause for thanksgiving, "because I hear" (v. 5), and purpose "and I pray that" (v. 6), which concludes with the petition that is closely tied to the subsequent appeal. Joined both thematically and grammatically with what precedes it, v. 7 concludes the thanksgiving section and provides a smooth transition into the body of the letter (Moule, *Colossians and Philemon,* 140; Lohmeyer, *Briefe,* 192; Lohse, *Colossians and Philemon,* 192; O'Brien, *Colossians, Philemon,* 276). Tightly packed into one single sentence, the formal thanksgiving (vv. 4-6) contains three participial clauses that follow the main verb *eucharistō,* "give thanks." Following this expression of gratitude to God, the first clause, "as I remember you in my prayers" (v. 4), places the entire section within a prayerful context of relationship with God. The second, causal phrase (v. 5) provides the reason for Paul's gratitude. The final purpose clause (v. 6) concludes with the prayer that looks forward to the present request, with the hope for an extension of this graciousness (White, *Form and Function,* 31–32). While the thanksgiving section can function rhetorically to enlist the recipient's good will *(captatio benevolentiae),* in this, as in all of Paul's letters, the aim seems more to guide and enkindle the spirit of love and partnership that is already vibrant and active. Paul's goal is always to motivate Christians toward full maturity and mutuality in faith and love.

In preparation for Paul's appeal, the thanksgiving section introduces a number of significant theological terms that are repeated throughout the letter and appear to serve as important interpretative keys that help to open up the text's meaning. These fundamental concepts include *agapē* ("love"), repeated twice in vv. 5 and 7 and again in vv. 9 (as the basis for the appeal) and 16 (with regard to Onesimus' status as "beloved brother"), *koinōnia* ("partnership") in v. 6 and repeated in v. 17 (for Philemon as Paul's partner), and *agathou tou* ("the good") in v. 6 and again in v. 14 (for the specific good that Paul desires). Additionally, another cluster of three terms, "heart" *(splagchna),* "refresh" *(anapepautai),* and "brother" *(adelphe),* provides the content that frames the body of the letter, just preceding its opening and at its closing (vv. 7 and 20). And although the lengthy theological exposition that often precedes Paul's paraenetic sections (e.g., Rom 12:1-6) is absent from this one-page letter, it appears that these weighty terms are all the theological foundation Paul needs to ground his appeal and elicit his friend's acquiescence. Perhaps, given his close relationship with Philemon as friend, coworker, and even spiritual father (v. 19), Paul may already know that this is sufficient.

Without providing any specific details Paul simply mentions what he has heard of the ongoing pastoral care, concern, and generosity Philemon has shown toward his fellow Christians. Besides Onesimus, traveling coworkers and other missionaries are the likely sources of this good news. As mentioned in the notes, the difficulties in translating v. 5 have been worked out in a variety of ways. Past scholarly attempts to relate "love" *(agapē)* and "faith" *(pistis)* to both the "Lord Jesus" and "all the saints" have required a dual translation of *pistis* as "faith" in the Lord Jesus and "faithfulness" or fidelity toward the saints. The more recent discovery of the chiastic pattern (ABB'A') within this sentence, joining "love" (A) with "all the saints" (A') and "faith" (B) with "the Lord Jesus" (B'), not only resolves this difficulty but has the effect of placing "faith in the Lord Jesus" in the central position it merits as the source and continuing wellspring of this love. It also preserves the priority given to *agapē* in this letter, as love is the determining factor for Paul's appeal (v. 9). Internal evidence that supports this chiastic reading (ABB'A'), which inverts or criss-crosses the association of love (A) and faith (B) with the Lord Jesus (B') and all the saints (A'), is provided by the following verses, which clearly affirm these associations in linking "faith" with the "Lord Jesus" (BB') in v. 6, and "love" with "all the saints" (AA') in v. 7.

In Paul's theology, as is evident in this letter, *agapē* occupies the central and premier position (cf. 1 Cor 13:13), whether he is speaking of God and God's activity or of human response. As first fruit of the Spirit's presence and action (Gal 5:22), love empowers the fulfillment of God's will as it unites believers with God and one another (Rom 13:8). In extending love toward another, believers participate in God's own love, which has been given to them through the Holy Spirit (Rom 5:5). Love was the driving force effecting the abundant goodness that had already provided Paul with much joy and encouragement (v. 7). It is the same love that encourages Paul to seek its expansion in the present circumstance, as he appeals to the love he has every hope of receiving.

In both Old and New Testaments the love that draws the faithful together as God's own chosen people is always in response to a prior experience of God's love for them (Exod 34:6; Deut 7:8; Ps 86:15; Rom 5:8; Gal 2:20; cf. Rom 8:31-39). It is the experience of God's love that elicits in its recipients the desire to respond to that love, and that response makes loving relations with others possible, for the genuine reception of divine love effects an inner transformation that calls for mutuality and uncalculated reciprocity. From the OT (2 Sam 1:26; Ruth 4:15) through the NT (Rom 5:8), such love always breaks through established conventions and expectations. For Paul, God's love is incarnate in the one who was totally free to live his life on behalf of others. In dying and rising, the exalted Lord continues to free believers to move beyond their own concerns to share in Christ's loving care and service of others (Gal 5:13-14). Such love always seeks the good of others, especially loved ones, as it hopes for their continued growth and maturation in faith (Schnackenburg, *Moral Teaching*, 219–20). Paul's own love for his converts and for the Christian communities to whom he writes demonstrates a prayerful and attentive pastoral guidance that always seeks an increase in that love and goodness and in the mutual relations they share (cf. Rom 1:11-12; 15:14-15).

Love and faith are inseparably related. Faith always seeks to express itself in love. Being relational and mutual, faith, like love, seems compelled to make some return as it seeks to respond to God's loving graciousness (Furnish, *Love Command,* 97). Faith is a trusting reliance in God's abiding presence and promise to bring about the future that God intends. Faith is receptive to God's will and willing to be transformed by the grace that places it within a family of believers. Faith is trusting in God's grace to shape the new life and the new community it creates (2 Cor 1:21-22; 4:13; Gal 2:9-10; 5:5; Phil 3:8-9; cf. Rom 14:22-23). For Paul, trusting in God's saving activity in Christ meant accepting the call to participate in Jesus' own life of faith (2 Cor 4:11-15).

Since faith is a gift that compels response, "faith in the Lord Jesus" means precisely the faith that, in acknowledging Jesus as Lord, accepts his claim upon one's life. Philemon's loving actions on behalf of God's people had already demonstrated this faith in concrete and practical terms. In Pauline terms, his faith can be described as an obedient response to the Lord. The Pauline expression "the obedience of faith" (Rom 1:5) stresses the active component of the demand that the gift of faith warrants. It also assists in the interpretation of Paul's meaning of faith in this letter, as Paul makes use of both terms ("faith" in vv. 5 and 6 and "obedience" in v. 21) in two key locations. Evidence for the close correspondence between "faith" (in vv. 5-6) and "obedience to God" (in v. 21) can be found in the threefold repetition of terms in their adjacent verses (vv. 7 and 20) and suggests a deliberate connection. Thus, just as Paul concludes his appeal with the repetition of "brother" and "refresh my heart in Christ" (v. 20), it becomes apparent that Paul had intended the correspondence when his final comment brings the hearer back to his introduction of the appeal. Clearly Paul understands Philemon's faith and love in terms of obedience to Christ. It is what gives Paul every assurance that his friend will provide all that he requests.

The love of God that fills the believer always moves to expand that love in building up the life of the community into a communion that both reflects God's life and draws the faithful more deeply into it. It is this participation in God's creation of a whole new family standing under the sovereign lordship of Jesus Christ that is meant by the term *koinōnia. Koinōnia* was an important early Christian expression that may best be described as an "ecclesial communion" (so Lohfink, *Jesus and Community,* 99–102) that unites into one community all those who belong to Christ (Rom 15:26; 2 Cor 8:4; 9:14; Gal 2:9; Phil 2:1; Acts 2:42; Heb 13:16). Described by Paul in a variety of ways, as "fellowship with Christ Jesus" (1 Cor 1:9), "members of the body of Christ" (1 Cor 12:27; cf. 1 Cor 10:16), partners/participating in the Spirit (2 Cor 13:13; Phil 2:1), *koinōnia* entails sharing in both the joys and sufferings that are inherent in every committed partnership. This vibrant and vital communion of saints makes God's purposes and action visible and concrete in the lives of believers. It is what John Koenig so aptly describes as "practical incarnations of the divine will" (*Galatians, Philippians, Philemon,* 195).

While the horizon of Paul's thought surely presses toward "all the good" that awaits its eschatological salvation and fulfillment (Phil 1:6), for the present, knowledge of all the good requires discerning God's will in ever-changing situations. This ongoing discernment also opens up new possibilities for expressing one's faith in these new circumstances. Unlike most letters, where Paul is responding in gratitude or writing to address new problems, crises, and tensions as they arise, in this letter Paul writes to notify his friend of Onesimus' conversion and baptism and the new opportunity this presents for their shared partnership and, particularly for Philemon, for the possibility of a renewed relationship with Onesimus, who is now his beloved brother in Christ. Paul's prayer (v. 6) invites Philemon to welcome this good news, "the new reality of sisterly and brotherly community which comes from the new beginning made possible by the Spirit" (Lohfink, *Jesus and Community,* 109). For Philemon, this also involves the challenge of the new reality that allows for no distinctions among people (cf. Gal 3:28) and how he will appropriate this understanding in his concrete relations with Onesimus.

Paul's prayer for the efficacy of their mutual "partnership in faith" prepares for the appeal that will call upon this partnership (repeating the expression *koinōnon*) to once again express love and faith in upbuilding the community that is to welcome Onesimus within its fellowship (v. 17). N. T. Wright characterizes v. 6 as the "driving center" of the letter (*Colossians and Philemon,* 175–78), as scholars have begun to notice that the thanksgiving prepares for the subsequent appeal by securing the theological basis that will support and even motivate the generous reciprocity it seeks (Brown, *Introduction to the New Testament,* 503; and especially Soards, "Neglected Dimensions," 209–19).

While not a necessary component of the formal thanksgiving, v. 7 brings to completion the expansion of the chiasmus in v. 5 and moves the basis for the appeal (*agapē,* v. 9) back to a concluding emphasis. Just as v. 6 joins together the central parts of the chiastic pair (BB' of v. 5) to elaborate on what "faith" (B) in "the Lord Jesus" (B') means, so the response (in v. 7) of the "love" (A) shown to "all the saints" (A') demonstrates how faith's expression in love elicits the joy and encouragement that motivate Paul's appeal to this love (v. 9). This transitional verse creates an atmosphere of almost jubilant appreciation as Paul frames his appeal within a context of prayer that seems already to anticipate an assured response. Even in imprisonment Paul holds his eschatological vision wide open in the joyful expectation that God's promises for "all the good" will in fact work themselves out (cf. Phil 1:20; Rom 8:38-39).

What begins in the thanksgiving as a personal and singular address to his friend (vv. 4-5) opens up to include the entire community as Paul turns his attention toward Philemon's participation *(koinōnia)* in the faith (v. 6) and his care for "the saints" (v. 7). It discloses an underlying pastoral concern at work in this appeal that involves not only Philemon and Onesimus, but the entire community who are also called to effect the reception that the apostle requests and the Gospel demands (v. 17; cf. vv. 8-9). Given such a commendable account of Philemon's character and demonstrable goodness, it would appear that Paul fully expects his pastoral associate to lead his community in yet another witness to his love and faith as his response once again gives Paul cause to be grateful to God.

For Reference and Further Study

Boers, Hendrikus. "Αγάπη and Χάρις in Paul's Thought," *CBQ* 59 (1997) 693–713.

Campbell, John. "'*Koinonia.*' Its Cognates in the New Testament," in idem, *Three New Testament Studies.* Leiden: Brill, 1965, 1–28.

Harrington, Daniel J. "Love as the Primary Virtue," in Daniel J. Harrington and James F. Keenan, eds., *Jesus and Virtue Ethics: Building Bridges Between New Testament Studies and Moral Theology.* Lanham, MD: Sheed & Ward, 2002.

Hooker, Morna D. *"Pistis Christou,"* in eadem, *From Adam to Christ: Essays in Paul.* New York and Cambridge: Cambridge University Press, 1990, 165–86.

Mullins, Terence Y. "The Thanksgivings of Philemon and Colossians," *NTS* 30 (1984) 288–93.

Panikulam, George. *Koinōnia in the New Testament: A Dynamic Expression of Christian Life.* AnBib 85. Rome: Biblical Institute Press, 1979, 8–16.

Pao, David W. *Thanksgiving: An Investigation of a Pauline Theme.* Downers Grove, IL: InterVarsity Press, 2002.

Riesenfeld, Harold. "Faith and Love Promoting Hope. An Interpretation of Philemon v. 6," in Morna D. Hooker and S. G. Wilson, eds., *Paul and Paulinism: Essays in Honour of C. K. Barrett.* London: S.P.C.K., 1982.

Sakenfeld, Katherine Doob. "Loyalty, Love: The Language of Human Interconnection in the Hebrew Bible," in Michael P. O'Connor and David Noel Freedman, eds., *Backgrounds for the Bible.* Winona Lake, IN: Eisenbrauns, 1987.

Schubert, Paul. *Form and Function of the Pauline Thanksgivings.* BZNW 20. Berlin: Töpelmann, 1939.

Wright, N. T. "*Christos* as Messiah in Paul: Philemon 6," in idem, *The Climax of the Covenant: Christ and Law in Pauline Theology.* Edinburgh: T & T Clark, 1991, 41–55.

3. *Basis for the Appeal and Relevant New Details* (8-14)

8. Therefore, as I am bold enough in Christ to demand that you do what is necessary, 9. on account of love I prefer to appeal, I, Paul, as ambassador and now, as well, a prisoner of Christ Jesus, 10. I appeal on behalf of my own child, whose father I have become in my imprisonment, Onesimus, 11. who was once useless to you, but is now exceedingly useful both to you and to me. 12. I am sending him back to you, that is, my own heart. 13. I would have liked to keep him with me that he might serve on your behalf during my imprisonment for the gospel, 14. but I chose to do nothing without your consent, so that the good that you do might not be forced but of your own free will.

Notes

8. *Therefore, as I am bold enough in Christ:* The inferential conjunction *dio* ("therefore," BDAG 250) links the transitional verse (v. 7) of the thanksgiving to the body opening (O'Brien, *Colossians, Philemon,* 287). The particular use of *dio* makes this connection intentional as *gar* or *de* would normally perform this function (Dunn, *Colossians and Philemon,* 324). Paul's appeal to love follows directly from the love and faith just affirmed in the previous section. Most scholars interpret *echōn* ("having") as concessive, "as I am/while I am." The literal translation of *pollēn en Christǭ parrēsian* as "having much boldness in Christ" best captures Paul's own task: to proclaim boldly the Gospel of God, to announce what it is that God is bringing about. *Pollēn* is translated here as "enough" (BDAG 849), meaning that God has provided him with all he needs to proclaim this Gospel with power and effectiveness. To translate this as "full right" imposes a personal authority or claim (*pace* Lohse, *Colossians and Philemon,* 198) that Paul never uses and fails to see the distinction between *parrēsia* ("boldness," "outspokenness," "freedom of speech," BDAG 1344) and *exousia,* ("authority," "right," BDAG 352–53), which Paul could have used if he wanted to stress his apostolic "authority" (2 Cor 10:8; 13:10). As used elsewhere (2 Cor 3:12–4:2), *parrēsia* expresses the public proclamation of God's will as it openly confronts people with the powerful truth claim of God's word. "In Christ" is a favored expression Paul uses to speak of all those who are baptized in Christ, that is, who are already living in the realm of God's powerful rule, the new eschatological community still living in the midst of the old world.

   to demand that you do what is necessary: So emboldened to speak, Paul follows up with rather strong language. Paul needs to emphasize the importance of his appeal as he stresses what "is right" (*to anēkon,* BDAG 79), and even "necessary" (as I have chosen to translate it in this context) if the Gospel is to effect its claim on Philemon and his community. The infinitive of *epitassein* ("order" or "demand," BDAG 383) suggests that the apostle has some clear-cut expectations for Philemon to attend to. Its cognate noun, *epitagē,* is also employed by Paul to express God's imperative (Rom 16:26; 1 Cor 7:6, 25; 2 Cor 8:8; see O'Brien, *Colossians, Philemon,* 287–88 for additional NT usage). While

Heinrich Schlier emphasizes its legally binding character, taking "what is right" in the sense of an OT covenant demand (*anēkei, TDNT* 1:360), John Koenig's preference for "what is fitting" leaves almost too much room for flexibility (*Galatians, Philippians, Philemon* 196). "What is necessary" seems best to convey the importance of what this claim intends to accomplish, as it also keeps in mind that Paul is seeking the full cooperation of a respected friend and colleague. Even though love cannot coerce or compel, it still can make its demands known. *Soi* ("you") is dative after the infinitive and continues Paul's singular address to Philemon.

9\. *on account of love I prefer to appeal:* With *dia tēn agapēn* ("on account of/because of love" or "for love's sake") Paul introduces the basis and motivation for both the appeal and the act of sending Onesimus back to Philemon (v. 12; cf. vv. 13-14). The article *tēn* (with *agapēn*) is anaphoric and refers back to the previous expression of love (vv. 5, 7) that Paul wishes to re-ignite in the present appeal (BDF §252, 258, 491). Paul's decision to appeal *(parakalō)* also recalls his use of the corresponding expression, *paraklēsis* (v. 7), the encouragement that obviously figures into this decision. Koenig calls attention to other *parakalō-paraklēsis* combinations in Paul's letters (cf. Phil 2:1 and 4:2; *Galatians, Philippians, Philemon,* 196). *Parakalein* has a range of meanings, from what is perhaps the most memorable of God's consoling words in the Isaian proclamation, "Comfort, comfort my people" (Isa 40:1; cf. 2 Cor 5:20) to the familiar Pauline paraenesis or "exhortation" (Rom 12:1; 1 Cor 10:1; Phil 4:2; 1 Thess 4:15; 5:14, etc.). In this verse both friendship and encouragement seem to be the sense Paul wants to convey. *Mallon* is best translated as "prefer" instead of its more literal translation as "rather," which appeals to some scholars as it brings out the contrast with the preceding *epitassein,* often translated as "order" or "command." But since the Gospel's imperative (or "demand" as I translate it) does not clash in any way with love's appeal, the less contrastive "I prefer to appeal" seems to best fit the intended meaning.

I, Paul, as ambassador and now, as well, a prisoner of Christ Jesus: Toioutos joins *ōn* (present participle of *eimi,* "to be") with the particle *hōs,* having a causal sense, "as I am" (BDAG 1105; cf. 1 Cor 3:10). The introductory "I," needed in the English translation, gives voice to the first-person inflection of *parakalō* (as *egō* is not present in the Greek) and is added to the Greek name *Paulos.* The apostle takes care to make his request on behalf of Christ, whose ambassador he is and whom he represents. This makes it clear that Paul is not drawing upon his own apostolic authority; rather it is as Christ's envoy that he makes this appeal. Just as in the political arena that still exists today and like any ambassador, Paul seeks to advance a mutual bond of cooperation but carries no special authority except that of persuasion and entreaty. Where employed elsewhere by Paul, "ambassador" is used in connection with the divinely-commissioned ministry of reconciliation as "ambassadors of Christ," Christ "making his appeal through us" (2 Cor 5:20). The Gospel is always presented as God's rightful claim, not Paul's. The various translations of *presbytēs,* as either "ambassador" or "old man," arise from contemporary usage of the term, which in Paul's day could be translated both ways. While the precise spelling for "ambassador" is *presbeytēs,* the other form used here, *presbytēs,* with the original meaning "old man," was also used for "ambassador" (2 Chr 32:31; 1 Macc 14:22; 2 Macc 11:34; BDAG 1462; Günther Bornkamm, *presbytēs, TDNT* 6:683; Lightfoot, *Epistles,* 336–37). Scholars remain divided over whether to translate *presbytēs* as "ambassador" (O'Brien, Moule, Martin, Wright, Peterson) or as "old man" (Fitzmyer, Lohse, Stuhlmacher). Those who opt for "old man," which is never used elsewhere in Paul, do so because they equate being "ambassador" with the apostolic authority Paul refuses to claim. But "ambassador" carries no such authoritative weight, nor should the term be linked with apostolic authority in a letter in which Paul does not even mention being an apostle. It is helpful to think of present-day ambassadors whose role requires much in the way of persuasive ability in mediating and facilitating dialogue but who wield no power other than as personally-commissioned representatives. However, as an "ambassador of Christ," Paul shares none of the privileges the world generally offers most ambassadors, especially that of immunity from trial and imprisonment. In a sense, the combination of "ambassador" and "prisoner" would seem almost paradoxical if it were not for the qualifying *Christou Iēsou* (see the Interpretation). Providing emphasis but without adding contrast, *nuni de kai* ("and now, as well") brings "ambassador" and "prisoner" together as Paul states in what capacity he both belongs and witnesses to Christ: as one who proclaims his Gospel and participates in his suffering. *Nuni* adds greater emphasis than the more common *nun* (BDAG 682) but should not be taken to indicate that Paul had just recently been imprisoned (*pace* Martin, *Philemon,* 163). It appears that the Deutero-Pauline school also understood *presbytēs* as "ambassador" in coining the phrase that joins both terms as "ambassador in chains" with the use of the unambiguous *presbeytēs* (Eph 6:20; see MacDonald, *Colossians and Ephesians,* 347, for an expanded discussion of Paul as Christ's ambassador). Later use of *presbyteros* for church "elders" (Acts 11:30; 14:23; 20:17; Titus 1:5; Jas 5:14; 1 Pet 5:1) should not influence the interpretation of this earlier text (so Osiek, *Families,* 135–36).

10. *I appeal on behalf of my own child, whose father I have become in my imprisonment, Onesimus*: In this verse Paul finally states that the appeal concerns Onesimus. *Parakalō se* ("I appeal to you") repeats the main verb of the preceding verse and adds the direct object *se* ("you"). In context *peri* has a more personal character of "on behalf of" rather than simply "concerning" (Zerwick, *Analysis,* 652; Lohse, *Colossians and Philemon,* 199 n. 23; Fitzmyer, *Philemon,* 105–106), especially as it is complemented by the possessive and even emphatic *emou* ("my own" child: Harris, *Philemon,* 261; cf. v. 19). Reference to Onesimus as Paul's own "child" *(teknou)* is a clear indication that Onesimus had been brought to faith in Jesus Christ by the apostle, even without the additional *hon egennēsa* ("whose father I have become"). Paul's use of familial terms reflects the personal intimacy he shares with his own converts, such as Timothy (1 Cor 4:17; cf. Phil 2:22) and Philemon (Phlm 19). Paul also refers to whole communities he helped to found as his own beloved children in the Lord (cf. 1 Cor 4:14-15; Gal 4:19; 1 Thess 2:11). Even as, occasionally, Jewish and Greco-Roman teachers would refer to their disciples or pupils as "sons," the personal relationship that unites Paul with his converts in Christ goes far beyond normal secular usage (cf. 1 Cor 4:15; Karl H. Rengstorf and Friedrich Büchsel,

gennaō, TDNT 1:668–75). The masculine relative pronoun *hon* ("whom") is in agreement with Onesimus. *Egennēsa* means literally "beget" or "give birth to" (BDAG 193; see Gottlob Schrenk, *patēr, TDNT* 5:1005, for more on Paul's use of the parental metaphor). Such fatherly love seeks not only to nurture but also to bring the child to full maturity in mutual love and equal partnership (cf. v. 17). Bringing Onesimus to faith in Christ Jesus, however, does not necessarily imply that the apostle himself baptized him (cf. 1 Cor 1:14-17). And while whole households were known to have been converted (1 Cor 16:15-16; cf. Acts 18:8), this was apparently not the case in Philemon's household. Like Timothy (v. 1), Apphia ("the sister," v. 2), and Philemon (vv. 7, 20), Onesimus is also called by the familial name "brother," yet this relation to Philemon remains unexpressed until the time when Paul is prepared to announce it along with the appeal, when he asks Philemon to receive his "beloved brother" as he would receive the apostle himself (vv. 16-17). At this early point in the letter Paul simply provides notice of Onesimus' conversion, their close relationship, and the beneficial service he now provides. The preposition *en* ("during") is circumstantial, and *desmois,* meaning "prisoner" (BDAG 219), with possessive *mou,* is translated as "my imprisonment." The name *Onēsimos* has been found in many inscriptions throughout Ephesus and Asia Minor and is thought to have been a popular name for male slaves at that time (see Lightfoot, *Epistles,* 308; Fitzmyer, *Philemon,* 107).

11. *who was once useless to you, but is now exceedingly useful both to you and to me:* The placement of Onesimus' name at the end of the previous verse could serve to facilitate the word play that seems to be operative in this one. This verse is also dependent on the previous one as it contains no verb in Greek, although translations provide one. It may well be the first time that Philemon has heard any word concerning his absentee slave since his departure, and Paul's notice does not give any reason to think that Philemon had been aware either of his conversion by Paul or of the exemplary service mentioned here. Thus the word play could serve to lighten any tension, as it seems to play off the meaning of Onesimus' name ("useful" or "beneficial") by contrasting his former "useless" *(achrēstos)* behavior with his present "useful" *(euchrēstos)* service. Temporal terms that compare his pre- and post-Christian status, "once" *(pote)* . . . "but now" *(nuni de),* function to accentuate Onesimus' transformation in Christ. The prefix *eu* in *euchrēstos* designates this service as not only "useful" but genuinely and exceedingly so. The curious benefit to Philemon that is included in *kai soi kai emoi* ("both to you and to me") prepares for the implied appeal in v. 13, "so that he might serve on your behalf." Although many commentaries note the disparagement of Phrygian slaves as useless and unreliable (Lightfoot, *Epistles,* 310; Callahan, *Embassy of Onesimus,* 361), as the word play indicates, Onesimus' previous uselessness may have had less to do with any character flaw and more to do with the reality that, as a Christian, Onesimus may now be able to perform many services in a Christian household that he could not do prior to his baptism. This may be especially true in a household that hosts the local community's fellowship and worship. What appears to be a deliberate pun on Onesimus' name, perhaps as a way to lighten any tension with regard to Onesimus' absence from the household, also appears to extend

to a later word play in v. 20, where the apostle requests some "profit" or "benefit" *(onaimēn)* from his friend, as the "even more" of v. 21 clearly refers to the expectation that Philemon will send Onesimus back to Paul to assist in his useful service of the Gospel.

12. *I am sending him back to you, that is, my own heart:* It is out of love that the decision is made to send Onesimus back to Philemon (noting again the singular *soi*). While the apostle's direct concern and love for Philemon will be stated in v. 14, at this point Paul expresses the depth of his personal bond with Onesimus and the obvious personal sacrifice he is making in sending back his own child (v. 10), whom he also identifies as his "own heart" *(ta ema splagchna).* This strongly emotive and personal identification with his new convert will resurface at the apex of the appeal, when Paul asks Philemon to welcome Onesimus as if he were the apostle himself (v. 17). This verse, which begins with the relative clause *hon anepempsa soi* ("I am sending back to you"), is linked with what precedes and follows in a series of relative clauses (*hon egennēsa* [v. 10] . . . *hon anepempsa* [v. 12] . . . *hon egō eboulomēn* [v. 13]) that begins to gather together all the necessary information Paul must provide to build up to his appeal. The verb, *anapempein,* can mean either "send" or "send back" (BDAG 70), and is usually taken as an epistolary aorist (BDF §334; Moule, *Idiom Book,* 12; Fitzmyer, *Philemon,* 109–10). The personal pronoun *ema* is emphatic ("my own"), and *splagchna,* as in v. 7, is translated as "heart" (cf. v. 20). Synonymous with *kardia* (also "heart") and *pneuma* ("spirit"), *splagchna* is also a term that conveys such depth that, with this personal identification with Onesimus, Paul expresses one of the closest personal bonds of love that can unite one person with another.

13. *I would have liked to keep him with me that he might serve on your behalf during my imprisonment for the gospel:* No sooner has Paul stated his decision to send Onesimus back home (v. 12) than he mentions his own desire to have Onesimus remain with him, with the pronoun *hon* ("whom I would have liked to retain") referring back to the relative connective *hon* in v. 12 ("whom I am sending back," BDF §458). *Egō* ("I") adds emphasis and continues the previous emotional appeal as the conditional sense of *eboulomēn* ("would have liked," BDF §359.2; ZBG 356) makes it clear what the apostle would have chosen if he had only himself to consider. *Katechein,* "to keep" (BDAG 926) conveys the sense of "holding on to" or "holding fast," as it is used in 2 Cor 11:2, "to hold fast to one's faith," or 2 Cor 15:2, "to hold fast to the gospel message," and similarly in 1 Thess 5:21, "to hold on to what is good." In Onesimus, Paul has a valued companion and coworker by his side (cf. v. 11). The preposition *pros* denotes friendly relations (BDAG 874) and takes the accusative reflexive pronoun, *emauton,* meaning "with me," "beside me," or "at my side" (BDAG 321; Zerwick, *Analysis,* 653; Moule, *Idiom Book,* 52–53). With the *hina* clause Onesimus' usefulness to both Paul and Philemon (cf. v. 11) is now specified as service exercised on behalf of Philemon. And since Philemon was previously introduced as the apostle's coworker, this service must be related to the Gospel mission, perhaps even preaching. The present subjunctive *diakonę̄* also serves to move Paul's stated desire to an implied request that only Philemon is in a position to

grant. Thus this purpose clause apprises Philemon of Paul's need, especially while in prison, as it provides an opening for his friend to respond to his need without compelling him to do so. *Hyper sou* ("on your behalf" or "in your place") was a common expression used by scribes in writing letters for someone else (so Lohse, *Colossians and Philemon,* 202 n. 48). Here Paul employs the phrase to suggest that Onesimus can render service for Philemon even in his absence from the household. It also points out Philemon's opportunity to provide Paul with some useful assistance, especially at this time, *en tois desmois tou euaggeliou* ("during my imprisonment for the gospel"; cf. Phil 1:7). It is here that Philemon is given the actual reason for Paul's imprisonment, which is undoubtedly his public proclamation of the Gospel and its mission. In the singular technical sense, as here, *to euaggelion* ("the gospel") appears twenty-five times in the undisputed letters of Paul (and six times in the Deutero-Pauline letters). Peter Stuhlmacher (*Philemon,*153) notes that when Paul uses the expression *euaggelion tou theou* (Rom 1:1; 15:16; 2 Cor 11:7; 1 Thess 2:2, 8, 9) he is speaking in terms of the origin and authority of the Gospel, and when proclaiming the *euaggelion tou Christou* (Rom 15:19; 1 Cor 9:12; 2 Cor 2:12; 9:13; 10:14; Gal 1:7; Phil 1:27; 1 Thess 3:2) he is speaking of its content, that is, what the Gospel proclaims.

14. *but I chose to do nothing without your consent, so that the good that you do might not be forced, but of your own free will:* The adversative *de* ("but") refers back to Paul's decision not to retain Onesimus, but to send him back to Philemon (v. 12). Once again Paul speaks of his decision as based upon his own "choice" or "preference" *(ēthelēsa)* "to do" *(poiēsai)* nothing without Philemon's consent. The use of *sēs* instead of *sou* for "your" consent adds greater emphasis (BDAG 934). Paul's decision not to do anything *(ouden)* without or "apart from" *(chōris)* his friend's response may also presume Paul's understanding of partnership with Philemon (cf. "coworker," v. 1, and "partner," v. 17). The noun *gnōmē,* meaning "knowledge" as well as "consent," could also indicate that Philemon had, up to this point, been unaware of Onesimus' conversion and his help to Paul in the Gospel mission. The second *hina* clause (v. 14b) of this rather lengthy sentence (vv. 13-14) is related to the first (v. 13b) in specifying Onesimus' service on Philemon's behalf as "the good" *(to agathon)* that Paul desires. While "the good" here does give some concrete notion of what Paul meant by "all the good" (*pantos agathou tou,* v. 6), used earlier, it does not limit it to just this action. The close connection between the two purpose clauses is also clear if we place the protases and apodoses of each clause side by side so that "I would have liked" . . . "but I chose" (*eboulomēn,* v. 13a . . . *ēthelēsa,* v. 14a) serves as a bridge that equates Onesimus' service on Philemon's behalf (v. 13b) with "the good" that Paul seeks for his friend (v. 14b). The implication is clear: to his friend's credit, Paul would like Philemon to voluntarily release his slave to join Paul in serving the Gospel. The connection is also observed in the relationship between the subjunctive verbs in each verse, as the future possibility that Onesimus "might serve" (*diakonę̄,* v. 13b) is tied to the condition that it "might be" (*ę̄,* v. 14b) freely given by Philemon. The particle *hōs* ("as") introduces the comparison "not as" . . . "but" *(mē hōs . . . alla)* to emphasize the

distinction between "by compulsion" or "force" *(kata anagkēn)* and "of free will" *(kata hekousion). Hekousion* ("free will") is found only here in Paul's letters (Lohse, *Colossians and Philemon,* 202 n. 53). Fitzmyer (*Philemon,* 112) finds a resemblance between this phrase, *kata hekousion,* and the expression for the biblical "free-will" offering (*kat' hekousion,* Num 15:3 LXX) used in voluntary cultic acts (cf. Friedrich Hauck, *hekousios, TDNT* 2:470). This is certainly in line with Paul's understanding of his own mission as priestly service in bringing the Gentiles to faith in Jesus (cf. Rom 15:15-18; see especially Walter Radl, "Kult und Evangelium," 58–75, and C. E. B. Cranfield, *Romans,* 755).

Interpretation

The body of Paul's letter to Philemon presents the same general structure as that of any Hellenistic letter: opening (vv. 8-14), middle (vv. 15-17), and concluding segment (vv. 18-20). The opening, which usually conveys both the motive for sending the letter and relevant information, is rather extensive here in comparison with other letters, including Paul's, as he establishes the basis that will ground the appeal to be proposed in v. 17. The middle section further develops and carries forward all the information Paul needs to present before he can actually make his request. Once the appeal is made, it is in the concluding segment that Paul provides its guarantee of acceptance by removing any and all obstacles that could possibly impede Philemon's response (vv. 18-19). Paul concludes the body of the letter with the same joyful note that prepared for it (v. 7), as he summarily asks his friend to "refresh my heart in Christ" (v. 20).

Within the opening of the body of the letter (vv. 8-14) Paul already employs the available conventions of persuasive rhetoric *(pathos, logos, ethos)* to elicit his friend's support. The apostle's appeal to his personal and emotional relations with Philemon *(pathos)* is given prominent emphasis in the appeal to his friend on the basis of *agapē* (v. 9), in the attention given to the parent-child relationship that the conversion of Onesimus creates (v. 10), and in Paul's own identification with Philemon's slave as "my own heart" (v. 12). Paul's appeal to reason *(logos)* follows from his request to keep Onesimus by his side, where he is most useful to the mission and could even provide such service on Philemon's behalf. This implied request for Philemon to send Onesimus back to Paul is stated as the apostle's intent to evoke his friend's goodness by an appeal to his good character (*ethos;* cf. vv. 4-7). All three persuasive strategies continue into the central body of Paul's appeal. *Pathos* is at the heart of his appeal with its emphasis on Onesimus as a "beloved brother" (v. 16) with whom Paul once again identifies in asking Philemon to welcome him "as me" (v. 17). *Ethos* comes to the fore as Paul solicits this favor from his "partner" (v. 17) and finally spells out "what is necessary" (v. 8) in an invitation that appears to expect an affirmative response to love's demand (v. 9). *Logos* also appears to preface the request as Paul discerns the divine purpose and plan unfolding in all the events that have led up to this request (v. 15).

The close connection between the body opening and the preceding thanksgiving section is supported both structurally, by the inferential conjunction "therefore," and functionally, as the "love" that Paul so highly commends (vv. 5, 7) goes to the very basis of his appeal "to love" (v. 9). The essential and weighty theological terms introduced in the thanksgiving section are also repeated in key places throughout the body of the letter as Paul spells out how "love," "faith," "partnership," and "knowledge of all the good that is ours in Christ" pertain to this specific request and situation.

The boldness of Paul's initial expression (v. 8) reflects the boldness of a request that effectively eliminates the distinction between master and slave within the Christian community and new household of God (v. 16). Paul's right to even make such a request rests on his own apostolic task to proclaim and interpret the Gospel in every particular and concrete circumstance that presents itself (Beker, "Recasting Pauline Theology," 15–24). And yet, as Peter O'Brien rightly insists, Paul is not asserting his apostolic authority here (*Colossians, Philemon,* 268). Nowhere in this letter does he refer to himself as an "apostle." While one could posit that Paul had no need to present his apostolic credentials in writing to his own spiritual son (v. 19), it has also been suggested that Paul may have deliberately omitted any such use of dignified status in a letter that aims at leveling status and class distinctions, especially as "no longer as a slave but . . . a beloved brother" (v. 16) sets their fraternal bond in Christ over against the master-slave relationship (see the Introduction for a fuller discussion; see also Lewis, "Triangle," 239–46). The issue is not what Paul wants, but what God wills and rightfully demands. The necessity of the demand is made clear at the outset as the indicative of Onesimus' baptism in Christ (v. 10) leads to the imperative that he be treated accordingly, as one who belongs to Christ and can claim equal status as "brother" along with Philemon and Paul (v. 16; cf. vv. 1, 2, 7, 20). As commissioned by the risen Christ for this mission and given the eschatological knowledge and vision it entails, Paul is in position to guide his converts and churches in the direction of God's plans for the new eschatological community that has already begun in Christ (cf. Rom 1:1, 5; 1 Cor 9:16-17). Paul's bold announcement of "what is necessary" or "needed" right from the beginning of the letter indicates that he knows exactly what God wants in this situation. Paul's appeal is not based on any authority of his own, but rather on the claim and power of the Gospel to bring about what God demands from those who claim to belong to Christ (Sampley, *Pauline Partnership,* 98 n. 7).

Nevertheless, Paul cedes to love's appeal even as it makes the same demand. While love leaves Philemon's freedom intact (and actually empowers it!), it does not give him the choice of another option, as the condition of his being Paul's "partner" in his response (v. 17) makes clear. But Paul does not treat his colleague as if he were a new convert who needed guidance, either. In basing his appeal on love, Paul elicits Philemon's gracious support, respectful of the authority he already has as his coworker and especially as host to the community that is to welcome Onesimus. Love, by its very nature, cannot coerce or compel (cf. 1 Cor 13:5; 2 Cor 10:1-2, 10; 1 Thess 2:6-7). Yet for love to be received, a response must be made, and the mutuality inherent in love expects a response in kind (cf. 1 Cor 4:14). Partnership with Paul means heeding what Christ demands. And because Philemon is host to the community that is also addressed in the letter (vv. 3, 22, 25), it is likely that Paul expects his friend to lead the community in its response.

The rather odd placement of Paul's self-description in v. 9b, which repeats his unique use of "prisoner" in the letter opening (v. 1) and adds "ambassador," is directly related to the basis of the appeal to love (v. 9a). This suggests that Paul does not approach his friend as the apostle who exhorts and teaches, but instead as an ambassador whose more cordial and ingratiating role is to deepen the relationship that already exists between them. It also affirms that, as Christ's ambassador, Paul is speaking on behalf of Christ in a request that comes from God, not Paul. Elsewhere in his letters Paul refers to his mission as Christ's ambassador in a ministry of reconciliation (2 Cor 5:20; see the Notes for the choice of "ambassador" over "old man"). Although Paul does not use the expression here, the image of an ambassador of reconciliation does appear to suit the letter's goal as it seeks to reunite the absentee slave, Onesimus, with the head of his household, Philemon.

Paul's use of "prisoner of Christ Jesus" is striking, especially in its initial and unique appearance in v. 1 and with the additional references to his imprisonment throughout the letter pointing to its obvious significance (vv. 9, 10, 13, and 23). Paul's other letters may provide some insight that the present reader, perhaps unlike Philemon, needs in order to appreciate its meaning. The apostle's thoughts concerning his imprisonment, as with his many hardships and suffering in general (2 Cor 11:23-28), call attention to his willingness to suffer for the sake of Christ, his people, and his Gospel. For Paul, suffering and vulnerability are an expected aspect of his mission. Ties to the OT concept of witness also show a close connection with another of his commonly used self-designations, "servant of God," placing him in a clear line of continuity with the suffering OT prophets (Rom 1:1, 5; cf. 2 Cor 1:1). Also, all the suffering this mission brings him binds him more completely with Christ, who "was crucified in weakness, but now he lives by the power of God" (2 Cor 13:4). Thus in imitating the pattern of the life of Christ, whose life he now lives, Paul comes to know Christ ever more experientially and deeply. And when Paul calls attention to his hardships, including several imprisonments, he does so to boast of the power of God at work in human weakness and limitation (cf. 2 Cor 11:30). The seeming incongruity in pairing the dignified title of "ambassador" with "prisoner" seems less peculiar in light of Paul's understanding of the mysterious and paradoxical ways in which God works for good in the world (Wright, *Colossians and Philemon,* 180). As the apostle states in writing to the Corinthians, "God's power is made perfect in weakness." Paul continues, "I am content with weaknesses, insults, hardships, persecutions, and constraints for the sake of Christ, for whenever I am weak, then I am strong" (2 Cor 12:9-10). This is both paradoxical and countercultural, as most people boast of their strengths, not their weaknesses.

Paul's letters, then, provide at least three possible meanings that might fit in with the use of the expression *desmios Christou Iesou:* The first is that of being in the "bonds" of Christ (taking *desmios* as Cassidy does in *Paul in Chains,* 146), in the sense of belonging to Christ, somewhat similar to being a "servant" or "slave." This could be the sense implied in v. 1, where Paul also gives a short notice to Philemon and his community about his present imprisonment (as Cassidy surmises, ibid. 146, as does Peterson, who views ambassador, prisoner, and slave as functional equivalents: *Rediscovering Paul,* 128). Here in v. 9, and in his role as "ambassador of Christ," Paul appears to be once again stressing his role as Christ's representative, both in his commissioned task as "ambassador" and in his experience of living as Christ did, sharing in Christ's suffering, and witnessing to God's power in the midst of it (see especially 2 Cor 4:7-12; also Rom 8:17; Phil 1:29; 3:10). While Paul does not explicitly speak of this divine power at work in this imprisonment as he does in the Philippian letter (1:12-14), it is at least implied by Onesimus' conversion (v. 10), by his surprisingly useful service while Paul is in prison for the sake of the Gospel (v. 13), and in his discernment of divine providence at work in all that has taken place (v. 15). If this expression is to be read as "prisoner of Christ" rather than "prisoner for Christ," Paul could also be stating that it is Christ, and not his Greco-Roman captors, who holds him captive and is truly in control of the eventual outcome of the situation. Christ's sovereign rule is already present, moving all peoples and their history toward the future that God is creating, a future that belongs to God alone.

The affectionate, fatherly love the apostle expresses toward Onesimus is not unusual for Paul. It is likely to elicit a surge of emotion from Philemon, who is also Paul's beloved child in Christ, as interpreters have always read v. 19. Both Philemon and Onesimus stand in the company of others, like Timothy (1 Cor 4:17; Phil 2:19-22) and probably Apphia and Archippus

(Phlm 2), who have been personally brought to faith by the apostle. With much tenderness and deep affection Paul also refers to the churches he founded as his own beloved children, "For I became your father in Christ Jesus through the gospel" (1 Cor 4:14). The apostle appears to be modeling this relation on God's own parental love for God's chosen people, both paternal (e.g., Isa 63:16; 64:7) and maternal (e.g., Isa 49:15; see Johnson, *She Who Is*). This approach continues through Jesus' own gentle outreach and ingathering of Israel (cf. Jesus' maternal lament in Matt 23:37 and its parallel, Luke 13:34) and in Paul's own characterization of his parental concern for his churches. Like God, who continues to love and redeem even those children who have grieved the Holy Spirit (Isa 63:10, 16; cf. Isa 43:4; 54:10; Rom 11:25-32), and like all good parents, Paul continues his vigilant care for his "little children" even when they have turned away from his Gospel for another (Gal 4:19). Throughout his letters, like mothers and fathers and as one of God's coworkers (2 Cor 3:9), Paul nourishes (1 Cor 3:2), consoles (1 Thess 2:7-9), exhorts (1 Thess 2:11), and admonishes when necessary (1 Cor 4:14; 2 Cor 6:13). Like typical parents he bears all the anxiety and tears it takes to bring them to maturity ("willing to be spent for your sakes," 2 Cor 12:15; cf. Phil 2:17) as well as all the joy that delights in their accomplishments (Phil 1:5-7; 1 Thess 1:8; 3:9; cf. Phil 4:1; 1 Thess 2:20). Paul continues the tradition of using masculine and feminine images to describe his own task of "giving birth" (*gennēsa,* v. 10) to their faith and bringing them to full maturity (2 Cor 11:28; 1 Thess 3:5). And good parent that he is, Paul never counts the cost (v. 19) because he considers his task to be a gift, not a burden (George R. Beasley-Murray, "Parental Metaphors," *DPL* 655–58).

At this emotionally charged point in the letter, when Paul will inform Philemon that he is sending Onesimus, "his own heart" (v. 12), back to him, he inserts what appears to be a parenthetical touch of lightness and humor that plays on the meaning of Onesimus' name as "useful" (v. 11). This may be the first news Philemon is hearing of his slave Onesimus since his departure. News of his conversion by Paul may have come as quite a surprise, hence the need for some pause and perhaps a little lightness. At the same time this is no mere parenthetical remark, as Paul makes the essential point of Onesimus' "useful" contribution to the mission. It is likely that Onesimus has told Paul of his former uselessness to Philemon, which may also have been a factor in his leaving the household. It is possible that more of a point than a pun was intended as Paul affirms the God-given transformation that has changed Onesimus' life. For, in what seems to be a mere pun, Paul is actually providing this formerly "useless" slave with a superb recommendation, the details of which extend into the following verses (vv. 13-14).

The emotional appeal that accompanied notice of Onesimus' arrival is continued as Paul expresses his desire to keep Onesimus by his side and so retain his help (v. 13). This verse also explains what the apostle meant when he described Onesimus' useful service as beneficial "both to you and to me" (v. 11). Here the rhetorical persuasion that begins with *pathos* also moves to include an appeal to logic as Paul seeks to cause this useful service to continue. Onesimus' activity is in some way or another connected with the Gospel mission, as service on Philemon's behalf, that is, most likely in his capacity as Paul's missionary coworker. The verb Paul uses to describe this service *(diakoneō)* belongs to the same word group as *diakonia,* an important early expression for Christian ministry in all its various capacities (BDAG 229–30).

Letting Philemon know of his wishes (and his need during his imprisonment) is a gentle way of requesting a favor from a friend who is certain to take notice without having to make a direct request. It is also a way of making sure that Philemon's decision is not forced, especially given Paul's explicit statement that he is basing his appeal on love and not coercion (vv. 8-9). The implicit appeal continues the earlier tone of respect that Paul accorded his dear friend and partner in the thanksgiving section. It is also at this point that Paul begins to shift his focus from Onesimus (and all the preliminary details that needed to be mentioned) back to Philemon. Paul's concern for his friend's growth in virtue ("the good you do") recalls his earlier prayer ("that your partnership may be effective in realizing all the good that is ours in Christ Jesus") and provides a genuine opportunity for Philemon to extend to Paul the gracious hospitality he has already given to others. The lengthy sentence (vv. 13-14) that begins with Paul's wish ("I would have liked") and ends with the final purpose clause ("so that the good you do might not be forced but voluntary") can only mean that Paul's implied request will be granted when Philemon sends Onesimus back to Paul and to the service of the Gospel.

As several interpreters rightly note (Koenig, *Galatians, Philippians, Philemon,* 198; Wright, *Colossians and Philemon,* 183), there may be more persuasive power in Paul's wishful implication than in any straightforward request he might have made. This would, of course, be effective only in a friendly correspondence, especially one that exists between friends who are aware of each other's care and concern and who share important values and goals. People generally do not express their desires in official letters. Such an expectation of mutual care and concern can only work between trusted friends.

We know from Paul's other letters that even his acceptance of any assistance is rare (Phil 4:15, 17-18; cf. 2 Cor 11: 9). When he does accept help it is only from his closest friends, such as his partners in the Philippian church, who are mature in faith (Phil 2:25, 30; cf. 1:5, 7). Here Paul seeks assistance similar to that provided by the Philippian congregation, who sent Epaphroditus to assist Paul while in prison. And although it remains unstated, it is likely that Philemon's action will have an important impact on the community, as such concrete action can only more strongly witness to their union in Christ, the effective *koinōnia* that Paul prays will lead to yet another experience of what he means by "all the good that is ours in Christ" (v. 6).

For Reference and Further Study

Aune, David E. *The New Testament in Its Literary Environment*. Philadelphia: Westminster, 1985.

Best, Ernest. "Paul's Apostolic Authority — ?" *JSNT* 27 (1986) 3–25.

Lapsley, Jacqueline E. "Feeling Our Way: Love for God in Deuteronomy," *CBQ* 65 (2003) 350–69.

Marrow, Stanley B. *Speaking the Word Fearlessly: Boldness in the New Testament*. New York, NY, and Ramsey, NJ: Paulist, 1982.

Post, Stephen G. *A Theory of Agapē: On the Meaning of Christian Love*. Lewisburg, PA: Bucknell University Press; Cranberry, NJ: Associated University Presses, 1990.

Sanders, Jack T. "The Transition from Opening Epistolary Thanksgivings to the Body of the Letters of the Pauline Corpus," *JBL* 81 (1962) 348–62.

Schütz, John H. *Paul and the Anatomy of Apostolic Authority*. Cambridge: Cambridge University Press, 1975.

Taylor, N. H. "Onesimus: A Case Study of Slave Conversion in Early Christianity," *Religion and Theology* 3 (1996) 259–81.

Unnik, W. C. van. "The Christian's Freedom of Speech in the New Testament," *BJRL* 44 (1962) 466–88.

Vacek, Edward Collins. *Love, Human and Divine: The Heart of Christian Ethics*. Washington, DC: Georgetown University Press, 1994.

Wedderburn, A. J. M. "Some Observations on Paul's Use of the Phrases 'in Christ' and 'with Christ,'" *JSNT* 25 (1985) 83–97.

Witherup, Ronald D. *Conversion in the New Testament*. Collegeville: Liturgical Press, 1994.

4. *Central Request: Providential Discernment, Love's Imperative, Explicit Appeal, and Guarantee of Acceptance* (15-20)

15. For perhaps this is why he was parted from you for a while, that you might have him back forever, 16. no longer as a slave, but much more than a slave, a beloved brother, especially to me, but how much more to you, both in the flesh and in the Lord. 17. So if you regard me as a partner, welcome him as you would me. 18. And if he has wronged you in any way, or owes you anything, charge that to me. 19. I, Paul, write this with my own hand. I will repay it, to say nothing of your owing me even your own self. 20. Yes, brother, I want some benefit from you in the Lord. Refresh my heart in Christ.

Notes

15. *For perhaps this is why he was parted from you for a while:* The postpositive conjunction *gar* ("for") expresses both continuation and cause (BDAG 189–90) as Paul, with great tact, for the first and only time mentions Onesimus' absence from Philemon's household. The possibility that God's providential guidance lies behind all that has transpired is advanced by the prepositional phrase *dia touto* ("this is why," "for this reason," BDAG 225–26, *ZBG* §112). With the adverb *tacha* ("perhaps"), Philemon is invited to share the apostle's discerning perspective on the situation. The verb *echōristhē* ("he was parted") is to be taken as a "theological passive" (*ZBG* §236; Fitzmyer, *Philemon,* 112; Lohse, *Colossians and Philemon,* 202; O'Brien, *Colossians, Philemon,* 295; Harris, *Colossians & Philemon,* 265) that shifts the focus to God's providential action and away from Onesimus' departure which, some commentators suspect, may have involved his running away from the household. The idiom *pros hōran* ("for a while"), meaning literally "for an hour" (BDAG 1102), especially in contrast to *aiōnion* ("forever"), also works to mitigate an absence that apparently included enough time for Paul to catechize Onesimus, not to mention the possible additional period of "useful service" he has provided (vv. 10-11; Dunn, *Colossians and Philemon,* 333). The comparison between "for a while" and "forever" makes the benefit to Philemon far outweigh any temporary trouble and inconvenience.

that you might have him back forever: The spatial proximity between "for a while" and "forever" facilitates the obvious comparison. The *hina* clause, "that you might have him back forever," cannot simply refer to Onesimus' return in his capacity as a slave, since the master-slave relation does not exist forever. *Aiōnion* generally refers to what is everlasting and eternal, without end (BDAG 33). But even if it is taken as "a slave for life" (so Hermann Sasse, *aiōnios, TDNT* 1:209) the phrase in the next verse, "no longer as a slave," rules out this possibility. Thus "having him back forever" can only refer to the new relation the two men now share as brothers in Christ, precisely the point Paul will stress in the following verse. While *apechēs* is best translated in this sentence as "to have back," a nuance of its alternative meaning "to have fully/completely" may also be in mind in light of the relationship they now share ("both in the flesh and in the Lord," v. 16; Winter, "Paul's Letter," 10). *Auton* ("him") in "have him back forever" refers to Onesimus as it picks up the *auton* of v. 12, where Paul speaks of Onesimus as "my own self"; it also provides the next verse (v. 16) with its subject.

16. *no longer as a slave, but more than a slave, a beloved brother:* The combination *ouketi* ("no longer") . . . *all' hyper* ("but more than") sets up the comparison that, in light of his baptism, Onesimus is no longer to be considered *hōs doulon* ("as a slave") but *hyper doulon* ("much more than a slave"), a "beloved brother" *(adelphon agapēton).* "Much more" best translates the meaning of *hyper* (BDAG 1031; Harald Riesenfeld, *hyper, TDNT* 8:515). *Ouketi* also provides an even stronger contrast and comparison than the *mē* of v. 14. This first and only indication that Onesimus is Philemon's slave is quickly redirected toward his new identity in Christ as a "brother." And while nothing has happened to change his legal status as slave, the reality of his baptism in Christ has completely transformed the nature of his relationship with other Christian "sisters" and "brothers" whom he joins in calling God *Abba,* and Jesus "Lord." Joseph Fitzmyer (*Philemon,* 114) correctly identifies the inaccurate translation of *hōs* by Allan D. Callahan ("as if" instead of "as," *Embassy of Onesimus,* 373) that led him to suggest that Onesimus had not been Philemon's slave, but was only treated as such (cf. Mitchell, "Chrysostom on Philemon"). This new relationship in Christ stands at the center of Paul's argument from lesser to greater when he compares Onesimus' former slave status to that of a "beloved brother." Whether or not Onesimus retained his position as Philemon's slave, it is clear from Paul's statement that he is no longer to be regarded as a slave but is, by virtue of his baptism, a beloved brother to all within the church whether Philemon chooses to recognize this fact and act accordingly or not (O'Brien, *Colossians, Philemon,* 297).

especially to me, but how much more to you, both in the flesh and in the Lord: This fraternal relationship, also qualified by *agapēton* ("beloved"), draws Onesimus into the circle of personal intimacy that Paul already shares with Philemon (v. 1; also v. 19). *Malista emoi* ("especially to me") also recalls prior use of personal pronouns, *emou* ("my child," v. 10), *emoi* (describing Onesimus' usefulness "to me," v. 11), *ema* (indicating whom Paul is sending back, "my own heart," v. 12), and *pros emauton* (expressing the desire to keep Onesimus "beside me," v. 13), all of which function to describe the closeness that has developed between Paul and his convert. While using the superlative *malista* in an elative sense ("especially") for his relationship with Onesimus, Paul presses the relatedness between Onesimus and Philemon even further with *posǭ mallon* ("how much more") and the dual condition *kai . . . kai* ("both . . . and") to describe the bond that is both "in the flesh" and "in the Lord." *En Kyriǭ* ("in the Lord") characterizes the relationship all Christians share, making them brothers and sisters both to the Lord Jesus and to each other. Unlike other letters in which "flesh" and "spirit" are often contrasted (cf. Rom 8:12-14; Gal 3:3; 4:29), in this, the only Pauline text to combine both phrases (so Lohmeyer, *Philemon,* 189), "in the flesh" and "in the Lord" work to support each other. *En sarki* ("in the flesh") pertains to the natural realm of human and social relations that makes for the additional bond between Philemon and Onesimus as members of the same household. It is thought that slaves and their families were considered members of the extended family of the household unit, which in Greco-Roman society would have included the expectation of loyalty and protection (R. J. Erickson, *DPL* 304; Peterson, *Rediscovering Paul,* 174). "In the Lord" represents the greater sphere of God's action and involvement in human life and community that establishes their new relation as siblings and equals (cf. Gal 3:27-29; 1 Cor 7:22), which would certainly transcend the master-slave connection. Here Paul's primary concern is not whether or not Onesimus is given his freedom, but that he be acknowledged as the "brother" he truly is.

17. *So if you regard me as a partner, welcome him as you would me:* The stage is now set for Paul to announce his central appeal, that Onesimus be welcomed as if he were the apostle himself, *hōs eme* ("as me"), which moves the previous comparison from "no longer as a slave" all the way to identification with Paul himself. The sustained emotional appeal continues with the apposition between *hōs eme* and *auton* ("him"). Postpositive *oun* ("so," BDAG 736) is resumptive in continuing the line of thought from v. 15 and also providing the essential content of the appeal that was first noted in vv. 9 and 10 (Lohse, *Colossians and Philemon,* 203; O'Brien, *Colossians, Philemon,* 298). The conditional nature of the request only serves to heighten its importance for Paul. The simple condition is indicated by *ei* ("if," *ZBG* §303) and the second person indicative of *echō* (*echeis,* "if you consider/regard": BDAG 420–21), which takes the double accusative in the direct object *me* ("me") and the noun *koinōnon* ("partner," treated as a predicative adjective: BDAG 553–54; cf. 2 Cor 8:23). The verb *echeis* is also used in vv. 5 and 8, indicating Philemon's love and faith and Paul's boldness in speech respectively. *Koinōnia* ("partner") also retrieves the content of Paul's prayer in the introductory thanksgiving (*hē koinōnia tēs pisteōs,* v. 5). The whole weight of the letter comes to rest on this appeal to welcome *(proslabou)* Onesimus as if he were Paul. As Eduard Lohse writes, this does much to elevate Onesimus' status, especially for a runaway slave (*Colossians and Philemon,* 204). *Proslabou* is the first in a series of imperatives, to be followed by *elloga* ("charge," v. 18), *anapauson* ("refresh," v. 20), and *etoimaze* ("prepare," v. 22), that help to pave the way for Philemon's response yet in no way force his decision. In contemporary Hellenistic usage the imperative mood can at times follow the indicative without the force of an imperative. The only true imperative here is that of love's appeal. Theologically one could say that the indicative of Onesimus' baptism in Christ leads to the imperative that Philemon graciously welcome Onesimus as his beloved brother.

18. *And if he has wronged you in any way, or owes you anything, charge that to me:* The conditional statement of v. 17 is followed by another, with *ei* ("if") introducing the second imperative, *elloga* ("to charge"). The verb *ellogeō* is only found twice in the NT, here and in Rom 5:13 (Herbert Preisker, *ellogeō, TDNT* 2:517; for a discussion of the unusual form of *elloga* see Fitzmyer, *Philemon,* 118; also BDF

§90; Lohse, *Colossians and Philemon,* 204 nn. 69 and 70). The entire expression *touto emoi elloga* ("charge that to me") can also be seen as continuing the response to the initial condition, "If you consider me your partner. . . ." The aorist verb, *ēdikēsen,* "to wrong someone or to treat unjustly" (BDAG 20), looks to some past event and could hint at some possible wrongdoing or some injustice suffered by Philemon, even as it leaves unspecified what that could be. Paul uses this verb with the same sense in other letters (1 Cor 6:8; 2 Cor 7:2, 12a). Only in 2 Pet 2:13 does it appear to have a strict financial meaning (Gottlob Schrenk, *adikeō, TDNT* 1:161). Here Paul may be referring to the temporary loss of service (cf. v. 15) that resulted from Onesimus' absence from the household. The aorist verb takes a double accusative, *se* ("you"), specifying Philemon as the person wronged, and *ti,* "anything," "any matter," or "any way" in which he may have been offended, with no specific injury indicated. This aorist verb looks to some past event that many commentators think is associated with Onesimus' flight from the household (see the discussion in the Introduction). The second verb, *opheilei* ("owe," BDAG 743; and, as *prosopheilei,* for the debt owed Paul in v. 19) is commonly employed in the language of commerce and finance and could leave open the possibility that some monetary debt could be owed to Philemon, if only from services lost in Onesimus' absence. Again *touto* ("anything") leaves the putative debt unspecified. Paul makes certain that nothing stands in the way of the reunion he seeks as he assumes personal responsibility for any outstanding debt that Onesimus might have incurred. The entire sentence not only continues the apostle's identification with his new convert, whose debt he will cover, but also shows Paul's consistent sensitivity and respect for Philemon as his friend and partner.

19. *I, Paul, write this with my own hand. I will repay it:* Here is a distinctive and recognizable Pauline stamp (2 Cor 10:1; Gal 5:2; 1 Thess 2:18), joining the emphatic *egō* ("I") and the apostle's signature *(Paulos),* as Paul declares that he is writing this with his own hand. *Egrapsa* ("I write this") is an epistolary aorist (Moule, *Idiom Book,* 148; BDF §334). *Tę emę cheiri* ("with my own hand," cf. 1 Cor 16:21; Gal 6:11; Col 4:18; 2 Thess 3:17) also employs the emphatic and personal *emę* ("my own"). Paul's promise of repayment of any outstanding debt is given further assurance with the second emphatic *egō* and the verb *apotisō* ("I will repay"), using what can be taken as a legal term for payment in full (so Lohse, *Colossians and Philemon,* 204; BDAG 124; *MM* 71). While the signature statement by itself could simply confirm that it is Paul himself who authors the letter, the additional mention of repayment is taken by some scholars to have all the force of a legally binding statement (Bahr, "Subscriptions in the Pauline Letters," 27–41; Dunn, *Colossians and Philemon,* 340; O'Brien, *Colossians, Philemon,* 300), while others see it as more of a parenthetical note (Lohse, *Colossians and Philemon,* 204).

to say nothing of your owing me even your own self: In the same breath Paul assumes all responsibility for any and all debt Onesimus may owe his friend and reverses any need to do so. Repayment becomes totally unnecessary with the words of this accompanying statement that, as far as Paul is concerned, settles all accounts. With this final remark, described as an elliptical construction known as a *praeteritio* (or *paraleipsis,* so Fitzmyer, *Philemon,* 118; also Harris, *Colossians & Philemon,* 274), which actually states what one would rather not say, *hina mē legō* ("to say nothing," "not to mention"), Paul effectively cancels any debt Onesimus might have owed Philemon. The verb *ophlein* ("owe," v. 18) is repeated here with the prefix *pros,* which gives *prosopheleis* even greater emphasis, "to owe in addition" (BDAG 883). The *soi* ("you") . . . *moi* ("me") combination refers to the spiritual debt Philemon owes Paul. *Kai seauton* ("even your own self") clearly refers to Philemon's life in Christ, for which Paul takes credit. The contrasting combination of statements in this verse adds quite a bit of irony that is not without some humor as it totally reorients claims of indebtedness. No matter what Onesimus may owe his slaveowner, it can never compare with the debt of gratitude Philemon owes to Paul. And as it is a debt that can only be repaid by love, it goes directly to the basis of Paul's appeal.

20. *Yes, brother, I want some benefit from you in the Lord:* Positioned both at the beginning of the body of the letter (as the last word of v. 7) and in the first words of its concluding sentence (v. 20), the vocative singular *adelphe* focuses all the attention on Philemon as Paul's "brother," the relationship that goes to the central core of his appeal to receive Onesimus as "beloved brother in Christ" (vv. 16-17). The adverb *nai* ("yes") also adds a concluding note as it prepares for an affirmative response and the confidence Paul will express in summary (vv. 21-22). *Adelphe* also continues the letter's affectionate tone (Fitzmyer, *Philemon,* 119). In this final summary statement it is clear that Paul expects a positive and concrete response from Philemon. But the request for a hospitable welcome for Onesimus does not exclude the possibility of his manumission (*pace* Lohse, *Colossians and Philemon,* 205). Nevertheless, the benefit Paul wants "in the Lord" does recall the only other time Paul uses the identical expression, in v. 16, where Philemon is to acknowledge his new relationship with Onesimus, "no longer as a slave . . . but as a beloved brother . . . in the Lord." Suggestions that the verb *onaimēn* ("to benefit" or "to profit") provides yet another word play on the name Onesimus (which also means "profitable" or "useful"; cf. v. 11 and the Notes) could function as a lighthearted way of recalling Onesimus' useful service, which Paul has made possible, and for which he now seeks some return in kind (Wright, *Colossians and Philemon,* 189; *pace* Fitzmyer, who, in agreement with Lightfoot and Bahr, finds this too farfetched, *Philemon,* 119). The verb *oninēmi* also means "to derive joy or comfort" (BDAG 711) and is an instance of Paul's use of the rare optative (an optative proper, BDF §384), here to express an attainable desire or wish, which in this context reads like an imperative (so Fitzmyer, *Philemon,* 119).

Refresh my heart in Christ: Together with the vocative "brother," this phrase, which concludes the body of the letter, also repeats, in reverse order ("hearts," "refreshed," "brother," in v. 7, with "brother," "refresh," "heart," as here), the statement that concluded the thanksgiving and prepared for the body of the letter. Here also, as the active voice of the verb "to refresh" *(anapauson)* replaces the previous passive reminiscence (*anapepautai,* v. 7), Paul directly invites Philemon to extend to him that same refreshment he has been so good at providing for other Christians. This recollection of the graciousness of the thanksgiving section (vv. 4-7) also recalls "all the good that is ours in Christ," and so does not limit Paul's request to the immediately preceding appeal. Gracious host that Philemon is, he cannot fail to refresh the heart of the one from whom he has received his own life of faith.

Interpretation

Other than indirectly, in v. 15, Paul never mentions the fact that Onesimus may have run away, nor does he indicate how much time he may have spent away from the household. Instead, Paul tactfully provides an alternative perspective that turns Onesimus' departure into a working out of God's will that actually serves to benefit Philemon. Even as there is also no mention of the circumstances that brought Paul and Onesimus together, what is stated, his conversion and baptism into Christ and his useful service (for Philemon and Paul, v. 11), is enough for Paul to discern God's providential action bringing these past events toward the outcome Paul desires and anticipates (vv. 16-17). The hint of divine guidance, assisted by the apostle's use of the "theological passive" voice of the verb in "he was parted from you," rests on the biblical conviction that God's plan and guidance lie behind and guide human action and the events of history (Sir 44:17, 21; 45:24; Wis 16:1, 25; Ethelbert Stauffer, *hina, TDNT* 3:323–33). Paul turns what could easily be a negative situation into a positive one by shifting the focus from Onesimus' departure to God's involvement in all that has taken place. His absence is also minimized by comparing the temporal master-slave relation with the lasting and permanent relation they share as brothers in Christ. Thus all the information Paul brings to light so far leads to only one conclusion, that Philemon ought to be reunited with Onesimus, "no longer as a slave, but much more than a slave, a beloved brother, especially to me, but how much more to you, both in the flesh and in the Lord" (v. 16). In v. 16 Paul moves into the heart of his request, reaching back to his initial mention of the appeal to "what is necessary" (v. 8). Paul continues the line of thought begun in v. 15, which spoke of lasting relations between Philemon and Onesimus, as he now announces the way in which they are related as "beloved brothers." "What is necessary" is for Philemon to relate to Onesimus as his brother in Christ and not as his slave. This is the abiding relationship that God has made possible in Christ, and it is the only one Paul considers valid if we take seriously what Paul means by the phrase "no longer as a slave." The addition of "both in the flesh and in the Lord" guarantees that this new fraternal relation is to exist in every dimension of their lives together. Paul's use of "in the Lord" in this verse is significant precisely because use of the title "Lord" emphasizes Jesus' sovereign claim in establishing communities in which all who are baptized share equal status: "There is neither Jew nor Greek, there is neither slave nor free, there is neither male nor female; for you are all one in Christ Jesus . . . heirs according to the promise" (Gal 3:26-29).

Familial terms that abound in the Pauline corpus receive special emphasis throughout this brief letter. Besides the references to Timothy and Apphia as "brother" and "sister," Philemon is called "brother" in two key locations, both as a preface to the appeal that is about to open and in the closing summary (vv. 7, 20), an obvious repetition that enables these two verses to form an *inclusio* around the body of the letter. Paul's use of the vocative singular *adelphe* in directly addressing Philemon heightens the fraternal emphasis. The centerpiece of Paul's appeal focuses on the relationship that both he and Philemon share with Onesimus as "beloved brothers" (v. 16). Here, too, with the emphasis "especially to me" Paul reaffirms his already stated personal bond with Onesimus (vv. 10, 11, 12, 13) even as he stresses the more extensive relationship between Onesimus and Philemon "both in the flesh and in the Lord." The additional relationship "in the flesh" may include a lifetime of experiences they share in common as members of the same Greco-Roman household. In this correspondence Paul mentions no contrast or conflict between secular and spiritual spheres of existence, as he does in other letters (cf. Rom 6:19; 8:12-14; Gal 3:3; 4:29). Instead, in this instance Paul has both realms of existence working cooperatively to support his argument and the Lord's sovereign claim over all creation (Cassidy, "Roman Imprisonment," 154, 162–63).

What begins as providential guidance (v. 15) and extends to the Lord's claim (v. 16) finally reaches its goal as Paul expresses the concrete action he asks of his friend and partner: to welcome Onesimus as a beloved brother and even as if he were the apostle himself (v. 17). This is the response Paul seeks and has a right to expect from his partner in faith. That Paul should have to make this request, and even so carefully prepare such a theologically sound and exceptionally persuasive kind of appeal, suggests that much more is at stake. Paul's request demands that a former (and likely runaway) slave be embraced as a beloved brother, as an equal and coheir in Christ. In such a slave-dependent economy and status-dominated society this was no small request. It goes to the very heart of a countercultural Gospel for which Paul and his companions are continually being beaten, persecuted, and imprisoned. What seems so obvious and right to a contemporary social consciousness and mindset must have been quite radical in Paul's day. While manumission was a possible and accepted practice, it was mostly limited to slaves who could afford to purchase their own freedom and whose life of dedicated service was far spent. But beyond any thought of possible manumission for Onesimus, Paul, in calling for brotherly affection, is seeking a relationship that would have been unheard-of and even considered impossible to establish, as it would mean the leveling of the distinction that the master-slave combination establishes and epitomizes. The request that Philemon greet Onesimus as he would greet Paul himself presses the importance of this reunion and reconciliation. "Partner" certainly underscores the fundamental task Philemon shares as Paul's coworker and host to the local community, for the hospitality Paul seeks is a core concern of his letters. When he wrote to Christians in Corinth he was concerned for equal treatment of poor and rich at eucharistic meals and worship. In Galatia he focused on the acceptance of baptized Gentiles as full and equal members of the faithful community. In Romans this same concern is central to his paraenesis: "Welcome one another, therefore, as Christ has welcomed you" (Rom 15:7), as Paul places loving concern for the people of God above concerns over "unclean" food and feastdays. Here it completes Paul's prayer that Philemon "may realize all the good that is ours in Christ" (v. 6). This realization or effectiveness for which Paul prays extends to his partner's ability to persuade and lead his community to join him in the gracious reception he seeks for Onesimus.

Many commentators take Paul's promise of compensation for any debt owed or injustice done to Philemon as an indication that Onesimus may have stolen some money from the household, perhaps to provide the resources he would need to run away (Stuhlmacher, *Philemon*, 49; Fitzmyer, *Philemon*, 117; Wright, *Colossians and Philemon*, 187). Even beyond the financial loss, there is also the possible harm done through unfairness and dishonor that would be especially significant in an honor-shame culture. Other possible scenarios have also been suggested, including that of F. F. Bruce, who maintains that Philemon had sent Onesimus to Paul but he had overstayed his leave (*Paul, Apostle of the Heart Set Free*, 400). Yet, curiously, no mention is made of any remorse or need for forgiveness or even of reconciliation. It appears that the letter from the apostle and the presence of Onesimus, the letter's likely carrier (and obviously Paul's personal envoy or representative), are sufficient to warrant the hospitable reception that is expected.

Whatever else lies behind vv. 18-19, there is the certain goal of removing any possible obstacle that could stand in the way of this hospitable and filial reunion Paul seeks. In assuming personal responsibility for all compensation due his friend, Paul not only exercises parental care in covering any possible infraction by Onesimus (so O'Brien, *Colossians, Philemon*, 300); he also demonstrates concern for any loss or dishonor suffered by Philemon (cf. Koenig, *Galatians, Philippians, Philemon*, 200). Thus the customary signature that appears to certify that it is the apostle himself who authors this letter may be more than a mere courtesy (especially in an honor-shame culture), although I think treating it as a legal promissory note (so Stuhlmacher, *Philemon*, 49; O'Brien, *Colossians, Philemon*, 300) goes too far, especially with the concluding words, "to say nothing of your owing me your own self," which effectively cancels all debts. I agree with Fitzmyer (*Philemon*, 117) who counters the claim that this could include possible manumission fees (*pace* Winter, "Paul's Letter," 1–15), as it moves too far in advance of the request just made in v. 17.

Paul demonstrates the rhetorician's skill and tact in both delaying any mention of debt or injury until after he states his appeal and saving his best argument for last, with the words that cancel all debts. The amount Philemon owes his spiritual father—as Paul describes it, "his own life"—makes any debt Onesimus could have incurred pale in comparison. Philemon, as Paul's own convert, should recognize how Onesimus' conversion to Jesus Christ changes everything. And as a leader of the community that gathers in his home he is entrusted with the pastoral responsibility to implement and effect these changes.

The rhetorical strategy that serves gently to remind Philemon of his spiritual debt to Paul continues the letter's personal nature and light-heartedness despite the seriousness of the request. Another punctual reminder of their relationship comes in the subsequent expression with the affirmative, *nai adelphe* (yes, brother!). The very nature of the close bond they share makes it possible for Paul to come out and quite naturally tell his friend and brother, "I want some benefit from you in the Lord. Refresh my heart in Christ!"

This notion of mutual indebtedness, a reciprocity of material and spiritual gifts depending on need and circumstance, is well documented in Paul, especially in connection with the special collection for the poor in Jerusalem (cf. Rom 15:26-27). In this letter, however, any and all financial obligation quickly disappears in face of the weightier relational claims and appeals to love (cf. Rom 13:8).

Verse 20 brings the body of Paul's appeal full circle by repeating several key terms and the essential content of v. 7 with the concluding phrase, *anapauson mou ta splagchna en Christọ* ("Refresh my heart in Christ!"). What started off sounding more like an official appeal (v. 8) becomes a request between friends, a friendly imperative. As N. T. Wright states, the "gentle irony" continues as the one who appeals is actually the one with all the rightful claim, that is, Paul, both as Christ's ambassador and suffering witness in prison and as Philemon's spiritual father. But for Paul it is not a question of rightful claim or authority; it is about the debt every Christian owes, the debt to love one another as Christ has loved us (1 Cor 9:11-12).

For Reference and Further Study

Hooker, Morna D. "A Partner in the Gospel: Paul's Understanding of His Ministry," in Eugene H. Lovering, Jr., and Jerry L. Sumney, eds., *Theology and Ethics in Paul and His Interpreters: Essays in Honor of Victor Paul Furnish.* Nashville: Abingdon, 1996, 83–100.

Lewis, Lloyd A. "An African-American Appraisal of the Philemon-Paul-Onesimus Triangle," in Cain Hope Felder, ed., *Stony the Road We Trod: African American Biblical Interpretation.* Minneapolis: Fortress, 1991, 232–46.

Lohfink, Gerhard. *Jesus and Community: The Social Dimensions of Christian Faith.* Trans. John P. Galvin. Philadelphia: Fortress; New York, NY, and Mahwah, NJ: Paulist, 1984.

Martin, Clarice J. "The Rhetorical Function of Commercial Language in Paul's Letter to Philemon (Verse 18)," in Duane F. Watson, ed., *Persuasive Artistry: Studies in New Testament Rhetoric in Honor of George Kennedy.* JSNTSup 50. Sheffield: JSOT Press, 1991, 321–37.

Martyn, J. Louis. *Theological Issues in the Letters of Paul.* Nashville: Abingdon, 1997.

Mitchell, Margaret. "John Chrysostom on Philemon: A Second Look," *HTR* 88 (1995) 135–48.

Peperzak, Adriaan. "Giving," in Jean-Joseph Goux, Edith Wyschogrod, and Eric Boynton, eds., *The Enigma of Gift and Sacrifice.* New York: Fordham University Press, 2002, 161–75.

Plevnik, Joseph. "The Understanding of God at the Basis of Pauline Theology," *CBQ* 65 (2003) 554–67.

Schüssler Fiorenza, Elisabeth. "The Praxis of Coequal Discipleship," in Richard A. Horsley, ed., *Paul and Empire: Religion and Power in Roman Imperial Society.* Harrisburg, PA: Trinity Press International, 1997, 224–41.

Wilson, Andrew. "The Pragmatics of Politeness and Pauline Epistolography: A Case Study of the Letter to Philemon," *JSNT* 48 (1992) 107–19.

5. *Conclusion: Expression of Confidence, Plans to Visit, Final Greetings and Blessing* (21-25)

21. Confident of your obedience, I write to you, knowing that you will do even more than I ask. 22. At the same time, prepare a guest room for me, for I am hoping through your prayers to be granted to you. 23. Epaphras, my fellow prisoner in Christ Jesus, sends greetings to you, 24. and so do Mark, Aristarchus, Demas, and Luke, my coworkers. 25. The grace of the Lord Jesus Christ be with your spirit.

Notes

21. *Confident of your obedience, I write to you:* Given the conclusive note of v. 20, and with no linking particle, v. 21 is thought to start the letter closing (White, *Form and Function,* 104–106; Dunn, *Colossians and Philemon,* 343). The perfect participle *pepoithōs,* literally "being persuaded" or "confident" (Fitzmyer, *Philemon,* 121) reflects Paul's confirmed trust in his friend's faith (cf. 2 Cor 1:15; 2:3 for similar usage; see also Gal 5:10; Phil 2:24 for confidence and trust in the Lord). *Hypakoē,* which means "obedience," is used by the apostle in numerous instances as "obedience of faith," that is, as the obedience that faith is or expresses (cf. Rom 1:5; 6:6; 15:18; 16:19, 26; 2 Cor 7:15; 10:5-6). For Paul it always denotes faith that manifests itself in concrete terms, a faith that is responsive to and carries out the Lord's will (Rudolf Bultmann, *peithō, TDNT* 6:1–11; idem, *Theology of the New Testament,* 323; Conzelmann, *Outline of the Theology of the New Testament,* 172; Gnilka, *Philemonbrief,* 87–88; Stuhlmacher, *Philemon,* 52). Paul's confidence in Philemon's obedience corresponds with his commendation of his friend's faith "toward the Lord Jesus," expressed in love for "all the holy ones" (v. 5). *Hypakoē* is also used by Paul in discussing the obedience of Christ (Rom 5:10; 2 Cor 10:5). Peter T. O'Brien suggests that this obedience includes heeding the words of Christ's ambassador, and that Paul is also expressing confidence that his prayers (cf. vv. 4-6) will be answered (*Colossians, Philemon,* 305; cf. 2 Cor 7:13; 10:6). With *egrapsa soi* ("I write to you") Paul uses the epistolary aorist that conveys the sense that he is writing this as Philemon reads (or hears) the letter. This only serves to accentuate the letter's function to mediate one's personal presence to the recipient (Doty, *Letters in Primitive Christianity,* 12, 36). A number of scholars take the second *egrapsa* ("I write") to indicate that Paul penned this brief letter himself, without any scribal assistance (so Lightfoot, *Epistles,* 342; Dibelius, *An die Kolosser, Epheser, an Philemon,* 107; Gnilka, *Philemonbrief,* 87).

    knowing that you will do even more than I ask: The perfect participle of *oida, eidōs* ("knowing"), qualifies *pepoithōs,* as Paul reaffirms his confident expectation that Philemon will provide (*poiēseis,* the future indicative meaning "do" or "make") an appropriate response (Harris, *Colossians & Philemon,* 278). The *hoti* clause introduces Paul's second use of *hyper* (cf. v. 16), in the comparative sense, as *kai hyper* ("even more than"), of going even beyond what Paul had just requested in v. 17 (BDAG 1031; BDF §230; Harald Riesenfeld, *hyper, TDNT* 8:515). *Ha legō,* literally "what I say," is best translated here as "what I ask" (cf. 1 Cor 10:13; 2 Cor 1:8, etc; BDAG 589–90; Lohse, *Philemon,* 206 n. 5).

22. *At the same time, prepare a guest room for me: Hama de kai* ("at the same time") suggests that the following action is to coincide with Philemon's response in v. 21. The adverb *hama* denotes the coincidence of two actions (BDAG 49; BDF §425) as the particle *de* simply provides the connection, but without contrast (BDAG 222), and joins the adjunctive *kai* (Harris, *Colossians & Philemon,* 279). The accompanying imperative *hetoimaze,* literally "prepare" or "keep ready," also adds to the impression that the location of Paul's imprisonment is not too far away from Philemon's residence. *Moi* follows *hetoimaze* directly and is

literally translated "prepare for me" (Fitzmyer, *Philemon,* 122). Paul's final request of Philemon is that he keep a "guest room" *(xenian)* waiting for him as he promises to visit his friend as soon as he is released from prison. More commonly the term is used to describe the "hospitality" that is offered rather than as an actual place, as it is meant here (BDAG 683; cf. Acts 28:23 where it is used for the apostle's "lodging" during his house arrest in Rome; also *xenos* for "host" in Rom 16:23; BDF §294.5, 378).

for I am hoping through your prayers to be granted to you: Elpizō, literally "I hope," here in epistolary form, "I am hoping" (as in Rom 15:24; 1 Cor 16:7; Phil 1:25; 2:9, 23; Fitzmyer, *Philemon,* 123) completes the Pauline triad of love and faith as it adds an element of patient endurance to that of trust and confidence (cf. 1 Cor 13:13; Rudolf Bultmann, *elpis, TDNT* 2:517–35). The conjunctive *gar* ("for") introduces Paul's reason for this request as he asks for their prayers *(tōn proseuchōn)* on his behalf. Such an indirect request for prayers signifies the closeness of the bond between Paul and the addressee, as also seen in his request for prayers from the Philippians (Phil 1:19; see Wiles, *Paul's Intercessory Prayers,* 281–82). The plural *hymōn* in "your prayers" resumes, at least for the moment, Paul's address to the entire community, not included since the opening blessing and not mentioned again until the closing benediction. While not a private correspondence, this letter is unique among the Pauline letters in its singular appeal to Paul's personal friend and colleague. *Charisthēsomai hymin* ("to be granted to you") includes the sense of being given freely or graciously, as a gift or favor (O'Brien, *Colossians, Philemon,* 307; see also, for its secular usage in the release of captives, Fitzmyer, *Philemon,* 123). The passive voice points to the necessity of divine action and is taken as a "theological passive" (Lohse, *Philemon,* 206). Both the meaning and voice of the verb express total reliance on God's graciousness, while *dia tōn proseuchōn hymōn* ("through your prayers") includes the importance of their participation in securing Paul's freedom. For similar requests for prayer see also Rom 15:30; 1 Thess 5:25.

23. *Epaphras, my fellow prisoner in Christ Jesus, sends greetings to you:* Epaphras (the name is thought to be a shortened form of Epaphroditus [BDAG 360; BDF §125.1], although not the same Epaphroditus sent by the Philippians [Phil 2:25; 4:18; see Fitzmyer, *Philemon,* 123]), is someone whose name appears only here and in the Deutero-Pauline letter to the Colossians, where he is given the status of a Pauline coworker who acted as intermediary between the apostle and the Colossians and was also a founder of the community (Col 1:7-8; 4:12-13). In the letter to Philemon he has the distinction of being Paul's only *synaichmalōtos mou* ("my fellow prisoner"), a term also used elsewhere for Andronicus and Junia (Rom 16:7) and Aristarchus (Col 4:10), who is also mentioned as Paul's coworker in the next verse. Margaret MacDonald notes the unusual choice of a term that means literally "fellow prisoner of war" (*Colossians,* 179–80) when Paul could have used the more common words *syndedemenos* (cf. Heb 13:13) or *syndesmotes* for "fellow prisoner" (see also Gerhard Kittel, *aiteō, TDNT* 1:196–97). That he is a prisoner *en Christǭ Iēsou* ("in Christ Jesus") denotes that he, like Paul, is imprisoned for proclaiming the Gospel of Jesus Christ. The special greeting that he alone sends to Philemon, who is

saluted with the singular *se* ("you"), suggests that they, too, are friends (so O'Brien, *Colossians, Philemon,* 307). *Aspazetai* ("sends greetings," BDAG 144) employs the formal epistolary term that is commonly used (Rom 16:3, 5-16; 1 Cor 16:19-20; 2 Cor 13:12; Phil 4:21-22; Mullins, "Visit Talk," 350–58). Tradition also mentions someone named Epaphras who became the bishop of Colossae and was later martyred (see Fitzmyer, *Philemon,* 123).

24. *and so do Mark, Aristarchus, Demas, and Luke, my coworkers: Markos* ("Mark") is first in the list of four other coworkers who send greetings to Philemon, all four of whom, plus Epaphras, are mentioned in the longer list of greeters in the Colossian letter where more details are provided. There Mark, who is introduced as Barnabas' cousin, is apparently unknown to the Colossians, who are asked to "receive him" (Col 4:10). He is joined by Aristarchus, in reverse order in the Colossian letter, who is described at that time as Paul's fellow prisoner (see above). Both Mark and Aristarchus are mentioned in Acts. Mark, also known as John Mark, appears to be the same person who earlier had accompanied Paul and Barnabas (Acts 12:12, 25; but note 15:37-39). In Acts, Aristarchus is described as a Macedonian from Thessalonica (Acts 20:4) who was charged with rioting with Paul and Gaius in Ephesus for rejecting their gods (Acts 19:29, 40) and who later accompanied a captive Paul by sea to Rome (Acts 27:2). Demas and Luke are also mentioned in reverse order in the Colossian correspondence (Col 4:14), but only Luke is described in more detail as "the beloved physician." While later tradition ascribes the second and third gospels and Acts to Mark and Luke respectively (Fitzmyer, *Philemon,* 124–25), it may be the same Demas who is less honorably presented in 2 Tim 4:10: "for Demas, enamored of the present world, deserted me and went to Thessalonica." However, Ignatius also mentions a Demas (with a slightly different spelling) as bishop of Magnesia (see Fitzmyer, *Philemon,* 125). In the Philemon letter, and more in keeping with his usual brevity in these greetings, Paul only mentions the four as *hoi synergoi mou* ("my coworkers").

25. *The grace of the Lord Jesus Christ be with your spirit: Hē charis* ("grace") recalls the initial blessing as opening and closing benedictions enclose the letter and place Paul's words within the sphere of God's powerful domain and action. The subjective genitive, *tou Kyriou Iēsou Christou,* the full title and name of the Lord (vv. 3, 25), signifies the grace that comes from the Lord Jesus Christ. *Hymōn* ("your"), in *meta tou pneumatos hymōn* ("with your spirit"), is plural and corresponds to the opening blessing of the entire community. "Your spirit" clearly refers to the human spirit that Paul prays will be open and receptive to God's word and the promptings of the Holy Spirit.

Interpretation

The confident summary of v. 21 introduces the epilogue so characteristic of Paul's letters, complete with travel plans (v. 22), extended greetings (vv. 23-24), and final blessing (v. 25; cf. 1 Cor 16:22; 2 Cor 13:11; Gal 6:11-18;

Weima, *Neglected Endings*, 234–36). This final and emphatic expression of confidence in Philemon's obedience to the Lord also serves to bring the letter together as a cohesive whole, as it corresponds with his "faith toward the Lord Jesus" (v. 5) and the apostle's prayer for its continued effective realization (v. 6; Miller, *Obedience of Faith*, 50–51). This also expresses Paul's assurance that his partner will "do what is necessary" (v. 8) and heed the appeal that comes from Christ's ambassador (v. 9).

John L. White finds that this confidence formula represents one of the most significant formal differences between Paul's letters and Hellenistic ones, having no parallel in the Greek papyri (*Form and Function*, 104). While he affirms that this is a genuine expression of confidence in Philemon, White is also right in stating that for Paul it also signifies his assurance "that the divine message which he proclaims will effectively run its course" (ibid. 105–106). For, as Paul writes to the Romans, the Gospel "is the power of God for the salvation of everyone who believes" (Rom 1:16).

This second mention of Paul's writing this letter, "I write to you" (v. 21), aside from giving the impression that Paul penned the entire letter himself without scribal assistance (see the Notes), should also alert the letter's interpreter to the fact that Paul is not merely writing another letter of recommendation similar to those Greco-Roman letters written by a slaveowner's friend that typically appeal for mercy on behalf of a returning slave. Paul is writing on his own and Christ's behalf with a personal request for his partner in faith. Nowhere in this letter does Paul ask for leniency or forgiveness for Onesimus who returns not "as a slave" but as a beloved "brother" in the Lord (v. 16).

With the confident assurance "knowing that you will do even more than I ask," Paul announces what Fitzmyer calls the second climax of the letter (*Philemon*, 122), the first being the declaration of Onesimus as "no longer as a slave, but as a brother, beloved . . . in the Lord" (v. 16) just before the apostle states his request (v. 17; cf. also O'Brien, *Colossians, Philemon*, 305). Here "even more than I ask" must refer back to the implied request for Onesimus' subsequent return to useful service of the Gospel beside the apostle himself. While this can mean service on Philemon's behalf or not, the implications for manumission are obvious from Paul's request that Onesimus be considered "no longer as a slave, but as a brother . . . both in the flesh and in the Lord" (v. 16). The addition of "in the flesh," which includes his secular relations with Onesimus, can only mean that this fraternal relationship is to extend even beyond that of the Christian community. Most scholars at least entertain the possibility that Paul has Onesimus' freedom in view with this statement (see especially O"Brien, who calls Paul's expression "tantalizing," *Colossians, Philemon*, 305; Bruce, *Paul, Apostle of the Heart Set Free*, 206; Harrison, "Onesimus and Philemon," 276–80; Houlden, *Paul's Letters from Prison*, 232; Knox, *Philemon among the Letters,* 24–26; Lohmeyer, *Philemon,* 191; Wiles, *Paul's Intercessory Prayers,* 216–21).

Paul mentions no travel plans other than his hope to visit his friend as soon as he is released from prison. His simultaneous request to have a room ready for him suggests that Paul has some reason to think this possible and soon, unlike the Philippian letter, where life and death still lay in the balance (Phil 1:20). It also implies that Paul does not have far to travel, making Ephesus as the location of his imprisonment seem all the more probable. It certainly casts quite a bit of doubt upon a possible Roman imprisonment (see the Introduction for a fuller discussion). Given Paul's confident assurance, it also seems improbable that Paul would plan such a visit to press his appeal upon Philemon. As Paul had emphatically stated, his intention was not to compel any decision (vv. 8-9; cf. v. 14). It would also go against the whole tenor of the letter, with its lighthearted humor (vv. 11, 20) and so personal an appeal between such close friends and partners (vv. 17, 19; Dunn, *Colossians and Philemon,* 345; see especially Mullins, "Visit Talk," 350–58). However, the compliant response from the rest of the community is another matter that Paul's promised visit could influence.

Knowing that Philemon would delight in graciously welcoming him into his home (cf. v. 17), Paul promises to visit him as soon as possible. Founded on the OT practice of welcoming and providing for the needs of strangers (Lev 19:34; Deut 10:19) as well as Jesus' own ministry of table fellowship as both host and guest (especially prominent in the Gospel of Luke and Acts), such gracious hospitality is one of the most prominent features of early Christianity. Not only the success, but the very survival of the early Christian mission depended on Christians who were willing to open their homes and provide support and sustenance to traveling preachers such as Paul and his companions. This may well be part of why Paul expresses gratitude to Philemon in the earlier thanksgiving (v. 7). Philemon's home certainly appears to have the necessary size and accommodations, as he also hosts the local community gathering (v. 2).

The apostle's request for prayers is not uncommon, and a similar request for his freedom is found in the Philippian letter, where he also asks the community to intercede on his behalf (Phil 1:19). On other occasions he requests prayers for their safety (cf. Rom 15:30; 1 Thess 5:25). All of Paul's letters typically open and close with prayers and blessings for those he addresses. Epaphras, who is given prominence both as Paul's fellow prisoner "in Christ Jesus" and in sending his own special greetings to Philemon, is most likely to be well known to the host, if not also to his community. By the time the Deutero-Pauline letter to the Colossians is written, Epaphras, a Colossian himself, is well known in Laodicea and Hierapolis and is spoken of highly as a beloved servant of Christ Jesus and faithful minister to their needs (Col 1:7-8; 4:12-13). Now imprisoned with Paul, Epaphras may also have been sent by Paul and his companions to preach to the Colossians, possibly founding their community (cf. Col 1:7-8; MacDonald, *Colossians,* 181–82). Epaphras is joined by four more coworkers, Mark, Aristarchus, Demas, and Luke, who send greetings. Whether Philemon had known or worked with them previously cannot be known for certain. All but Mark seem to be known to the Colossians in that later correspondence, which included the additional names of Tychicus (who, together with Onesimus, delivers the Deutero-Pauline letter [Col 4:7-9]), Jesus, who is called Justus (Col 4:11), and Nympha and her church (Col 4:15), to whom the letter is also to be read.

The close, almost parallel listing of names between the two letters has led many to place Philemon's house church in Colossae (see the Introduction). But the absence of any mention of Philemon and Apphia makes this less certain. Similarly, the dating of this letter around the same time as the Colossian correspondence (Dunn, *Colossians and Philemon,* 37–41) has a number of difficulties, not the least of which is the shift from the honorable mention of Archippus as Paul's "fellow soldier" (Phlm 2) to the rather brisk admonition "See that you fulfill the ministry which you have received in the Lord" (Col 4:17).

Basically the same as saying "may the Lord's Spirit be with your spirit" (Rom 8:16; Eduard Schweizer, *pneuma, TDNT* 6:435) to lead and guide it, Paul's closing benediction "The grace of the Lord Jesus Christ be with your spirit" is his characteristic epistolary blessing (Rom 16:20; Phil 4:23; 1 Thess 5:28), with only slight variations in his other letters ("Lord Jesus" in 1 Cor 16:23 and "brothers" in Gal 6:18), including an expansion in the second extant letter to the Corinthian community, "The grace of the Lord Jesus Christ and the love of God and the fellowship of the Holy Spirit be with you all" (2 Cor 13:14).

For Reference and Further Study

Cox, Claude E. "The Reading of the Personal Letters as the Background for the Reading of the Scriptures in the Early Church," in Abraham J. Malherbe, Frederick W. Norris, and James W. Thompson, eds., *The Early Church in its Context: Essays in Honor of Everett Ferguson.* Leiden and Boston: Brill, 1998, 74–91.

Funk, Robert W. "The Apostolic *Parousia:* Form and Significance," in William R. Farmer, C. F. D. Moule, and Richard R. Niebuhr, eds., *Christian History and Interpretation: Studies Presented to John Knox.* Cambridge: Cambridge University Press, 1967, 249–68.

Miller, James C. *The Obedience of Faith, the Eschatological People of God, and the Purpose of Romans.* SBLDS 177. Atlanta: Society of Biblical Literature, 2000.

Mullins, Terence Y. "Greeting as New Testament Form," *JBL* 87 (1968) 418–26.
________. "Visit Talk in New Testament Letters," *CBQ* 35 (1973) 350–58.
Olson, Stanley N. "Pauline Expressions of Confidence in His Addressees," *CBQ* 47 (1985) 282–95.
Weima, Jeffrey A. *Neglected Endings: The Significance of the Pauline Letter Closings.* JSNTSup 101. Sheffield: Sheffield Academic Press, 1994.

INDEXES

PHILIPPIANS—INDEX OF SCRIPTURE AND OTHER ANCIENT WRITINGS

The Old Testament

The New Testament

Various Ancient Writings

PHILIPPIANS—INDEX OF AUTHORS

PHILEMON—INDEX OF SCRIPTURE AND OTHER ANCIENT WRITINGS

The Old Testament

Early Jewish Literature

Early Christian Literature

Greco-Roman Literature

PHILEMON—INDEX OF AUTHORS